nephew's indebtedne[...] deception in order for [...] cons both Lucre and his rival, Hoard, [...] cial gain in a romantic scheme, further enforcing the corrupting power of money.

First performed in 1598, Ben Jonson's play *Every Man in His Humour* remained popular for centuries after its original publication and performance in the early 1600s. "Humour," in addition to its relationship to comedy, was believed to be an inherent temperament—choleric, melancholic, phlegmatic, or sanguine— that determined a person's character. First used in Greek and Latin drama, the later use of the "typè" could, for example, identify an obsession. Kitely, a merchant, is motivated by jealousy (choleric). Edward Know'well, overly concerned for his son's future, is driven to act by his anxiety (melancholic). William Shakespeare performed in the play, possibly as Know'well. The edition reprinted here is the revised Folio edition (1616), which replaced the original Italian setting and names with English names, and was set in London.

FRIAR BACON AND
FRIAR BUNGAY

Robert Greene

[Characters of the Play

KING HENRY THE THIRD
EDWARD, PRINCE OF WALES, *his son*
EMPEROR OF GERMANY
KING OF CASTILE
DUKE OF SAXONY
LACY, *Earl of Lincoln* ⎫
WARREN, *Earl of Sussex* ⎬ *Edward's friends*
ERMSBY, *a Gentleman* ⎭
RAFE SIMNELL, *the King's fool*
FRIAR BACON
MILES, *his poor scholar*
FRIAR BUNGAY
JACQUES VANDERMAST, *a German magician*
BURDEN ⎫
MASON ⎬ *Oxford doctors*
CLEMENT ⎭
LAMBERT ⎫
SERLSBY ⎬ *Country squires*
TWO SCHOLARS, *their sons*
THE KEEPER OF FRESSINGFIELD
HIS FRIEND
THOMAS ⎫
RICHARD ⎬ *Rustics*
A CONSTABLE
A POST, *serving Lacy*

LORDS, GENTLEMEN, SERVANTS, *attending King Henry's court*
COUNTRY CLOWNS *at Harleston Fair*

ELEANOR, *daughter to the King of Castile*
MARGARET, *the Keeper's daughter, called the Fair Maid of Fressingfield*
JOAN, *a country wench*
HOSTESS OF THE BELL, *at Henley*

TWO DEVILS
THE VOICE OF BACON'S BRAZEN HEAD
A SPIRIT IN THE SHAPE OF HERCULES]

[i]

Enter [Prince Edward], *malcontented; with* Lacy, Earl of Lincoln;
John Warren, Earl of Sussex; *and* Ermsby, Gentleman; Rafe
Simnell, *the King's fool*; [*other lords and gentlemen*].

LACY. Why looks my lord like to a troubled sky
When heaven's bright shine is shadowed with a fog?
Alate we ran the deer, and through the lawns
Stripp'd with our nags the lofty frolic bucks
That scudded 'fore the teasers like the wind.
Ne'er was the deer of merry Fressingfield
So lustily pull'd down by jolly mates,
Nor shar'd the farmers such fat venison,
So frankly dealt, this hundred years before;
Nor have I seen my lord more frolic in the chase,
And now chang'd to a melancholy dump.
  WARREN. After the Prince got to the keeper's lodge
And had been jocund in the house a while,
Tossing of ale and milk in country cans,
Whether it was the country's sweet content,
Or else the bonny damsel fill'd us drink,
That seem'd so stately in her stammel red,
Or that a qualm did cross his stomach then,
But straight he fell into his passions.
  ERMSBY. Sirrah Rafe, what say you to your master,
Shall he thus all amort live malcontent?
  RAFE. Hearest thou, Ned? Nay, look if he will speak to me.
  EDWARD. What say'st thou to me, fool?
  RAFE. I prithee tell me, Ned, art thou in love with the
keeper's daughter?
  EDWARD. How if I be, what then?

3

RAFE. Why then, sirrah, I'll teach thee how to deceive love.

EDWARD. How, Rafe?

RAFE. Marry, sirrah Ned, thou shalt put on my cap and my coat and my dagger, and I will put on thy clothes and thy sword, and so thou shalt be my fool.

EDWARD. And what of this?

RAFE. Why, so thou shalt beguile Love, for Love is such a proud scab that he will never meddle with fools nor children. Is not Rafe's counsel good, Ned?

EDWARD. Tell me, Ned Lacy, didst thou mark the maid,
How lively in her country weeds she look'd?
A bonnier wench all Suffolk cannot yield.
All Suffolk! Nay, all England holds none such.

RAFE. Sirrah Will Ermsby, Ned is deceived.

ERMSBY. Why, Rafe?

RAFE. He says all England hath no such, and I say, and I'll stand to it, there is one better in Warwickshire.

WARREN. How provest thou that, Rafe?

RAFE. Why, is not the Abbot a learned man and hath read many books, and thinkest thou he hath not more learning than thou to choose a bonny wench? Yes, I warrant thee, by his whole grammar.

ERMSBY. A good reason, Rafe.

EDWARD. I tell thee, Lacy, that her sparkling eyes
Do lighten forth sweet love's alluring fire;
And in her tresses she doth fold the looks
Of such as gaze upon her golden hair;
Her bashful white mix'd with the morning's red
Luna doth boast upon her lovely cheeks;
Her front is beauty's table, where she paints
The glories of her gorgeous excellence;
Her teeth are shelves of precious margarites
Richly enclosed with ruddy coral cleeves.
Tush, Lacy, she is beauty's over-match,
If thou survey'st her curious imagery.

LACY. I grant, my lord, the damsel is as fair
As simple Suffolk's homely towns can yield;
But in the court be quainter dames than she,
Whose faces are enrich'd with honor's taint,
Whose beauties stand upon the stage of fame
And vaunt their trophies in the courts of Love.

EDWARD. Ah, Ned, but hadst thou watch'd her as myself,
And seen the secret beauties of the maid,
Their courtly coyness were but foolery.

ERMSBY. Why, how watch'd you her, my lord?

EDWARD. When as she swept like Venus through the house,
And in her shape fast folded up my thoughts,
Into the milkhouse went I with the maid,
And there amongst the cream bowls she did shine
As Pallas 'mongst her princely huswifery.
She turn'd her smock over her lily arms
And dived them into milk to run her cheese;
But, whiter than the milk, her crystal skin,
Checked with lines of azure, made her blush,
That art or nature durst bring for compare.
Ermsby, if thou hadst seen as I did note it well,
How beauty play'd the huswife, how this girl,
Like Lucrece, laid her fingers to the work,
Thou wouldest with Tarquin hazard Rome and all
To win the lovely maid of Fressingfield.

RAFE. Sirrah Ned, wouldst fain have her?

EDWARD. Ay, Rafe.

RAFE. Why, Ned, I have laid the plot in my head thou shalt
have her already.

EDWARD. I'll give thee a new coat, and learn me that.

RAFE. Why, sirrah Ned, we'll ride to Oxford to Friar Bacon.
Oh, he is a brave scholar, sirrah; they say he is a brave nigromancer,
that he can make women of devils, and he can juggle cats into
costermongers.

EDWARD. And how then, Rafe?

RAFE. Marry, sirrah, thou shalt go to him, and because thy
father Harry shall not miss thee, he shall turn me into thee; and
I'll to the court and I'll prince it out, and he shall make thee
either a silken purse, full of gold, or else a fine wrought smock.

EDWARD. But how shall I have the maid?

RAFE. Marry, sirrah, if thou beest a silken purse full of gold,
then on Sundays she'll hang thee by her side, and you must not
say a word. Now, sir, when she comes into a great press of
people, for fear of the cutpurse, on a sudden she'll swap thee
into her plackerd; then, sirrah, being there, you may plead for
yourself.

ERMSBY. Excellent policy!

EDWARD. But how if I be a wrought smock?

RAFE. Then she'll put thee into her chest and lay thee into lavender, and upon some good day she'll put thee on, and at night when you go to bed, then being turn'd from a smock to a man, you may make up the match.

LACY. Wonderfully wisely counseled, Rafe.

EDWARD. Rafe shall have a new coat.

RAFE. God thank you when I have it on my back, Ned.

EDWARD. Lacy, the fool hath laid a perfect plot;
For why our country Margaret is so coy
And stands so much upon her honest points,
That marriage or no market with the maid,
Ermsby, it must be nigromantic spells
And charms of art that must enchain her love,
Or else shall Edward never win the girl.
Therefore, my wags, we'll horse us in the morn,
And post to Oxford to this jolly friar.
Bacon shall by his magic do this deed.

WARREN. Content, my lord; and that's a speedy way
To wean these headstrong puppies from the teat.

EDWARD. I am unknown, not taken for the prince;
They only deem us frolic courtiers
That revel thus among our liege's game;
Therefore I have devised a policy.
Lacy, thou know'st next Friday is Saint James',
And then the country flocks to Harleston fair;
Then will the keeper's daughter frolic there,
And over-shine the troop of all the maids
That come to see and to be seen that day.
Haunt thee disguis'd among the country swains;
Feign th'art a farmer's son not far from thence;
Espy her loves, and who she liketh best;
Cote him, and court her to control the clown.
Say that the courtier 'tired all in green,
That help'd her handsomely to run her cheese
And fill'd her father's lodge with venison,
Commends him, and sends fairings to herself.
Buy something worthy of her parentage,
Not worth her beauty, for, Lacy, then the fair
Affords no jewel fitting for the maid.
And when thou talkest of me, note if she blush;

Oh, then she loves; but if her cheeks wax pale,
Disdain it is. Lacy, send how she fares,
And spare no time nor cost to win her loves.

LACY. I will, my lord, so execute this charge
As if that Lacy were in love with her.

EDWARD. Send letters speedily to Oxford of the news.

RAFE. And sirrah Lacy, buy me a thousand thousand million
of fine bells.

LACY. What wilt thou do with them, Rafe?

RAFE. Marry, every time that Ned sighs for the keeper's daughter, I'll tie a bell about him; and so within three or four days I
will send word to his father Harry that his son and my master
Ned is become love's morris-dance.

EDWARD. Well, Lacy, look with care unto thy charge,
And I will haste to Oxford to the friar,
That he by art, and thou by secret gifts,
Mayst make me lord of merry Fressingfield.

LACY. God send your honor your heart's desire.   *Exeunt.*

[*ii*]

Enter Friar Bacon *with* Miles, *his poor scholar, with books under his
arm; with them* Burden, Mason, Clement, *three doctors.*

BACON. Miles, where are you?

MILES. *Hic sum, dostissime et reverendissime doctor.*

BACON. *Attulisti nos libros meos de necromantia?*

MILES. *Ecce quam bonum et quam jocundum, habitares libros in
unum.*

BACON. Now, masters of our academic state,
That rule in Oxford, viceroys in your place,
Whose heads contain maps of the liberal arts,
Spending your time in depth of learned skill,
Why flock you thus to Bacon's secret cell,
A friar newly stall'd in Brazen-nose?
Say what's your mind, that I may make reply.

BURDEN. Bacon, we hear that long we have suspect,
That thou art read in magic's mystery;
In pyromancy to divine by flames;
To tell by hydromantic ebbs and tides;
By aeromancy to discover doubts,

To plain out questions, as Apollo did.

BACON. Well, Master Burden, what of all this?

MILES. Marry, sir, he doth but fulfill by rehearsing of these names the Fable of the Fox and the Grapes: that which is above us pertains nothing to us.

BURDEN. I tell thee, Bacon, Oxford makes report,
Nay, England, and the court of Henry says
Th'art making of a brazen head by art
Which shall unfold strange doubts and aphorisms
And read a lecture in philosophy,
And by the help of devils and ghastly fiends,
Thou mean'st, ere many years or days be past,
To compass England with a wall of brass.

BACON. And what of this?

MILES. What of this, master? Why, he doth speak mystically, for he knows if your skill fail to make a brazen head, yet Mother Waters' strong ale will fit his turn to make him have a copper nose.

CLEMENT. Bacon, we come not grieving at thy skill,
But joying that our academy yields
A man suppos'd the wonder of the world;
For if thy cunning work these miracles,
England and Europe shall admire thy fame,
And Oxford shall in characters of brass
And statues such as were built up in Rome
Eternize Friar Bacon for his art.

MASON. Then, gentle friar, tell us thy intent.

BACON. Seeing you come as friends unto the friar,
Resolve you, doctors, Bacon can by books
Make storming Boreas thunder from his cave
And dim fair Luna to a dark eclipse.
The great arch-ruler, potentate of hell,
Trembles, when Bacon bids him or his fiends
Bow to the force of his pentageron.
What art can work, the frolic friar knows;
And therefore will I turn my magic books
And strain out nigromancy to the deep.
I have contriv'd and fram'd a head of brass
(I made Belcephon hammer out the stuff),
And that by art shall read philosophy;
And I will strengthen England by my skill,

That if ten Caesars liv'd and reign'd in Rome,
With all the legions Europe doth contain,
They should not touch a grass of English ground.
The work that Ninus rear'd at Babylon,
The brazen walls fram'd by Semiramis,
Carved out like to the portal of the sun,
Shall not be such as rings the English strond
From Dover to the market place of Rye.

BURDEN. Is this possible?

MILES. I'll bring ye two or three witnesses.

BURDEN. What be those?

MILES. Marry, sir, three or four as honest devils and good companions as any be in hell.

MASON. No doubt but magic may do much in this,
For he that reads but mathematic rules
Shall find conclusions that avail to work
Wonders that pass the common sense of men.

BURDEN. But Bacon roves a bow beyond his reach,
And tells of more than magic can perform,
Thinking to get a fame by fooleries.
Have I not pass'd as far in state of schools,
And read of many secrets? Yet to think
That heads of brass can utter any voice,
Or more, to tell of deep philosophy—
This is a fable Aesop had forgot.

BACON. Burden, thou wrong'st me in detracting thus;
Bacon loves not to stuff himself with lies.
But tell me 'fore these doctors, if thou dare,
Of certain questions I shall move to thee.

BURDEN. I will; ask what thou can.

MILES. Marry, sir, he'll straight be on your pick-pack to know whether the feminine or the masculine gender be most worthy.

BACON. Were you not yesterday, Master Burden, at Henley upon the Thames?

BURDEN. I was; what then?

BACON. What book studied you thereon all night?

BURDEN. I? None at all; I read not there a line.

BACON. Then, doctors, Friar Bacon's art knows naught.

CLEMENT. What say you to this, Master Burden? Doth he not touch you?

BURDEN. I pass not of his frivolous speeches.

MILES. Nay, Master Burden, my master, ere he hath done with you, will turn you from a doctor to a dunce, and shake you so small that he will leave no more learning in you than is in Balaam's ass.

BACON. Masters, for that learned Burden's skill is deep,
And sore he doubts of Bacon's cabalism,
I'll show you why he haunts to Henley oft:
Not, doctors, for to taste the fragrant air,
But there to spend the night in alchemy,
To multiply with secret spells of art.
Thus private steals he learning from us all.
To prove my sayings true, I'll show you straight
The book he keeps at Henley for himself.

MILES. Nay, now my master goes to conjuration, take heed.

BACON. Masters, stand still; fear not. I'll show you but his book.

Here he conjures.

Per omnes deos infernales, Belcephon.

Enter a woman with a shoulder of mutton on a spit, and a devil.

MILES. Oh, master, cease your conjuration, or you spoil all, for here's a she-devil come with a shoulder of mutton on a spit. You have marr'd the devil's supper; but no doubt he thinks our college fare is slender, and so hath sent you his cook with a shoulder of mutton to make it exceed.

HOSTESS. Oh, where am I, or what's become of me?

BACON. What art thou?

HOSTESS. Hostess at Henley, mistress of the Bell.

BACON. How camest thou here?

HOSTESS. As I was in the kitchen 'mongst the maids,
Spitting the meat against supper for my guess,
A motion moved me to look forth of door.
No sooner had I pried into the yard,
But straight a whirlwind hoisted me from thence
And mounted me aloft unto the clouds.
As in a trance, I thought nor feared naught,
Nor know I where or whither I was ta'en,
Nor where I am, nor what these persons be.

BACON. No? Know you not Master Burden?

HOSTESS. Oh, yes, good sir, he is my daily guest.

What, Master Burden, 'twas but yesternight
That you and I at Henley play'd at cards.

BURDEN. I know not what we did; a pox of all conjuring friars!

CLEMENT. Now, jolly friar, tell us, is this the book
That Burden is so careful to look on?

BACON. It is; but, Burden, tell me now,
Thinkest thou that Bacon's nigromantic skill
Cannot perform his head and wall of brass,
When he can fetch thine hostess in such post?

MILES. I'll warrant you, master, if Master Burden could conjure
as well as you, he would have his book every night from Henley
to study on at Oxford.

MASON. Burden, what, are you mated by this frolic friar?
Look how he droops; his guilty conscience
Drives him to bash and makes his hostess blush.

BACON. Well, mistress, for I will not have you miss'd,
You shall to Henley to cheer up your guests
'Fore supper 'gin. Burden, bid her adieu,
Say farewell to your hostess 'fore she goes.
Sirrah, away, and set her safe at home.

HOSTESS. Master Burden, when shall we see you at Henley?

Exeunt Hostess *and the devil.*

BURDEN. The devil take thee and Henley too.

MILES. Master, shall I make a good motion?

BACON. What's that?

MILES. Marry, sir, now that my hostess is gone to provide
supper, conjure up another spirit, and send Doctor Burden flying
after.

BACON. Thus, rulers of our academic state,
You have seen the friar frame his art by proof;
And as the college called Brazen-nose
Is under him, and he the master there,
So surely shall this head of brass be fram'd,
And yield forth strange and uncouth aphorisms;
And hell and Hecate shall fail the friar,
But I will circle England round with brass.

MILES. So be it, *et nunc et semper.* Amen.   *Exeunt omnes.*

[*iii*]

Enter Margaret, *the fair maid of Fressingfield, with*
Thomas, [Richard,] *and* Joan, *and other clowns;* Lacy,
disguised in country apparel.

THOMAS. By my troth, Margaret, here's a weather is able to
make a man call his father whoreson. If this weather hold, we
shall have hay good cheap, and butter and cheese at Harleston
will bear no price.

MARGARET. Thomas, maids, when they come to see the fair,
Count not to make a cope for dearth of hay.
When we have turn'd our butter to the salt,
And set our cheese safely upon the racks,
Then let our fathers price it as they please.
We country sluts of merry Fressingfield
Come to buy needless naughts to make us fine,
And look that young men should be frank this day,
And court us with such fairings as they can.
Phoebus is blithe, and frolic looks from heaven
As when he courted lovely Semele,
Swearing the pedlars shall have empty packs,
If that fair weather may make chapmen buy.

LACY. But, lovely Peggy, Semele is dead,
And therefore Phoebus from his palace pries,
And, seeing such a sweet and seemly saint,
Shows all his glories for to court yourself.

MARGARET. This is a fairing, gentle sir, indeed,
To soothe me up with such smooth flattery;
But learn of me, your scoff's too broad before.
Well, Joan, our beauties must abide their jests;
We serve the turn in jolly Fressingfield.

JOAN. Margaret, a farmer's daughter for a farmer's son.
I warrant you the meanest of us both
Shall have a mate to lead us from the church.
But, Thomas, what's the news? What, in a dump?
Give me your hand, we are near a pedlar's shop;
Out with your purse; we must have fairings now.

THOMAS. Faith, Joan, and shall. I'll bestow a fairing on you,
and then we will to the tavern and snap off a pint of wine
or two.

All this while Lacy *whispers* Margaret *in the ear.*

MARGARET. Whence are you, sir? Of Suffolk? For your terms
Are finer than the common sort of men.

LACY. Faith, lovely girl, I am of Beccles by,
Your neighbor not above six miles from hence,
A farmer's son that never was so quaint
But that he could do courtesy to such dames.
But trust me, Margaret, I am sent in charge
From him that revel'd in your father's house,
And fill'd his lodge with cheer and venison,
'Tired in green. He sent you this rich purse,
His token that he help'd you run your cheese,
And in the milkhouse chatted with yourself.

MARGARET. To me? You forget yourself.

LACY. Women are often weak in memory.

MARGARET. Oh, pardon, sir, I call to mind the man.
'Twere little manners to refuse his gift,
And yet I hope he sends it not for love;
For we have little leisure to debate of that.

JOAN. What, Margaret, blush not; maids must have their loves.

THOMAS. Nay, by the mass, she looks pale as if she were angry.

RICHARD. Sirrah, are you of Beccles? I pray, how doth Goodman
Cob? My father bought a horse of him. I'll tell you, Marget, 'a
were good to be a gentleman's jade, for of all things the foul
hilding could not abide a dungcart.

MARGARET [*aside*]. How different is this farmer from the rest
That erst as yet hath pleas'd my wand'ring sight.
His words are witty, quickened with a smile,
His courtesy gentle, smelling of the court;
Facile and debonair in all his deeds,
Proportion'd as was Paris, when, in gray,
He courted Œnon in the vale by Troy.
Great lords have come and pleaded for my love—
Who but the keeper's lass of Fressingfield?
And yet methinks this farmer's jolly son
Passeth the proudest that hath pleas'd mine eye.
But, Peg, disclose not that thou art in love,
And show as yet no sign of love to him,
Although thou well wouldst wish him for thy love;
Keep that to thee, till time doth serve thy turn
To show the grief wherein thy heart doth burn.

Come, Joan and Thomas, shall we to the fair?
You, Beccles man, will not forsake us now?

LACY. Not whilst I may have such quaint girls as you.

MARGARET. Well, if you chance to come by Fressingfield,
Make but a step into the keeper's lodge,
And such poor fare as woodmen can afford—
Butter and cheese, cream, and fat venison—
You shall have store, and welcome therewithal.

LACY. Gramercies, Peggy; look for me ere long.   *Exeunt omnes.*

[iv]

Enter [King] Henry the Third; *the* Emperor [of Germany]; *the*
King of Castile; Eleanor, *his daughter;* Jacques Vandermast, *a*
German [*scientist*].

HENRY. Great men of Europe, monarchs of the west,
Ring'd with the walls of old Oceanus,
Whose lofty surge is like the battlements
That compass'd high-built Babel in with towers,
Welcome, my lords, welcome, brave western kings,
To England's shore, whose promontory cleeves
Shows Albion is another little world.
Welcome says English Henry to you all;
Chiefly unto the lovely Eleanor,
Who dar'd for Edward's sake cut through the seas,
And venture as Agenor's damsel through the deep,
To get the love of Henry's wanton son.

CASTILE. England's rich monarch, brave Plantagenet,
The Pyren Mounts swelling above the clouds,
That ward the wealthy Castile in with walls,
Could not detain the beauteous Eleanor;
But hearing of the fame of Edward's youth,
She dar'd to brook Neptunus' haughty pride
And bide the brunt of froward Æolus.
Then may fair England welcome her the more.

ELEANOR. After that English Henry, by his lords,
Had sent Prince Edward's lovely counterfeit,
A present to the Castile Eleanor,
The comely portrait of so brave a man,
The virtuous fame discoursed of his deeds,

Edward's courageous resolution
Done at the Holy Land 'fore Damas' walls,
Led both mine eye and thoughts in equal links
To like so of the English monarch's son
That I attempted perils for his sake.

EMPEROR. Where is the prince, my lord?

HENRY. He posted down, not long since, from the court
To Suffolk side, to merry Framingham,
To sport himself amongst my fallow deer;
From thence, by packets sent to Hampton House,
We hear the prince is ridden with his lords
To Oxford, in the academy there
To hear dispute amongst the learned men.
But we will send forth letters for my son,
To will him come from Oxford to the court.

EMPEROR. Nay, rather, Henry, let us, as we be,
Ride for to visit Oxford with our train.
Fain would I see your universities
And what learned men your academy yields.
From Hapsburg have I brought a learned clerk
To hold dispute with English orators.
This doctor, surnam'd Jacques Vandermast,
A German born, pass'd into Padua,
To Florence, and to fair Bolonia,
To Paris, Rheims, and stately Orleans,
And, talking there with men of art, put down
The chiefest of them all in aphorisms,
In magic, and the mathematic rules.
Now let us, Henry, try him in your schools.

HENRY. He shall, my lord; this motion likes me well.
We'll progress straight to Oxford with our trains,
And see what men our academy brings.
And, wonder Vandermast, welcome to me;
In Oxford shalt thou find a jolly friar
Called Friar Bacon, England's only flower.
Set him but nonplus in his magic spells,
And make him yield in mathematic rules,
And for thy glory I will bind thy brows
Not with a poet's garland made of bays,
But with a coronet of choicest gold.
Whilst then we fit to Oxford with our troops,

Let's in and banquet in our English court. [*Exeunt.*]

[v]

Enter Rafe Simnell *in Edward's apparel;* Edward, Warren,
Ermsby, *disguised.*

RAFE. Where be these vagabond knaves, that they attend no
better on their master?

EDWARD. If it please your honor, we are all ready at an inch.

RAFE. Sirrah, Ned, I'll have no more post horse to ride on.
I'll have another fetch.

ERMSBY. I pray you, how is that, my lord?

RAFE. Marry, sir, I'll send to the Isle of Ely for four or five
dozen of geese, and I'll have them tied six and six together with
whipcord. Now upon their backs will I have a fair field-bed with
a canopy; and so, when it is my pleasure, I'll flee into what place
I please. This will be easy.

WARREN. Your honor hath said well; but shall we to Brazen-
nose College before we pull off our boots?

ERMSBY. Warren, well motioned; we will to the friar
Before we revel it within the town.
Rafe, see you keep your countenance like a prince.

RAFE. Wherefore have I such a company of cutting knaves to
wait upon me, but to keep and defend my countenance against
all mine enemies? Have you not good swords and bucklers?

Enter Bacon *and* Miles.

ERMSBY. Stay, who comes here?

WARREN. Some scholar; and we'll ask him where Friar
Bacon is.

BACON. Why, thou arrant dunce, shall I never make thee good
scholar? Doth not all the town cry out and say, Friar Bacon's
subsizar is the greatest blockhead in all Oxford? Why, thou canst
not speak one word of true Latin.

MILES. No, sir? Yes; what is this else? *Ego sum tuus homo,* "I
am your man." I warrant you, sir, as good Tully's phrase as any
is in Oxford.

BACON. Come on, sirrah, what part of speech is *Ego?*

MILES. *Ego,* that is "I"; marry, *nomen substantivo.*

BACON. How prove you that?

MILES. Why, sir, let him prove himself and 'a will; "I" can be heard, felt, and understood.

BACON. Oh, gross dunce!

Here beat him.

EDWARD. Come, let us break off this dispute between these two. Sirrah, where is Brazen-nose College?

MILES. Not far from Coppersmiths' Hall.

EDWARD. What, dost thou mock me?

MILES. Not I, sir; but what would you at Brazen-nose?

ERMSBY. Marry, we would speak with Friar Bacon.

MILES. Whose men be you?

ERMSBY. Marry, scholar, here's our master.

RAFE. Sirrah, I am the master of these good fellows; mayst thou not know me to be a lord by my reparel?

MILES. Then here's good game for the hawk; for here's the master fool and a covey of coxcombs. One wise man, I think, would spring you all.

EDWARD. Gog's wounds! Warren, kill him.

WARREN. Why, Ned, I think the devil be in my sheath; I cannot get out my dagger.

ERMSBY. Nor I mine. 'Swones, Ned, I think I am bewitch'd.

MILES. A company of scabs. The proudest of you all draw your weapon, if he can. [*Aside.*] See how boldly I speak, now my master is by.

EDWARD. I strive in vain; but if my sword be shut
And conjured fast by magic in my sheath,
Villain, here is my fist.

Strike him a box on the ear.

MILES. Oh, I beseech you, conjure his hands, too, that he may not lift his arms to his head, for he is light-fingered.

RAFE. Ned, strike him. I'll warrant thee by mine honor.

BACON. What means the English prince to wrong my man?

EDWARD. To whom speakest thou?

BACON. To thee.

EDWARD. Who art thou?

BACON. Could you not judge when all your swords grew fast

That Friar Bacon was not far from hence?
Edward, King Henry's son, and Prince of Wales,
Thy fool disguis'd cannot conceal thyself.
I know both Ermsby and the Sussex earl,
Else Friar Bacon had but little skill.
Thou comest in post from merry Fressingfield,
Fast-fancied to the keeper's bonny lass,
To crave some succor of the jolly friar;
And Lacy, Earl of Lincoln, hast thou left
To 'treat fair Margaret to allow thy loves;
But friends are men, and love can baffle lords.
The earl both woos and courts her for himself.

    WARREN. Ned, this is strange; the friar knoweth all.

    ERMSBY. Apollo could not utter more than this.

    EDWARD. I stand amazed to hear this jolly friar
Tell even the very secrets of my thoughts.
But, learned Bacon, since thou knowest the cause
Why I did post so fast from Fressingfield,
Help, friar, at a pinch, that I may have
The love of lovely Margaret to myself,
And, as I am true Prince of Wales, I'll give
Living and lands to strength thy college state.

    WARREN. Good friar, help the prince in this.

    RAFE. Why, servant Ned, will not the friar do it? Were not
my sword glued to my scabbard by conjuration, I would cut off
his head, and make him do it by force.

    MILES. In faith, my lord, your manhood and your sword is all
alike; they are so fast conjured that we shall never see them.

    ERMSBY. What, doctor, in a dump? Tush, help the prince,
And thou shalt see how liberal he will prove.

    BACON. Crave not such actions greater dumps than these?
I will, my lord, strain out my magic spells;
For this day comes the earl to Fressingfield,
And 'fore that night shuts in the day with dark,
They'll be betrothed each to other fast.
But come with me; we'll to my study straight,
And in a glass prospective I will show
What's done this day in merry Fressingfield.

    EDWARD. Gramercies, Bacon; I will quite thy pain.

    BACON. But send your train, my lord, into the town;
My scholar shall go bring them to their inn.

Meanwhile we'll see the knavery of the earl.

EDWARD. Warren, leave me; and, Ermsby, take the fool;
Let him be master, and go revel it
Till I and Friar Bacon talk awhile.

WARREN. We will, my lord.

RAFE. Faith, Ned, and I'll lord it out till thou comest. I'll be
Prince of Wales over all the blackpots in Oxford.

Exeunt [all except Bacon *and* Edward].

[vi]

Bacon and Edward *goes into the study.*

BACON. Now, frolic Edward, welcome to my cell.
Here tempers Friar Bacon many toys,
And holds this place his consistory court,
Wherein the devils pleads homage to his words.
Within this glass prospective thou shalt see
This day what's done in merry Fressingfield
'Twixt lovely Peggy and the Lincoln earl.

EDWARD. Friar, thou glad'st me. Now shall Edward try
How Lacy meaneth to his sovereign lord.

BACON. Stand there and look directly in the glass.

Enter Margaret *and* Friar Bungay.

What sees my lord?

EDWARD. I see the keeper's lovely lass appear
As bright-sun as the paramour of Mars,
Only attended by a jolly friar.

BACON. Sit still, and keep the crystal in your eye.

MARGARET. But tell me, Friar Bungay, is it true
That this fair courteous country swain,
Who says his father is a farmer nigh,
Can be Lord Lacy, Earl of Lincolnshire?

BUNGAY. Peggy, 'tis true, 'tis Lacy, for my life,
Or else mine art and cunning both doth fail,
Left by Prince Edward to procure his loves;
For he in green that holp you run your cheese
Is son to Henry, and the Prince of Wales.

MARGARET. Be what he will, his lure is but for lust.

But did Lord Lacy like poor Margaret,
Or would he deign to wed a country lass,
Friar, I would his humble handmaid be,
And, for great wealth, quite him with courtesy.

BUNGAY. Why, Margaret, dost thou love him?

MARGARET. His personage, like the pride of vaunting Troy,
Might well avouch to shadow Helen's scape;
His wit is quick, and ready in conceit,
As Greece afforded in her chiefest prime;
Courteous, ah, friar, full of pleasing smiles.
Trust me, I love too much to tell thee more;
Suffice to me he is England's paramour.

BUNGAY. Hath not each eye that view'd thy pleasing face
Surnamed thee Fair Maid of Fressingfield?

MARGARET. Yes, Bungay, and would God the lovely earl
Had that in *esse* that so many sought.

BUNGAY. Fear not, the friar will not be behind
To show his cunning to entangle love.

EDWARD. I think the friar courts the bonny wench.
Bacon, methinks he is a lusty churl.

BACON. Now look, my lord.

Enter Lacy.

EDWARD. Gog's wounds, Bacon, here comes Lacy!

BACON. Sit still, my lord, and mark the comedy.

BUNGAY. Here's Lacy. Margaret, step aside awhile.

LACY. Daphne, the damsel that caught Phoebus fast,
And lock'd him in the brightness of her looks,
Was not so beauteous in Apollo's eyes
As is fair Margaret to the Lincoln earl.
Recant thee, Lacy, thou art put in trust.
Edward, thy sovereign's son, hath chosen thee,
A secret friend, to court her for himself,
And darest thou wrong thy prince with treachery?
Lacy, love makes no exception of a friend,
Nor deems it of a prince but as a man.
Honor bids thee control him in his lust;
His wooing is not for to wed the girl,
But to entrap her and beguile the lass.
Lacy, thou lovest; then brook not such abuse,

But wed her, and abide thy prince's frown,
For better die, than see her live disgrac'd.

MARGARET. Come, friar, I will shake him from his dumps.
How cheer you, sir? A penny for your thought.
You're early up; pray God it be the near.
What, come from Beccles in a morn so soon?

LACY. Thus watchful are such men as live in love,
Whose eyes brook broken slumbers for their sleep.
I tell thee, Peggy, since last Harleston fair
My mind hath felt a heap of passions.

MARGARET. A trusty man, that court it for your friend.
Woo you still for the courtier all in green?
I marvel that he sues not for himself.

LACY. Peggy, I pleaded first to get your grace for him,
But when mine eyes survey'd your beauteous looks,
Love, like a wag, straight dived into my heart,
And there did shrine the idea of yourself.
Pity me, though I be a farmer's son,
And measure not my riches but my love.

MARGARET. You are very hasty; for to garden well,
Seeds must have time to sprout before they spring;
Love ought to creep as doth the dial's shade,
For timely ripe is rotten too too soon.

BUNGAY. *Deus hic;* room for a merry friar.
What, youth of Beccles, with the keeper's lass?
'Tis well. But, tell me, hear you any news?

MARGARET. No, friar. What news?

BUNGAY. Hear you not how the pursevants do post
With proclamations through each country town?

LACY. For what, gentle friar? Tell the news.

BUNGAY. Dwell'st thou in Beccles and hear'st not of these
news?
Lacy, the Earl of Lincoln, is late fled
From Windsor court, disguised like a swain,
And lurks about the country here unknown.
Henry suspects him of some treachery,
And therefore doth proclaim in every way
That who can take the Lincoln earl shall have,
Paid in the Exchequer, twenty thousand crowns.

LACY. The Earl of Lincoln! Friar, thou art mad.
It was some other; thou mistakest the man.

The Earl of Lincoln! Why, it cannot be.

MARGARET. Yes, very well, my lord, for you are he.
The keeper's daughter took you prisoner.
Lord Lacy, yield; I'll be your jailer once.

EDWARD. How familiar they be, Bacon.

BACON. Sit still, and mark the sequel of their loves.

LACY. Then am I double prisoner to thyself.
Peggy, I yield. But are these news in jest?

MARGARET. In jest with you, but earnest unto me;
For why these wrongs do wring me at the heart.
Ah, how these earls and noble men of birth
Flatter and feign to forge poor women's ill.

LACY. Believe me, lass, I am the Lincoln earl
I not deny; but 'tired thus in rags
I lived disguis'd to win fair Peggy's love.

MARGARET. What love is there where wedding ends not love?

LACY. I meant, fair girl, to make thee Lacy's wife.

MARGARET. I little think that earls will stoop so low.

LACY. Say, shall I make thee countess ere I sleep?

MARGARET. Handmaid unto the earl, so please himself;
A wife in name, but servant in obedience.

LACY. The Lincoln countess, for it shall be so.
I'll plight the bands, and seal it with a kiss.

EDWARD. Gog's wounds, Bacon, they kiss! I'll stab them!

BACON. Oh, hold your hands, my lord, it is the glass!

EDWARD. Choler to see the traitors 'gree so well
Made me think the shadows substances.

BACON. 'Twere a long poinard, my lord, to reach between
Oxford and Fressingfield. But sit still and see more.

BUNGAY. Well, Lord of Lincoln, if your loves be knit,
And that your tongues and thoughts do both agree,
To avoid ensuing jars, I'll hamper up the match.
I'll take my portace forth and wed you here;
Then go to bed and seal up your desires.

LACY. Friar, content. Peggy, how like you this?

MARGARET. What likes my lord is pleasing unto me.

BUNGAY. Then handfast hand, and I will to my book.

BACON. What sees my lord now?

EDWARD. Bacon, I see the lovers hand in hand,
The friar ready with his portace there
To wed them both; then am I quite undone.

Bacon, help now, if e'er thy magic serv'd;
Help, Bacon; stop the marriage now,
If devils or nigromancy may suffice,
And I will give thee forty thousand crowns.
  BACON. Fear not, my lord, I'll stop the jolly friar
For mumbling up his orisons this day.
  LACY. Why speak'st not, Bungay? Friar, to thy book.

Bungay *is mute, crying, "Hud, hud."*

  MARGARET. How lookest thou, friar, as a man distraught?
Reft of thy senses, Bungay? Show by signs,
If thou be dumb, what passions holdeth thee.
  LACY. He's dumb indeed. Bacon hath with his devils
Enchanted him, or else some strange disease
Or apoplexy hath possess'd his lungs.
But Peggy, what he cannot with his book,
We'll 'twixt us both unite it up in heart.
  MARGARET. Else let me die, my lord, a miscreant.
  EDWARD. Why stands Friar Bungay so amaz'd?
  BACON. I have struck him dumb, my lord; and if your honor
please, I'll fetch this Bungay straightway from Fressingfield,
And he shall dine with us in Oxford here.
  EDWARD. Bacon, do that and thou contentest me.
  LACY. Of courtesy, Margaret, let us lead the friar
Unto thy father's lodge, to comfort him
With broths, to bring him from this hapless trance.
  MARGARET. Or else, my lord, we were passing unkind
To leave the friar so in his distress.

Enter a devil, and carry [off] Bungay on his back.

  MARGARET. Oh, help, my lord, a devil! a devil, my lord!
Look how he carries Bungay on his back!
Let's hence, for Bacon's spirits be abroad.   *Exeunt.*
  EDWARD. Bacon, I laugh to see the jolly friar
Mounted upon the devil, and how the earl
Flees with his bonny lass for fear.
As soon as Bungay is at Brazen-nose,
And I have chatted with the merry friar,
I will in post hie me to Fressingfield

And quite these wrongs on Lacy ere it be long.

BACON. So be it, my lord. But let us to our dinner;
For ere we have taken our repast awhile,
We shall have Bungay brought to Brazen-nose. *Exeunt.*

[*vii*]

Enter three doctors, Burden, Mason, Clement.

MASON. Now that we are gathered in the Regent House,
It fits us talk about the king's repair;
For he, troop'd with all the western kings
That lie alongst the Dansig seas by east,
North by the clime of frosty Germany,
The Almain monarch, and the Saxon duke,
Castile, and lovely Eleanor with him,
Have in their jests resolved for Oxford town.

BURDEN. We must lay plots of stately tragedies,
Strange comic shows, such as proud Roscius
Vaunted before the Roman emperors,
To welcome all the western potentates.

CLEMENT. But more, the king by letters hath foretold
That Frederick, the Almain emperor,
Hath brought with him a German of esteem,
Whose surname is Don Jacques Vandermast,
Skillful in magic and those secret arts.

MASON. Then must we all make suit unto the friar,
To Friar Bacon, that he vouch this task,
And undertake to countervail in skill
The German; else there's none in Oxford can
Match and dispute with learned Vandermast.

BURDEN. Bacon, if he will hold the German play,
We'll teach him what an English friar can do.
The devil, I think, dare not dispute with him.

CLEMENT. Indeed, Mas Doctor, he pleasured you
In that he brought your hostess with her spit
From Henley, posting unto Brazen-nose.

BURDEN. A vengeance on the friar for his pains;
But, leaving that, let's hie to Bacon straight
To see if he will take this task in hand.

CLEMENT. Stay, what rumor is this? The town is up in a mutiny.
What hurly-burly is this?

Enter a Constable, *with* Rafe, Warren, Ermsby, *and* Miles.

CONSTABLE. Nay, masters, if you were ne'er so good, you shall
before the doctors to answer your misdemeanor.

BURDEN. What's the matter, fellow?

CONSTABLE. Marry, sir, here's a company of rufflers that drinking in the tavern have made a great brawl, and almost kill'd the
vintner.

MILES. *Salve,* Doctor Burden. This lubberly lurden,
Ill-shap'd and ill-faced, disdain'd and disgraced,
What he tells unto *vobis, mentitur de nobis.*

BURDEN. Who is the master and chief of this crew?

MILES. *Ecce asinum mundi, fugura rotundi,*
Neat, sheat, and fine, as brisk as a cup of wine.

BURDEN. What are you?

RAFE. I am, father doctor, as a man would say, the bellwether
of this company. These are my lords, and I the Prince of Wales.

CLEMENT. Are you Edward, the king's son?

RAFE. Sirrah Miles, bring hither the tapster that drew the wine,
and I warrant when they see how soundly I have broke his head,
they'll say 'twas done by no less man than a prince.

MASON. I cannot believe that this is the Prince of Wales.

WARREN. And why so, sir?

MASON. For they say the prince is a brave and a wise gentleman.

WARREN. Why, and thinkest thou, doctor, that he is not so?
Dar'st thou detract and derogate from him,
Being so lovely and so brave a youth?

ERMSBY. Whose face, shining with many a sugar'd smile,
Bewrays that he is bred of princely race?

MILES. And yet, Master Doctor, to speak like a proctor,
And tell unto you what is veriment and true,
To cease of this quarrel, look but on his apparel;
Then mark but my talis, he is great Prince of Walis,
The chief of our *gregis,* and *filius regis.*
Then 'ware what is done, for he is Henry's white son.

RAFE. Doctors, whose doting nightcaps are not capable of my
ingenious dignity, know that I am Edward Plantagenet, whom

if you displease, will make a ship that shall hold all your colleges, and so carry away the Niniversity with a fair wind to the Bankside in Southwark. How say'st thou, Ned Warren, shall I not do it?

WARREN. Yes, my good lord; and if it please your lordship, I will gather up all your old pantofles, and with the cork make you a pinnace of five hundred ton, that shall serve the turn marvelous well, my lord.

ERMSBY. And I, my lord, will have pioners to undermine the town, that the very gardens and orchards be carried away for your summer walks.

MILES. And I with *scientia* and great *diligentia*
Will conjure and charm to keep you from harm;
That *utrum horum mavis,* your very great *navis,*
Like Bartlet's ship, from Oxford do skip,
With colleges and schools full loaden with fools.
Quid dices ad hoc, worshipful *domine* Dawcock?

CLEMENT. Why, hare-brain'd courtiers, are you drunk or mad,
To taunt us up with such scurrility?
Deem you us men of base and light esteem,
To bring us such a fop for Henry's son?
Call out the beadles and convey them hence,
Straight to Bocardo; let the roisters lie
Close clapp'd in bolts, until their wits be tame.

ERMSBY. Why, shall we to prison, my lord?

RAFE. What say'st, Miles, shall I honor the prison with my presence?

MILES. No, no; out with your blades, and hamper these jades;
Have a flirt and a crash, now play revel-dash,
And teach these *sacerdos* that the Bocardos,
Like peasants and elves, are meet for themselves.

MASON. To the prison with them, constable.

WARREN. Well, doctors, seeing I have sported me
With laughing at these mad and merry wags,
Know that Prince Edward is at Brazen-nose,
And this, attired like the Prince of Wales,
Is Rafe, King Henry's only loved fool;
I, Earl of Sussex; and this, Ermsby,
One of the privy chamber to the king,
Who, while the prince with Friar Bacon stays,
Have revel'd it in Oxford as you see.

MASON. My lord, pardon us; we knew not what you were;
But courtiers may make greater scapes than these.

Will't please your honor dine with me today?

WARREN. I will, Master Doctor, and satisfy the vintner for his hurt; only I must desire you to imagine him all this forenoon the Prince of Wales.

MASON. I will, sir.

RAFE. And upon that, I will lead the way; only I will have Miles go before me, because I have heard Henry say that wisdom must go before majesty. *Exeunt omnes.*

[*viii*]

Enter Prince Edward *with his poniard in his hand,* Lacy *and* Margaret.

EDWARD. Lacy, thou canst not shroud thy trait'rous thoughts,
Nor cover as did Cassius all his wiles;
For Edward hath an eye that looks as far
As Lynceus from the shores of Grecia.
Did not I sit in Oxford by the friar,
And see thee court the maid of Fressingfield,
Sealing thy flattering fancies with a kiss?
Did not proud Bungay draw his portace forth
And, joining hand in hand, had married you,
If Friar Bacon had not stroke him dumb
And mounted him upon a spirit's back,
That we might chat at Oxford with the friar?
Traitor, what answer'st? Is not all this true?

LACY. Truth all, my lord, and thus I make reply.
At Harleston Fair, there courting for your grace,
When as mine eye survey'd her curious shape,
And drew the beauteous glory of her looks
To dive into the center of my heart,
Love taught me that your honor did but jest,
That princes were in fancy but as men,
How that the lovely maid of Fressingfield
Was fitter to be Lacy's wedded wife
Than concubine unto the Prince of Wales.

EDWARD. Injurious Lacy, did I love thee more
Than Alexander his Hephestion?
Did I unfold the passion of my love
And lock them in the closet of thy thoughts?
Wert thou to Edward second to himself,

Sole friend, and partner of his secret loves?
And could a glance of fading beauty break
Th' enchained fetters of such private friends?
Base coward, false, and too effeminate
To be corrival with a prince in thoughts!
From Oxford have I posted since I din'd
To quite a traitor 'fore that Edward sleep.

 MARGARET. 'Twas I, my lord, not Lacy stepp'd awry;
For oft he sued and courted for yourself,
And still woo'd for the courtier all in green;
But I, whom fancy made but over-fond,
Pleaded myself with looks as if I lov'd.
I fed mine eye with gazing on his face,
And, still bewitch'd, lov'd Lacy with my looks.
My heart with sighs, mine eyes pleaded with tears,
My face held pity and content at once,
And more I could not cipher out by signs
But that I lov'd Lord Lacy with my heart.
Then, worthy Edward, measure with thy mind
If women's favors will not force men fall,
If beauty and if darts of piercing love
Is not of force to bury thoughts of friends.

 EDWARD. I tell thee, Peggy, I will have thy loves.
Edward or none shall conquer Margaret.
In frigates bottom'd with rich Sethin planks,
Topp'd with the lofty firs of Lebanon,
Stemm'd and incas'd with burnish'd ivory,
And overlaid with plates of Persian wealth,
Like Thetis shalt thou wanton on the waves,
And draw the dolphins to thy lovely eyes,
To dance lavoltas in the purple streams.
Sirens, with harps and silver psalteries,
Shall wait with music at thy frigate's stem
And entertain fair Margaret with their lays.
England and England's wealth shall wait on thee;
Britain shall bend unto her prince's love
And do due homage to thine excellence,
If thou wilt be but Edward's Margaret.

 MARGARET. Pardon, my lord. If Jove's great royalty
Sent me such presents as to Danaë,
If Phoebus, 'tired in Latona's weeds,

Come courting from the beauty of his lodge,
The dulcet tunes of frolic Mercury,
Not all the wealth heaven's treasury affords,
Should make me leave Lord Lacy or his love.

EDWARD. I have learn'd at Oxford, then, this point of schools:
Ablata causa, tollitur effectus.
Lacy, the cause that Margaret cannot love
Nor fix her liking on the English prince,
Take him away, and then the effects will fail.
Villain, prepare thyself; for I will bathe
My poinard in the bosom of an earl.

LACY. Rather than live and miss fair Margaret's love,
Prince Edward, stop not at the fatal doom,
But stab it home; end both my loves and life.

MARGARET. Brave Prince of Wales, honored for royal deeds,
'Twere sin to stain fair Venus' courts with blood.
Love's conquests ends, my lord, in courtesy;
Spare Lacy, gentle Edward; let me die,
For so both you and he do cease your loves.

EDWARD. Lacy shall die as traitor to his lord.

LACY. I have deserved it; Edward, act it well.

MARGARET. What hopes the prince to gain by Lacy's death?

EDWARD. To end the loves 'twixt him and Margaret.

MARGARET. Why, thinks King Henry's son that Margaret's
love
Hangs in the uncertain balance of proud time,
That death shall make a discord of our thoughts?
No; stab the earl, and 'fore the morning sun
Shall vaunt him thrice over the lofty east,
Margaret will meet her Lacy in the heavens.

LACY. If aught betides to lovely Margaret
That wrongs or wrings her honor from content,
Europe's rich wealth nor England's monarchy
Should not allure Lacy to overlive.
Then, Edward, short my life and end her loves.

MARGARET. Rid me, and keep a friend worth many loves.

LACY. Nay, Edward, keep a love worth many friends.

MARGARET. And if thy mind be such as fame hath blaz'd,
Then, princely Edward, let us both abide
The fatal resolution of thy rage;
Banish thou fancy and embrace revenge,

And in one tomb knit both our carcasses,
Whose hearts were linked in one perfect love.

EDWARD [*aside*]. Edward, art thou that famous Prince of Wales
Who at Damasco beat the Saracens,
And brought'st home triumph on thy lance's point,
And shall thy plumes be pull'd by Venus down?
Is it princely to dissever lovers' leagues,
To part such friends as glory in their loves?
Leave, Ned, and make a virtue of this fault,
And further Peg and Lacy in their loves.
So in subduing fancy's passion,
Conquering thyself, thou get'st the richest spoil.—
Lacy, rise up. Fair Peggy, here's my hand.
The Prince of Wales hath conquered all his thoughts,
And all his loves he yields unto the earl.
Lacy, enjoy the maid of Fressingfield;
Make her thy Lincoln countess at the church,
And Ned, as he is true Plantagenet,
Will give her to thee frankly for thy wife.

LACY. Humbly I take her of my sovereign,
As if that Edward gave me England's right,
And rich'd me with the Albion diadem.

MARGARET. And doth the English prince mean true?
Will he vouchsafe to cease his former loves,
And yield the title of a country maid
Unto Lord Lacy?

EDWARD. I will, fair Peggy, as I am true lord.

MARGARET. Then, lordly sir, whose conquest is as great,
In conquering love, as Caesar's victories,
Margaret, as mild and humble in her thoughts
As was Aspasia unto Cyrus' self,
Yields thanks, and, next Lord Lacy, doth enshrine
Edward the second secret in her heart.

EDWARD. Gramercy, Peggy. Now that vows are pass'd,
And that your loves are not to be revolt,
Once, Lacy, friends again, come, we will post
To Oxford; for this day the king is there,
And brings for Edward Castile Eleanor.
Peggy, I must go see and view my wife;
I pray God I like her as I loved thee.
Beside, Lord Lincoln, we shall hear dispute

'Twixt Friar Bacon and learned Vandermast.
Peggy, we'll leave you for a week or two.

MARGARET. As it please Lord Lacy; but love's foolish looks
Think footsteps miles and minutes to be hours.

LACY. I'll hasten, Peggy, to make short return.
But, please your honor, go unto the lodge;
We shall have butter, cheese, and venison;
And yesterday I brought for Margaret
A lusty bottle of neat claret wine.
Thus can we feast and entertain your grace.

EDWARD. 'Tis cheer, Lord Lacy, for an emperor,
If he respect the person and the place.
Come, let us in; for I will all this night
Ride post until I come to Bacon's cell.   *Exeunt.*

[ix]

Enter Henry, Emperor, [Duke of Saxony,] Castile, Eleanor,
    Vandermast, Bungay, [*other lords and attendants*].

EMPEROR. Trust me, Plantagenet, these Oxford schools
Are richly seated near the river side;
The mountains full of fat and fallow deer,
The battling pastures laid with kine and flocks,
The town gorgeous with high-built colleges,
And scholars seemly in their grave attire,
Learned in searching principles of art.
What is thy judgment, Jaques Vandermast?

VANDERMAST. That lordly are the buildings of the town,
Spacious the rooms and full of pleasant walks;
But for the doctors, how that they be learned,
It may be meanly, for aught I can hear.

BUNGAY. I tell thee, German, Hapsburg holds none such,
None read so deep as Oxenford contains.
There are within our academic state
Men that may lecture it in Germany
To all the doctors of your Belgic schools.

HENRY. Stand to him, Bungay. Charm this Vandermast,
And I will use thee as a royal king.

VANDERMAST. Wherein darest thou dispute with me?

BUNGAY. In what a doctor and a friar can.

VANDERMAST. Before rich Europe's worthies put thou forth
The doubtful question unto Vandermast.

BUNGAY. Let it be this: whether the spirits of pyromancy or
geomancy be most predominant in magic?

VANDERMAST. I say, of pyromancy.

BUNGAY. And I, of geomancy.

VANDERMAST. The cabalists that write of magic spells,
As Hermes, Melchie, and Pythagoras,
Affirm that 'mongst the quadruplicity
Of elemental essence, *terra* is but thought
To be a *punctum* squared to the rest;
And that the compass of ascending elements
Exceed in bigness as they do in height;
Judging the concave circle of the sun
To hold the rest in his circumference.
If, then, as Hermes says, the fire be great'st,
Purest, and only giveth shapes to spirits,
Then must these demones that haunt that place
Be every way superior to the rest.

BUNGAY. I reason not of elemental shapes,
Nor tell I of the concave latitudes,
Noting their essence nor their quality,
But of the spirits that pyromancy calls,
And of the vigor of the geomantic fiends.
I tell thee, German, magic haunts the grounds,
And those strange necromantic spells,
That work such shows and wondering in the world,
Are acted by those geomantic spirits
That Hermes calleth *terrae filii*.
The fiery spirits are but transparent shades
That lightly pass as heralds to bear news;
But earthly fiends, clos'd in the lowest deep,
Dissever mountains, if they be but charg'd,
Being more gross and massy in their power.

VANDERMAST. Rather these earthly geomantic spirits
Are dull and like the place where they remain;
For, when proud Lucifer fell from the heavens,
The spirits and angels that did sin with him
Retain'd their local essence as their faults,
All subject under Luna's continent.
They which offended less hang in the fire,

And second faults did rest within the air;
But Lucifer and his proud-hearted fiends
Were thrown into the center of the earth,
Having less understanding than the rest,
As having greater sin and lesser grace.
Therefore such gross and earthly spirits do serve
For jugglers, witches, and vild sorcerers;
Whereas the pyromantic genii
Are mighty, swift, and of far-reaching power.
But grant that geomancy hath most force;
Bungay, to please these mighty potentates,
Prove by some instance what thy art can do.

BUNGAY. I will.

EMPEROR. Now, English Harry, here begins the game;
We shall see sport between these learned men.

VANDERMAST. What wilt thou do?

BUNGAY. Show thee the tree leav'd with refined gold,
Whereon the fearful dragon held his seat,
That watch'd the garden call'd Hesperides,
Subdued and won by conquering Hercules.

VANDERMAST. Well done.

Here Bungay *conjures, and the tree appears with the
dragon shooting fire.*

HENRY. What say you, royal lordings, to my friar?
Hath he not done a point of cunning skill?

VANDERMAST. Each scholar in the nicromantic spells
Can do as much as Bungay hath perform'd.
But as Alcmena's bastard raz'd this tree,
So will I raise him up as when he lived,
And cause him pull the dragon from his seat,
And tear the branches piecemeal from the root.
Hercules, *prodi, prodi,* Hercules!

Hercules *appears in his lion's skin.*

HERCULES. *Quis me vult?*

VANDERMAST. Jove's bastard son, thou Libyan Hercules,
Pull off the sprigs from off the Hesperian tree,
As once thou didst to win the golden fruit.

HERCULES. *Fiat.*

Here he begins to break the branches.

VANDERMAST. Now, Bungay, if thou canst by magic charm
The fiend appearing like great Hercules
From pulling down the branches of the tree,
Then art thou worthy to be counted learned.
    BUNGAY. I cannot.
    VANDERMAST. Cease, Hercules, until I give thee charge.
Mighty commander of this English isle,
Henry, come from the stout Plantagenets,
Bungay is learned enough to be a friar,
But to compare with Jacques Vandermast,
Oxford and Cambridge must go seek their cells
To find a man to match him in his art.
I have given nonplus to the Paduans,
To them of Sien, Florence, and Bologna,
Reimes, Louvain, and fair Rotherdam,
Frankford, Utrech, and Orleans;
And now must Henry, if he do me right,
Crown me with laurel, as they all have done.

Enter Bacon.

BACON. All hail to this royal company,
That sit to hear and see this strange dispute.
Bungay, how stand'st thou as a man amaz'd?
What, hath the German acted more than thou?
    VANDERMAST. What art thou that questions thus?
    BACON. Men call me Bacon.
    VANDERMAST. Lordly thou lookest, as if that thou wert learn'd;
Thy countenance, as if science held her seat
Between the circled arches of thy brows.
    HENRY. Now, monarchs, hath the German found his match.
    EMPEROR. Bestir thee, Jacques, take not now the foil,
Lest thou dost lose what foretime thou didst gain.
    VANDERMAST. Bacon, wilt thou dispute?
    BACON. No, unless he were more learn'd than Vandermast;
For yet, tell me; what hast thou done?
    VANDERMAST. Rais'd Hercules to ruinate that tree

That Bungay mounted by his magic spells.

BACON. Set Hercules to work.

VANDERMAST. Now, Hercules, I charge thee to thy task.
Pull off the golden branches from the root.

HERCULES. I dare not. Seest thou not great Bacon here,
Whose frown doth act more than thy magic can?

VANDERMAST. By all the thrones and dominations,
Virtues, powers, and mighty hierarchies,
I charge thee to obey to Vandermast.

HERCULES. Bacon, that bridles headstrong Belcephon,
And rules Asmenoth, guider of the north,
Binds me from yielding unto Vandermast.

HENRY. How now, Vandermast, have you met with your
match?

VANDERMAST. Never before was't known to Vandermast
That men held devils in such obedient awe.
Bacon doth more than art, or else I fail.

EMPEROR. Why, Vandermast, art thou overcome?
Bacon, dispute with him and try his skill.

BACON. I come not, monarchs, for to hold dispute
With such a novice as is Vandermast.
I come to have your royalties to dine
With Friar Bacon here in Brazen-nose;
And for this German troubles but the place,
And holds this audience with a long suspense,
I'll send him to his academy hence.
Thou, Hercules, whom Vandermast did raise,
Transport the German unto Hapsburg straight,
That he may learn by travail, 'gainst the spring,
More secret dooms and aphorisms of art.
Vanish the tree and thou away with him.

Exit the spirit with Vandermast *and the tree.*

EMPEROR. Why, Bacon, whither dost thou send him?

BACON. To Hapsburg; there your highness at return
Shall find the German in his study safe.

HENRY. Bacon, thou hast honored England with thy skill,
And made fair Oxford famous by thine art;
I will be English Henry to thyself.
But tell me, shall we dine with thee today?

BACON. With me, my lord; and while I fit my cheer,
See where Prince Edward comes to welcome you,

Gracious as the morning star of heaven.   *Exit.*

    Enter Edward, Lacy, Warren, Ermsby.

EMPEROR. Is this Prince Edward, Henry's royal son?
How martial is the figure of his face,
Yet lovely and beset with amorets.
    HENRY. Ned, where hast thou been?
    EDWARD. At Framingham, my lord, to try your bucks
If they could 'scape the teasers or the toil;
But hearing of these lordly potentates
Landed and progress'd up to Oxford town,
I posted to give entertain to them—
Chief, to the Almain monarch; next to him,
And joint with him, Castile and Saxony,
Are welcome as they may be to the English court.
Thus for the men. But see, Venus appears,
Or one that over-matcheth Venus in her shape.
Sweet Eleanor, beauty's high-swelling pride,
Rich nature's glory and her wealth at once,
Fair of all fairs, welcome to Albion;
Welcome to me, and welcome to thine own,
If that thou deign'st the welcome from myself.
    ELEANOR. Martial Plantagenet, Henry's high-minded son,
The mark that Eleanor did count her aim,
I lik'd thee 'fore I saw thee; now, I love,
And so as in so short a time I may;
Yet so as time shall never break that so,
And therefore so accept of Eleanor.
    CASTILE. Fear not, my lord, this couple will agree,
If love may creep into their wanton eyes;
And therefore, Edward, I accept thee here,
Without suspense as my adopted son.
    HENRY. Let me that joy in these consorting greets,
And glory in these honors done to Ned,
Yield thanks for all these favors to my son,
And rest a true Plantagenet to all.

    Enter Miles *with a cloth and trenchers and salt.*

    MILES. *Salvete, omnes reges,* that govern your *greges,*

In Saxony and Spain, in England and in Almain;
For all this frolic rable must I cover thee, table,
With trenchers, salt, and cloth, and then look for your broth.

EMPEROR. What pleasant fellow is this?

HENRY. 'Tis, my lord, Doctor Bacon's poor scholar.

MILES [aside]. My master hath made me sewer of these great lords, and God knows I am as serviceable at a table as a sow is under an apple tree. 'Tis no matter; their cheer shall not be great, and therefore what skills where the salt stand, before or behind?   [Exit.]

CASTILE. These scholars knows more skill in axioms,
How to use quips and sleights of sophistry,
Than for to cover courtly for a king.

Enter Miles with a mess of pottage and broth, and after him, Bacon.

MILES. Spill, sir? Why, do you think I never carried twopenny chop before in my life?
By your leave, nobile decus, for here comes Doctor Bacon's pecus,
Being in his full age, to carry a mess of pottage.

BACON. Lordings, admire not if your cheer be this,
For we must keep our academic fare.
No riot where philosophy doth reign;
And therefore, Henry, place these potentates,
And bid them fall unto their frugal cates.

EMPEROR. Presumptuous friar, what, scoff'st thou at a king?
What, dost thou taunt us with thy peasants' fare,
And give us cates fit for country swains?
Henry, proceeds this jest of thy consent,
To twit us with such a pittance of such price?
Tell me, and Frederick will not grieve thee long.

HENRY. By Henry's honor and the royal faith
The English monarch beareth to his friend,
I knew not of the friar's feeble fare;
Nor am I pleas'd he entertains you thus.

BACON. Content thee, Frederick, for I show'd the cates
To let thee see how scholars use to feed,
How little meat refines our English wits.
Miles, take away, and let it be thy dinner.

MILES. Marry, sir, I will. This day shall be a festival day with me,

For I shall exceed in the highest degree.   *Exit* Miles.

    BACON. I tell thee, monarch, all the German peers
Could not afford thy entertainment such,
So royal and so full of majesty,
As Bacon will present to Frederick.
The basest waiter that attends thy cups
Shall be in honors greater than thyself;
And for thy cates, rich Alexandria drugs,
Fetch'd by carvels from Egypt's richest straits,
Found in the wealthy strond of Africa,
Shall royalize the table of my king.
Wines richer than the 'Gyptian courtesan
Quaff'd to Augustus' kingly counter-match
Shall be carous'd in English Henry's feasts;
Kandy shall yield the richest of her canes;
Persia, down her Volga by canoes,
Send down the secrets of her spicery;
The Afric dates, mirobolans of Spain,
Conserves and suckets from Tiberias,
Cates from Judea, choicer than the lamp
That fired Rome with sparks of gluttony,
Shall beautify the board for Frederick;
And therefore grudge not at a friar's feast.   [*Exeunt.*]

[*x*]

    Enter two gentlemen, Lambert *and* Serlsby, *with the* keeper.

    LAMBERT. Come, frolic keeper of our liege's game,
Whose table spread hath ever venison
And jacks of wine to welcome passengers,
Know I am in love with jolly Margaret,
That over-shines our damsels as the moon
Dark'neth the brightest sparkles of the night.
In Laxfield here my land and living lies;
I'll make thy daughter jointer of it all,
So thou consent to give her to my wife;
And I can spend five hundred marks a year.
    SERLSBY. I am the lands-lord, keeper, of thy holds;
By copy all thy living lies in me;
Laxfield did never see me raise my due.

I will enfeoff fair Margaret in all,
So she will take her to a lusty squire.

KEEPER. Now, courteous gentles, if the keeper's girl
Hath pleased the liking fancy of you both,
And with her beauty hath subdued your thoughts,
'Tis doubtful to decide the question.
It joys me that such men of great esteem
Should lay their liking on this base estate,
And that her state should grow so fortunate
To be a wife to meaner men than you.
But sith such squires will stoop to keeper's fee,
I will, to avoid displeasure of you both,
Call Margaret forth, and she shall make her choice.   *Exit.*

LAMBERT. Content, keeper, send her unto us.
Why, Serlsby, is thy wife so lately dead,
Are all thy loves so lightly passed over,
As thou canst wed before the year be out?

SERLSBY. I live not, Lambert, to content the dead;
Nor was I wedded but for life to her.
The grave ends and begins a married state.

Enter Margaret.

LAMBERT. Peggy, the lovely flower of all towns,
Suffolk's fair Helen and rich England's star,
Whose beauty tempered with her huswifery
Makes England talk of merry Fressingfield!

SERLSBY. I cannot trick it up with poesies,
Nor paint my passions with comparisons,
Nor tell a tale of Phoebus and his loves;
But this believe me: Laxfield here is mine,
Of ancient rent seven hundred pounds a year,
And, if thou canst but love a country squire,
I will enfeoff thee, Margaret, in all.
I cannot flatter; try me, if thou please.

MARGARET. Brave neighboring squires, the stay of Suffolk's clime,
A keeper's daughter is too base in 'gree
To match with men accompted of such worth.
But might I not displease, I would reply.

LAMBERT. Say, Peggy. Naught shall make us discontent.

MARGARET. Then, gentles, note that love hath little stay,
Nor can the flames that Venus sets on fire
Be kindled but by fancy's motion.
Then pardon, gentles, if a maid's reply
Be doubtful, while I have debated with myself,
Who or of whom love shall constrain me like.

SERLSBY. Let it be me; and trust me, Margaret,
The meads environed with the silver streams,
Whose battling pastures fatt'neth all my flocks,
Yielding forth fleeces stapled with such wool
As Lempster cannot yield more finer stuff,
And forty kine with fair and burnish'd heads,
With strouting dugs that paggle to the ground,
Shall serve thy dairy if thou wed with me.

LAMBERT. Let pass the country wealth, as flocks and kine,
And lands that wave with Ceres' golden sheaves,
Filling my barns with plenty of the fields;
But, Peggy, if thou wed thyself to me,
Thou shalt have garments of embroder'd silk,
Lawns, and rich networks for thy head-attire.
Costly shall be thy fair 'abiliments,
If thou wilt be but Lambert's loving wife.

MARGARET. Content you, gentles. You have proffered fair,
And more than fits a country maid's degree.
But give me leave to counsel me a time;
For fancy blooms not at the first assault.
Give me but ten days respite and I will reply
Which or to whom myself affectionates.

SERLSBY. Lambert, I tell thee thou art importunate;
Such beauty fits not such a base esquire.
It is for Serlsby to have Margaret.

LAMBERT. Think'st thou with wealth to over-reach me?
Serlsby, I scorn to brook thy country braves.
I dare thee, coward, to maintain this wrong
At dint of rapier, single in the field.

SERLSBY. I'll answer, Lambert, what I have avouch'd.
Margaret, farewell; another time shall serve.   *Exit* Serlsby.

LAMBERT. I'll follow. Peggy, farewell to thyself;
Listen how well I'll answer for thy love.   *Exit* Lambert.

MARGARET. How Fortune tempers lucky haps with frowns,
And wrongs me with the sweets of my delight.

Love is my bliss; and love is now my bale.
Shall I be Helen in my froward fates,
As I am Helen in my matchless hue,
And set rich Suffolk with my face afire?
If lovely Lacy were but with his Peggy,
The cloudy darkness of his bitter frown
Would check the pride of these aspiring squires.
Before the term of ten days be expired,
When as they look for answer of their loves,
My lord will come to merry Fressingfield
And end their fancies and their follies both;
Till when, Peggy, be blithe and of good cheer.

Enter a post with a letter and a bag of gold.

POST. Fair lovely damsel, which way leads this path?
How might I post me unto Fressingfield?
Which footpath leadeth to the keeper's lodge?
MARGARET. Your way is ready and this path is right.
Myself do dwell hereby in Fressingfield,
And, if the keeper be the man you seek,
I am his daughter. May I know the cause?
POST. Lovely and once beloved of my lord—
No marvel if his eye was lodg'd so low,
When brighter beauty is not in the heavens—
The Lincoln earl hath sent you letters here,
And with them, just an hundred pounds in gold.
Sweet bonny wench, read them and make reply.
MARGARET. The scrolls that Jove sent Danaë,
Wrapp'd in rich closures of fine burnish'd gold,
Were not more welcome than these lines to me.
Tell me, whilst that I do unrip the seals,
Lives Lacy well? How fares my lovely lord?
POST. Well, if that wealth may make men to live well.

The letter, and Margaret reads it.

"The blooms of the almond tree grow in a night, and vanish in
a morn; the flies *haemerae,* fair Peggy, take life with the sun, and
die with the dew; fancy, that slippeth in with a gaze, goeth out
with a wink; and too timely loves have ever the shortest length.

I write this as thy grief, and my folly, who at Fressingfield lov'd
that which time hath taught me to be but mean dainties. Eyes
are dissemblers, and fancy is but queasy. Therefore know, Margaret,
I have chosen a Spanish lady to be my wife, chief waiting-woman
to the Princess Eleanor: a lady fair, and no less fair than thyself,
honorable and wealthy. In that I forsake thee, I leave thee to
thine own liking; and for thy dowry I have sent thee an hundred
pounds, and ever assure thee of my favor, which shall avail thee
and thine much. Farewell.

                              Not thine nor his own,
                                    Edward Lacy"

Fond Ate, doomer of bad-boding fates,
That wraps proud Fortune in thy snaky locks,
Didst thou enchant my birthday with such stars
As lighten'd mischief from their infancy?
If heavens had vow'd, if stars had made decree,
To show on me their froward influence,
If Lacy had but lov'd, heavens, hell, and all,
Could not have wrong'd the patience of my mind.
    POST. It grieves me, damsel, but the earl is forc'd
To love the lady by the king's command.
    MARGARET. The wealth combin'd within the English shelves,
Europe's commander, nor the English king
Should not have mov'd the love of Peggy from her lord.
    POST. What answer shall I return to my lord?
    MARGARET. First, for thou cam'st from Lacy whom I lov'd—
Ah, give me leave to sigh at every thought!—
Take thou, my friend, the hundred pound he sent;
For Margaret's resolution craves no dower.
The world shall be to her as vanity;
Wealth, trash; love, hate; pleasure, despair.
For I will straight to stately Framingham,
And in the abbey there be shorn a nun,
And yield my loves and liberty to God.
Fellow, I give thee this, not for the news,
For those be hateful unto Margaret,
But for th'art Lacy's man, once Margaret's love.
    POST. What I have heard, what passions I have seen,
I'll make report of them unto the earl.   *Exit* Post.
    MARGARET. Say that she joys his fancies be at rest,

And prays that his misfortune may be hers.   *Exit.*

[*xi*]

Enter Friar Bacon *drawing the curtains with a white stick, a book in his hand, and a lamp lighted by him, and the* brazen head; *and* Miles, *with weapons by him.*

BACON. Miles, where are you?

MILES. Here, sir.

BACON. How chance you tarry so long?

MILES. Think you that the watching of the brazen head craves no furniture? I warrant you, sir, I have so armed myself that if all your devils come I will not fear them an inch.

BACON. Miles, thou knowest that I have dived into hell
And sought the darkest palaces of fiends;
That with my magic spells great Belcephon
Hath left his lodge and kneeled at my cell;
The rafters of the earth rent from the poles,
And three-form'd Luna hid her silver looks,
Trembling upon her concave continent,
When Bacon read upon his magic book.
With seven years' tossing nigromantic charms,
Poring upon dark Hecat's principles,
I have fram'd out a monstrous head of brass,
That, by th' enchanting forces of the devil,
Shall tell out strange and uncouth aphorisms,
And girt fair England with a wall of brass.
Bungay and I have watch'd these threescore days,
And now our vital spirits crave some rest.
If Argus liv'd, and had his hundred eyes,
They could not overwatch Phobeter's night.
Now, Miles, in thee rests Friar Bacon's weal;
The honor and renown of all his life
Hangs in the watching of this brazen head.
Therefore, I charge thee by the immortal God,
That holds the souls of men within his fist,
This night thou watch; for, ere the morning star
Sends out his glorious glister on the north,
The head will speak. Then, Miles, upon thy life,

Wake me; for then by magic art I'll work
To end my seven years' task with excellence.
If that a wink but shut thy watchful eye,
Then farewell Bacon's glory and his fame.
Draw close the curtains, Miles. Now, for thy life,
Be watchful, and—   *Here he falleth asleep.*

MILES. So. I thought you would talk yourself asleep anon; and
'tis no marvel, for Bungay on the days and he on the nights have
watch'd just these ten-and-fifty days. Now this is the night, and
'tis my task and no more. Now, Jesus bless me, what a goodly
head it is; and a nose! you talk of *nos autem glorificare,* but here's
a nose that I warrant may be call'd *nos autem popelare* for the
people of the parish. Well, I am furnished with weapons. Now,
sir, I will set me down by a post, and make it as good as a watch-
man to wake me if I chance to slumber. I thought, Goodman
Head, I would call you out of your memento.

                          Sit down and knock your head.
Passion a' God, I have almost broke my pate! Up, Miles, to your
task; take your brown bill in your hand; here's some of your
master's hobgoblins abroad.

                    With this a great noise. The Head *speaks.*
HEAD. Time is.

MILES. Time is? Why, Master Brazen-head, have you such a
capital nose, and answer you with syllables, "Time is"? Is this all
my master's cunning, to spend seven years' study about "Time
is"? Well, sir, it may be we shall have some better orations of it
anon. Well, I'll watch you as narrowly as ever you were watch'd,
and I'll play with you as the nightingale with the slowworm: I'll
set a prick against my breast. [*Places the point of the halberd against
his breast.*] Now, rest there, Miles. [*Falls asleep.*] Lord have mercy
upon me, I have almost kill'd myself! [*Noise again.*] Up, Miles;
list how they rumble.

HEAD. Time was.

MILES. Well, Friar Bacon, you spent your seven years' study
well, that can make your head speak but two words at once.
"Time was." Yea, marry, time was when my master was a wise
man, but that was before he began to make the brazen head. You
shall lie, while your arse ache and your head speak no better.
Well, I will watch, and walk up and down, and be a peripatetian
and a philosopher of Aristotle's stamp. [*Noise again.*] What, a fresh
noise? Take thy pistols in hand, Miles.

Here the Head *speaks; and a lightning flasheth forth, and a hand
appears that breaketh down the* Head *with a hammer.*

HEAD. Time is past.

MILES. Master, master, up! Hell's broken loose; your head
speaks, and there's such a thunder and lightning that I warrant
all Oxford is up in arms. Out of your bed, and take a brown bill
in your hand. The latter day is come.

BACON. Miles, I come. Oh, passing warily watch'd;
Bacon will make thee next himself in love.
When spake the head?

MILES. When spake the head! Did not you say that he should
tell strange principles of philosophy? Why, sir, it speaks but two
words at a time.

BACON. Why, villain, hath it spoken oft?

MILES. Oft? Ay, marry, hath it, thrice. But in all those three
times it hath uttered but seven words.

BACON. As how?

MILES. Marry, sir, the first time he said, "Time is." As if Fabius
Cumentator should have pronounc'd a sentence, he said, "Time
was." And the third time, with thunder and lightning, as in great
choler, he said, "Time is past."

BACON. 'Tis past indeed. Ah, villain, time is past;
My life, my fame, my glory, all are past.
Bacon, the turrets of thy hope are ruin'd down;
Thy seven years' study lieth in the dust;
Thy brazen head lies broken through a slave
That watch'd, and would not when the head did will.
What said the head first?

MILES. Even, sir, "Time is."

BACON. Villain, if thou hadst call'd to Bacon then,
If thou hadst watch'd, and wak'd the sleepy friar,
The brazen head had uttered aphorisms,
And England had been circled round with brass.
But proud Astmeroth, ruler of the north,
And Demogorgon, master of the fates,
Grudge that a mortal man should work so much.
Hell trembled at my deep, commanding spells;
Fiends frown'd to see a man their over-match.
Bacon might boast more than a man might boast,
But now the braves of Bacon hath an end;

Europe's conceit of Bacon hath an end;
His seven years' practice sorteth to ill end;
And, villain, sith my glory hath an end,
I will appoint thee fatal to some end.
Villain, avoid; get thee from Bacon's sight.
Vagrant, go roam and range about the world,
And perish as a vagabond on earth.

MILES. Why then, sir, you forbid me your service.

BACON. My service, villain, with a fatal curse
That direful plagues and mischief fall on thee.

MILES. 'Tis no matter. I am against you with the old proverb, "The more the fox is curs'd, the better he fares." God be with you, sir. I'll take but a book in my hand, a wide-sleeved gown on my back, and a crowned cap on my head, and see if I can want promotion. [*Exit.*]

BACON. Some fiend or ghost haunt on thy weary steps,
Until they do transport thee quick to hell;
For Bacon shall have never merry day,
To lose the fame and honor of his head. *Exit.*

[xii]

Enter Emperor, Castile, Henry, Eleanor, Edward, Lacy, Rafe,
[*and attendants*].

EMPEROR. Now, lovely prince, the prince of Albion's wealth,
How fares the Lady Eleanor and you?
What, have you courted and found Castile fit
To answer England in equivalence?
Will't be a match 'twixt bonny Nell and thee?

EDWARD. Should Paris enter in the courts of Greece
And not lie fettered in fair Helen's looks?
Or Phoebus 'scape those piercing amorets
That Daphne glanced at his deity?
Can Edward then sit by a flame and freeze,
Whose heat puts Helen and fair Daphne down?
Now, monarchs, ask the lady if we 'gree.

HENRY. What, madam, hath my son found grace or no?

ELEANOR. Seeing, my lord, his lovely counterfeit,
And hearing how his mind and shape agreed,
I come not, troop'd with all this warlike train,

Doubting of love, but so affectionate
As Edward hath in England what he won in Spain.

CASTILE. A match, my lord; these wantons needs must love.
Men must have wives and women will be wed.
Let's haste the day to honor up the rites.

RAFE. Sirrah Harry, shall Ned marry Nell?

HENRY. Ay, Rafe; how then?

RAFE. Marry, Harry, follow my counsel. Send for Friar Bacon
to marry them, for he'll so conjure him and her with his nigromancy, that they shall love together like pig and lamb whilst
they live.

CASTILE. But hear'st thou, Rafe, art thou content to have
Eleanor to thy lady?

RAFE. Ay, so she will promise me two things.

CASTILE. What's that, Rafe?

RAFE. That she will never scold with Ned, nor fight with me.
Sirrah Harry, I have put her down with a thing unpossible.

HENRY. What's that, Rafe?

RAFE. Why, Harry, didst thou ever see that a woman could
both hold her tongue and her hands? No. But when egg-pies
grows on apple trees, then will thy gray mare prove a bagpiper.

EMPEROR. What says the Lord of Castile and the Earl of Lincoln,
that they are in such earnest and secret talk?

CASTILE. I stand, my lord, amazed at his talk,
How he discourseth of the constancy
Of one surnam'd, for beauty's excellence,
The Fair Maid of merry Fressingfield.

HENRY. 'Tis true, my lord, 'tis wondrous for to hear;
Her beauty passing Mars's paramour,
Her virgin's right as rich as Vesta's was.
Lacy and Ned hath told me miracles.

CASTILE. What says Lord Lacy? Shall she be his wife?

LACY. Or else Lord Lacy is unfit to live.
May it please your highness give me leave to post
To Fressingfield, I'll fetch the bonny girl,
And prove in true appearance at the court
What I have vouched often with my tongue.

HENRY. Lacy, go to the querry of my stable
And take such coursers as shall fit thy turn.
Hie thee to Fressingfield and bring home the lass;
And for her fame flies through the English coast,

If it may please the Lady Eleanor,
One day shall match your excellence and her.

ELEANOR. We Castile ladies are not very coy.
Your highness may command a greater boon;
And glad were I to grace the Lincoln earl
With being partner of his marriage day.

EDWARD. Gramercy, Nell; for I do love the lord
As he that's second to myself in love.

RAFE. You love her? Madam Nell, never believe him you
though he swears he loves you.

ELEANOR. Why, Rafe?

RAFE. Why, his love is like unto a tapster's glass that is broken
with every touch; for he loved the Fair Maid of Fressingfield once,
out of all ho. Nay, Ned, never wink upon me; I care not, I.

HENRY. Rafe tells all; you shall have a good secretary of him.
But Lacy, haste thee post to Fressingfield,
For ere thou hast fitted all things for her state,
The solemn marriage day will be at hand.

LACY. I go, my lord.   *Exit* Lacy.

EMPEROR. How shall we pass this day, my lord?

HENRY. To horse, my lord. The day is passing fair;
We'll fly the partridge or go rouse the deer.
Follow, my lords; you shall not want for sport.   *Exeunt.*

[*xiii*]

Enter Friar Bacon *with* Friar Bungay *to his cell.*

BUNGAY. What means the friar that frolick'd it of late
To sit as melancholy in his cell
As if he had neither lost nor won today?

BACON. Ah, Bungay, my brazen head is spoil'd,
My glory gone, my seven years' study lost.
The fame of Bacon, bruited through the world,
Shall end and perish with this deep disgrace.

BUNGAY. Bacon hath built foundation on his fame
So surely on the wings of true report,
With acting strange and uncouth miracles,
As this cannot infringe what he deserves.

BACON. Bungay, sit down; for by prospective skill
I find this day shall fall out ominous.

Some deadly act shall 'tide me ere I sleep,
But what and wherein little can I guess.

    BUNGAY. My mind is heavy, whatso'er shall hap.

Enter two Scholars, *sons to Lambert and Serlsby. Knock.*

    BACON. Who's that knocks?

    BUNGAY. Two scholars that desires to speak with you.

    BACON. Bid them come in. Now, my youths, what would you have?

    1ST SCHOLAR. Sir, we are Suffolk men and neighboring friends,
Our fathers, in their countries, lusty squires;
Their lands adjoin. In Crackfield mine doth dwell,
And his in Laxfield. We are college mates,
Sworn brothers, as our fathers lives as friends.

    BACON. To what end is all this?

    2ND SCHOLAR. Hearing your worship kept within your cell
A glass prospective wherein men might see
Whatso their thoughts or hearts' desire could wish,
We come to know how that our fathers fare.

    BACON. My glass is free for every honest man.
Sit down and you shall see ere long
How or in what state your friendly fathers lives.
Meanwhile, tell me your names.

    1ST SCHOLAR. Mine Lambert.

    2ND SCHOLAR. And mine Serlsby.

    BACON. Bungay, I smell there will be a tragedy.

Enter Lambert *and* Serlsby, *with rapiers and daggers.*

    LAMBERT. Serlsby, thou hast kept thine hour like a man.
Th'art worthy of the title of a squire
That durst, for proof of thy affection,
And for thy mistress' favor, prize thy blood.
Thou know'st what words did pass at Fressingfield,
Such shameless braves as manhood cannot brook;
Ay, for I scorn to bear such piercing taunts,
Prepare thee, Serlsby; one of us will die.

    SERLSBY. Thou see'st I single thee the field,
And what I spake, I'll maintain with my sword.
Stand on thy guard; I cannot scold it out.

And if thou kill me, think I have a son,
That lives in Oxford, in the Broadgates Hall,
Who will revenge his father's blood with blood.

LAMBERT. And, Serlsby, I have there a lusty boy
That dares at weapon buckle with thy son,
And lives in Broadgates too, as well as thine.
But draw thy rapier, for we'll have a bout.

BACON. Now, lusty younkers, look within the glass,
And tell me if you can discern your sires.

1ST SCHOLAR. Serlsby, 'tis hard; thy father offers wrong,
To combat with my father in the field.

2ND SCHOLAR. Lambert, thou liest; my father's is the abuse,
And thou shalt find it, if my father harm.

BUNGAY. How goes it, sirs?

1ST SCHOLAR. Our fathers are in combat hard by Fressingfield.

BACON. Sit still, my friends, and see the event.

LAMBERT. Why stand'st thou, Serlsby? Doubt'st thou of thy life?
A veney, man; fair Margaret craves so much.

SERLSBY. Then this, for her!

1ST SCHOLAR. Ah, well thrust.

2ND SCHOLAR. But mark the ward.

They fight and kill each other.

LAMBERT. Oh, I am slain!

SERLSBY. And I; Lord have mercy on me.

1ST SCHOLAR. My father slain! Serlsby, ward that.

The two Scholars *stab one another.*

2ND SCHOLAR. And so is mine. Lambert, I'll quite thee well.

BUNGAY. Oh, strange stratagem.

BACON. See, friar, where the fathers both lie dead.
Bacon, thy magic doth effect this massacre.
This glass prospective worketh many woes;
And therefore, seeing these brave, lusty brutes,
These friendly youths did perish by thine art,
End all thy magic and thine art at once.
The poniard that did end the fatal lives
Shall break the cause efficiat of their woes.

So fade the glass, and end with it the shows
That nigromancy did infuse the crystal with.

He breaks the glass.

  BUNGAY. What means learned Bacon thus to break his glass?
  BACON. I tell thee, Bungay, it repents me sore
That ever Bacon meddled in this art.
The hours I have spent in pyromantic spells,
The fearful tossing in the latest night
Of papers full of nigromantic charms,
Conjuring and adjuring devils and fiends,
With stole and albe and strange pentaganon,
The wresting of the holy name of God,
As Sother, Eloim, and Adonai,
Alpha, Manoth, and Tetragrammaton,
With praying to the five-fold powers of heaven,
Are instances that Bacon must be damn'd
For using devils to countervail his God.
Yet, Bacon, cheer thee; drown not in despair.
Sins have their salves. Repentance can do much.
Think Mercy sits where Justice holds her seat,
And from those wounds those bloody Jews did pierce,
Which by thy magic oft did bleed afresh,
From thence for thee the dew of mercy drops
To wash the wrath of high Jehovah's ire,
And make thee as a new-born babe from sin.
Bungay, I'll spend the remnant of my life
In pure devotion, praying to my God
That he would save what Bacon vainly lost.

Exit [with Bungay].

[*xiv*]

Enter Margaret *in nun's apparel;* Keeper, *her father; and their friend.*

  KEEPER. Margaret, be not so headstrong in these vows.
Oh, bury not such beauty in a cell,
That England hath held famous for the hue.
Thy father's hair, like to the silver blooms
That beautify the shrubs of Africa,
Shall fall before the dated time of death,

Thus to forgo his lovely Margaret.

MARGARET. Ah, father, when the harmony of heaven
Soundeth the measures of a lively faith,
The vain illusions of this flattering world
Seems odious to the thoughts of Margaret.
I loved once; Lord Lacy was my love;
And now I hate myself for that I lov'd,
And doted more on him than on my God.
For this, I scourge myself with sharp repents.
But now, the touch of such aspiring sins
Tells me all love is lust but love of heavens,
That beauty us'd for love is vanity.
The world contains naught but alluring baits,
Pride, flattery, and inconstant thoughts.
To shun the pricks of death I leave the world,
And vow to meditate on heavenly bliss,
To live in Framingham a holy nun,
Holy and pure in conscience and in deed;
And for to wish all maids to learn of me
To seek heaven's joy before earth's vanity.

FRIEND. And will you then, Margaret, be shorn a nun, and so
leave us all?

MARGARET. Now, farewell, world, the engine of all woe.
Farewell to friends and father; welcome, Christ.
Adieu to dainty robes; this base attire
Better befits an humble mind to God
Than all the show of rich 'abiliments.
Love, oh love, and, with fond love, farewell,
Sweet Lacy, whom I loved once so dear;
Ever be well, but never in my thoughts,
Lest I offend to think on Lacy's love.
But even to that, as to the rest, farewell.

Enter Lacy, Warren, Ermsby, *booted and spurred.*

LACY. Come on, my wags, we're near the keeper's lodge.
Here have I oft walk'd in the wat'ry meads,
And chatted with my lovely Margaret.

WARREN. Sirrah Ned, is not this the keeper?

LACY. 'Tis the same.

ERMSBY. The old lecher hath gotten holy mutton to him. A nun, my lord.

LACY. Keeper, how farest thou? Holla, man, what cheer?
How doth Peggy, thy daughter and my love?

KEEPER. Ah, good my lord, oh, woe is me for Peg!
See where she stands, clad in her nun's attire,
Ready for to be shorn in Framingham.
She leaves the world because she left your love.
Oh, good my lord, persuade her if you can.

LACY. Why, how now, Margaret; what, a malcontent?
A nun? What holy father taught you this,
To task yourself to such a tedious life
As die a maid? 'Twere injury to me
To smother up such beauty in a cell.

MARGARET. Lord Lacy, thinking of thy former 'miss,
How fond the prime of wanton years were spent
In love—oh, fie upon that fond conceit,
Whose hap and essence hangeth in the eye—
I leave both love and love's content at once,
Betaking me to Him that is true love,
And leaving all the world for love of Him.

LACY. Whence, Peggy, comes this metamorphosis?
What, shorn a nun? And I have from the court
Posted with coursers to convey thee hence
To Windsor, where our marriage shall be kept.
Thy wedding robes are in the tailors' hands.
Come, Peggy, leave these peremptory vows.

MARGARET. Did not my lord resign his interest,
And make divorce 'twixt Margaret and him?

LACY. 'Twas but to try sweet Peggy's constancy.
But will fair Margaret leave her love and lord?

MARGARET. Is not heaven's joy before earth's fading bliss,
And life above sweeter than life in love?

LACY. Why, then Margaret will be shorn a nun?

MARGARET. Margaret hath made a vow which may not be revok'd.

WARREN. We cannot stay, my lord; and if she be so strict,
Our leisure grants us not to woo afresh.

ERMSBY. Choose you, fair damsel; yet the choice is yours.
Either a solemn nunnery or the court;

God or Lord Lacy. Which contents you best,
To be a nun, or else Lord Lacy's wife?

LACY. A good motion. Peggy, your answer must be short.

MARGARET. The flesh is frail. My lord doth know it well,
That when he comes with his enchanting face,
Whatso'er betide, I cannot say him nay.
Off goes the habit of a maiden's heart;
And, seeing Fortune will, fair Framingham,
And all the show of holy nuns, farewell.
Lacy for me, if he will be my lord.

LACY. Peggy, thy lord, thy love, thy husband.
Trust me, by truth of knighthood, that the king
Stays for to marry matchless Eleanor
Until I bring thee richly to the court,
That one day may both marry her and thee.
How sayst thou, keeper? Art thou glad of this?

KEEPER. As if the English king had given
The park and deer of Fressingfield to me.

ERMSBY. I pray thee, my Lord of Sussex, why art thou in a
brown study?

WARREN. To see the nature of women, that be they never so
near
God, yet they love to die in a man's arms.

LACY. What have you fit for breakfast? We have hied
And posted all this night to Fressingfield.

MARGARET. Butter and cheese and humbles of a deer,
Such as poor keepers have within their lodge.

LACY. And not a bottle of wine?

MARGARET. We'll find one for my lord.

LACY. Come, Sussex, let's in; we shall have more,
For she speaks least to hold her promise sure.   *Exeunt.*

[xv]

Enter a devil *to seek Miles.*

DEVIL. How restless are the ghosts of hellish spirits
When every charmer with his magic spells
Calls us from nine-fold trenched Phlegiton,
To scud and over-scour the earth in post
Upon the speedy wings of swiftest winds.

Now Bacon hath rais'd me from the darkest deep
To search about the world for Miles his man,
For Miles, and to torment his lazy bones
For careless watching of his brazen head.
See where he comes. Oh, he is mine.

Enter Miles *with a gown and a cornercap.*

MILES. A scholar, quoth you? Marry, sir, I would I had been made a bottle maker when I was made a scholar; for I can get neither to be a deacon, reader, nor schoolmaster; no, not the clerk of a parish. Some call me dunce; another saith my head is as full of Latin as an egg's full of oatmeal. Thus I am tormented that the devil and Friar Bacon haunts me. Good Lord, here's one of my master's devils. I'll go speak to him. What, Master Plutus, how cheer you?

DEVIL. Dost thou know me?

MILES. Know you, sir? Why, are not you one of my master's devils that were wont to come to my master, Doctor Bacon, at Brazen-nose?

DEVIL. Yes, marry, am I.

MILES. Good Lord, Master Plutus, I have seen you a thousand times at my master's, and yet I had never the manners to make you drink. But, sir, I am glad to see how conformable you are to the statute. I warrant you he's as yeomanly a man as you shall see; mark you, masters, here's a plain, honest man, without welt or guard. But I pray you, sir, do you come lately from hell?

DEVIL. Ay, marry; how then?

MILES. Faith, 'tis a place I have desired long to see. Have you not good tippling houses there? May not a man have a lusty fire there, a pot of good ale, a pair of cards, a swinging piece of chalk, and a brown toast that will clap a white waistcoat on a cup of good drink?

DEVIL. All this you may have there.

MILES. You are for me, friend, and I am for you. But I pray you, may I not have an office there?

DEVIL. Yes, a thousand. What wouldst thou be?

MILES. By my troth, sir, in a place where I may profit myself. I know hell is a hot place, and men are marvelous dry, and much drink is spent there. I would be a tapster.

DEVIL. Thou shalt.

MILES. There's nothing lets me from going with you, but that 'tis a long journey, and I have never a horse.

DEVIL. Thou shalt ride on my back.

MILES. Now surely here's a courteous devil, that for to pleasure his friend will not stick to make a jade of himself. But I pray you, goodman friend, let me move a question to you.

DEVIL. What's that?

MILES. I pray you, whether is your pace a trot or an amble?

DEVIL. An amble.

MILES. 'Tis well. But take heed it be not a trot. But 'tis no matter; I'll prevent it.

DEVIL. What dost?

MILES. Marry, friend, I put on my spurs; for if I find your pace either a trot or else uneasy, I'll put you to a false gallop; I'll make you feel the benefit of my spurs.

DEVIL. Get up upon my back.

MILES. Oh, Lord, here's even a goodly marvel, when a man rides to hell on the devil's back.   *Exeunt roaring*.

[*xvi*]

Enter the Emperor *with a pointless sword; next, the* King of
Castile, *carrying a sword with a point;* Lacy, *carrying the globe;*
Ed[ward]; Warr[en], *carrying a rod of gold with a dove on it;*
Ermsby, *with a crown and scepter;* [Princess Eleanor],
with the Fair Maid of Fressingfield *on her left hand;* Henry,
Bacon, *with other Lords attending.*

EDWARD. Great potentates, earth's miracles for state,
Think that Prince Edward humbles at your feet,
And, for these favors, on his martial sword
He vows perpetual homage to yourselves,
Yielding these honors unto Eleanor.

HENRY. Gramercies, lordlings. Old Plantagenet,
That rules and sways the Albion diadem,
With tears discovers these conceived joys,
And vows requital, if his men-at-arms,
The wealth of England, or due honors done
To Eleanor, may quite his favorites.
But all this while, what say you to the dames,
That shine like to the crystal lamps of heaven?

EMPEROR. If but a third were added to these two,
They did surpass those gorgeous images
That gloried Ida with rich beauty's wealth.

MARGARET. 'Tis I, my lords, who humbly on my knee
Must yield her orisons to mighty Jove,
For lifting up his handmaid to this state,
Brought from her homely cottage to the court,
And grac'd with kings, princes, and emperors;
To whom, next to the noble Lincoln earl,
I vow obedience and such humble love
As may a handmaid to such mighty men.

ELEANOR. Thou martial man that wears the Almain crown,
And you the western potentates of might,
The Albion princess, English Edward's wife,
Proud that the lovely star of Fressingfield,
Fair Margaret, countess to the Lincoln earl,
Attends on Eleanor—gramercies, lord, for her—
'Tis I give thanks for Margaret to you all,
And rest, for her, due bounden to yourselves.

HENRY. Seeing the marriage is solemnized,
Let's march in triumph to the royal feast.
But why stands Friar Bacon here so mute?

BACON. Repentant for the follies of my youth,
That magic's secret mysteries misled,
And joyful that this royal marriage
Portends such bliss unto this matchless realm.

HENRY. Why, Bacon, what strange event shall happen to this
land?
Or what shall grow from Edward and his queen?

BACON. I find by deep prescience of mine art,
Which once I temper'd in my secret cell,
That here where Brute did build his Troynovant,
From forth the royal garden of a king
Shall flourish out so rich and fair a bud
Whose brightness shall deface proud Phoebus' flower,
And over-shadow Albion with her leaves.
Till then Mars shall be master of the field;
But then the stormy threats of wars shall cease.
The horse shall stamp as careless of the pike;
Drums shall be turn'd to timbrels of delight;
With wealthy favors plenty shall enrich

The strond that gladded wand'ring Brute to see,
And peace from heaven shall harbor in these leaves
That gorgeous beautifies this matchless flower.
Apollo's hellitropian then shall stoop,
And Venus' hyacinth shall vail her top;
Juno shall shut her gilliflowers up,
And Pallas' bay shall bash her brightest green;
Ceres' carnation, in consort with those,
Shall stoop and wonder at Diana's rose.
   HENRY. This prophecy is mystical.
But, glorious commanders of Europa's love,
That makes fair England like that wealthy isle
Circled with Gihon and swift Euphrates,
In royalizing Henry's Albion
With presence of your princely mightiness,
Let's march. The tables all are spread,
And viands such as England's wealth affords
Are ready set to furnish out the boards.
You shall have welcome, mighty potentates;
It rests to furnish up this royal feast.
Only your hearts be frolic, for the time
Craves that we taste of naught but jouissance.
Thus glories England over all the west.   *Exeunt omnes.*

Finis Friar Bacon, made by Robert Greene,
Master of Arts.
Omne tulit punctum qui miscuit utile dulci.

THE SHOEMAKER'S HOLIDAY,
OR THE GENTLE CRAFT

Thomas Dekker

THE FIRST THREE-MAN'S SONG

O the month of May, the merry month of May,
  So frolick, so gay, and so green, so green, so green!
O, and then did I unto my true love say:
  'Sweet Peg, thou shalt be my summer's queen!

'Now the nightingale, the pretty nightingale,
  The sweetest singer in all the forest's choir,
Entreats thee, sweet Peggy, to hear thy true love's tale;
  Lo, yonder she sitteth, her breast against a brier.

'But O, I spy the cuckoo, the cuckoo, the cuckoo;
  See where she sitteth: come away, my joy;
Come away, I prithee: I do not like the cuckoo
  Should sing where my Peggy and I kiss and toy.'

O the month of May, the merry month of May,
  So frolick, so gay, and so green, so green, so green!
And then did I unto my true love say:
  'Sweet Peg, thou shalt be my summer's queen!'

THE SECOND THREE-MAN'S SONG

This is to be sung at the latter end.

Cold's the wind, and wet's the rain,
  Saint Hugh be our good speed:
Ill is the weather that bringeth no gain,
  Nor helps good hearts in need.

Trowl the bowl, the jolly nut-brown bowl,
   And here, kind mate, to thee:
Let's sing a dirge for Saint Hugh's soul,
   And down it merrily.

Down a down heydown a down,
                  [Close with the tenor boy.]
   Hey derry derry, down a down!
Ho, well done; to me let come!
   Ring compass, gentle joy.

Trowl the bowl, the nut-brown bowl,
   And here, kind mate, to thee: &c.
      [Repeat as often as there be men to drink;
        and at last when all have drunk, this verse:

Cold's the wind, and wet's the rain,
   Saint Hugh be our good speed:
Ill is the weather that bringeth no gain,
   Nor helps good hearts in need.

THE PROLOGUE

AS IT WAS PRONOUNCED BEFORE THE QUEEN'S MAJESTY

As wretches in a storm (expecting day),
With trembling hands and eyes cast up to heaven,
Make prayers the anchor of their conquered hopes,
So we, dear goddess, wonder of all eyes,
Your meanest vassals, through mistrust and fear
To sink into the bottom of disgrace
By our imperfect pastimes, prostrate thus
On bended knees, our sails of hope do strike,
Dreading the bitter storms of your dislike.
Since then, unhappy men, our hap is such,
That to ourselves ourselves no help can bring,
But needs must perish, if your saint-like ears
(Locking the temple where all mercy sits)
Refuse the tribute of our begging tongues:
Oh grant, bright mirror of true chastity,
From those life-breathing stars, your sun-like eyes
One gracious smile: for your celestial breath
Must send us life, or sentence us to death.

DRAMATIS PERSONÆ.

THE KING
THE EARL OF CORNWALL
SIR HUGH LACY, *Earl of Lincoln*
ROWLAND LACY, *otherwise* HANS, ⎫
ASKEW, ⎭ *His Nephews*
SIR ROGER OTELEY, *Lord Mayor of London*
MASTER HAMMON, ⎫
MASTER WARNER, ⎬ *Citizens of London*
MASTER SCOTT, ⎭
SIMON EYRE, *the Shoemaker*
ROGER, *commonly called* HODGE, ⎫
FIRK, ⎬ *Eyre's Journeymen*
RALPH, ⎭
LOVELL, a *Courtier*
DODGER, *Servant to the* EARL OF LINCOLN
A DUTCH SKIPPER
A BOY
Courtiers, Attendants, Officers, Soldiers, Hunters, Shoemakers,
  Apprentices, Servants
ROSE, *Daughter of* SIR ROGER
SYBIL, *her Maid*
MARGERY, *Wife of* SIMON EYRE
JANE, *Wife of* RALPH

SCENE.—London and Old Ford

ACT THE FIRST

[SCENE I]

[A Street in London]

Enter the LORD MAYOR *and the* EARL OF LINCOLN

LINCOLN. My lord mayor, you have sundry times
Feasted myself and many courtiers more:
Seldom or never can we be so kind
To make requital of your courtesy.
But leaving this, I hear my cousin Lacy
Is much affected to your daughter Rose.

LORD MAYOR. True, my good lord, and she loves him so well
That I mislike her boldness in the chase.

LINCOLN. Why, my lord mayor, think you it then a shame,
To join a Lacy with an Oteley's name?

LORD MAYOR. Too mean is my poor girl for his high birth;
Poor citizens must not with courtiers wed,
Who will in silks and gay apparel spend
More in one year than I am worth, by far:
Therefore your honour need not doubt my girl.

LINCOLN. Take heed, my lord, advise you what you do,
A verier unthrift lives not in the world,
Than is my cousin; for I'll tell you what:
'Tis now almost a year since he requested
To travel countries for experience;
I furnished him with coin, bills of exchange,
Letters of credit, men to wait on him,
Solicited my friends in Italy
Well to respect him. But to see the end:

Scant had he journeyed through half Germany,
But all his coin was spent, his men cast off,
His bills embezzled, and my jolly coz,
Ashamed to show his bankrupt presence here,
Became a shoemaker in Wittenberg,
A goodly science for a gentleman
Of such descent! Now judge the rest by this:
Suppose your daughter have a thousand pound,
He did consume me more in one half year;
And make him heir to all the wealth you have,
One twelvemonth's rioting will waste it all.
Then seek, my lord, some honest citizen
To wed your daughter to.

    LORD MAYOR. I thank your lordship.
[*Aside*] Well, fox, I understand your subtilty.—
As for your nephew, let your lordship's eye
But watch his actions, and you need not fear,
For I have sent my daughter far enough.
And yet your cousin Rowland might do well,
Now he hath learned an occupation;
And yet I scorn to call him son-in-law.

    LINCOLN. Ay, but I have a better trade for him:
I thank his grace, he hath appointed him
Chief colonel of all those companies
Mustered in London and the shires about,
To serve his highness in those wars of France.
See where he comes!—

Enter LOVELL, LACY, *and* ASKEW

                          Lovell, what news with you?
    LOVELL. My Lord of Lincoln, 'tis his highness' will,
That presently your cousin ship for France
With all his powers; he would not for a million,
But they should land at Dieppe within four days.

    LINCOLN. Go certify his grace, it shall be done.

                               Exit LOVELL

Now, cousin Lacy, in what forwardness
Are all your companies?

    LACY. All well prepared.

The men of Hertfordshire lie at Mile-end,
Suffolk and Essex train in Tothill-fields,
The Londoners and those of Middlesex,
All gallantly prepared in Finsbury,
With frolic spirits long for their parting hour.

    LORD MAYOR. They have their imprest, coats, and furniture;
And, if it please your cousin Lacy come
To the Guildhall, he shall receive his pay;
And twenty pounds besides my brethren
Will freely give him, to approve our loves
We bear unto my lord, your uncle here.

    LACY. I thank your honour.

    LINCOLN. Thanks, my good lord mayor.

    LORD MAYOR. At the Guildhall we will expect your coming.

                                   Exit

    LINCOLN. To approve your loves to me? No subtilty!
Nephew, that twenty pound he doth bestow
For joy to rid you from his daughter Rose.
But, cousins both, now here are none but friends,
I would not have you cast an amorous eye
Upon so mean a project as the love
Of a gay, wanton, painted citizen.
I know, this churl even in the height of scorn
Doth hate the mixture of his blood with thine.
I pray thee, do thou so! Remember, coz,
What honourable fortunes wait on thee:
Increase the king's love, which so brightly shines,
And gilds thy hopes. I have no heir but thee,—
And yet not thee, if with a wayward spirit
Thou start from the true bias of my love.

    LACY. My lord, I will for honour, not desire
Of land or livings, or to be your heir,
So guide my actions in pursuit of France,
As shall add glory to the Lacys' name.

    LINCOLN. Coz, for those words here's thirty Portuguese,
And, Nephew Askew, there a few for you.
Fair Honour, in her loftiest eminence,
Stays in France for you, till you fetch her thence.
Then, nephews, clap swift wings on your designs:
Begone, begone, make haste to the Guildhall;

There presently I'll meet you. Do not stay:
Where honour beckons, shame attends delay.   *Exit*

   ASKEW. How gladly would your uncle have you gone!
   LACY. True, coz, but I'll o'erreach his policies.
I have some serious business for three days,
Which nothing but my presence can dispatch.
You, therefore, cousin, with the companies,
Shall haste to Dover; there I'll meet with you:
Or, if I stay past my prefixèd time,
Away for France; we'll meet in Normandy.
The twenty pounds my lord mayor gives to me
You shall receive, and these ten Portuguese,
Part of mine uncle's thirty. Gentle coz,
Have care to our great charge; I know, your wisdom
Hath tried itself in higher consequence.

   ASKEW. Coz, all myself am yours: yet have this care,
To lodge in London with all secrecy;
Our uncle Lincoln hath, besides his own,
Many a jealous eye, that in your face
Stares only to watch means for your disgrace.

   LACY. Stay, cousin, who be these?

Enter SIMON EYRE, MARGERY *his wife,* HODGE, FIRK, JANE, *and*
RALPH *with a piece*

   EYRE. Leave whining, leave whining! Away with this
whimpering, this puling, these blubbering tears, and these wet
eyes! I'll get thy husband discharged, I warrant thee, sweet Jane;
go to!

   HODGE. Master, here be the captains.

   EYRE. Peace, Hodge; husht, ye knave, husht!

   FIRK. Here be the cavaliers and the colonels, master.

   EYRE. Peace, Firk; peace, my fine Firk! Stand by with your
pishery-pashery, away! I am a man of the best presence; I'll speak
to them, an they were Popes.—Gentlemen, captains, colonels,
commanders! Brave men, brave leaders, may it please you to give
me audience. I am Simon Eyre, the mad shoemaker of Tower
Street; this wench with the mealy mouth that will never tire is
my wife, I can tell you; here's Hodge, my man and my foreman;
here's Firk, my fine firking journeyman, and this is blubbered
Jane. All we come to be suitors for this honest Ralph. Keep him

at home, and as I am a true shoemaker and a gentleman of the Gentle Craft, buy spurs yourselves, and I'll find ye boots these seven years.

MARGERY. Seven years, husband?

EYRE. Peace, midriff, peace! I know what I do. Peace!

FIRK. Truly, master cormorant, you shall do God good service to let Ralph and his wife stay together. She's a young new-married woman; if you take her husband away from her a night, you undo her; she may beg in the daytime; for he's as good a workman at a prick and an awl, as any is in our trade.

JANE. O let him stay, else I shall be undone.

FIRK. Ay, truly, she shall be laid at one side like a pair of old shoes else, and be occupied for no use.

LACY. Truly, my friends, it lies not in my power: The Londoners are pressed, paid, and set forth By the lord mayor, I cannot change a man.

HODGE. Why, then you were as good be a corporal as a colo-nel, if you cannot discharge one good fellow; and I tell you true, I think you do more than you can answer, to press a man within a year and a day of his marriage.

EYRE. Well said, melancholy Hodge; gramercy, my fine foreman.

MARGERY. Truly, gentlemen, it were ill done for such as you, to stand so stiffly against a poor young wife; considering her case, she is new-married, but let that pass: I pray, deal not roughly with her; her husband is a young man, and but newly entered, but let that pass.

EYRE. Away with your pishery-pashery, your pols and your edipols! Peace, midriff; silence, Cicely Bumtrinket! Let your head speak.

FIRK. Yea, and the horns too, master.

EYRE. Too soon, my fine Firk, too soon! Peace, scoundrels! See you this man? Captains, you will not release him? Well, let him go; he's a proper shot; let him vanish! Peace, Jane, dry up thy tears, they'll make his powder dankish. Take him, brave men; Hector of Troy was an hackney to him, Hercules and Termagant scoundrels, Prince Arthur's Round-table—by the Lord of Ludgate—ne'er fed such a tall, such a dapper swordsman; by the life of Pharaoh, a brave resolute swordsman! Peace, Jane! I say no more, mad knaves.

FIRK. See, see, Hodge, how my master raves in commendation of Ralph!

HODGE. Ralph, th' art a gull, by this hand, an thou goest not.

ASKEW. I am glad, good Master Eyre, it is my hap
To meet so resolute a soldier.
Trust me, for your report and love to him,
A common slight regard shall not respect him.

LACY. Is thy name Ralph?

RALPH.   Yes, sir.

LACY. Give me thy hand;
Thou shalt not want, as I am a gentleman.
Woman, be patient; God, no doubt, will send
Thy husband safe again; but he must go,
His country's quarrel says it shall be so.

HODGE. Th' art a gull, by my stirrup, if thou dost not go
I will not have thee strike thy gimlet into these weak vessels;
prick thine enemies, Ralph.

Enter DODGER

DODGER. My lord, your uncle on the Tower-hill
Stays with the lord mayor and the aldermen,
And doth request you with all speed you may,
To hasten thither.

ASKEW.   Cousin, come let's go.

LACY. Dodger, run you before, tell them we come.—

Exit DODGER

This Dodger is mine uncle's parasite.
The arrant'st varlet that e'er breathed on earth;
He sets more discord in a noble house
By one day's broaching of his pickthank tales,
Than can be salved again in twenty years,
And he, I fear, shall go with us to France,
To pry into our actions.

ASKEW.   Therefore, coz,
It shall behove you to be circumspect.

LACY. Fear not, good cousin.—Ralph, hie to your colours.

RALPH. I must, because there is no remedy;
But, gentle master and my loving dame,
As you have always been a friend to me,
So in my absence think upon my wife.

JANE. Alas, my Ralph.

MARGERY.   She cannot speak for weeping.

EYRE. Peace, you cracked groats, you mustard tokens, disquiet not the brave soldier. Go thy ways, Ralph!

JANE. Ay, ay, you bid him go; what shall I do
When he is gone?

FIRK. Why, be doing with me or my fellow Hodge; be not idle.

EYRE. Let me see thy hand, Jane. This fine hand, this white hand, these pretty fingers must spin, must card, must work; work, you bombast-cotton-candle-quean; work for your living, with a pox to you.—Hold thee, Ralph, here's five sixpences for thee; fight for the honour of the Gentle Craft, for the gentlemen shoe-makers, the courageous cordwainers, the flower of St. Martin's, the mad knaves of Bedlam, Fleet Street, Tower Street and Whitechapel; crack me the crowns of the French knaves; a pox on them, crack them; fight, by the Lord of Ludgate; fight, my fine boy!

FIRK. Here, Ralph, here's three twopences: two carry into France, the third shall wash our souls at parting, for sorrow is dry. For my sake, firk the *Basa mon cues*.

HODGE. Ralph, I am heavy at parting; but here's a shilling for thee. God send thee to cram thy slops with French crowns, and thy enemies' bellies with bullets.

RALPH. I thank you, master, and I thank you all.
Now, gentle wife, my loving lovely Jane,
Rich men, at parting, give their wives rich gifts,
Jewels and rings, to grace their lily hands.
Thou know'st our trade makes rings for women's heels:
Here take this pair of shoes, cut out by Hodge,
Stitched by my fellow Firk, seamed by myself,
Made up and pinked with letters for thy name.
Wear them, my dear Jane, for thy husband's sake,
And every morning, when thou pull'st them on,
Remember me, and pray for my return.
Make much of them; for I have made them so,
That I can know them from a thousand mo.

Drum sounds. Enter the LORD MAYOR, *the* EARL OF LINCOLN,
LACY, ASKEW, DODGER, *and* Soldiers. *They pass over the stage;*
RALPH *falls in amongst them;* FIRK *and the rest cry* 'Farewell,' *&c.,
and so exeunt.*

ACT THE SECOND

[SCENE I]

[*A Garden at Old Ford*]

Enter ROSE, *alone, making a garland*

ROSE. Here sit thou down upon this flow'ry bank,
And make a garland for thy Lacy's head.
These pinks, these roses, and these violets,
These blushing gilliflowers, these marigolds,
The fair embroidery of his coronet,
Carry not half such beauty in their cheeks,
As the sweet countenance of my Lacy doth.
O my most unkind father! O my stars,
Why lowered you so at my nativity,
To make me love, yet live robbed of my love?
Here as a thief am I imprisonèd
For my dear Lacy's sake within those walls,
Which by my father's cost were builded up
For better purposes; here must I languish
For him that doth as much lament, I know,
Mine absence, as for him I pine in woe.

Enter SYBIL

SYBIL. Good morrow, young mistress. I am sure you make
that garland for me; against I shall be Lady of the Harvest.

ROSE. Sybil, what news at London?

SYBIL. None but good; my lord mayor, your father, and master Philpot, your uncle, and Master Scot, your cousin, and Mistress Frigbottom by Doctors' Commons, do all, by my troth, send you most hearty commendations.

ROSE. Did Lacy send kind greetings to his love?

SYBIL. O yes, out of cry, by my troth. I scant knew him; here 'a wore a scarf; and here a scarf, here a bunch of feathers, and here precious stones and jewels, and a pair of garters,—O, monstrous! like one of our yellow silk curtains at home here in Old Ford house, here in Master Bellymount's chamber. I stood at our door in Cornhill, looked at him, he at me indeed, spake to him, but he not to me, not a word; marry go-up, thought I, with a wanion! He passed by me as proud—Marry foh! are you grown humorous, thought I; and so shut the door, and in I came.

ROSE. O Sybil, how dost thou my Lacy wrong!
My Rowland is as gentle as a lamb,
No dove was ever half so mild as he.

SYBIL. Mild? yea, as a bushel of stamped crabs. He looked upon me as sour as verjuice. Go thy ways, thought I; thou may'st be much in my gaskins, but nothing in my nether-stocks. This is your fault, mistress, to love him that loves not you; he thinks scorn to do as he's done to; but if
I were as you, I'd cry: Go by, Jeronimo, go by!
I'd set mine old debts against my new driblets,
And the hare's foot against the goose giblets,
For if ever I sigh, when sleep I should take,
Pray God I may lose my maidenhead when I wake.

ROSE. Will my love leave me then, and go to France?

SYBIL. I know not that, but I am sure I see him stalk before the soldiers. By my troth, he is a proper man; but he is proper that proper doth. Let him go snick up, young mistress.

ROSE. Get thee to London, and learn perfectly,
Whether my Lacy go to France, or no.
Do this, and I will give thee for thy pains
My cambric apron and my Romish gloves,
My purple stockings and a stomacher.
Say, wilt thou do this, Sybil, for my sake?

SYBIL. Will I, quoth a? At whose suit? By my troth, yes I'll go. A cambric apron, gloves, a pair of purple stockings, and a stomacher! I'll sweat in purple, mistress, for you; I'll take anything that comes a God's name. O rich! a cambric apron! Faith, then have at 'up tails all'. I'll go jiggy-joggy to London, and be here in a trice, young mistress.

Exit

ROSE. Do so, good Sybil. Meantime wretched I
Will sit and sigh for his lost company.   *Exit*

[*SCENE II*]

[*A Street in London*]

Enter ROWLAND LACY, *like a Dutch Shoemaker*

LACY. How many shapes have gods and kings devised,
Thereby to compass their desired loves!
It is no shame for Rowland Lacy, then,
To clothe his cunning with the Gentle Craft,
That, thus disguised, I may unknown possess
The only happy presence of my Rose.
For her have I forsook my charge in France,
Incurred the king's displeasure, and stirred up
Rough hatred in mine uncle Lincoln's breast.
O love, how powerful art thou, that canst change
High birth to baseness, and a noble mind
To the mean semblance of a shoemaker!
But thus it must be. For her cruel father,
Hating the single union of our souls,
Hath secretly conveyed my Rose from London,
To bar me of her presence; but I trust,
Fortune and this disguise will further me
Once more to view her beauty, gain her sight.
Here in Tower Street with Eyre the shoemaker
Mean I a while to work; I know the trade,
I learnt it when I was in Wittenberg.
Then cheer thy hoping spirits, be not dismayed,
Thou canst not want: do Fortune what she can,
The Gentle Craft is living for a man.   *Exit*

[*SCENE III*]

[*An open Yard before Eyre's House*]

Enter EYRE, *making himself ready*

EYRE. Where be these boys, these girls, these drabs, these
scoundrels? They wallow in the fat brewis of my bounty, and
lick up the crumbs of my table, yet will not rise to see my walks
cleansed. Come out, you powder-beef queans! What, Nan! what,
Madge Mumble-crust! Come out, you fat midriff-swag-belly-

whores, and sweep me these kennels that the noisome stench offend not the noses of my neighbours. What, Firk, I say; what, Hodge! Open my shop-windows! What, Firk, I say!

Enter FIRK

FIRK. O master, is't you that speak bandog and Bedlam this morning? I was in a dream, and mused what madman was got into the street so early; have you drunk this morning that your throat is so clear?

EYRE. Ah, well said, Firk; well said, Firk. To work, my fine knave, to work! Wash thy face, and thou'lt be more blest.

FIRK. Let them wash my face that will eat it. Good master, send for a souse-wife, if you will have my face cleaner.

Enter HODGE

EYRE. Away, sloven! avaunt, scoundrel!—Good-morrow, Hodge; good-morrow, my fine foreman.

HODGE. O master, good-morrow; y'are an early stirrer. Here's a fair morning.—Good-morrow, Firk, I could have slept this hour. Here's a brave day towards.

EYRE. Oh, haste to work, my fine foreman, haste to work.

FIRK. Master, I am dry as dust to hear my fellow Roger talk of fair weather; let us pray for good leather, and let clowns and ploughboys and those that work in the fields pray for brave days. We work in a dry shop; what care I if it rain?

Enter MARGERY

EYRE. How now, Dame Margery, can you see to rise? Trip and go, call up the drabs, your maids.

MARGERY. See to rise? I hope 'tis time enough, 'tis early enough for any woman to be seen abroad. I marvel how many wives in Tower Street are up so soon. Gods me, 'tis not noon,—here's a yowling!

EYRE. Peace, Margery, peace! Where's Cicely Bumtrinket, your maid? She has a privy fault, she f—ts in her sleep. Call the quean up; if my men want shoe-thread, I'll swinge her in a stirrup.

FIRK. Yet, that's but a dry beating; here's still a sign of drought.

Enter LACY, *as* HANS, *singing*

HANS. Der was een bore van Gelderland
    Frolick sie byen;
He was als dronck he cold nyet stand,
    Upsolce sie byen.
Tap eens de canneken,
Drincke, schone mannekin.

FIRK. Master, for my life, yonder's a brother of the Gentle Craft; if he bear not Saint Hugh's bones, I'll forfeit my bones; he's some uplandish workman: hire him, good master, that I may learn some gibble-gabble; 'twill make us work the faster.

EYRE. Peace, Firk! A hard world! Let him pass, let him vanish; we have journeymen enow. Peace, my fine Firk!

MARGERY. [*Sarcastically*] Nay, nay, y' are best follow your man's counsel; you shall see what will come on't: we have not men enow, but we must entertain every butter-box; but let that pass.

HODGE. Dame, 'fore God, if my master follow your counsel, he'll consume little beef. He shall be glad of men, an he can catch them.

FIRK. Ay, that he shall.

HODGE. 'Fore God, a proper man, and I warrant, a fine workman. Master, farewell; dame, adieu; if such a man as he cannot find work, Hodge is not for you.

Offers to go

EYRE. Stay, my fine Hodge.

FIRK. Faith, an your foreman go, dame, you must take a journey to seek a new journeyman; if Roger remove, Firk follows. If Saint Hugh's bones shall not be set a-work, I may prick mine awl in the walls, and go play. Fare ye well, master; good-bye, dame.

EYRE. Tarry, my fine Hodge, my brisk foreman! Stay, Firk!— Peace, pudding-broth! By the Lord of Ludgate, I love my men as my life. Peace, you gallimafry!—Hodge, if he want work, I'll hire him. One of you to him; stay,—he comes to us.

HANS. Goeden dach, meester, ende u vro oak.

FIRK. Nails, if I should speak after him without drinking, I should choke. And you, friend Oake, are you of the Gentle Craft?

HANS. Yaw, yaw, ik bin den skomawker.

FIRK. Den skomaker, quoth a! And hark you, skomaker, have you all your tools, a good rubbing-pin, a good stopper, a good dresser, your four sorts of awls, and your two balls of wax, your paring knife, your hand- and thumb-leathers, and good St. Hugh's bones to smooth up your work?

HANS. Yaw, yaw; be niet vorveard. Ik hab all de dingen voour mack skooes groot and cleane.

FIRK. Ha, ha! Good master, hire him; he'll make me laugh so that I shall work more in mirth than I can in earnest.

EYRE. Hear ye, friend, have ye any skill in the mystery of cordwainers?

HANS. Ik weet niet wat yow seg; ich verstaw you niet.

FIRK. Why, thus, man: [*Imitating by gesture a shoemaker at work.*] Ich verste u niet, quoth a.

HANS. Yaw, yaw, yaw; ick can dat wel doen.

FIRK. Yaw, yaw! He speaks yawing like a jackdaw that gapes to be fed with cheese-curds. Oh, he'll give a villanous pull at a can of double-beer; but Hodge and I have the vantage, we must drink first, because we are the eldest journeymen.

EYRE. What is thy name?

HANS. Hans—Hans Meulter.

EYRE. Give my thy hand; th' art welcome.—Hodge, entertain him; Firk, bid him welcome; come, Hans. Run, wife, bid your maids, your trullibubs, make ready my fine men's breakfasts. To him, Hodge!

HODGE. Hans, th' art welcome; use thyself friendly, for we are good fellows; if not, thou shalt be fought with, wert thou bigger than a giant.

FIRK. Yea, and drunk with, wert thou Gargantua. My master keeps no cowards, I tell thee.—Ho, boy, bring him an heel-block, here's a new journeyman.

Enter Boy

HANS. O, ich wersto you; ich moet een halve dossen cans betaelen; here, boy, nempt dis skilling, tap eens freelicke.

Exit Boy

EYRE. Quick, snipper-snapper, away! Firk, scour thy throat, thou shalt wash it with Castilian liquor.

Enter Boy

Come, my last of the fives, give me a can. Have to thee, Hans; here, Hodge; here, Firk; drink, you mad Greeks, and work like true Trojans, and pray for Simon Eyre, the shoemaker.—Here, Hans, and th' art welcome.

FIRK. Lo, dame, you would have lost a good fellow that will teach us to laugh. This beer came hopping in well.

MARGERY. Simon, it is almost seven.

EYRE. Is't so, Dame Clapper-dudgeon? Is't seven a clock, and my men's breakfast not ready? Trip and go, you soused conger, away! Come, you mad hyperboreans; follow me, Hodge; follow me, Hans; come after, my fine Firk; to work, to work a while, and then to breakfast! *Exit*

FIRK. Soft! Yaw, yaw, good Hans, though my master have no more wit but to call you afore me, I am not so foolish to go behind you, I being the elder journeyman. *Exeunt*

[SCENE IV]

[A Field near Old Ford]

Holloaing within. Enter Master WARNER *and* Master HAMMON, *attired as Hunters*

HAMMON. Cousin, beat every brake, the game's not far.
This way with winged feet he fled from death,
Whilst the pursuing hounds, scenting his steps,
Find out his highway to destruction.
Besides, the miller's boy told me even now,
He saw him take soil, and he halloaed him,
Affirming him to have been so embost
That long he could not hold.

WARNER.   If it be so,
'Tis best we trace these meadows by Old Ford.

A noise of Hunters within. Enter a Boy

HAMMON. How now, boy? Where's the deer? speak, saw'st thou him?

BOY. O yea; I saw him leap through a hedge, and then over a ditch, then at my lord mayor's pale. Over he skipped me, and in he went me, and 'holla' the hunters cried, and 'there, boy; there, boy!' But there he is, 'a mine honesty.

HAMMON. Boy, God amercy. Cousin, let's away; I hope we shall find better sport to-day. *Exeunt*

[SCENE V]

[Another part of the Field]

Hunting within. Enter ROSE *and* SYBIL

ROSE. Why, Sybil, wilt thou prove a forester?

SYBIL. Upon some, no; forester, go by; no, faith, mistress. The deer came running into the barn through the orchard and over the pale; I wot well, I looked as pale as a new cheese to see him. But whip, says goodman Pinclose, up with his flail, and our Nick with a prong, and down he fell, and they upon him, and I upon them. By my troth, we had such sport; and in the end we ended him; his throat we cut, flayed him, unhorned him, and my lord mayor shall eat of him anon, when he comes. *Horns sound within*

ROSE. Hark, hark, the hunters come; y' are best take heed,
They'll have a saying to you for this deed.

Enter Master HAMMON, *Master* WARNER, *Huntsmen, and* Boy

HAMMON. God save you, fair ladies.

SYBIL.   Ladies! O gross!

WARNER. Came not a buck this way?

ROSE.   No, but two does.

HAMMON. And which way went they? Faith, we'll hunt at those.

SYBIL. At those? upon some, no: when, can you tell?

WARNER. Upon some, ay.

SYBIL.   Good Lord!

WARNER.   Wounds! Then farewell!

HAMMON. Boy, which way went he?

BOY.   This way sir he ran.

HAMMON. This way he ran indeed, fair Mistress Rose;
Our game was lately in your orchard seen.

WARNER. Can you advise, which way he took his flight?

SYBIL. Follow your nose; his horns will guide you right.

WARNER. Th' art a mad wench.

SYBIL.   O, rich!

ROSE.   Trust me, not I.
It is not like that the wild forest-deer
Would come so near to places of resort;

You are deceived, he fled some other way.

    WARNER. Which way, my sugar-candy, can you shew?

    SYBIL. Come up, good honeysops, upon some, no.

    ROSE. Why do you stay, and not pursue your game?

    SYBIL. I'll hold my life, their hunting-nags be lame.

    HAMMON. A deer more dear is found within this place.

    ROSE. But not the deer, sir, which you had in chase.

    HAMMON. I chased the deer, but this dear chaseth me.

    ROSE. The strangest hunting that ever I see.

But where's your park?   *She offers to go away*

    HAMMON. [My park?] 'Tis here: O stay!

    ROSE. Impale me [in't], and then I will not stray.

    WARNER. They wrangle, wench; we are more kind than they.

    SYBIL. What kind of hart is that dear heart, you seek?

    WARNER. A hart, dear heart.

    SYBIL.   Who ever saw the like?

    ROSE. To lose your heart, is't possible you can?

    HAMMON. My heart is lost.

    ROSE.   Alack, good gentleman!

    HAMMON. This poor lost heart would I wish you might find.

    ROSE. You, by such luck, might prove your hart a hind.

    HAMMON. Why, Luck had horns, so have I heard some say.

    ROSE. Now, God, an't be his will, send Luck into your way.

Enter the LORD MAYOR *and Servants*

    LORD MAYOR. What, Master Hammon? Welcome to Old Ford!

    SYBIL. Gods pittikins, hands off, sir! Here's my lord.

    LORD MAYOR. I hear you had ill luck, and lost your game.

    HAMMON. 'Tis true, my lord.

    LORD MAYOR.   I am sorry for the same.

What gentleman is this?

    HAMMON.   My brother-in-law.

    LORD MAYOR. Y' are welcome both; sith Fortune offers you

Into my hands, you shall not part from hence,

Until you have refreshed your wearied limbs.—

Go, Sybil, cover the board!—You shall be guest

To no good cheer, but even a hunter's feast.

    HAMMON. I thank your lordship.—Cousin, on my life,

For our lost venison I shall find a wife.   *Exeunt*

LORD MAYOR. In, gentlemen; I'll not be absent long.—
This Hammon is a proper gentleman.
A citizen by birth, fairly allied;
How fit an husband were he for my girl!
Well, I will in, and do the best I can,
To match my daughter to this gentleman.   *Exit*

ACT THE THIRD

[SCENE I]

[*A Room in Eyre's House*]

Enter HANS, Skipper, HODGE, *and* FIRK

SKIPPER. Ick sal yow wat seggen, Hans; dis skip, dat comen
from Candy, is al vol, by Got's sacrament, van sugar, civet,
almonds, cambrick, end alle dingen, towsand towsand ding.
Nempt it, Hans, nempt it vor v meester. Daer be de bils van
laden. Your meester Simon Eyre sal hae good copen. Wat seggen
yow, Hans?

FIRK. Wat seggen de reggen, de copen slopen—laugh, Hodge,
laugh!

HANS. Mine liever broder Firk, bringt Meester Eyre tot det
signe vn Swannekin; daer sal yow finde dis skipper end me. Wat
seggen yow, broder Firk? Doot it, Hodge. Come, skipper.
                                        Exeunt HANS *and* Skipper

FIRK. Bring him, quoth you? Here's no knavery, to bring my
master to buy a ship worth of lading of two or three hundred
thousand pounds. Alas, that's nothing; a trifle, a bauble, Hodge.

HODGE. The truth is, Firk, that the merchant owner of the
ship dares not shew his head, and therefore this skipper that deals
for him, for the love he bears to Hans, offers my master Eyre a
bargain in the commodities. He shall have a reasonable day of
payment; he may sell the wares by that time, and be an huge
gainer himself.

FIRK. Yea, but can my fellow Hans lend my master twenty porpentines as an earnest penny?

HODGE. Portegues, thou wouldst say; here they be, Firk; hark, they jingle in my pocket like St. Mary Overy's bells.

Enter EYRE *and* MARGERY

FIRK. Mum, here comes my dame and my master. She'll scold, on my life, for loitering this Monday; but all's one, let them all say what they can, Monday's our holiday.

MARGERY. You sing, Sir Sauce, but I beshrew your heart, I fear, for this your singing we shall smart.

FIRK. Smart for me, dame; why, dame, why?

HODGE. Master, I hope you'll not suffer my dame to take down your journeymen.

FIRK. If she take me down, I'll take her up; yea, and take her down too, a button-hole lower.

EYRE. Peace, Firk; not I, Hodge; by the life of Pharaoh, by the Lord of Ludgate, by this beard, every hair whereof I value at a king's ransom, she shall not meddle with you.—Peace, you bombast-cotton-candle-quean; away, queen of clubs; quarrel not with me and my men, with me and my fine Firk; I'll firk you, if you do.

MARGERY. Yea, yea, man, you may use me as you please; but let that pass.

EYRE. Let it pass, let it vanish away; peace! Am I not Simon Eyre? Are not these my brave men, brave shoemakers, all gentlemen of the Gentle Craft? Prince am I none, yet am I nobly born, as being the sole son of a shoemaker. Away, rubbish! vanish, melt; melt like kitchen-stuff.

MARGERY. Yea, yea, 'tis well; I must be called rubbish kitchen-stuff, for a sort of knaves.

FIRK. Nay, dame, you shall not weep and wail in woe for me. Master, I'll stay no longer; here's an inventory of my shop-tools. Adieu, master; Hodge, farewell.

HODGE. Nay, stay, Firk, thou shalt not go alone.

MARGERY. I pray, let them go; there be more maids than Mawkin, more men than Hodge, and more fools than Firk.

FIRK. Fools? Nails! if I tarry now, I would my guts might be turned to shoe-thread.

HODGE. And if I stay, I pray God I may be turned to a Turk, and set in Finsbury for boys to shoot at.—Come, Firk.

EYRE. Stay, my fine knaves, you arms of my trade, you pillars of my profession. What, shall a tittle-tattle's words make you forsake Simon Eyre?—Avaunt, kitchen-stuff! Rip, you brown-bread Tannikin; out of my sight! Move me not! Have not I ta'en you from selling tripes in East-cheap, and set you in my shop, and made you hail-fellow with Simon Eyre, the shoemaker? And now do you deal thus with my journeymen? Look, you powder-beef-quean, on the face of Hodge, here's a face for a lord.

FIRK. And here's a face for any lady in Christendom.

EYRE. Rip, you chitterling, avaunt! Boy, bid the tapster of the Boar's Head fill me a dozen cans of beer for my journeymen.

FIRK. A dozen, cans? O brave! Hodge, now I'll stay.

EYRE. [Aside to the Boy]. An the knave fills any more than two, he pays for them. [Exit Boy. Aloud.] A dozen cans of beer for my journeymen. [Re-enter Boy.] Here, you mad Mesopotamians, wash your livers with this liquor. Where be the odd ten? [Aside] No more, Madge, no more.—Well said. Drink and to work!—What work dost thou, Hodge? what work?

HODGE. I am a-making a pair of shoes for my lord mayor's daughter, Mistress Rose.

FIRK. And I a pair of shoes for Sybil, my lord's maid. I deal with her.

EYRE. Sybil? Fie, defile not thy fine workmanly fingers with the feet of kitchen-stuff and basting-ladles. Ladies of the court, fine ladies, my lads, commit their feet to our apparelling; put gross work to Hans. Yark and seam, yark and seam!

FIRK. For yarking and seaming let me alone, an I come to 't.

HODGE. Well, Master, all this is from the bias. Do you remember the ship my fellow Hans told you of? The Skipper and he are both drinking at the Swan. Here be the Portigues to give earnest. If you go through with it, you cannot choose but be a lord at least.

FIRK. Nay, dame, if my master prove not a lord, and you a lady, hang me.

MARGERY. Yea, like enough, if you may loiter and tipple thus.

FIRK. Tipple, dame? No, we have been bargaining with Skellum Skanderbag: can you Dutch spreaken for a ship of silk Cyprus, laden with sugar-candy?

Enter the Boy *with a velvet coat and an Alderman's gown.* EYRE
puts them on

EYRE. Peace, Firk; silence, Tittle-tattle! Hodge, I'll go through
with it. Here's a seal-ring, and I have sent for a guarded gown
and a damask cassock. See where it comes; look here, Maggy;
help me, Firk; apparel me, Hodge; silk and satin, you mad
Philistines, silk and satin.

FIRK. Ha, ha, my master will be as proud as a dog in a doublet,
all in beaten damask and velvet.

EYRE. Softly, Firk, for rearing of the nap, and wearing threadbare my garments. How dost thou like me, Firk? How do I look,
my fine Hodge?

HODGE. Why, now you look like yourself, master. I warrant
you, there's few in the city, but will give you the wall, and come
upon you with the right worshipful.

FIRK. Nails, my master looks like a threadbare cloak new turned
and dressed. Lord, Lord, to see what good raiment doth! Dame,
dame, are you not enamoured?

EYRE. How say'st thou, Maggy, am I not brisk? Am I not
fine?

MARGERY. Fine? By my troth, sweetheart, very fine! By my
troth, I never liked thee so well in my life, sweetheart; but let
that pass. I warrant, there be many women in the city have not
such handsome husbands, but only for their apparel; but let that
pass too.

Re-enter HANS *and* Skipper

HANS. Godden day, mester. Dis be de skipper dat heb de skip
van marchandice; de commodity ben good; nempt it, master,
nempt it.

EYRE. Godamercy, Hans; welcome, skipper. Where lies this
ship of merchandise?

SKIPPER. De skip ben in revere; dor be van Sugar, cyvet,
almonds, cambrick, and a towsand towsand tings, gotz sacrament;
nempt it, mester: ye sal heb good copen.

FIRK. To him, master! O sweet master! O sweet wares! Prunes,
almonds, sugar-candy, carrot-roots, turnips, O brave fatting meat!
Let not a man buy a nutmeg but yourself.

EYRE. Peace, Firk! Come, skipper, I'll go aboard with you.—
Hans, have you made him drink?

SKIPPER. Yaw, yaw, ic heb veale gedrunck.

EYRE. Come, Hans, follow me. Skipper, thou shalt have my countenance in the city.   *Exeunt*

FIRK. Yaw, heb veale gedrunck, quoth a. They may well be called butter-boxes, when they drink fat veal and thick beer too. But come, dame, I hope you'll chide us no more.

MARGERY. No, faith, Firk; no, perdy, Hodge. I do feel honour creep upon me, and which is more, a certain rising in my flesh; but let that pass.

FIRK. Rising in your flesh do you feel, say you? Ay, you may be with child, but why should not my master feel a rising in his flesh, having a gown and a gold ring on? But you are such a shrew, you'll soon pull him down.

MARGERY. Ha, ha! prithee, peace! Thou mak'st my worship laugh; but let that pass. Come, I'll go in; Hodge, prithee, go before me; Firk, follow me.

FIRK. Firk doth follow: Hodge, pass out in state.

                                                        Exeunt

[SCENE II]

[London: a Room in Lincoln's House]

Enter the EARL OF LINCOLN *and* DODGER

LINCOLN. How now, good Dodger, what's the news in France?

DODGER. My lord, upon the eighteenth day of May
The French and English were prepared to fight;
Each side with eager fury gave the sign
Of a most hot encounter. Five long hours
Both armies fought together; at the length
The lot of victory fell on our sides.
Twelve thousand of the Frenchmen that day died,
Four thousand English, and no man of name
But Captain Hyam and young Ardington,
Two gallant gentlemen, I knew them well.

LINCOLN. But, Dodger, prithee, tell me, in this fight
How did my cousin Lacy bear himself?

DODGER. My lord, your cousin Lacy was not there.

LINCOLN. Not there?

DODGER.   No, my good lord.

LINCOLN.   Sure, thou mistakest.

I saw him shipped, and a thousand eyes beside
Were witnesses of the farewells which he gave,
When I, with weeping eyes, bid him adieu.
Dodger, take heed.

DODGER.   My lord, I am advised,
That what I spake is true: to prove it so,
His cousin Askew, that supplied his place,
Sent me for him from France, that secretly
He might convey himself thither.

LINCOLN.   Is't ever so?
Dares he so carelessly venture his life
Upon the indignation of a king?
Has he despised my love, and spurned those favours
Which I with prodigal hand poured on his head?
He shall repent his rashness with his soul;
Since of my love he makes no estimate,
I'll make him wish he had not known my hate.
Thou hast no other news?

DODGER.   None else, my lord.

LINCOLN. None worse I know thou hast.—Procure the king
To crown his giddy brows with ample honours,
Send him chief colonel, and all my hope
Thus to be dashed! But 'tis in vain to grieve,
One evil cannot a worse [one] relieve.
Upon my life, I have found out his plot;
That old dog, Love, that fawned upon him so,
Love to that puling girl, his fair-cheeked Rose,
The lord mayor's daughter, hath distracted him,
And in the fire of that love's lunacy
Hath he burnt up himself, consumed his credit.
Lost the king's love, yea, and I fear, his life,
Only to get a wanton to his wife,
Dodger, it is so.

DODGER.   I fear so, my good lord.

LINCOLN. It is so—nay, sure it cannot be!
I am at my wits' end. Dodger!

DODGER.   Yea, my lord.

LINCOLN. Thou art acquainted with my nephew's haunts;
Spend this gold for thy pains; go seek him out;
Watch at my lord mayor's—there if he live,
Dodger, thou shalt be sure to meet with him.

Prithee, be diligent.—Lacy, thy name
Lived once in honour, now ['tis] dead in shame.—
Be circumspect.   *Exit*
   DODGER.   I warrant you, my lord.   *Exit*

[SCENE III]

[London: a Room in the Lord Mayor's House]

Enter the LORD MAYOR *and* Master SCOTT

   LORD MAYOR. Good Master Scott, I have been bold with you,
To be a witness to a wedding-knot
Betwixt young Master Hammon and my daughter.
O, stand aside; see where the lovers come.

Enter Master HAMMON *and* ROSE

   ROSE. Can it be possible you love me so?
No, no, within those eyeballs I espy
Apparent likelihoods of flattery.
Pray now, let go my hand.
   HAMMON.   Sweet Mistress Rose,
Misconstrue not my words, nor misconceive
Of my affection, whose devoted soul
Swears that I love thee dearer than my heart.
   ROSE. As dear as your own heart? I judge it right;
Men love their hearts best when th' are out of sight.
   HAMMON. I love you, by this hand.
   ROSE.   Yet hands off now!
If flesh be frail, how weak and frail's your vow!
   HAMMON. Then by my life I swear.
   ROSE.   Then do not brawl;
One quarrel loseth wife and life and all.
Is not your meaning thus?
   HAMMON.   In faith, you jest.
   ROSE. Love loves to sport; therefore leave love, y' are best.
   LORD MAYOR. What? square they, Master Scott?
   SCOTT.   Sir, never doubt,
Lovers are quickly in, and quickly out.
   HAMMON. Sweet Rose, be not so strange in fancying me.

Nay, never turn aside, shun not my sight:
I am not grown so fond, to fond my love
On any that shall quit it with disdain;
If you will love me, so—if not, farewell.

LORD MAYOR. Why, how now, lovers, are you both agreed?

HAMMON. Yes, faith, my lord.

LORD MAYOR. 'Tis well, give me your hand.
Give me yours, daughter.—How now, both pull back?
What means this, girl?

ROSE.   I mean to live a maid.

HAMMON. [*Aside.*] But not to die one; pause, ere that be said.

LORD MAYOR. Will you still cross me, still be obstinate?

HAMMON. Nay, chide her not, my lord, for doing well;
If she can live an happy virgin's life,
'Tis far more blessed than to be a wife.

ROSE. Say, sir, I cannot: I have made a vow,
Whoever be my husband, 'tis not you.

LORD MAYOR. Your tongue is quick; but Master Hammon, know,
I bade you welcome to another end.

HAMMON. What, would you have me pule and pine and pray,
        With 'lovely lady', 'mistress of my heart',
        'Pardon your servant', and the rhymer play,
            Railing on Cupid and his tyrant's-dart;
Or shall I undertake some martial spoil,
Wearing your glove at tourney and at tilt,
And tell how many gallants I unhorsed—
Sweet, will this pleasure you?

ROSE.   Yea, when wilt begin?
What, love rhymes, man? Fie on that deadly sin!

LORD MAYOR. If you will have her, I'll make her agree.

HAMMON. Enforced love is worse than hate to me.
[*Aside.*] There is a wench keeps shop in the Old Change.
To her will I; it is not wealth I seek,
I have enough, and will prefer her love
Before the world.—[*Aloud.*] My good lord mayor, adieu.
Old love for me, I have no luck with new.   *Exit*

LORD MAYOR. Now, mammet, you have well behaved yourself,
But you shall curse your coyness if I live.—
Who's within there? See you convey your mistress
Straight to th' Old Ford! I'll keep you straight enough.

Fore God, I would have sworn the puling girl
Would willingly accept of Hammon's love;
But banish him, my thoughts!—Go, minion, in!   *Exit* ROSE
Now tell me, Master Scott, would you have thought
That Master Simon Eyre, the shoemaker,
Had been of wealth to buy such merchandise?

SCOTT. 'Twas well, my lord, your honour and myself
Grew partners with him; for your bills of lading
Shew that Eyre's gains in one commodity
Rise at the least to full three thousand pound
Besides like gain in other merchandise.

LORD MAYOR. Well, he shall spend some of his thousands now.
For I have sent for him to the Guildhall.

Enter EYRE

See, where he comes. Good morrow, Master Eyre.

EYRE. Poor Simon Eyre, my lord, your shoemaker.

LORD MAYOR. Well, well, it likes yourself to term you so.
Now, Master Dodger, what's the news with you?

DODGER. I'd gladly speak in private to your honour.

LORD MAYOR. You shall, you shall.—Master Eyre and Master
Scott,
I have some business with this gentleman;
I pray, let me entreat you to walk before
To the Guildhall; I'll follow presently.
Master Eyre, I hope ere noon to call you sheriff.

EYRE. I would not care, my lord, if you might call me
King of Spain.—Come, Master Scott.

Exeunt EYRE *and* SCOTT

LORD MAYOR. Now, Master Dodger, what's the news you
bring?

DODGER. The Earl of Lincoln by me greets your lordship,
And earnestly requests you, if you can,
Inform him, where his nephew Lacy keeps.

LORD MAYOR. Is not his nephew Lacy now in France?

DODGER. No, I assure your lordship, but disguised
Lurks here in London.

LORD MAYOR.   London? is't even so?
It may be; but upon my faith and soul,
I know not where he lives, or whether he lives:

So tell my Lord of Lincoln.—Lurks in London?
Well, Master Dodger, you perhaps may start him;
Be but the means to rid him into France,
I'll give you a dozen angels for your pains:
So much I love his honour, hate his nephew.
And, prithee, so inform thy lord from me.

DODGER. I take my leave. *Exit* DODGER
LORD MAYOR. Farewell, good Master Dodger.
Lacy in London? I dare pawn my life,
My daughter knows thereof, and for that cause
Denied young Master Hammon in his love.
Well, I am glad I sent her to Old Ford.
Gods Lord, 'tis late; to Guildhall I must hie;
I know my brethren stay my company. *Exit*

[SCENE IV]

[London: a Room in Eyre's House]

Enter FIRK, MARGERY, HANS, *and* HODGE

MARGERY. Thou goest too fast for me, Roger. O, Firk!

FIRK. Ay, forsooth.

MARGERY. I pray thee, run—do you hear?—run to Guildhall, and learn if my husband, Master Eyre, will take that worshipful vocation of Master Sheriff upon him. Hie thee, good Firk.

FIRK. Take it? Well, I go; an he should not take it, Firk swears to forswear him. Yes, forsooth, I go to Guildhall.

MARGERY. Nay, when? thou art too compendious and tedious.

FIRK. O rare, your excellence is full of eloquence. [*Aside*] How like a new cart-wheel my dame speaks, and she looks like an old musty ale-bottle going to scalding.

MARGERY. Nay, when? thou wilt make me melancholy.

FIRK. God forbid your worship should fall into that humour;—I run. *Exit*

MARGERY. Let me see now, Roger and Hans.

HODGE. Ay, forsooth, dame—mistress I should say, but the old term so sticks to the roof of my mouth, I can hardly lick it off.

MARGERY. Even what thou wilt, good Roger; dame is a fair name for any honest Christian; but let that pass. How dost thou, Hans?

HANS. Mee tanck you, vro.

MARGERY. Well, Hans and Roger, you see, God hath blest your master, and, perdy, if ever he comes to be Master Sheriff of London—as we are all mortal—you shall see, I will have some odd thing or other in a corner for you: I will not be your back-friend; but let that pass. Hans, pray thee, tie my shoe.

HANS. Yaw, ic sal, vro.

MARGERY. Roger, thou know'st the length of my foot; as it is none of the biggest, so I thank God, it is handsome enough; prithee, let me have a pair of shoes made, cork, good Roger, wooden heel too.

HODGE. You shall.

MARGERY. Art thou acquainted with never a farthingale-maker, nor a French hood-maker? I must enlarge my bum, ha, ha! How shall I look in a hood, I wonder! Perdy, oddly, I think.

HODGE. [*Aside*] As a cat out of a pillory.—Very well, I warrant you, mistress.

MARGERY. Indeed, all flesh is grass; and, Roger, canst thou tell where I may buy a good hair?

HODGE. Yes, forsooth, at the poulterer's in Gracious Street.

MARGERY. Thou art an ungracious wag; perdy, I mean a false hair for my periwig.

HODGE. Why, mistress, the next time I cut my beard, you shall have the shavings of it; but they are all true hairs.

MARGERY. It is very hot, I must get me a fan or else a mask.

HODGE. [*Aside.*] So you had need, to hide your wicked face.

MARGERY. Fie upon it, how costly this world's calling is; perdy, but that it is one of the wonderful works of God, I would not deal with it. Is not Firk come yet? Hans, be not so sad, let it pass and vanish, as my husband's worship says.

HANS. Ick bin vrolicke, lot see yow soo.

HODGE. Mistress, will you drink a pipe of tobacco?

MARGERY. Oh, fie upon it, Roger, perdy! These filthy tobacco-pipes are the most idle slavering baubles that ever I felt. Out upon it! God bless us, men look not like men that use them.

Enter RALPH, *being lame*

HODGE. What, fellow Ralph? Mistress, look here, Jane's husband! Why, how now, lame? Hans, make much of him, he's a brother of our trade, a good workman, and a tall soldier.

HANS. You be welcome, broder.

MARGERY. Perdy, I knew him not. How dost thou, good Ralph? I am glad to see thee well.

RALPH. I would [to] God you saw me, dame, as well
As when I went from London into France.

MARGERY. Trust me, I am sorry, Ralph, to see thee impotent. Lord, how the wars have made him sunburnt! The left leg is not well; 'twas a fair gift of God the infirmity took not hold a little higher, considering thou camest from France; but let that pass.

RALPH. I am glad to see you well, and I rejoice
To hear that God hath blest my master so
Since my departure.

MARGERY. Yea, truly, Ralph, I thank my Maker; but let that pass.

HODGE. And, sirrah Ralph, what news, what news in France?

RALPH. Tell me, good Roger, first, what news in England?
How does my Jane? When didst thou see my wife?
Where lives my poor heart? She'll be poor indeed,
Now I want limbs to get whereon to feed.

HODGE. Limbs? Hast thou not hands, man?
Thou shalt never see a shoemaker want bread, though he have but three fingers on a hand.

RALPH. Yet all this while I hear not of my Jane.

MARGERY. O Ralph, your wife,—perdy, we know not what's become of her. She was here a while, and because she was married, grew more stately than became her, I checked her, and so forth; away she flung, never returned, nor said bye nor bah; and, Ralph, you know, 'ka me, ka thee.' And so, as I tell ye— Roger, is not Firk come yet?

HODGE. No, forsooth.

MARGERY. And so, indeed, we heard not of her, but I hear she lives in London; but let that pass. If she had wanted, she might have opened her case to me or my husband, or to any of my men; I am sure, there's not any of them, perdy, but would have done her good to his power. Hans, look if Firk be come.

HANS. Yaw, ik sal, vro.   *Exit* HANS

MARGERY. And so, as I said—but, Ralph, why dost thou weep? Thou knowest that naked we came out of our mother's womb, and naked we must return; and, therefore, thank God for all things.

HODGE. No, faith, Jane is a stranger here; but, Ralph, pull up a good heart, I know thou hast one. Thy wife, man, is in London;

one told me, he saw her awhile ago very brave and neat; we'll ferret her out, an London hold her.

MARGERY. Alas, poor soul, he's overcome with sorrow; he does but as I do, weep for the loss of any good thing, but, Ralph, get thee in, call for some meat and drink, thou shalt find me worshipful towards thee.

RALPH. I thank you, dame; since I want limbs and lands, I'll trust to God, my good friends and my hands.   *Exit*

Enter HANS *and* FIRK *running*

FIRK. Run, good Hans! O Hodge, O mistress! Hodge, heave up thine ears; mistress, smug up your looks; on with your best apparel; my master is chosen, my master is called, nay, condemned by the cry of the country to be sheriff of the city for this famous year now to come. And time now being, a great many men in black gowns were asked for their voices and their hands, and my master had all their fists about his ears presently, and they cried 'Ay, ay, ay, ay',—and so I came away—

Wherefore without all other grieve
I do salute you, Mistress Shrieve.

HANS. Yaw, my mester is de groot man, de shrieve.

HODGE. Did not I tell you, mistress? Now I may boldly say: Good-morrow to your worship.

MARGERY. Good-morrow, good Roger. I thank you, my good people all.—Firk, hold up thy hand: here's a three-penny piece for thy tidings.

FIRK. 'Tis but three-half-pence, I think. Yes, 'tis three-pence, I smell the rose.

HODGE. But, mistress, be ruled by me, and do not speak so pulingly.

FIRK. 'Tis her worship speaks so, and not she. No, faith, mistress, speak me in the old key: 'To it, Firk', 'there, good Firk', 'ply your business, Hodge', 'Hodge, with a full mouth', 'I'll fill your bellies with good cheer, till they cry twang'.

Enter EYRE *wearing a gold chain*

HANS. See, myn liever broder, heer compt my meester.

MARGERY. Welcome home, Master Shrieve; I pray God continue you in health and wealth.

EYRE. See here, my Maggy, a chain, a gold chain for Simon Eyre. I shall make thee a lady; here's a French hood for thee; on with it, on with it! dress thy brows with this flap of a shoulder of mutton, to make thee look lovely. Where be my fine men? Roger, I'll make over my shop and tools to thee; Firk, thou shalt be the foreman; Hans, thou shalt have an hundred for twenty. Be as mad knaves as your master Sim Eyre hath been, and you shall live to be Sheriffs of London.—How dost thou like me, Margery? Prince am I none, yet am I princely born. Firk, Hodge, and Hans!

ALL THREE. Ay, forsooth, what says your worship, Master Sheriff?

EYRE. Worship and honour, you Babylonian knaves, for the Gentle Craft. But I forgot myself; I am bidden by my lord mayor to dinner to Old Ford; he's gone before, I must after. Come, Madge, on with your trinkets! No, my true Trojans, my fine Firk, my dapper Hodge, my honest Hans, some device, some odd crotchets, some morris, or such like, for the honour of the gentlemen shoemakers. Meet me at Old Ford, you know my mind. Come, Madge, away. Shut up the shop, knaves, and make holiday.   *Exeunt*

FIRK. O rare! O brave! Come, Hodge; follow me, Hans; We'll be with them for a morris-dance.   *Exeunt*

[SCENE V]

[A Room at Old Ford]

Enter the LORD MAYOR, ROSE, EYRE, MARGERY *in a French hood,* SYBIL, *and other Servants*

LORD MAYOR. Trust me, you are as welcome to Old Ford
As I myself.

MARGERY.   Truly, I thank your lordship.

LORD MAYOR. Would our bad cheer were worth the thanks you give.

EYRE. Good cheer, my lord mayor, fine cheer! A fine house, fine walls, all fine and neat.

LORD MAYOR. Now, by my troth, I'll tell thee, Master Eyre,
It does me good, and all my brethren,

That such a madcap fellow as thyself
Is entered into our society.

MARGERY. Ay, but, my lord, he must learn now to put on gravity.

EYRE. Peace, Maggy, a fig for gravity! When I go to Guildhall in my scarlet gown, I'll look as demurely as a saint, and speak as gravely as a justice of peace; but now I am here at Old Ford, at my good lord mayor's house, let it go by, vanish, Maggy, I'll be merry; away with flip-flap, these fooleries, these gulleries. What, honey? Prince am I none, yet am I princely born. What says my lord mayor?

LORD MAYOR. Ha, ha, ha! I had rather than a thousand pound, I had an heart but half so light as yours.

EYRE. Why, what should I do, my lord? A pound of care pays not a dram of debt. Hum, let's be merry, whiles we are young; old age, sack and sugar will steal upon us, ere we be aware.

LORD MAYOR. It's well done; Mistress Eyre, pray, give good counsel
To my daughter.

MARGERY. I hope, Mistress Rose will have the grace to take nothing that's bad.

LORD MAYOR. Pray God she do; for i' faith, Mistress Eyre,
I would bestow upon that peevish girl
A thousand marks more than I mean to give her
Upon condition she'd be ruled by me.
The ape still crosseth me. There came of late
A proper gentleman of fair revenues,
Whom gladly I would call [a] son-in-law:
But my fine cockney would have none of him.
You'll prove a coxcomb for it, ere you die:
A courtier, or no man must please your eye.

EYRE. Be ruled; sweet Rose: th' art ripe for a man. Marry not with a boy that has no more hair on his face than thou hast on thy cheeks. A courtier? wash, go by! stand not upon pishery-pashery: those silken fellows are but painted images, outsides, outsides, Rose; their inner linings are torn. No, my fine mouse, marry me with a gentleman grocer like my lord mayor, your father; a grocer is a sweet trade: plums, plums. Had I a son or daughter should marry out of the generation and blood of the shoemakers, he should pack; what, the Gentle Trade is a living for a man through Europe, through the world.

> *A noise within of a tabor and a pipe*

LORD MAYOR. What noise is this?

EYRE. O my lord mayor, a crew of good fellows that for love to your honour are come hither with a morris-dance. Come in, my Mesopotamians, cheerily.

Enter HODGE, HANS, RALPH, FIRK, *and other* Shoemakers, *in a morris; after a little dancing the* LORD MAYOR *speaks*

LORD MAYOR. Master Eyre, are all these shoemakers?

EYRE. All cordwainers, my good lord mayor.

ROSE. [*Aside*] How like my Lacy looks yond' shoemaker!

HANS. [*Aside*] O that I durst but speak unto my love!

LORD MAYOR. Sybil, go fetch some wine to make these drink. You are all welcome.

ALL.   We thank your lordship.

> *Rose takes a cup of wine and goes to* HANS

ROSE. For his sake whose fair shape thou represent'st,
Good friend, I drink to thee.

HANS. Ic bedancke, good frister.

MARGERY. I see, Mistress Rose, you do not want judgment; you have drunk to the properest man I keep.

FIRK. Here be some have done their parts to be as proper as he.

LORD MAYOR. Well, urgent business calls me back to London:
Good fellows, first go in and taste our cheer;
And to make merry as you homeward go,
Spend these two angels in beer at Stratford-Bow.

EYRE. To these two, my mad lads, Sim Eyre adds another; then cheerily, Firk; tickle it, Hans, and all for the honour of shoemakers.   *All go dancing out*

LORD MAYOR. Come, Master Eyre, let's have your company.   *Exeunt*

ROSE. Sybil, what shall I do?

SYBIL.   Why, what's the matter?

ROSE. That Hans the shoemaker is my love Lacy,
Disguised in that attire to find me out.
How should I find the means to speak with him?

SYBIL. What, mistress, never fear; I dare venture my maiden-head to nothing, and that's great odds, that Hans the Dutchman, when we come to London, shall not only see and speak with

you, but in spite of all your father's policies steal you away and
marry you. Will not this please you?

    ROSE. Do this, and ever be assured of my love.

    SYBIL. Away, then, and follow your father to London, lest your
absence cause him to suspect something:
To-morrow, if my counsel be obeyed,
I'll bind you prentice to the Gentle Trade.

Exeunt

ACT THE FOURTH

[SCENE I]

[A Street in London]

JANE in a Seamster's shop, working.
Enter Master HAMMON, muffled; he stands aloof

    HAMMON. Yonder's the shop, and there my fair love sits.
She's fair and lovely, but she is not mine.
O, would she were! Thrice have I courted her,
Thrice hath my hand been moistened with her hand,
Whilst my poor famished eyes do feed on that
Which made them famish. I am infortunate:
I still love one, yet nobody loves me.
I muse, in other men what women see,
That I so want! Fine Mistress Rose was coy,
And this too curious! Oh, no, she is chaste,
And for she thinks me wanton, she denies
To cheer my cold heart with her sunny eyes.
How prettily she works, oh pretty hand!
Oh happy work! It doth me good to stand
Unseen to see her. Thus I oft have stood
In frosty evenings, a light burning by her,
Enduring biting cold, only to eye her.
One only look hath seemed as rich to me
As a king's crown; such is love's lunacy.
Muffled I'll pass along, and by that try

Whether she know me.

JANE.   Sir, what is't you buy?
What is't you lack, sir, calico, or lawn,
Fine cambric shirts, or bands, what will you buy?

HAMMON. [*Aside*] That which thou wilt not sell. Faith, yet I'll try;
How do you sell this handkercher?

JANE.   Good cheap.

HAMMON. And how these ruffs?

JANE.   Cheap too.

HAMMON.   And how this band?

JANE. Cheap too.

HAMMON.   All cheap; how sell you then this hand?

JANE. My hands are not to be sold.

HAMMON.   To be given then!
Nay, faith, I come to buy.

JANE.   But none knows when.

HAMMON. Good sweet, leave work a little while; let's play.

JANE. I cannot live by keeping holiday.

HAMMON. I'll pay you for the time which shall be lost.

JANE. With me you shall not be at so much cost.

HAMMON. Look how you wound this cloth, so you wound me.

JANE. It may be so.

HAMMON.   'Tis so.

JANE.   What remedy?

HAMMON. Nay, faith, you are too coy.

JANE.   Let go my hand.

HAMMON. I will do any task at your command;
I would let go this beauty, were I not
In mind to disobey you by a power
That controls kings: I love you!

JANE.   So, now part.

HAMMON. With hands I may, but never with my heart.
In faith, I love you.

JANE.   I believe you do.

HAMMON. Shall a true love in me breed hate in you?

JANE. I hate you not.

HAMMON.   Then you must love?

JANE.   I do.

What are you better now? I love not you.

   HAMMON. All this, I hope, is but a woman's fray,

That means: come to me, when she cries: away!

In earnest, mistress, I do not jest,

A true chaste love hath entered in my breast.

I love you dearly, as I love my life,

I love you as a husband loves a wife;

That, and no other love, my love requires.

Thy wealth, I know, is little; my desires

Thirst not for gold. Sweet, beauteous Jane, what's mine

Shall, if thou make myself thine, all be thine.

Say, judge, what is thy sentence, life or death?

Mercy or cruelty lies in thy breath.

   JANE. Good sir, I do believe you love me well;

For 'tis a silly conquest, silly pride

For one like you—I mean a gentleman—

To boast that by his love-tricks he hath brought

Such and such women to his amorous lure;

I think you do not so, yet many do,

And make it even a very trade to woo.

I could be coy, as many women be,

Feed you with sunshine smiles and wanton looks,

But I detest witchcraft; say that I

Do constantly believe you, constant have——

   HAMMON. Why dost thou not believe me?

   JANE.   I believe you;

But yet, good sir, because I will not grieve you

With hopes to taste fruit which will never fall,

In simple truth this is the sum of all:

My husband lives, at least, I hope he lives.

Pressed was he to these bitter wars in France;

Bitter they are to me by wanting him.

I have but one heart, and that heart's his due.

How can I then bestow the same on you?

Whilst he lives, his I live, be it ne'er so poor,

And rather be his wife than a king's whore.

   HAMMON. Chaste and dear woman, I will not abuse thee,

Although it cost my life, if thou refuse me.

Thy husband, pressed for France, what was his name?

   JANE. Ralph Damport.

HAMMON.   Damport?—Here's a letter sent
From France to me, from a dear friend of mine,
A gentleman of place; here he doth write
Their names that have been slain in every fight.

JANE. I hope death's scroll contains not my love's name.

HAMMON. Cannot you read?

JANE.   I can.

HAMMON.   Peruse the same.
To my remembrance such a name I read
Amongst the rest. See here.

JANE.   Ay me, he's dead!
He's dead! if this be true, my dear heart's slain!

HAMMON. Have patience, dear love.

JANE.   Hence, hence!

HAMMON.   Nay, sweet Jane,
Make not poor sorrow proud with these rich tears.
I mourn thy husband's death, because thou mourn'st.

JANE. That bill is forged; 'tis signed by forgery.

HAMMON. I'll bring thee letters sent besides to many,
Carrying the like report: Jane, 'tis too true.
Come, weep not: mourning, though it rise from love,
Helps not the mourned, yet hurts them that mourn.

JANE. For God's sake, leave me.

HAMMON.   Wither dost thou turn?
Forget the dead, love them that are alive;
His love is faded, try how mine will thrive.

JANE. 'Tis now no time for me to think on love.

HAMMON. 'Tis now best time for you to think on love,
Because your loves lives not.

JANE.   Though he be dead,
My love to him shall not be buried;
For God's sake, leave me to myself alone.

HAMMON. 'Twould kill my soul, to leave thee drowned in
moan.
Answer me to my suit, and I am gone;
Say to me yea or no.

JANE.   No.

HAMMON.   Then farewell!
One farewell will not serve, I come again;
Come, dry these wet cheeks; tell me, faith, sweet Jane,
Yea or no, once more.

JANE.   Once more I say, no;
Once more be gone, I pray; else will I go.

HAMMON. Nay, then I will grow rude, by this white hand,
Until you change that cold 'no'; here I'll stand
Till by your hard heart——

JANE.   Nay, for God's love, peace!
My sorrows by your presence more increase.
Not that you thus are present, but all grief
Desires to be alone; therefore in brief
Thus much I say, and saying bid adieu:
If ever I wed man, it shall be you.

HAMMON. O blessed voice! Dear Jane, I'll urge no more;
Thy breath hath made me rich.

JANE.   Death makes me poor.

Exeunt

[SCENE II]

[London: a Street before Hodge's Shop]

HODGE, *at his shop-board,* RALPH, FIRK, HANS, *and* Boy *at work*

ALL. Hey, down a down, derry.

HODGE. Well said, my hearts; ply your work to-day, we loitered
yesterday; to it pell-mell, that we may live to be lord mayors, or
aldermen at least.

FIRK. Hey, down a down, derry.

HODGE. Well said, i' faith! How say'st thou, Hans, doth not
Firk tickle it?

HANS. Yaw, mester.

FIRK. Not so neither, my organ-pipe squeaks this morning for
want of liquoring. Hey, down a down, derry!

HANS. Forward, Firk, tow best un jolly yongster. Hort, ay,
mester, ic bid yo, cut me un pair vampres vor Mester Jeffre's
boots.

HODGE. Thou shalt, Hans.

FIRK. Master!

HODGE. How now, boy?

FIRK. Pray, now you are in the cutting vein, cut me out a pair
of counterfeits, or else my work will not pass current; hey, down
a down!

HODGE. Tell me, sirs, are my cousin Mistress Priscilla's shoes done?

FIRK. Your cousin? No, master; one of your aunts, hang her; let them alone.

RALPH. I am in hand with them; she gave charge that none but I should do them for her.

FIRK. Thou do for her? then 'twill be a lame doing, and that she loves not. Ralph, thou might'st have sent her to me, in faith, I would have yearked and firked your Priscilla. Hey, down a down, derry. This gear will not hold.

HODGE. How say'st thou, Firk, were we not merry at Old Ford?

FIRK. How, merry? why, our buttocks went jiggy-joggy like a quagmire. Well, Sir Roger Oatmeal, if I thought all meal of that nature, I would eat nothing but bagpuddings.

RALPH. Of all good fortunes my fellow Hans had the best.

FIRK. 'Tis true, because Mistress Rose drank to him.

HODGE. Well, well, work apace. They say, seven of the aldermen be dead, or very sick.

FIRK. I care not, I'll be none.

RALPH. No, nor I; but then my Master Eyre will come quickly to be lord mayor.

Enter SYBIL

FIRK. Whoop, yonder comes Sybil.

HODGE. Sybil, welcome, i' faith; and how dost thou, mad wench?

FIRK. Syb-whore, welcome to London.

SYBIL. Godamercy, sweet Firk; good lord, Hodge, what a delicious shop you have got! You tickle it, i' faith.

RALPH. Godamercy, Sybil, for our good cheer at Old Ford.

SYBIL. That you shall have, Ralph.

FIRK. Nay, by the mass, we had tickling cheer, Sybil; and how the plague dost thou and Mistress Rose and my lord mayor? I put the women in first.

SYBIL. Well, Godamercy; but God's me, I forget myself, where's Hans the Fleming?

FIRK. Hark, butter-box, now you must yelp out some spreken.

HANS. Wat begaie you? Vat vod you, Frister?

SYBIL. Marry, you must come to my young mistress, to pull on her shoes you made last.

HANS. Vare ben your egle fro, vare ben your mistris?

SYBIL. Marry, here at our London house in Cornhill.

FIRK. Will nobody serve her turn but Hans?

SYBIL. No, sir. Come, Hans, I stand upon needles.

HODGE. Why then, Sybil, take heed of pricking.

SYBIL. For that let me alone. I have a trick in my budget. Come, Hans.

HANS. Yaw, yaw, ic sall meete yo gane.

Exit HANS *and* SYBIL

HODGE. Go, Hans, make haste again. Come, who lacks work?

FIRK. I, master, for I lack my breakfast; 'tis munching-time and past.

HODGE. Is't so? why, then leave work, Ralph. To breakfast! Boy, look to the tools. Come, Ralph; come, Firk.

Exeunt

Enter a Serving-man

SERVING-MAN. Let me see now, the sign of the Last in Tower Street. Mass, yonder's the house. What, haw! Who's within?

Enter RALPH

RALPH. Who calls there? What want you, sir?

SERVING-MAN. Marry, I would have a pair of shoes made for a gentlewoman against to-morrow morning. What, can you do them?

RALPH. Yes, sir, you shall have them. But what's length her foot?

SERVING-MAN. Why, you must make them in all parts like this shoe; but, at any hand, fail not to do them, for the gentlewoman is to be married very early in the morning.

RALPH. How? by this shoe must it be made? by this? Are you sure, sir, by this?

SERVING-MAN. How, by this? Am I sure, by this? Art thou in thy wits? I tell thee, I must have a pair of shoes, dost thou mark me? a pair of shoes, two shoes, made by this very shoe, this same shoe, against to-morrow morning by four a clock. Dost understand me? Canst thou do 't?

RALPH. Yes, sir, yes—ay, ay!—I can do 't. By this shoe, you say? I should know this shoe. Yes, sir, yes, by this shoe, I can do 't. Four a clock, well. Whither shall I bring them?

SERVING-MAN. To the sign of the Golden Ball in Watling Street;
enquire for one Master Hammon, a gentleman, my master.

RALPH. Yea, sir, by this shoe, you say?

SERVING-MAN. I say, Master Hammon at the Golden Ball; he's
the bridegroom, and those shoes are for his bride.

RALPH. They shall be done by this shoe; well, well, Master
Hammon at the Golden Shoe—I would say, the Golden Ball;
very well, very well. But I pray you, sir, where must Master
Hammon be married?

SERVING-MAN. At Saint Faith's Church, under Paul's.
But what's that to thee? Prithee, dispatch those shoes, and so
farewell.   *Exit*

RALPH. By this shoe, said he. How am I amazed
At this strange accident! Upon my life,
This was the very shoe I gave my wife,
When I was pressed for France; since when, alas!
I never could hear of her: 'tis the same,
And Hammon's bride no other but my Jane.

Enter FIRK

FIRK. 'Snails, Ralph, thou hast lost thy part of three pots, a
countryman of mine gave me to breakfast.

RALPH. I care not; I have found a better thing.

FIRK. A thing? away! Is it a man's thing, or a woman's thing?

RALPH. Firk, dost thou know this shoe?

FIRK. No, by my troth; neither doth that know me! I have no
acquaintance with it, 'tis a mere stranger to me.

RALPH. Why, then I do; this shoe, I durst be sworn,
Once covered the instep of my Jane.
This is her size, her breadth, thus trod my love;
These true-love knots I pricked; I hold my life,
By this old shoe I shall find out my wife.

FIRK. Ha, ha! Old shoe, that wert new! How a murrain came
this ague-fit of foolishness upon thee?

RALPH. Thus, Firk: even now here came a serving-man;
By this shoe would he have a new pair made
Against to-morrow morning for his mistress,
That's to be married to a gentleman.
And why may not this be my sweet Jane?

FIRK. And why may'st not thou be my sweet ass? Ha, ha!

RALPH. Well, laugh and spare not! But the truth is this:
Against to-morrow morning I'll provide
A lusty crew of honest shoemakers,
To watch the going of the bride to church.
If she prove Jane, I'll take her in despite
From Hammon and the devil, were he by.
If it be not my Jane, what remedy?
Hereof I am sure, I shall live till I die,
Although I never with a woman lie.   *Exit*

FIRK. Thou lie with a woman, to build nothing but Cripple-
gates! Well, God sends fools fortune, and it may be, he may light
upon his matrimony by such a device; for wedding and hanging
goes by destiny.   *Exit*

[SCENE III]

[*London: a Room in the Lord Mayor's House in Cornhill*]

Enter HANS *and* ROSE, *arm in arm*

HANS. How happy am I by embracing thee!
Oh, I did fear such cross mishaps did reign,
That I should never see my Rose again.

ROSE. Sweet Lacy, since fair opportunity
Offers herself to further our escape,
Let not too over-fond esteem of me
Hinder that happy hour. Invent the means,
And Rose will follow thee through all the world.

HANS. Oh, how I surfeit with excess of joy,
Made happy by thy rich perfection!
But since thou pay'st sweet interest to my hopes,
Redoubling love on love, let me once more
Like to a bold-faced debtor crave of thee,
This night to steal abroad, and at Eyre's house,
Who now by death of certain aldermen
Is mayor of London, and my master once,
Meet thou thy Lacy, where in spite of change,
Your father's anger, and mine uncle's hate,

Our happy nuptials will we consummate.

Enter SYBIL

SYBIL. Oh God, what will you do, mistress? Shift for yourself,
your father is at hand! He's coming, he's coming! Master Lacy,
hide yourself in my mistress! For God's sake, shift for yourselves!

HANS. Your father come, sweet Rose—what shall I do? Where
shall I hide me? How shall I escape?

ROSE. A man, and want wit in extremity?
Come, come, be Hans still, play the shoemaker,
Pull on my shoe.

Enter the LORD MAYOR

HANS.   Mass, and that's well remembered.

SYBIL. Here comes your father.

HANS. Forware, metresse, 'tis un good skow, it sal vel dute,
or ye sal neit betallen.

ROSE. Oh God, it pincheth me; what will you do?

HANS. [*Aside*] Your father's presence pincheth, not the shoe.

LORD MAYOR. Well done; fit my daughter well, and she shall
please thee well.

HANS. Yaw, yaw, ick weit dat well; forware, 'tis un good skoo,
'tis gimait van neits leither; see euer, mine here.

Enter a Prentice

LORD MAYOR. I do believe it.—What's the news with you?

PRENTICE. Please you, the Earl of Lincoln at the gate
Is newly 'lighted, and would speak with you.

LORD MAYOR. The Earl of Lincoln come to speak with me?
Well, well, I know his errand. Daughter Rose,
Send hence your shoemaker, dispatch, have done!
Syb, make things handsome! Sir boy, follow me.   *Exit*

HANS. Mine uncle come! Oh, what may this portend?
Sweet Rose, this of our love threatens an end.

ROSE. Be not dismayed at this; whate'er befall,
Rose is thine own. To witness I speak truth,
Where thou appoint'st the place, I'll meet with thee.
I will not fix a day to follow thee,

But presently steal hence. Do not reply:
Love which gave strength to bear my father's hate,
Shall now add wings to further our escape.   *Exeunt*

[SCENE IV]

[*Another Room in the same House*]

Enter the LORD MAYOR *and the* EARL OF LINCOLN

LORD MAYOR. Believe me, on my credit, I speak truth:
Since first your nephew Lacy went to France,
I have not seen him. It seemed strange to me,
When Dodger told me that he stayed behind,
Neglecting the high charge the king imposed.

LINCOLN. Trust me, Sir Roger Oteley, I did think
Your counsel had given head to this attempt,
Drawn to it by the love he bears your child.
Here I did hope to find him in your house;
But now I see mine error, and confess,
My judgment wronged you by conceiving so.

LORD MAYOR. Lodge in my house, say you? Trust me, my
lord,
I love your nephew Lacy too too dearly,
So much to wrong his honour; and he hath done so,
That first gave him advice to stay from France.
To witness I speak truth, I let you know,
How careful I have been to keep my daughter
Free from all conference or speech of him;
Not that I scorn your nephew, but in love
I bear your honour, lest your noble blood
Should by my mean worth be dishonoured.

LINCOLN. [*Aside*] How far the churl's tongue wanders from his
heart!
—Well, well, Sir Roger Oteley, I believe you,
With more than many thanks for the kind love
So much you seem to bear me. But, my lord,
Let me request your help to seek my nephew,
Whom if I find, I'll straight embark for France.
So shall your Rose be free, my thoughts at rest,
And much care die which now lies in my breast.

Enter SYBIL

SYBIL. Oh Lord! Help, for God's sake! my mistress; oh, my young mistress!

LORD MAYOR. Where is thy mistress? What's become of her?

SYBIL. She's gone, she's fled!

LORD MAYOR. Gone! Whither is she fled?

SYBIL. I know not, forsooth; she's fled out of doors with Hans the shoemaker; I saw them scud, scud, scud, apace, apace!

LORD MAYOR. Which way? What, John! Where be my men? Which way?

SYBIL. I know not, an it please your worship.

LORD MAYOR. Fled with a shoemaker? Can this be true?

SYBIL. Oh Lord, sir, as true as God's in Heaven.

LINCOLN. [*Aside*] Her love turned shoemaker? I am glad of this.

LORD MAYOR. A Fleming butter-box, a shoemaker!
Will she forget her birth, requite my care
With such ingratitude? Scorned she young Hammon
To love a honnikin, a needy knave?
Well, let her fly, I'll not fly after her,
Let her starve, if she will; she's none of mine.

LINCOLN. Be not so cruel, sir.

Enter FIRK *with shoes*

SYBIL. [*Aside.*] I am glad, she's 'scaped.

LORD MAYOR. I'll not account of her as of my child.
Was there no better object for her eyes
But a foul drunken lubber, swill-belly,
A shoemaker? That's brave!

FIRK. Yea, forsooth; 'tis a very brave shoe, and as fit as a pudding.

LORD MAYOR. How now, what knave is this? From whence comest thou?

FIRK. No knave, sir. I am Firk the shoemaker, lusty Roger's chief lusty journeyman, and I come hither to take up the pretty leg of sweet Mistress Rose, and thus hoping your worship is in as good health, as I was at the making hereof, I bid you farewell, yours, Firk.

LORD MAYOR. Stay, stay, Sir Knave!

LINCOLN.   Come hither, shoemaker!

FIRK. 'Tis happy the knave is put before the shoemaker, or else I would not have vouchsafed to come back to you. I am moved, for I stir.

LORD MAYOR. My lord, this villain calls us knaves by craft.

FIRK. Then 'tis by the Gentle Craft, and to call one knave gently, is no harm. Sit your worship merry! [*Aside to* SYBIL] Syb, your young mistress—I'll so bob them, now my Master Eyre is lord mayor of London.

LORD MAYOR. Tell me, sirrah, whose man are you?

FIRK. I am glad to see your worship so merry. I have no maw to this gear, no stomach as yet to a red petticoat.

Pointing to SYBIL

LINCOLN. He means not, sir, to woo you to his maid,
But only doth demand whose man you are.

FIRK. I sing now to the tune of Rogero. Roger, my fellow, is now my master.

LINCOLN. Sirrah, know'st thou one Hans, a shoemaker?

FIRK. Hans, shoemaker? Oh yes, stay, yes, I have him. I tell you what, I speak it in secret: Mistress Rose and he are by this time—no, not so, but shortly are to come over one another with 'Can you dance the shaking of the sheets?' It is that Hans—[*Aside*] I'll so gull these diggers!

LORD MAYOR. Know'st thou, then, where he is?

FIRK. Yes, forsooth; yea, marry!

LINCOLN. Canst thou, in sadness?

FIRK. No, forsooth; no marry!

LORD MAYOR. Tell me, good honest fellow, where he is.
And thou shalt see what I'll bestow of thee.

FIRK. Honest fellow? No, sir; not so, sir; my profession is the Gentle Craft; I care not for seeing, I love feeling; let me feel it here; aurium tenus, ten pieces of gold; genuum tenus, ten pieces of silver; and then Firk is your man— [*Aside*] in a new pair of stretchers.

LORD MAYOR. Here is an angel, part of thy reward,
Which I will give thee; tell me where he is.

FIRK. No point! Shall I betray my brother? no! Shall I prove Judas to Hans? no! Shall I cry treason to my corporation? no, I shall be firked and yerked then. But give me your angel; your angel shall tell you.

LINCOLN. Do so, good fellow; 'tis no hurt to thee.

FIRK. Send simpering Syb away.

LORD MAYOR. Huswife, get you in.   *Exit* SYBIL

FIRK. Pitchers have ears, and maids have wide mouths; but for Hauns-prauns, upon my word, to-morrow morning he and young Mistress Rose go to this gear, they shall be married together, by this rush, or else turn Firk to a firkin of butter, to tan leather withal.

LORD MAYOR. But art thou sure of this?

FIRK. Am I sure that Paul's steeple is a handful higher than London Stone or that the Pissing-Conduit leaks nothing but pure Mother Bunch? Am I sure I am lusty Firk? God's nails, do you think I am so base to gull you?

LINCOLN. Where are they married? Dost thou know the church?

FIRK. I never go to church, but I know the name of it; it is a swearing church—stay a while, 'tis—Ay, by the mass, no, no,— 'tis—Ay, by my troth, no, nor that; 'tis—Ay, by my faith, that, that, 'tis, Ay, by my Faith's Church under Paul's Cross. There they shall be knit like a pair of stockings in matrimony; there they'll be inconie.

LINCOLN. Upon my life, my nephew Lacy walks
In the disguise of this Dutch shoemaker.

FIRK. Yes, forsooth.

LINCOLN. Doth he not, honest fellow?

FIRK. No, forsooth; I think Hans is nobody but Hans, no spirit.

LORD MAYOR. My mind misgives me now, 'tis so, indeed.

LINCOLN. My cousin speaks the language, knows the trade.

LORD MAYOR. Let me request your company, my lord;
Your honourable presence may, no doubt,
Refrain their headstrong rashness, when myself
Going alone perchance may be o'erborne.
Shall I request this favour?

LINCOLN.   This, or what else.

FIRK. Then you must rise betimes, for they mean to fall to their 'hey-pass and repass', 'pindy-pandy, which hand will you have', very early.

LORD MAYOR. My care shall every way equal their haste.
This night accept your lodging in my house,
The earlier shall we stir, and at Saint Faith's
Prevent this giddy hare-brained nuptial.
This traffic of hot love shall yield cold gains:
They ban our loves, and we'll forbid their banns.   *Exit*

LINCOLN. At Saint Faith's Church thou say'st?

FIRK. Yes, by my troth.

LINCOLN. Be secret, on thy life.   *Exit*

FIRK. Yes, when I kiss your wife! Ha, ha, here's no craft in the Gentle Craft. I came hither of purpose with shoes to Sir Roger's worship, whilst Rose, his daughter, be cony-catched by Hans. Soft now; these two gulls will be at Saint Faith's Church to-morrow morning, to take Master Bridegroom and Mistress Bride napping, and they, in the meantime, shall chop up the matter at the Savoy. But the best sport is, Sir Roger Oteley will find my fellow lame Ralph's wife going to marry a gentleman, and then he'll stop her instead of his daughter. Oh, brave! there will be fine tickling sport. Soft now, what have I to do? Oh, I know; now a mess of shoemakers meet at the Woolsack in Ivy Lane, to cozen my gentlemen of lame Ralph's wife, that's true.

> Alack, alack!
> Girls, hold out tack!
> For now smocks for this jumbling
> Shall go to wrack.   *Exit*

ACT THE FIFTH

[SCENE I]

[A Room in Eyre's House]

Enter EYRE, MARGERY, HANS, and ROSE

EYRE. This is the morning, then, say, my bully, my honest Hans, is it not?

HANS. This is the morning, that must make us two happy or miserable; therefore, if you——

EYRE. Away with these ifs and ans, Hans, and these et caeteras! By mine honour, Rowland Lacy, none but the king shall wrong thee. Come, fear nothing, am not I Sim Eyre? Is not Sim Eyre lord mayor of London? Fear nothing, Rose: let them all say what they can; dainty, come thou to me—laughest thou?

MARGERY. Good my lord, stand her friend in what thing you may.

EYRE. Why, my sweet Lady Madgy, think you Simon Eyre can forget his fine Dutch journeyman? No, vah! Fie, I scorn it, it shall never be cast in my teeth, that I was unthankful. Lady Madgy, thou had'st never covered thy Saracen's head with this French flap, nor loaden thy bum with this farthingale ('tis trash, trumpery, vanity); Simon Eyre had never walked in a red petticoat, nor wore a chain of gold, but for my fine journeyman's Portigues.—And shall I leave him? No! Prince am I none, yet bear a princely mind.

HANS. My lord, 'tis time for us to part from hence.

EYRE. Lady Madgy, Lady Madgy, take two or three of my pie-crust-eaters, my buff-jerkin varlets, that do walk in black gowns at Simon Eyre's heels; take them, good Lady Madgy; trip and go, my brown queen of periwigs, with my delicate Rose and my jolly Rowland to the Savoy; see them linked, countenance the marriage; and when it is done, cling, cling together, you Hamborow turtle-doves. I'll bear you out, come to Simon Eyre; come, dwell with me, Hans, thou shalt eat minced-pies and marchpane. Rose, away, cricket; trip and go, my Lady Madgy, to the Savoy; Hans, wed, and to bed; kiss, and away! Go, vanish!

MARGERY. Farewell, my lord.

ROSE. Make haste, sweet love.

MARGERY.   She'd fain the deed were done.

HANS. Come, my sweet Rose; faster than deer we'll run.

Exeunt all but EYRE

EYRE. Go, vanish, vanish! Avaunt, I say! By the Lord of Ludgate, it's a mad life to be a lord mayor; it's a stirring life, a fine life, a velvet life, a careful life. Well, Simon Eyre, yet set a good face on it, in the honour of Saint Hugh. Soft, the king this day comes to dine with me, to see my new buildings; his majesty is welcome, he shall have good cheer, delicate cheer, princely cheer. This day, my fellow prentices of London come to dine with me too; they shall have fine cheer, gentlemanlike cheer. I promised the mad Cappadocians, when we all served at the Conduit together, that if ever I came to be mayor of London, I would feast them all, and I'll do 't, I'll do 't, by the life of Pharaoh; by this beard, Sim Eyre will be no flincher. Besides, I have procured that upon every Shrove Tuesday, at the sound of the pancake bell, my fine dapper Assyrian lads shall clap up their shop windows, and away. This is the day, and this day they shall do 't, they shall do 't.

> Boys, that day are you free, let masters care,
> And prentices shall pray for Simon Eyre.   *Exit*

[SCENE II]

[*A Street near St. Faith's Church*]

Enter HODGE, FIRK, RALPH, *and five or six* Shoemakers, *all with cudgels or such weapons*

HODGE. Come, Ralph; stand to it, Firk. My masters, as we are the brave bloods of the shoemakers, heirs apparent to Saint Hugh, and perpetual benefactors to all good fellows, thou shalt have no wrong; were Hammon a king of spades, he should not delve in thy close without thy sufferance. But tell me, Ralph, art thou sure 'tis thy wife?

RALPH. Am I sure this is Firk? This morning, when I stroked on her shoes, I looked upon her, and she upon me, and sighed, asked me if ever I knew one Ralph. Yes, said I. For his sake, said she—tears standing in her eyes—and for thou art somewhat like him, spend this piece of gold. I took it; my lame leg and my travel beyond sea made me unknown. All is one for that: I know she's mine.

FIRK. Did she give thee this gold? O glorious glittering gold! She's thine own, 'tis thy wife, and she loves thee; for I'll stand to 't, there's no woman will give gold to any man, but she thinks better of him, than she thinks of them she gives silver to. And for Hammon, neither Hammon nor hangman shall wrong thee in London. Is not our old master Eyre, lord mayor? Speak, my hearts.

ALL. Yes, and Hammon shall know it to his cost.

Enter HAMMON, *his* Serving-man, JANE, *and others.*

HODGE. Peace, my bullies; yonder they come.

RALPH. Stand to 't, my hearts. Firk, let me speak first.

HODGE. No, Ralph, let me.—Hammon, whither away so early?

HAMMON. Unmannerly, rude slave, what's that to thee?

FIRK. To him, sir? Yes, sir, and to me, and others. Good-morrow, Jane, how dost thou? Good Lord, how the world is changed with you! God be thanked!

HAMMON. Villains, hands off! How dare you touch my love?

ALL THE SHOEMAKERS. Villains? Down with them! Cry clubs for prentices!

HODGE. Hold, my hearts! Touch her, Hammon? Yea, and more than that: we'll carry her away with us. My masters and gentlemen, never draw your bird-spits; shoemakers are steel to the back, men every inch of them, all spirit.

THOSE OF HAMMON'S SIDE. Well, and what of all this?

HODGE. I'll show you.—Jane, dost thou know this man? 'Tis Ralph, I can tell thee; nay, 'tis he in faith, though he be lamed by the wars. Yet look not strange, but run to him, fold him about the neck and kiss him.

JANE. Lives then my husband? Oh God, let me go,
Let me embrace my Ralph.

HAMMON.   What means my Jane?

JANE. Nay, what meant you, to tell me, he was slain?

HAMMON. [O] pardon me, dear love, for being misled. [*To Ralph*] 'Twas rumoured here in London, thou wert dead.

FIRK. Thou seest he lives. Lass, go, pack home with him. Now, Master Hammon, where's your mistress, your wife?

SERVING-MAN. 'Swounds, master, fight for her! Will you thus lose her?

SHOEMAKERS. Down with that creature! Clubs! Down with him!

HODGE. Hold, hold!

HAMMON. Hold, fool! Sirs, he shall do no wrong. Will my Jane leave me thus, and break her faith?

FIRK. Yea, sir! She must, sir! She shall, sir! What then? Mend it!

HODGE. Hark, fellow Ralph, follow my counsel: set the wench in the midst, and let her choose her man, and let her be his woman.

JANE. Whom should I choose? Whom should my thoughts affect
But him whom Heaven hath made to be my love?
Thou art my husband, and these humble weeds
Make thee more beautiful than all his wealth.
Therefore, I will but put off his attire,

Returning it into the owner's hand,
And after ever be thy constant wife.

HODGE. Not a rag, Jane! The law's on our side; he that sows in another man's ground, forfeits his harvest. Get thee home, Ralph; follow him, Jane; he shall not have so much as a busk-point from thee.

FIRK. Stand to that, Ralph; the appurtenances are thine own. Hammon, look not at her!

SERVING-MAN. O, 'swounds, no!

FIRK. Blue coat, be quiet, we'll give you a new livery else; we'll make Shrove Tuesday Saint George's Day for you. Look not, Hammon, leer not! I'll firk you! For thy head now, [not] one glance, one sheep's eye, anything, at her! Touch not a rag, lest I and my brethren beat you to clouts.

SERVING-MAN. Come, Master Hammon, there's no striving here.

HAMMON. Good fellows, hear me speak; and, honest Ralph,
Whom I have injured most by loving Jane,
Mark what I offer thee: here in fair gold
Is twenty pound, I'll give it for thy Jane;
If this content thee not, thou shalt have more.

HODGE. Sell not thy wife, Ralph; make her not a whore.

HAMMON. Say, wilt thou freely cease thy claim in her,
And let her be my wife?

ALL THE SHOEMAKERS.   No, do not, Ralph.

RALPH. Sirrah Hammon, Hammon, dost thou think a shoe-maker is so base to be a bawd to his own wife for commodity? Take thy gold, choke with it! Were I not lame, I would make thee eat thy words.

FIRK. A shoemaker sell his flesh and blood? Oh, indignity!

HODGE. Sirrah, take up your pelf, and be packing.

HAMMON. I will not touch one penny, but in lieu
Of that great wrong I offerèd thy Jane,
To Jane and thee I give that twenty pound.
Since I have failed of her, during my life,
I vow, no woman else shall be my wife.
Farewell, good fellows of the Gentle Trade:
Your morning mirth my mourning day hath made.   *Exit*

FIRK. [*To the Serving-man.*] Touch the gold, creature, if you dare! Y 're best be trudging. Here, Jane, take thou it. Now let's home, my hearts.

HODGE. Stay! Who comes here? Jane, on again with thy mask!

Enter the EARL OF LINCOLN, *the* LORD MAYOR, *and* Servants

LINCOLN. Yonder's the lying varlet mocked us so.

LORD MAYOR. Come hither, sirrah!

FIRK. I, sir? I am sirrah? You mean me, do you not?

LINCOLN. Where is my nephew married?

FIRK. Is he married? God give him joy, I am glad of it. They
have a fair day, and the sign is in a good planet, Mars in Venus.

LORD MAYOR. Villain, thou toldst me that my daughter Rose
This morning should be married at Saint Faith's;
We have watched there these three hours at the least,
Yet see we no such thing.

FIRK. Truly, I am sorry for 't; a bride's a pretty thing.

HODGE. Come to the purpose. Yonder's the bride and bridegroom you look for, I hope. Though you be lords, you are not
to bar by your authority men from women, are you?

LORD MAYOR. See, see, my daughter's masked.

LINCOLN.   True, and my nephew,
To hide his guilt, [now] counterfeits him lame.

FIRK. Yea, truly; God help the poor couple, they are lame and
blind.

LORD MAYOR. I'll ease her blindness.

LINCOLN.   I'll his lameness cure.

FIRK. [*Aside to the Shoemakers*] Lie down, sirs, and laugh! My
fellow Ralph is taken for Rowland Lacy, and Jane for Mistress
Damask Rose. This is all my knavery.

LORD MAYOR. What, have I found you, minion?

LINCOLN.   O base wretch!
Nay, hide thy face, the horror of thy guilt
Can hardly be washed off. Where are thy powers?
What battles have you made? O yes, I see,
Thou fought'st with Shame, and Shame hath conquered thee.
This lameness will not serve.

LORD MAYOR.   Unmask yourself.

LINCOLN. Lead home your daughter.

LORD MAYOR.   Take your nephew hence.

RALPH. Hence! 'Swounds, what mean you? Are you mad?
I hope you cannot enforce my wife from me. Where's Hammon?

LORD MAYOR. Your wife?

LINCOLN. What Hammon?

RALPH. Yea, my wife; and, therefore, the proudest of you that lays hands on her first, I'll lay my crutch 'cross his pate.

FIRK. To him, lame Ralph! Here's brave sport!

RALPH. Rose call you her? Why, her name is Jane. Look here else; do you know her now?   *Unmasking* JANE

LINCOLN. Is this your daughter?

LORD MAYOR.   No, nor this your nehpew.
My Lord of Lincoln, we are both abused
By this base, crafty varlet.

FIRK. Yea, forsooth, no varlet; forsooth, no base; forsooth, I am but mean; no crafty neither, but of the Gentle Craft.

LORD MAYOR. Where is my daughter Rose? Where is my child?

LINCOLN. Where is my nephew Lacy married?

FIRK. Why, here is good laced mutton, as I promised you.

LINCOLN. Villain, I'll have thee punished for this wrong.

FIRK. Punish the journeyman villain, but not the journeyman shoemaker.

Enter DODGER

DODGER. My lord, I come to bring unwelcome news.
Your nephew Lacy and your daughter Rose
Early this morning wedded at the Savoy,
None being present but the lady mayoress.
Besides, I learnt among the officers,
The lord mayor vows to stand in their defence
'Gainst any that shall seek to cross the match.

LINCOLN. Dares Eyre the shoemaker uphold the deed?

FIRK. Yes, sir, shoemakers dare stand in a woman's quarrel, I warrant you, as deep as another, and deeper too.

DODGER. Besides, his grace to-day dines with the mayor;
Who on his knees humbly intends to fall
And beg a pardon for your nephew's fault.

LINCOLN. But I'll prevent him! Come, Sir Roger Oteley;
The king will do us justice in this cause.
Howe'er their hands have made them man and wife,
I will disjoin the match, or lose my life.   *Exeunt*

FIRK. Adieu, Monsieur Dodger! Farewell, fools! Ha, ha! Oh, if they had stayed, I would have so lambed them with flouts! O heart, my codpiece-point is ready to fly in pieces every time I think upon Mistress Rose; but let that pass, as my lady mayoress says.

HODGE. This matter is answered. Come, Ralph; home with thy wife. Come, my fine shoemakers, let's to our master's, the new lord mayor, and there swagger this Shrove Tuesday. I'll promise you wine enough, for Madge keeps the cellar.

ALL. O rare! Madge is a good wench.

FIRK. And I'll promise you meat enough, for simp'ring Susan keeps the larder. I'll lead you to victuals, my brave soldiers; follow your captain. O brave! Hark, hark!

Bell rings

ALL. The pancake-bell rings, the pancake-bell! Trilill, my hearts!

FIRK. O brave! O sweet bell! O delicate pancakes! Open the doors, my hearts, and shut up the windows! keep in the house, let out the pancakes! Oh, rare, my hearts! Let's march together for the honour of Saint Hugh to the great new hall in Gracious Street-corner, which our master, the new lord mayor, hath built.

RALPH. O the crew of good fellows that will dine at my lord mayor's cost to-day!

HODGE. By the Lord, my lord mayor is a most brave man. How shall prentices be bound to pray for him and the honour of the gentlemen shoemakers! Let's feed and be fat with my lord's bounty.

FIRK. O musical bell, still! O Hodge, O my brethren! There's cheer for the heavens: venison-pasties walk up and down piping hot, like sergeants; beef and brewis comes marching in dry-fats, fritters and pancakes come trowling in in wheel-barrows; hens and oranges hopping in porters'-baskets, collops and eggs in scuttles, and tarts and custards come quavering in in malt-shovels.

Enter more Prentices

ALL. Whoop, look here, look here!

HODGE. How now, mad lads, whither away so fast?

FIRST PRENTICE. Whither? Why, to the great new hall, know you not why? The lord mayor hath bidden all the prentices in London to breakfast this morning.

ALL. Oh, brave shoemaker, oh, brave lord of incomprehensible good fellowship! Whoo! Hark you! The pancake-bell rings.   *Cast up caps*

FIRK. Nay, more, my hearts! Every Shrove Tuesday is our year of jubilee; and when the pancake-bell rings, we are as free as my lord mayor; we may shut up our shops, and make holiday. I'll have it called Saint Hugh's Holiday.

ALL. Agreed, agreed! Saint Hugh's Holiday.

HODGE. And this shall continue for ever.

ALL. Oh, brave! Come, come, my hearts! Away, away!

FIRK. O eternal credit to us of the Gentle Craft! March fair, my hearts! Oh, rare!   *Exeunt*

[SCENE III]

[A Street in London]

Enter the KING *and his Train over the stage*

KING. Is our lord mayor of London such a gallant?

NOBLEMAN. One of the merriest madcaps in your land.
Your grace will think, when you behold the man,
He's rather a wild ruffian than a mayor.
Yet thus much I'll ensure your majesty.
In all his actions that concern his state,
He is as serious, provident, and wise,
As full of gravity amongst the grave,
As any mayor hath been these many years.

KING. I am with child, till I behold this huffcap.
But all my doubt is, when we come in presence,
His madness will be dashed clean out of countenance.

NOBLEMAN. It may be so, my liege.

KING.   Which to prevent
Let some one give him notice, 'tis our pleasure
That he put on his wonted merriment.
Set forward!

ALL.   On afore!   *Exeunt*

[SCENE IV]

[A Great Hall]

Enter EYRE, HODGE, FIRK, RALPH, *and other* Shoemakers, *all
with napkins on their shoulders*

EYRE. Come, my fine Hodge, my jolly gentlemen shoemakers;
soft, where be these cannibals, these varlets, my officers? Let them
all walk and wait upon my brethren; for my meaning is, that
none but shoemakers, none but the livery of my company shall
in their satin hoods wait upon the trencher of my sovereign.

FIRK. O my lord, it will be rare!

EYRE. No more, Firk; come, lively! Let your fellow prentices
want no cheer; let wine be plentiful as beer, and beer as water.
Hang these penny-pinching fathers, that cram wealth in innocent
lambskins. Rip, knaves, avaunt! Look to my guests!

HODGE. My lord, we are at our wits' end for room; those
hundred tables will not feast the fourth part of them.

EYRE. Then cover me those hundred tables again, and again,
till all my jolly prentices be feasted. Avoid, Hodge! Run, Ralph!
Frisk about, my nimble Firk! Carouse me fathom-healths to the
honour of the shoemakers. Do they drink lively, Hodge? Do
they tickle it, Firk?

FIRK. Tickle it? Some of them have taken their liquor standing
so long that they can stand no longer; but for meat, they would
eat it, an they had it.

EYRE. Want they meat? Where's this swag-belly, this greasy
kitchenstuff cook? Call the varlet to me! Want meat? Firk, Hodge,
lame Ralph, run, my tall men, beleaguer the shambles, beggar
all Eastcheap, serve me whole oxen in chargers, and let sheep
whine upon the tables like pigs for want of good fellows to eat
them. Want meat? Vanish, Firk! Avaunt, Hodge!

HODGE. Your lordship mistakes my man Firk; he means, their
bellies want meat, not the boards; for they have drunk so much,
they can eat nothing.

Enter HANS, ROSE, *and* MARGERY

MARGERY. Where is my lord?

EYRE. How now, Lady Madgy?

MARGERY. The king's most excellent majesty is new come; he sends me for thy honour; one of his most worshipful peers bade me tell thou must be merry, and so forth; but let that pass.

EYRE. Is my sovereign come? Vanish, my tall shoemakers, my nimble brethren; look to my guests, the prentices. Yet stay a little! How now, Hans? How looks my little Rose?

HANS. Let me request you to remember me.
I know, your honour easily may obtain
Free pardon of the king for me and Rose,
And reconcile me to my uncle's grace.

EYRE. Have done, my good Hans, my honest journeyman; look cheerily! I'll fall upon both my knees, till they be as hard as horn, but I'll get thy pardon.

MARGERY. Good my lord, have a care what you speak to his grace.

EYRE. Away, you Islington whitepot! hence, you hopperarse! you barley-pudding, full of maggots! you broiled carbonado! avaunt, avaunt, avoid, Mephistophilus! Shall Sim Eyre learn to speak of you, Lady Madgy? Vanish, Mother Miniver-cap; vanish, go, trip and go; meddle with your partlets and your pishery-pashery, your flewes and your whirligigs; go, rub, out of mine alley! Sim Eyre knows how to speak to a Pope, to Sultan Soliman, to Tamburlaine, an he were here, and shall I melt, shall I droop before my sovereign? No, come, my Lady Madgy! Follow me, Hans! About your business, my frolic free-booters! Firk, frisk about, and about, and about, for the honour of mad Simon Eyre, lord mayor of London.

FIRK. Hey, for the honour of the shoemakers.   *Exeunt*

[SCENE V]

[An Open Yard before the Hall]

A long flourish, or two. Enter the KING, Nobles, EYRE, MARGERY, LACY, ROSE. LACY *and* ROSE *kneel*

KING. Well, Lacy, though the fact was very foul
Of your revolting from our kingly love
And your own duty, yet we pardon you.
Rise both, and, Mistress Lacy, thank my lord mayor
For your young bridegroom here.

EYRE. So, my dear liege, Sim Eyre and my brethren, the gentlemen shoemakers, shall set your sweet majesty's image cheek by jowl by Saint Hugh for this honour you have done poor Simon Eyre. I beseech your grace, pardon my rude behaviour; I am a handicraftsman, yet my heart is without craft; I would be sorry at my soul, that my boldness should offend my king.

KING. Nay, I pray thee, good lord mayor, be even as merry
As if thou wert among thy shoemakers;
It does me good to see thee in this humour.

EYRE. Say'st thou me so, my sweet Dioclesian? Then, humph! Prince am I none, yet am I princely born. By the Lord of Ludgate, my liege, I'll be as merry as a pie.

KING. Tell me, in faith, mad Eyre, how old thou art.

EYRE. My liege, a very boy, a stripling, a younker; you see not a white hair on my head, not a grey in this beard. Every hair, I assure thy majesty, that sticks in this beard, Sim Eyre values at the King of Babylon's ransom, Tamar Cham's beard was a rubbing brush to 't: yet I'll shave it off, and stuff tennis-balls with it, to please my bully king.

KING. But all this while I do not know your age.

EYRE. My liege, I am six and fifty year old, yet I can cry humph! with a sound heart for the honour of Saint Hugh. Mark this old wench, my king: I danced the shaking of the sheets with her six and thirty years ago, and yet I hope to get two or three young lord mayors, ere I die. I am lusty still, Sim Eyre still. Care and cold lodging brings white hairs. My sweet Majesty, let care vanish, cast it upon thy nobles, it will make thee look always young like Apollo, and cry humph! Prince am I none, yet am I princely born.

KING. Ha, ha!
Say, Cornwall, didst thou ever see his like?

CORNWALL. Not I, my lord.

Enter the EARL OF LINCOLN *and the* LORD MAYOR

KING.   Lincoln, what news with you?

LINCOLN. My gracious lord, have care unto yourself,
For there are traitors here.

ALL.   Traitors? Where? Who?

EYRE. Traitors in my house? God forbid! Where be my officers? I'll spend my soul, ere my king feel harm.

KING. Where is the traitor, Lincoln?

LINCOLN.   Here he stands.

KING. Cornwall, lay hold on Lacy!—Lincoln, speak,
What canst thou lay unto thy nephew's charge?

LINCOLN. This, my dear liege: your Grace, to do me honour,
Heaped on the head of this degenerous boy
Desertless favours; you made choice of him,
To be commander over powers in France.
But he——

KING. Good Lincoln, prithee, pause a while!
Even in thine eyes I read what thou wouldst speak.
I know how Lacy did neglect our love,
Ran himself deeply, in the highest degree,
Into vile treason——

LINCOLN.   Is he not a traitor?

KING. Lincoln, he was; now have we pardoned him.
'Twas not a base want of true valour's fire,
That held him out of France, but love's desire.

LINCOLN. I will not bear his shame upon my back.

KING. Nor shalt thou, Lincoln; I forgive you both.

LINCOLN. Then, good my liege, forbid the boy to wed
One whose mean birth will much disgrace his bed.

KING. Are they not married?

LINCOLN.   No, my liege.

BOTH.   We are.

KING. Shall I divorce them then? O be it far,
That any hand on earth should dare untie
The sacred knot, knit by God's majesty;
I would not for my crown disjoin their hands,
That are conjoined in holy nuptial bands.
How say'st thou, Lacy, wouldst thou lose thy Rose?

LACY. Not for all India's wealth, my sovereign.

KING. But Rose, I am sure, her Lacy would forgo?

ROSE. If Rose were asked that question, she'd say no.

KING. You hear them, Lincoln?

LINCOLN.   Yea, my liege, I do.

KING. Yet canst thou find i' th' heart to part these two?
Who seeks, besides you, to divorce these lovers?

LORD MAYOR. I do, my gracious lord, I am her father.

KING. Sir Roger Oteley, our last mayor, I think?

NOBLEMAN. The same, my liege.

KING.   Would you offend Love's laws?
Well, you shall have your wills. You sue to me,
To prohibit the match. Soft, let me see—
You both are married, Lacy, art thou not?

LACY. I am, dread sovereign.

KING.   Then, upon thy life,
I charge thee not to call this woman wife.

LORD MAYOR. I thank your grace.

ROSE.   O my most gracious lord!

                                        Kneels

KING. Nay, Rose, never woo me; I tell you true,
Although as yet I am a bachelor,
Yet I believe, I shall not marry you.

ROSE. Can you divide the body from the soul,
Yet make the body live?

KING.   Yea, so profound?
I cannot, Rose, but you I must divide.
This fair maid, bridegroom, cannot be your bride.
Are you pleased, Lincoln? Oteley, are you pleased?

BOTH. Yes, my lord.

KING.   Then must my heart be eased;
For, credit me, my conscience lives in pain,
Till these whom I divorced, be joined again.
Lacy, give me thy hand; Rose, lend me thine!
Be what you would be! Kiss now? So, that's fine.
At night, lovers, to bed!—Now, let me see,
Which of you all mislikes this harmony.

LORD MAYOR. Will you then take from me my child perforce?

KING. Why, tell me, Oteley: shines not Lacy's name
As bright in the world's eye as the gay beams
Of any citizen?

LINCOLN.   Yea, but, my gracious lord,
I do mislike the match far more than he;
Her blood is too too base.

KING.   Lincoln, no more.
Dost thou not know that love respects no blood,
Cares not for difference of birth or state?
The maid is young, well born, fair, virtuous,
A worthy bride for any gentleman.
Besides, your nephew for her sake did stoop
To bare necessity, and, as I hear,

Forgetting honours and all courtly pleasures,
To gain her love, became a shoemaker.
As for the honour which he lost in France,
Thus I redeem it: Lacy, kneel thee down!—
Arise, Sir Rowland Lacy! Tell me now,
Tell me in earnest, Oteley, canst thou chide,
Seeing thy Rose a lady and a bride?

    Lord Mayor. I am content with what your grace hath done.
    Lincoln. And I, my liege, since there's no remedy.
    King. Come on, then, all shake hands: I'll have you friends;
Where there is much love, all discord ends.
What says my mad lord mayor to all this love?

    Eyre. O my liege, this honour you have done to my fine journeyman here, Rowland Lacy, and all these favours which you have shown to me this day in my poor house, will make Simon Eyre live longer by one dozen of warm summers more than he should.

    King. Nay, my mad lord mayor, that shall be thy name,
If any grace of mine can length thy life,
One honour more I'll do thee: that new building,
Which at thy cost in Cornhill is erected,
Shall take a name from us; we'll have it called
The Leadenhall, because in digging it
You found the lead that covereth the same.

    Eyre. I thank your majesty.
    Margery. God bless your grace!
    King. Lincoln, a word with you!

Enter Hodge, Firk, Ralph, *and more* Shoemakers

    Eyre. How now, my mad knaves? Peace, speak softly, yonder is the king.

    King. With the old troop which there we keep in pay,
We will incorporate a new supply
Before one summer more pass o'er my head,
France shall repent England was injured.
What are all those?

    Lacy.   All shoemakers, my liege,
Sometime my fellows; in their companies
I lived as merry as an emperor.

    King. My mad lord mayor, are all these shoemakers?

EYRE. All shoemakers, my liege; all gentlemen of the Gentle Craft, true Trojans, courageous cordwainers; they all kneel to the shrine of holy Saint Hugh.

ALL THE SHOEMAKERS. God save your majesty!

KING. Mad Simon, would they anything with us?

EYRE. Mum, mad knaves! Not a word! I'll do 't; I warrant you.—They are all beggars, my liege; all for themselves, and I for them all, on both my knees do entreat, that for the honour of poor Simon Eyre and the good of his brethren, these mad knaves, your grace would vouchsafe some privilege to my new Leadenhall, that it may be lawful for us to buy and sell leather there two days a week.

KING. Mad Sim, I grant your suit, you shall have patent
To hold two market-days in Leadenhall,
Mondays and Fridays, those shall be the times.
Will this content you?

ALL.   Jesus bless your grace!

EYRE. In the name of these my poor brethren shoemakers, I most humbly thank your grace. But before I rise, seeing you are in the giving vein and we in the begging, grant Sim Eyre one boon more.

KING. What is it, my lord mayor?

EYRE. Vouchsafe to taste of a poor banquet that stands sweetly waiting for your sweet presence.

KING. I shall undo thee, Eyre, only with feasts;
Already have I been too troublesome;
Say, have I not?

EYRE. O my dear king, Sim Eyre was taken unawares upon a day of shroving, which I promised long ago to the prentices of London.

> For, an 't please your highness, in time past,
> I bare the water-tankard, and my coat
> Sits not a whit the worse upon my back;
> And then, upon a morning, some mad boys,
> It was Shrove Tuesday, even as 'tis now,

Gave me my breakfast, and I swore then by the stopple of my tankard, if ever I came to be lord mayor of London, I would feast all the prentices. This day, my liege, I did it, and the slaves had an hundred tables five times covered; they are gone home and vanished;

> Yet add more honour to the Gentle Trade,

    Taste of Eyre's banquet, Simon's happy made.
  KING. Eyre, I will taste of thy banquet, and will say,
I have not met more pleasure on a day.
Friends of the Gentle Craft, thanks to you all,
Thanks, my kind lady mayoress, for our cheer.—
Come, lords, a while let 's revel it at home!
When all our sports and banquetings are done,
Wars must right wrongs which Frenchmen have begun.

                                    Exeunt

ALL FOOLS

George Chapman

ACTORS

GOSTANZO
MARC ANTONIO } *knights*
VALERIO, *son to Gostanzo*
FORTUNIO, *elder son to Marc Antonio*
RINALDO, *the younger*
DARIOTTO
CLAUDIO } *courtiers*
CORNELIO, *a start-up gentleman*
CURIO, *a page*
KYTE, *a scrivener*
FRANCIS POCK, *a surgeon*
[DRAWERS]

GAZETTA, *wife to Cornelio*
BELLANORA, *daughter to Gostanzo*
GRATIANA, *stolen wife to Valerio*

PROLOGUS

The fortune of a stage (like Fortune's self)
Amazeth greatest judgments, and none knows
The hidden causes of those strange effects,
That rise from this hell, or fall from this heaven.
 Who can show cause why your wits, that in aim
At higher objects, scorn to compose plays
(Though we are sure they could, would they vouchsafe it!),
Should (without means to make) judge better far,
Than those that make? And yet ye see they can.
For without your applause wretched is he
That undertakes the stage, and he's more blest
That with your glorious favors can contest.
 Who can show cause why th'ancient comic vein
Of Eupolis and Cratinus (now reviv'd,
Subject to personal application)
Should be exploded by some bitter spleens,
Yet merely comical and harmless jests
(Though ne'er so witty) be esteem'd but toys,
If void of th'other satirism's sauce?
 Who can show cause why quick Venerian jests
Should sometimes ravish, sometimes fall far short
Of the just length and pleasure of your ears,
When our pure dames think them much less obscene
Than those that win your panegyric spleen?
But our poor dooms (alas) you know are nothing.
To your inspired censure ever we
Must needs submit, and there's the mystery.
 Great are the gifts given to united heads,
To gifts, attire, to fair attire, the stage
Helps much. For if our other audience see
You on the stage depart before we end,

Our wits go with you all, and we are fools.
So Fortune governs in these stage events,
That merit bears least sway in most contents.
Auriculas asini quis non habet?
How we shall then appear, we must refer
To magic of your dooms, that never err.

[*I. i*]

Enter Rinaldo, Fortunio, Valerio.

RINALDO. Can one self cause, in subjects so alike
As you two are, produce effects so unlike?
One like the turtle, all in mournful strains
Wailing his fortunes, th'other like the lark,
Mounting the sky in shrill and cheerful notes,
Chanting his joys aspir'd. And both for love.
In one, love raiseth by his violent heat
Moist vapors from the heart into the eyes,
From whence they drown his breast in daily showers.
In th'other, his divided power infuseth
Only a temperate and most kindly warmth,
That gives life to those fruits of wit and virtue,
Which the unkind hand of an uncivil father
Had almost nipp'd in the delightsome blossom.
FORTUNIO. O, brother, love rewards our services
With a most partial and injurious hand,
If you consider well our different fortunes.
Valerio loves, and joys the dame he loves.
I love, and never can enjoy the sight
Of her I love, so far from conquering
In my desire's assault, that I can come
To lay no batt'ry to the fort I seek,
All passages to it so strongly kept
By strait guard of her father.
RINALDO.   I dare swear,
If just desert in love measur'd reward,
Your fortune should exceed Valerio's far.
For I am witness (being your bedfellow)
Both to the daily and the nightly service

You do unto the deity of love,
In vows, sighs, tears, and solitary watches.
He never serves him with such sacrifice,
Yet hath his bow and shafts at his command.
Love's service is much like our humorous lords';
Where minions carry more than servitors,
The bold and careless servant still obtains;
The modest and respective, nothing gains.
You never see your love, unless in dreams,
He, Hymen puts in whole possession.
What different stars reign'd when your loves were born,
He forc'd to wear the willow, you the horn?
But, brother, are you not asham'd to make
Yourself a slave to the base lord of love,
Begot of Fancy, and of Beauty born?
And what is Beauty? A mere quintessence,
Whose life is not in being, but in seeming,
And therefore is not to all eyes the same,
But like a cozening picture, which one way
Shows like a crow, another like a swan.
And upon what ground is this Beauty drawn?
Upon a woman, a most brittle creature,
And would to God (for my part) that were all.
    FORTUNIO. But tell me, brother, did you never love?
    RINALDO. You know I did, and was belov'd again,
And that of such a dame as all men deem'd
Honor'd, and made me happy in her favors.
Exceeding fair she was not, and yet fair
In that she never studied to be fairer
Than Nature made her. Beauty cost her nothing.
Her virtues were so rare, they would have made
An Ethiop beautiful, at least so thought
By such as stood aloof, and did observe her
With credulous eyes. But what they were indeed
I'll spare to blaze, because I lov'd her once.
Only I found her such, as for her sake
I vow eternal wars against their whole sex.
Inconstant shuttlecocks, loving fools, and jesters,
Men rich in dirt and titles, sooner won
With the most vile than the most virtuous,
Found true to none. If one amongst whole hundreds

Chance to be chaste, she is so proud withal,
Wayward and rude, that one of unchaste life
Is oftentimes approv'd a worthier wife.
Undressed, sluttish, nasty to their husbands,
Spong'd up, adorn'd, and painted to their lovers.
All day in ceaseless uproar with their households,
If all the night their husbands have not pleas'd them.
Like hounds, most kind, being beaten and abus'd,
Like wolves, most cruel, being kindliest us'd.

   FORTUNIO. Fie, thou profan'st the deity of their sex.

   RINALDO. Brother, I read that Egypt heretofore
Had temples of the richest frame on earth,
Much like this goodly edifice of women.
With alabaster pillars were those temples
Upheld and beautified, and so are women.
Most curiously glaz'd, and so are women.
Cunningly painted too, and so are women.
In outside wondrous heavenly, so are women.
But when a stranger view'd those fanes within,
Instead of gods and goddesses, he should find
A painted fowl, a fury, or a serpent,
And such celestial inner parts have women.

   VALERIO. Rinaldo, the poor fox that lost his tail,
Persuaded others also to lose theirs.
Thyself, for one perhaps that for desert
Or some defect in thy attempts refus'd thee,
Revil'st the whole sex, beauty, love, and all.
I tell thee love is nature's second sun,
Causing a spring of virtues where he shines.
And as without the sun, the world's great eye,
All colors, beauties, both of art and nature,
Are given in vain to men, so without love
All beauties bred in women are in vain,
All virtues born in men lie buried.
For love informs them as the sun doth colors.
And as the sun, reflecting his warm beams
Against the earth, begets all fruits and flowers,
So love, fair shining in the inward man,
Brings forth in him the honorable fruits
Of valor, wit, virtue, and haughty thoughts,
Brave resolution, and divine discourse.

O, 'tis the Paradise, the Heaven of earth.
And didst thou know the comfort of two hearts
In one delicious harmony united,
As to joy one joy, and think both one thought,
Live both one life, and therein double life,
To see their souls met at an interview
In their bright eyes, at parley in their lips,
Their language kisses, and t'observe the rest,
Touches, embraces, and each circumstance
Of all love's most unmatched ceremonies,
Thou wouldst abhor thy tongue for blasphemy.
O, who can comprehend how sweet love tastes
But he that hath been present at his feasts?

    RINALDO. Are you in that vein too, Valerio?
'Twere fitter you should be about your charge,
How plow and cart goes foward. I have known
Your joys were all employ'd in husbandry.
Your study was how many loads of hay
A meadow of so many acres yielded,
How many oxen such a close would fat.
And is your rural service now converted
From Pan to Cupid, and from beasts to women?
O, if your father knew this, what a lecture
Of bitter castigation he would read you!

    VALERIO. My father? Why my father? Does he think
To rob me of myself? I hope I know
I am a gentleman. Though his covetous humor
And education hath transform'd me bailie,
And made me overseer of his pastures,
I'll be myself, in spite of husbandry.

Enter Gratiana.

And see, bright heaven, here comes my husbandry.

Amplectitur eam.

Here shall my cattle graze, here nectar drink,
Here will I hedge and ditch, here hide my treasure.
O poor Fortunio, how wouldst thou triumph,
If thou enjoy'dst this happiness with my sister!

    FORTUNIO. I were in heaven if once 'twere come to that.
    RINALDO. And methinks 'tis my heaven that I am past it.

And should the wretched Machiavellian,
The covetous knight, your father, see this sight,
Lusty Valerio?

VALERIO.   'Sfoot, sir, if he should,
He shall perceive ere long my skill extends
To something more than sweaty husbandry.

RINALDO. I'll bear thee witness, thou canst skill of dice,
Cards, tennis, wenching, dancing, and what not,
And this is something more than husbandry!
Th'art known in ordinaries, and tobacco shops,
Trusted in taverns and in vaulting houses,
And this is something more than husbandry.
Yet all this while, thy father apprehends thee
For the most tame and thrifty groom in Europe.

FORTUNIO. Well, he hath ventur'd on a marriage
Would quite undo him, did his father know it.

RINALDO. Know it? Alas sir, where can he bestow
This poor gentlewoman he hath made his wife,
But his inquisitive father will hear of it,
Who, like the dragon to th' Hesperian fruit,
Is to his haunts? 'Slight! Hence, the old knight comes.

Intrat Gostanzo. *Omnes aufugiunt.*

GOSTANZO. Rinaldo.

RINALDO.   Who's that calls? What, Sir Gostanzo?
How fares your knighthood, sir?

GOSTANZO.   Say, who was that
Shrunk at my entry here? Was't not your brother?

RINALDO. He shrunk not, sir. His business call'd him hence.

GOSTANZO. And was it not my son that went out with him?

RINALDO. I saw not him. I was in serious speech
About a secret business with my brother.

GOSTANZO. Sure 'twas my son. What made he here? I sent
him
About affairs to be dispatch'd in haste.

RINALDO. Well, sir, lest silence breed unjust suspect,
I'll tell a secret I am sworn to keep,
And crave your honored assistance in it.

GOSTANZO. What is't, Rinaldo?

RINALDO.   This, sir: 'twas your son.

GOSTANZO. And what young gentlewoman grac'd their company?

RINALDO. Thereon depends the secret I must utter.
That gentlewoman hath my brother married.

GOSTANZO. Married? What is she?

RINALDO.   'Faith, sir, a gentlewoman,
But her unnourishing dowry must be told
Out of her beauty.

GOSTANZO.   Is it true, Rinaldo?
And does your father understand so much?

RINALDO. That was the motion, sir, I was entreating
Your son to make to him, because I know
He is well spoken and may much prevail
In satisfying my father, who much loves him,
Both for his wisdom and his husbandry.

GOSTANZO. Indeed he's one can tell his tale, I tell you,
And for his husbandry—

RINALDO.   O, sir, had you heard
What thrifty discipline he gave my brother
For making choice without my father's knowledge
And without riches, you would have admir'd him.

GOSTANZO. Nay, nay, I know him well. But what was it?

RINALDO. That in the choice of wives men must respect
The chief wife, riches, that in every course
A man's chief lodestar should shine out of riches,
Love nothing heartily in this world but riches,
Cast off all friends, all studies, all delights,
All honesty, and religion for riches,
And many such, which wisdom sure he learn'd
Of his experient father. Yet my brother
So soothes his rash affection, and presumes
So highly on my father's gentle nature,
That he's resolv'd to bring her home to him,
And like enough he will.

GOSTANZO.   And like enough
Your silly father, too, will put it up.
An honest knight, but much too much indulgent
To his presuming children.

RINALDO.   What a difference
Doth interpose itself 'twixt him and you!
Had your son us'd you thus!

GOSTANZO.   My son? Alas,
I hope to bring him up in other fashion.
Follows my husbandry, sets early foot
Into the world. He comes not at the city,
Nor knows the city arts.

  RINALDO.   But dice and wenching.   *Aversus.*

  GOSTANZO. Acquaints himself with no delight but getting,
A perfect pattern of sobriety,
Temperance, and husbandry to all my household.
And what's his company, I pray? Not wenches.

  RINALDO. Wenches? I durst be sworn he never smelt
A wench's breath yet. But methinks 'twere fit
You sought him out a wife.

  GOSTANZO.   A wife, Rinaldo?
He dares not look a woman in the face.

  RINALDO. 'Sfoot, hold him to one. Your son such a sheep?

  GOSTANZO. 'Tis strange, in earnest.

  RINALDO. Well, sir, though for my thriftless brother's sake,
I little care how my wrong'd father takes it,
Yet for my father's quiet, if yourself
Would join hands with your wise and toward son,
I should deserve it some way.

  GOSTANZO.   Good Rinaldo,
I love you and your father, but this matter
Is not for me to deal in. And 'tis needless.
You say your brother is resolv'd, presuming
Your father will allow it.

Enter Marc Antonio.

  RINALDO.   See, my father.
Since you are resolute not to move him, sir,
In any case conceal the secret by way   *Abscondit se.*
Of an atonement. Let me pray you will.

  GOSTANZO. Upon mine honor.

  RINALDO.   Thanks, sir.

  MARC ANTONIO. God save thee, honorable Knight Gostanzo.

  GOSTANZO. Friend Marc Antonio? Welcome. And I think
I have good news to welcome you withal.

  RINALDO [*aside*]. He cannot hold.

  MARC ANTONIO.   What news, I pray you, sir?

GOSTANZO. You have a forward, valiant, eldest son,
But wherein is his forwardness and valor?

MARC ANTONIO. I know not wherein you intend him so.

GOSTANZO. Forward before, valiant behind, his duty,
That he hath dar'd before your due consent
To take a wife.

MARC ANTONIO.   A wife, sir? What is she?

GOSTANZO. One that is rich enough: her hair pure amber,
Her forehead mother of pearl, her fair eyes
Two wealthy diamonds, her lips mines of rubies.
Her teeth are orient pearl, her neck pure ivory.

MARC ANTONIO. Jest not, good sir, in an affair so serious.
I love my son, and if his youth reward me
With his contempt of my consent in marriage,
'Tis to be fear'd that his presumption builds not
Of his good choice, that will bear out itself,
And being bad, the news is worse than bad.

GOSTANZO. What call you bad? Is it bad to be poor?

MARC ANTONIO. The world accounts it so. But if my son
Have in her birth and virtues held his choice
Without disparagement, the fault is less.

GOSTANZO. Sits the wind there? Blows there so calm a gale
From a contemned and deserved anger?
Are you so easy to be disobey'd?

MARC ANTONIO. What should I do? If my enamor'd son
Have been so forward, I assure myself
He did it more to satisfy his love
Than to incense my hate, or to neglect me.

GOSTANZO. A passing kind construction. Suffer this,
You ope him doors to any villainy.
He'll dare to sell, to pawn, run ever riot,
Despise your love in all, and laugh at you.
And that knight's competency you have gotten
With care and labor, he with lust and idleness
Will bring into the stipend of a beggar,
All to maintain a wanton whirligig,
Worth nothing more than she brings on her back.
Yet all your wealth too little for that back.
By heaven, I pity your declining state,
For be assur'd your son hath set his foot
In the right pathway to consumption:

Up to the heart in love, and for that love
Nothing can be too dear his love desires.
And how insatiate and unlimited
Is the ambition and the beggarly pride
Of a dame hoised from a beggar's state
To a state competent and plentiful,
You cannot be so simple not to know.

MARC ANTONIO. I must confess the mischief, but, alas,
Where is in me the power of remedy?

GOSTANZO. Where? In your just displeasure. Cast him off.
Receive him not. Let him endure the use
Of their enforced kindness that must trust him
For meat and money, for apparel, house,
And everything belongs to that estate,
Which he must learn with want of misery,
Since pleasure and a full estate hath blinded
His dissolute desires.

MARC ANTONIO.   What should I do?
If I should banish him my house and sight,
What desperate resolution might it breed
To run into the wars, and there to live
In want of competency and perhaps
Taste th'unrecoverable loss of his chief limbs,
Which while he hath in peace, at home with me,
May, with his spirit, ransom his estate
From any loss his marriage can procure.

GOSTANZO. Is't true? Nay, let him run into the war,
And lose what limbs he can. Better one branch
Be lopp'd away, than all the whole tree should perish,
And for his wants, better young want than old.
You have a younger son at Padua.
I like his learning well. Make him your heir,
And let your other walk. Let him buy wit
At's own charge, not at's father's. If you lose him,
You lose no more than that was lost before.
If you recover him, you find a son.

MARC ANTONIO. I cannot part with him.

GOSTANZO.   If it be so,
And that your love to him be so extreme,
In needful dangers ever choose the least.
If he should be in mind to pass the seas,

Your son Rinaldo (who told me all this)
Will tell me that, and so we shall prevent it.
If by no stern course you will venture that,
Let him come home to me with his fair wife,
And if you chance to see him, shake him up,
As if your wrath were hard to be reflected,
That he may fear hereafter to offend
In other dissolute courses. At my house,
With my advice and my son's good example,
Who shall serve as a glass for him to see
His faults, and mend them to his precedent,
I make no doubt but of a dissolute son
And disobedient, to send him home
Both dutiful and thrifty.

MARC ANTONIO.   O, Gostanzo!
Could you do this, you should preserve yourself
A perfect friend of me, and me a son.

GOSTANZO. Remember you your part, and fear not mine.
Rate him, revile him, and renounce him too.
Speak, can you do't, man?

MARC ANTONIO.   I'll do all I can.

Exit Marc Antonio.

GOSTANZO. Alas, good man, how nature overweighs him.

Rinaldo *comes forth.*

RINALDO. God save you, sir.
GOSTANZO.   Rinaldo, all the news
You told me as a secret, I perceive
Is passing common, for your father knows it.
The first thing he related was the marriage.

RINALDO. And was extremely mov'd?
GOSTANZO.   Beyond all measure.
But I did all I could to quench his fury,
Told him how easy 'twas for a young man
To run that amorous course, and though his choice
Were nothing rich, yet she was gently born,
Well qualified and beautiful. But he still
Was quite relentless, and would needs renounce him.

RINALDO. My brother knows it well, and is resolv'd
To trail a pike in field, rather than bide

The more fear'd push of my vex'd father's fury.

GOSTANZO. Indeed that's one way. But are no more means
Left to his fine wits than t'incense his father
With a more violent rage, and to redeem
A great offense with greater?

RINALDO.   So I told him,
But to a desperate mind all breath is lost.

GOSTANZO. Go to, let him be wise, and use his friends,
Amongst whom I'll be foremost, to his father.
Without this desperate error he intends
Join'd to the other, I'll not doubt to make him
Easy return into his father's favor,
So he submit himself, as duty binds him.
For fathers will be known to be themselves,
And often when their angers are not deep
Will paint an outward rage upon their looks.

RINALDO. All this I told him, sir. But what says he?
"I know my father will not be reclaim'd.
He'll think that if he wink at this offense,
'Twill open doors to any villainy.
I'll dare to sell, to pawn, and run all riot,
To laugh at all his patience, and consume
All he hath purchas'd to an honor'd purpose
In maintenance of a wanton whirligig
Worth nothing more than she wears on her back."

GOSTANZO [aside]. The very words I us'd t'incense his father.—
But, good Rinaldo, let him be advis'd.
How would his father grieve, should he be maim'd,
Or quite miscarry in the ruthless war!

RINALDO. I told him so. But, "Better far," said he,
"One branch should utterly be lopp'd away,
Than the whole tree of all his race should perish;
And for his wants, better young want than eld."

GOSTANZO [aside]. By heaven, the same words still I us'd t'his
father.
Why comes this about?—Well, good Rinaldo,
If he dare not endure his father's looks,
Let him and his fair wife come home to me,
Till I have qualified his father's passion.
He shall be kindly welcome and be sure
Of all the intercession I can use.

RINALDO. I thank you, sir. I'll try what I can do,
Although I fear me I shall strive in vain.

GOSTANZO. Well, try him, try him.   *Exit.*

RINALDO.   Thanks, sir, so I will.—
See, this old, politic, dissembling knight,
Now he perceives my father so affectionate,
And that my brother may hereafter live
By him and his with equal use of either,
He will put on a face of hollow friendship.
But this will prove an excellent ground to sow
The seed of mirth amongst us. I'll go seek
Valerio and my brother, and tell them
Such news of their affairs as they'll admire.   *Exit.*

[I.ii]

Enter Gazetta, Bellanora, Gratiana.

GAZETTA. How happy are your fortunes above mine!
Both still being woo'd and courted, still so feeding
On the delights of love that still you find
An appetite to more, where I am cloy'd,
And being bound to love-sports, care not for them.

BELLANORA. That is your fault, Gazetta. We have loves
And wish continual company with them
In honor'd marriage-rites, which you enjoy.
But seld or never can we get a look
Of those we love. Fortunio, my dear choice,
Dare not be known to love me, nor come near
My father's house, where I as in a prison
Consume my lost days and the tedious nights,
My father guarding me for one I hate.
And Gratiana here, my brother's love,
Joys him by so much stealth that vehement fear
Drinks up the sweetness of their stol'n delights,
Where you enjoy a husband, and may freely
Perform all obsequies you desire to love.

GAZETTA. Indeed I have a husband, and his love
Is more than I desire, being vainly jealous.
Extremes, though contrary, have the like effects.
Extreme heat mortifies like extreme cold;

Extreme love breeds satiety as well
As extreme hatred, and too violent rigor
Tempts chastity as much as too much licence.
There's no man's eye fix'd on me but doth pierce
My husband's soul. If any ask my welfare,
He straight doubts treason practic'd to his bed,
Fancies but to himself all likelihoods
Of my wrong to him, and lays all on me
For certain truths. Yet seeks he with his best
To put disguise on all his jealousy,
Fearing perhaps lest it may teach me that
Which otherwise I should not dream upon.
Yet lives he still abroad at great expense,
Turns merely gallant from his farmer's state,
Uses all games and recreations,
Runs races with the gallants of the court,
Feasts them at home, and entertains them costly.
And then upbraids me with their company.

Enter Cornelio.

See, see, we shall be troubled with him now.
    CORNELIO. Now, ladies, what plots have we now in hand?
They say when only one dame is alone
She plots some mischief, but if three together,
They plot three hundred. Wife, the air is sharp.
Y'ad best to take the house lest you take cold.
    GAZETTA. Alas, this time of year yields no such danger.
    CORNELIO. Go in, I say. A friend of yours attends you.
    GAZETTA. He is of your bringing, and may stay.
    CORNELIO. Nay, stand not chopping logic. In, I pray.
    GAZETTA. Ye see, gentlewomen, what my happiness is.
These humors reign in marriage. Humors, humors.
                        Exit [Gazetta], *He followeth.*
    GRATIANA. Now by my sooth, I am no fortune-teller,
And would be loath to prove so, yet pronounce
This at adventure, that 'twere indecorum
This heifer should want horns.
    BELLANORA.   Fie on this love.
I rather wish to want than purchase so.
    GRATIANA. Indeed such love is like a smoky fire

In a cold morning. Though the fire be cheerful,
Yet is the smoke so sour and cumbersome,
'Twere better lose the fire than find the smoke.
Such an attendant then as smoke to fire
Is jealousy to love. Better want both
Than have both.

Enter Valerio *and* Fortunio.

VALERIO.   Come, Fortunio, now take hold
On this occasion, as myself on this.   [*Embraces* Gratiana.]
One couple more would make a barley-break.

FORTUNIO. I fear, Valerio, we shall break too soon.
Your father's jealous spy-all will displease us.

VALERIO. Well, wench, the day will come his Argus eyes
Will shut, and thou shalt open. 'Sfoot, I think
Dame Nature's memory begins to fail her.
If I write but my name in mercers' books,
I am as sure to have at six months' end
A rascal at my elbow with his mace,
As I am sure my father's not far hence.
My father yet hath ought Dame Nature debt
These threescore years and ten, yet calls not on him.
But if she turn her debt-book over once,
And finding him her debtor, do but send
Her sergeant, John Death, to arrest his body,
Our souls shall rest, wench, then, and the free light
Shall triumph in our faces, where now night,
In imitation of my father's frowns,
Lowers at our meeting.

Enter Rinaldo.

                    See where the scholar comes.

RINALDO. Down on your knees, poor lovers. Reverence
learning.

FORTUNIO. I pray thee, why, Rinaldo?

RINALDO.   Mark what cause
Flows from my depth of knowledge to your loves,
To make you kneel and bless me while you live.

VALERIO. I pray thee, good scholard, give us cause.

RINALDO. Mark then, erect your ears.—[*To* Valerio.] You
know what horror
Would fly on your love from your father's frowns,
If he should know it. And your sister here
(My brother's sweetheart) knows as well what rage
Would seize his powers for her, if he should know
My brother woo'd her, or that she lov'd him.
Is not this true? Speak all.

    OMNES.   All this is true.

    RINALDO. It is as true that now you meet by stealth
In depth of midnight, kissing out at grates,
Climb over walls. And all this I'll reform.

    VALERIO. By logic.

    RINALDO.   Well, sir, you shall have all means
To live in one house, eat and drink together,
Meet and kiss your fills.

    VALERIO.   All this by learning?

    RINALDO. Ay, and your frowning father know all this.

    VALERIO. Ay, marry, small learning may prove that.

    RINALDO. Nay, he shall know it, and desire it too,
Welcome my brother to him, and your wife,
Entreating both to come and dwell with him.
Is not this strange?

    FORTUNIO.   Ay, too strange to be true.

    RINALDO. 'Tis in this head shall work it. Therefore, hear.
Brother, this lady you must call your wife,
For I have told her sweetheart's father here
That she is your wife. And because my father
(Who now believes it) must be quieted
Before you see him, you must live awhile
As husband to her in his father's house.
Valerio, here's a simple mean for you
To lie at rack and manger with your wedlock,
And, brother, for yourself to meet as freely
With this your long-desir'd and barred love.

    FORTUNIO. You make us wonder.

    RINALDO.   Peace, be rul'd by me,
And you shall see to what a perfect shape
I'll bring this rude plot, which blind Chance (the ape
Of counsel and advice) hath brought forth blind.
Valerio, can your heat of love forbear

Before your father, and allow my brother
To use some kindness to your wife before him?

   VALERIO. Ay, before him I do not greatly care,
Nor anywhere indeed. My sister here
Shall be my spy. If she will wrong herself,
And give her right to my wife, I am pleas'd.

   FORTUNIO. My dearest life I know will never fear
Any such will or thought in all my powers.
When I court her then, think I think 'tis thee,
When I embrace her, hold thee in mine arms.
Come, let us practice gainst we see your father.

                          [*Offers to embrace* Gratiana.]

   VALERIO. Soft, sir, I hope you need not do it yet.
Let me take this time.   [*Embraces her.*]

   RINALDO.   Come, you must not touch her.

   VALERIO. No, not before my father!

   RINALDO.   No, nor now,
Because you are so soon to practice it,
For I must bring them to him presently.
Take her, Fortunio. Go hence man and wife.
We will attend you rarely with fix'd faces.
Valerio, keep your countenance, and conceive
Your father in your forged sheepishness,
Who thinks thou dar'st not look upon a wench,
Nor knowest at which end to begin to kiss her.   *Exeunt.*

Finis Actus Primi.

[*II.i*]

Gostanzo, Marc Antonio.

   GOSTANZO. It is your own too simple lenity
And doting indulgence shown to him still
That thus hath taught your son to be no son.
As you have us'd him, therefore, so you have him.
Durst my son thus turn rebel to his duty,
Steal up a match unsuiting his estate,
Without all knowledge of or friend or father,
And to make that good with a worse offense,
Resolve to run beyond sea to the wars,

Durst my son serve me thus? Well, I have stay'd him,
Though much against my disposition,
And this hour I have set for his repair
With his young mistress and concealed wife,
And in my house here they shall sojourn both,
Till your black anger's storm be overblown.

MARC ANTONIO. My anger's storm? Ah, poor Fortunio,
One gentle word from thee would soon resolve
The storm of my rage to a shower of tears.

GOSTANZO. In that vein still? Well, Marc Antonio,
Our old acquaintance and long neighborhood
Ties my affection to you and the good
Of your whole house; in kind regard whereof
I have advis'd you for your credit sake,
And for the tender welfare of your son,
To frown on him a little. If you do not,
But at first parley take him to your favor,
I protest utterly to renounce all care
Of you and yours and all your amities.
They say he's wretched that out of himself
Cannot draw counsel to his proper weal.
But he's thrice wretched that has neither counsel
Within himself, nor apprehension
Of counsel for his own good from another.

MARC ANTONIO. Well, I will arm myself against this weakness
The best I can. I long to see this Helen
That hath enchanted my young Paris thus,
And's like to set all our poor Troy on fire.

Enter Valerio *with a* Page.

GOSTANZO. Here comes my son. Withdraw, take up your
stand.
You shall hear odds betwixt your son and mine.

                                   Marc Antonio *retires himself*.

VALERIO. Tell him I cannot do't. Shall I be made
A foolish novice, my purse set abroach
By every cheating come-you-seven, to lend
My money and be laugh'd at? Tell him plain
I profess husbandry, and will not play
The prodigal like him gainst my profession.

GOSTANZO [*aside*]. Here's a son.

MARC ANTONIO [*aside*]. An admirable spark.

PAGE. Well, sir, I'll tell him so.   *Exit* Page.

VALERIO.   'Sfoot, let him lead
A better husband's life and live not idly,
Spending his time, his coin, and self on wenches.

GOSTANZO. Why, what's the matter, son?

VALERIO. Cry mercy, sir. Why, there come messengers
From this and that brave gallant, and such gallants
As I protest I saw but through a grate.

GOSTANZO. And what's this message?

VALERIO.   Faith, sir, he's disappointed
Of payments and disfurnish'd of means present.
If I would do him the kind office, therefore,
To trust him but some seven-night with the keeping
Of forty crowns for me, he deeply swears,
As he's a gentleman, to discharge his trust.
And that I shall eternally endear him
To my wish'd service, he protests and contests.

GOSTANZO. Good words, Valerio. But thou art too wise
To be deceiv'd by breath. I'll turn thee loose
To the most cunning cheater of them all.

VALERIO. 'Sfoot, he's not asham'd besides to charge me
With a late promise. I must yield, indeed,
I did (to shift him with some contentment)
Make such a frivol promise.

GOSTANZO.   Ay, well done.
Promises are no fetters. With that tongue
Thy promise pass'd, unpromise it again.
Wherefore has man a tongue of power to speak,
But to speak still to his own private purpose?
Beasts utter but one sound, but men have change
Of speech and reason, even by Nature given them,
Now to say one thing and another now,
As best may serve their profitable ends.

MARC ANTONIO [*aside*]. By'r-lady, sound instructions to a son.

VALERIO. Nay, sir, he makes his claim by debt of friendship.

GOSTANZO. Tush, friendship's but a term, boy. The fond world
Like to a doting mother glazes over
Her children's imperfections with fine terms.
What she calls friendship and true, humane kindness,

Is only want of true experience.
Honesty is but a defect of wit;
Respect but mere rusticity and clownery.

MARC ANTONIO [*aside*]. Better and better. Soft, here comes
my son.

Enter Fortunio, Rinaldo, *and* Gratiana.

RINALDO [*aside*]. Fortunio, keep your countenance.—[*To*
Gostanzo.] See, sir, here
The poor young married couple which you pleas'd
To send for to your house.

GOSTANZO.   Fortunio, welcome.
And in that welcome I employ your wife's,
Who I am sure you count your second self.   *He kisses her.*

FORTUNIO. Sir, your right noble favors do exceed
All power of worthy gratitude by words,
That in your care supply my father's place.

GOSTANZO. Fortunio, I cannot choose but love you,
Being son to him who long time I have lov'd,
From whose just anger my house shall protect you,
Till I have made a calm way to your meetings.

FORTUNIO. I little thought, sir, that my father's love
Would take so ill so slight a fault as this.

GOSTANZO. Call you it slight? Nay, though his spirit take it
In higher manner than for your lov'd sake
I would have wish'd him, yet I make a doubt,
Had my son done the like, if my affection
Would not have turn'd to more spleen than your father's.
And yet I qualify him all I can,
And doubt not but that time and my persuasion
Will work out your excuse, since youth and love
Were th'unresisted organs to seduce you.
But you must give him leave, for fathers must
Be won by penitence and submission,
And not by force or opposition.

FORTUNIO. Alas, sir, what advise you me to do?
I know my father to be highly mov'd,
And am not able to endure the breath
Of his express'd displeasure, whose hot flames
I think my absence soonest would have quench'd.

GOSTANZO. True, sir, as fire with oil, or else like them
That quench the fire with pulling down the house.
You shall remain here in my house conceal'd
Till I have won your father to conceive
Kinder opinion of your oversight.
Valerio, entertain Fortunio
And his fair wife, and give them conduct in.

VALERIO. Y'are welcome, sir.

GOSTANZO.   What, sirrah, is that all?
No entertainment to the gentlewoman?

VALERIO. Forsooth, y'are welcome by my father's leave.

GOSTANZO. What, no more compliment? Kiss her, you
sheepshead.
Why, when?—Go, go, sir, call your sister hither.

Exit Valerio.

Lady, you'll pardon our gross bringing up?
We dwell far off from court, you may perceive.
The sight of such a blazing star as you
Dazzles my rude son's wits.

GRATIANA.   Not so, good sir.
The better husband, the more courtly ever.

RINALDO. Indeed a courtier makes his lips go far,
As he doth all things else.

Enter Valerio, Bellanora.

GOSTANZO.   Daughter, receive
This gentlewoman home, and use her kindly.

She kisses her.

BELLANORA. My father bids you kindly welcome, lady,
And therefore you must needs come well to me.

GRATIANA. Thank you, forsooth.

GOSTANZO.   Go, dame, conduct 'em in.

Exeunt Rinaldo, Fortunio, Bellanora, Gratiana.

Ah, errant sheepshead, hast thou liv'd thus long,
And dar'st not look a woman in the face?
Though I desire especially to see
My son a husband, shall I therefore have him
Turn absolute cullion? Let's see, kiss thy hand.
Thou kiss thy hand? Thou wip'st thy mouth, by th' mass.

Fie on thee, clown. They say the world's grown finer,
But I for my part never saw young men
Worse fashion'd and brought up than nowadays.
'Sfoot, when myself was young, was not I kept
As far from court as you? I think I was.
And yet my father on a time invited
The Duchess of his house. I, being then
About some five-and-twenty years of age,
Was thought the only man to entertain her.
I had my congé—plant myself of one leg,
Draw back the tother with a deep-fetch'd honor,
Then with a bel-regard advant mine eye
With boldness on her very visnomy.
Your dancers all were counterfeits to me.
And for discourse in my fair mistress' presence
I did not as you barren gallants do,
Fill my discourses up drinking tobacco,
But on the present furnish'd evermore
With tales and practic'd speeches—as sometimes,
"What is't o'clock?" "What stuff's this petticoat?"
"What cost the making?" "What the fringe and all?"
And what she had under her petticoat,
And such-like witty compliments. And for need,
I could have written as good prose and verse
As the most beggarly poet of 'em all,
Either acrostic, exordium,
Epithalamions, satires, epigrams,
Sonnets in dozens, or your quatorzains
In any rhyme, masculine, feminine,
Or sdrucciola, or couplets, blank verse.
Y'are but bench-whistlers nowadays to them
That were in our times. Well, about your husbandry.
Go, for i'faith, th'art fit for nothing else.

                            Exit Valerio. *Prodit* Marc Antonio.

  MARC ANTONIO. By'r-lady, you have play'd the courtier rarely.

  GOSTANZO. But did you ever see so blank a fool,
When he should kiss a wench, as my son is?

  MARC ANTONIO. Alas, 'tis but a little bashfulness.
You let him keep no company, nor allow him
Money to spend at fence and dancing-schools.

Y'are too severe, i'faith.

GOSTANZO.　　　　　And you too supple.
Well, sir, for your sake I have stay'd your son
From flying to the wars. Now see you rate him,
To stay him yet from more expenseful courses,
Wherein your lenity will encourage him.

MARC ANTONIO. Let me alone. I thank you for this
kindness.　　　　　　　　　　　　　　　　*Exeunt.*

Enter Valerio *and* Rinaldo.

RINALDO. So, are they gone? Now tell me, brave Valerio,
Have I not won the wreath from all your wits,
Brought thee t'enjoy the most desired presence
Of thy dear love at home, and with one labor
My brother t'enjoy thy sister, where
It had been her undoing t'have him seen,
And make thy father crave what he abhors,
T'entreat my brother home t'enjoy his daughter,
Command thee kiss thy wench, chide for not kissing,
And work all this out of a Machiavel,
A miserable politician?
I think the like was never play'd before!

VALERIO. Indeed, I must commend thy wit of force.
And yet I know not whose deserves most praise,
Of thine or my wit. Thine for plotting well,
Mine, that durst undertake and carry it
With such true form.

RINALDO.　　　　　Well, th'evening crowns the day.
Persever to the end. My wit hath put
Blind Fortune in a string into your hand.
Use it discreetly, keep it from your father,
Or you may bid all your good days good-night.

VALERIO. Let me alone, boy.

RINALDO.　　　　　　　Well, sir, now to vary
The pleasures of our wits, thou know'st, Valerio,
Here is the new-turn'd gentleman's fair wife,
That keeps thy wife and sister company,
With whom the amorous courtier Dariotto
Is far in love, and of whom her sour husband
Is passing jealous, puts on eagle's eyes

To pry into her carriage. Shall we see
If he be now from home, and visit her?

Enter Gazetta *sewing,* Cornelio *following.*

See, see, the prisoner comes.

VALERIO.   But soft, sir, see
Her jealous jailor follows at her heels.
Come, we will watch some fitter time to board her,
And in the meantime seek out our mad crew.
My spirit longs to swagger.

RINALDO.   Go to, youth.
Walk not too boldly. If the sergeants meet you,
You may have swaggering work your bellyful.

     VALERIO. No better copesmates.

Gazetta sits and sings sewing.

I'll go seek 'em out with this light in my hand.
The slaves grow proud with seeking out of us.

                    Exeunt [Valerio *and* Rinaldo].

     CORNELIO. A pretty work. I pray what flowers are these?

     GAZETTA. The pansy this.

     CORNELIO.   O, that's for lover's thoughts.
What's that, a columbine?

     GAZETTA.   No, that thankless flower
Fits not my garden.

     CORNELIO.   Hmnn! Yet it may mine.
This were a pretty present for some friend,
Some gallant courtier, as for Dariotto,
One that adores you in his soul, I know.

     GAZETTA. Me? Why me more than yourself, I pray?

     CORNELIO. O yes, he adores you, and adhorns me.
I'faith, deal plainly, do not his kisses relish
Much better than such peasant's as I am?

     GAZETTA. Whose kisses?

     CORNELIO.   Dariotto's. Does he not
The thing you wot on?

     GAZETTA.   What thing, good lord?

     CORNELIO. Why, lady, lie with you!

     GAZETTA.   Lie with me?

CORNELIO. Ay, with you.

GAZETTA.   You with me, indeed!

CORNELIO. Nay, I am told that he lies with you too,
And that he is the only whoremaster
About the city.

GAZETTA.   If he be so only,
'Tis a good hearing that there are no more.

CORNELIO. Well, mistress, well. I will not be abus'd.
Think not you dance in nets, for though you do not
Make broad profession of your love to him,
Yet do I understand your darkest language,
Your treads o'th' toe, your secret jogs and wrings,
Your intercourse of glances. Every tittle
Of your close amorous rites I understand.
They speak as loud to me as if you said,
"My dearest Dariotto, I am thine."

GAZETTA. Jesus, what moods are these? Did ever husband
Follow his wife with jealousy so unjust?
That once I lov'd you, you yourself will swear.
And if I did, where did you lose my love?
Indeed, this strange and undeserved usage
Hath power to shake a heart were ne'er so settled.
But I protest all your unkindness never
Had strength to make me wrong you but in thought.

CORNELIO. No, not with Dariotto?

GAZETTA.   No, by heaven.

CORNELIO. No letters pass'd, nor no designs for meeting?

GAZETTA. No, by my hope of heaven.

CORNELIO.   Well, no time past.
Go, go; go in and sew.

GAZETTA.   Well, be it so.   *Exit* Gazetta.

CORNELIO. Suspicion is (they say) the first degree
Of deepest wisdom. And however others
Inveigh against this mood of jealousy,
For my part I suppose it the best curb
To check the ranging appetites that reign
In this weak sex. My neighbors point at me
For this my jealousy. But should I do
As most of them do, let my wife fly out
To feasts and revels, and invite home gallants,
Play Menelaus, give them time and place,

While I sit like a well-taught waiting-woman,
Turning her eyes upon some work or picture,
Read in a book, or take a feigned nap,
While her kind lady takes one to her lap?
No, let me still be pointed at, and thought
A jealous ass, and not a wittolly knave.
I have a shew of courtiers haunt my house,
In show my friends, and for my profit too.
But I perceive 'em, and will mock their aims
With looking to their mark, I warrant 'em.
I am content to ride abroad with them,
To revel, dice, and fit their other sports,
But by their leaves I'll have a vigilant eye
To the main chance still. See my brave comrades.

Enter Dariotto, Claudio, [*Page*] *and* Valerio,
Valerio *putting up his sword.*

DARIOTTO [*to* Valerio]. Well, wag, well. Wilt thou still deceive
thy father,
And being so simple a poor soul before him,
Turn swaggerer in all companies besides?
   CLAUDIO. Hadst thou been rested, all would have come forth.
   VALERIO. Soft, sir, there lies the point. I do not doubt
But t' have my pennyworths of these rascals one day.
I'll smoke the buzzing hornets from their nests,
Or else I'll make their leather jerkins stay.
The whoreson hungry horseflies. Foot, a man
Cannot so soon, for want of almanacs,
Forget his day but three or four bare months,
But straight he sees a sort of corporals
To lie in ambuscado to surprise him.
   DARIOTTO. Well, thou hadst happy fortune to escape 'em.
   VALERIO. But they thought theirs was happier to scape me.
I, walking in the place where men's lawsuits
Are heard and pleaded, not so much as dreaming
Of any such encounter, steps me forth
Their valiant foreman, with the word, "I rest you."
I made no more ado, but laid these paws
Close on his shoulders, tumbling him to earth.
And there sate he on his posteriors,

Like a baboon. And turning me about,
I straight espied the whole troop issuing on me.
I stepp'd me back, and drawing my old friend here,
Made to the midst of them, and all unable
T'endure the shock, all rudely fell in rout,
And down the stairs they ran with such a fury,
As meeting with a troop of lawyers there,
Mann'd by their clients, some with ten, some with twenty,
Some five, some three—he that had least, had one—
Upon the stairs they bore them down afore them.
But such a rattling then was there amongst them
Of ravish'd declarations, replications,
Rejoinders and petitions—all their books
And writings torn and trod on, and some lost—
That the poor lawyers coming to the bar,
Could say nought to the matter, but instead,
Were fain to rail and talk besides their books
Without all order.

    CLAUDIO.   Faith, that same vein of railing
Became now most applausive. Your best poet is
He that rails grossest.

    DARIOTTO.   True, and your best fool
Is your broad railing fool.

    VALERIO.   And why not, sir?
For by the gods, to tell the naked truth,
What objects see men in this world but such
As would yield matter to a railing humor,
When he that last year carried after one
An empty buckram bag now fills a coach,
And crowds the senate with such troops of clients
And servile followers, as would put a mad spleen
Into a pigeon?

    DARIOTTO.   Come, pray leave these cross capers.
Let's make some better use of precious time.
See, here's Cornelio. Come, lad, shall we to dice?

    CORNELIO. Anything, I.

    CLAUDIO.   Well said. How does thy wife?

    CORNELIO. In health, God save her.

    VALERIO.   But where is she, man?

    CORNELIO. Abroad about her business.

    VALERIO.   Why, not at home?

Foot, my masters, take her to the court,
And this rare lad, her husband. And—dost hear?—
Play me no more the miserable farmer,
But be advis'd by friends. Sell all i'th' country,
Be a flat courtier, follow some great man,
Or bring thy wife there, and she'll make thee great.

    CORNELIO. What, to the court? Then take me for a gull.

    VALERIO. Nay, never shun it to be call'd a gull,
For I see all the world is but a gull,
One man gull to another in all kinds.
A merchant to a courtier is a gull,
A client to a lawyer is a gull,
A married man to a bachelor, a gull,
A bachelor to a cuckold is a gull,
All to a poet, or a poet to himself.

    CORNELIO [*aside*]. Hark, Dariotto, shall we gull this guller?

    DARIOTTO [*aside*]. He gulls his father, man, we cannot gull
him.

    CORNELIO [*aside*]. Let me alone.—Of all men's wits alive
I most admire Valerio's, that hath stol'n
By his mere industry, and that by spurts,
Such qualities as no wit else can match
With plodding at perfection every hour,
Which, if his father knew each gift he has,
Were like enough to make him give all from him.
I mean, besides his dicing and his wenching,
He has stol'n languages, th'Italian, Spanish,
And some spice of the French, besides his dancing,
Singing, playing on choice instruments.
These has he got, almost against the hair.

    CLAUDIO. But hast thou stol'n all these, Valerio?

    VALERIO. Toys, toys, a pox. And yet they be such toys
As every gentleman would not be without.

    CORNELIO. Vainglory makes ye judge 'em light i'faith!

    DARIOTTO. Afore heaven I was much deceiv'd in him.
But he's the man indeed that hides his gifts,
And sets them not to sale in every presence.
I would have sworn his soul were far from music,
And that all his choice music was to hear
His fat beasts bellow.

    CORNELIO.   Sir, your ignorance

Shall eftsoon be confuted. Prithee, Val,
Take thy theorbo for my sake a little.

VALERIO. By heaven, this month I touch'd not a theorbo.

CORNELIO. Touch'd a theorbo! Mark the very word.
Sirrah, go fetch. *Exit* Page.

VALERIO. If you will have it, I must needs confess
I am no husband of my qualities. *He untrusses and capers.*

CORNELIO. See what a caper there was!

CLAUDIO. See again!

CORNELIO. The best that ever. And how it becomes him!

DARIOTTO. O that his father saw these qualities!

Enter a Page *with an instrument.*

CORNELIO. Nay, that's the very wonder of his wit,
To carry all without his father's knowledge.

DARIOTTO. Why, we might tell him now.

CORNELIO. No, but we could not,
Although we think we could. His wit doth charm us.
Come, sweet Val, touch and sing.

DARIOTTO [*aside*]. Foot, will you hear
The worst voice in Italy?

Enter Rinaldo.

CORNELIO. O God, sir! *He sings.*
Courtiers, how like you this?

DARIOTTO. Believe it, excellent!

CORNELIO. Is it not natural?

VALERIO. If my father heard me,
Foot, he'd renounce me for his natural son.

DARIOTTO. By heaven, Valerio, and I were thy father,
And lov'd good qualities as I do my life,
I'd disinherit thee, for I never heard
Dog howl with worse grace.

CORNELIO. Go to, Signor Courtier.
You deal not courtly now to be so plain,
Nor nobly, to discourage a young gentleman
In virtuous qualities, that has but stol'n 'em.

CLAUDIO. Call you this touching a theorbo?

OMNES. Ha, ha, ha!

Exeunt all but Valerio *and* Rinaldo.

VALERIO. How now, what's here?

RINALDO.   Zoons, a plot laid to gull thee.
Could thy wit think the voice was worth the hearing?
This was the courtier's and the cuckold's project.

VALERIO. And is't e'en so? 'Tis very well, Mast Courtier
And Dan Cornuto, I'll cry quit with both.
And first, I'll cast a jar betwixt them both,
With firing the poor cuckold's jealousy.
I have a tale will make him mad,
And turn his wife divorced loose amongst us.
But first let's home, and entertain my wife.
O father, pardon. I was born to gull thee.   *Exeunt.*

Finis Actus Secundi.

[III.i]

Enter Fortunio, Bellanora, Gratiana, Gostanzo *following closely.*

FORTUNIO. How happy am I, that by this sweet means
I gain access to your most loved sight,
And therewithal to utter my full love,
Which but for vent would burn my entrails up!

GOSTANZO [*aside*]. By th' mass they talk too softly.

BELLANORA.   Little thinks
The austere mind my thrifty father bears
That I am vow'd to you, and so am bound
From him who for more riches he would force
On my disliking fancy.

FORTUNIO.   'Tis no fault
With just deeds to defraud an injury.

GOSTANZO [*aside*]. My daughter is persuading him to yield
In dutiful submission to his father.

Enter Valerio.

VALERIO. Do I not dream? Do I behold this sight
With waking eyes? Or from the ivory gate
Hath Morpheus sent a vision to delude me?
Is't possible that I, a mortal man,

Should shrine within mine arms so bright a goddess,
The fair Gratiana, beauty's little world?

GOSTANZO [*aside*]. What have we here?

VALERIO. My dearest mine of gold,
All this that thy white arms enfold,
Account it as thine own freehold.

GOSTANZO [*aside*]. God's my dear soul, what sudden change
is here!
I smell how this gear will fall out, i'faith.

VALERIO. Fortunio, sister, come. Let's to the garden. *Exeunt.*

GOSTANZO. Sits the wind there, i'faith? See what example
Will work upon the dullest appetite.
My son, last day so bashful that he durst not
Look on a wench, now courts her, and, by'r lady,
Will make his friend Fortunio wear his head
Of the right modern fashion. What, Rinaldo!

Enter Rinaldo.

RINALDO. I fear I interrupt your privacy.

GOSTANZO. Welcome, Rinaldo, would't had been your hap
To come a little sooner, that you might
Have seen a handsome sight. But let that pass.
The short is that your sister Gratiana
Shall stay no longer here.

RINALDO.   No longer, sir?
Repent you then so soon your favor to her,
And to my brother?

GOSTANZO.   No so, good Rinaldo.
But to prevent a mischief that I see
Hangs over your abused brother's head.
In brief, my son has learn'd but too much courtship.
It was my chance even now to cast mine eye
Into a place where, to your sister, enter'd
My metamorphos'd son—I must conceal
What I saw there. But to be plain, I saw
More than I would see. I had thought to make
My house a kind receipt for your kind brother.
But I'd be loath his wife should find more kindness
Than she had cause to like of.

RINALDO.   What's the matter?

Perhaps a little compliment or so.

 GOSTANZO. Well, sir, such compliment perhaps may cost
Married Fortunio the setting on.
Nor can I keep my knowledge. He that lately
Before my face I could not get to look
Upon your sister, by this light, now kiss'd her,
Embrac'd and courted with as good a grace,
As any courtier could. And I can tell you
(Not to disgrace her) I perceiv'd the dame
Was as far forward as himself, by th' mass.

 RINALDO. You should have school'd him for't.

 GOSTANZO.   No, I'll not see't,
For shame once found, is lost. I'll have him think
That my opinion of him is the same
That it was ever. It will be a mean
To bridle this fresh humor bred in him.

 RINALDO. Let me then school him. Foot, I'll rattle him up.

 GOSTANZO. No, no, Rinaldo, th'only remedy
Is to remove the cause, carry the object
From his late tempted eyes.

 RINALDO.   Alas, sir, whither?
You know my father is incens'd so much
He'll not receive her.

 GOSTANZO.   Place her with some friend
But for a time, till I reclaim your father.
Meantime your brother shall remain with me.

 RINALDO (to himself). The care's the less then. He has still his longing
To be with this gull's daughter.

 GOSTANZO.   What resolve you?
I am resolv'd she lodges here no more.
My friend's son shall not be abus'd by mine.

 RINALDO. Troth, sir, I'll tell you what a sudden toy
Comes in my head. What think you if I brought her
Home to my father's house?

 GOSTANZO.   Ay, marry, sir.
Would he receive her?

 RINALDO.   Nay, you hear not all.
I mean with use of some device or other.

 GOSTANZO. As how, Rinaldo?

 RINALDO.   Marry, sir, to say

She is your son's wife, married past your knowledge.

GOSTANZO. I doubt last day he saw her, and will know her
To be Fortunio's wife.

    RINALDO.   Nay, as for that,
I will pretend she was even then your son's wife,
But feign'd by me to be Fortunio's
Only to try how he would take the matter.

    GOSTANZO. 'Fore heaven 'twere pretty.

    RINALDO.   Would it not do well?

GOSTANZO. Exceeding well, in sadness.

    RINALDO.   Nay, good sir,
Tell me unfeignedly, do ye like't indeed?

    GOSTANZO. The best that e'er I heard.

    RINALDO.   And do you think
He'll swallow down the gudgeon?

    GOSTANZO.   O' my life.
It were a gross gob would not down with him,
An honest knight, but simple, not acquainted
With the fine sleights and policies of the world,
As I myself am.

    RINALDO.   I'll go fetch her straight.
And this jest thrive, 'twill make us princely sport.
But you must keep our counsel, second all,
Which to make likely, you must needs sometimes
Give your son leave (as if you knew it not)
To steal and see her at my father's house.

    GOSTANZO. Ay, but see you then that you keep good guard
Over his forward, new-begun affections,
For, by the Lord, he'll teach your brother else
To sing the cuckoo's note. Spirit will break out,
Though never so suppress'd and pinioned.

    RINALDO. Especially your son's. What would he be,
If you should not restrain him by good counsel?

    GOSTANZO. I'll have an eye on him, I warrant thee.
I'll in and warn the gentlewoman to make ready.

    RINALDO. Well, sir, and I'll not be long after you.

                               Exit Gostanzo.

Heaven, heaven, I see these politicians
(Out of blind Fortune's hands) are our most fools.
'Tis she that gives the luster to their wits,
Still plodding at traditional devices.

But take 'em out of them to present actions,
A man may grope and tickle 'em like a trout,
And take 'em from their close dear holes as fat
As a physician, and as giddy-headed,
As if by miracle heaven had taken from them
Even that which commonly belongs to fools.
Well, now let's note what black ball of debate
Valerio's wit hath cast betwixt Cornelio
And the enamor'd courtier. I believe
His wife and he will part. His jealousy
Hath ever watch'd occasion of divorce,
And now Valerio's villainy will present it.
See, here comes the twin-courtier, his companion.

Enter Claudio.

CLAUDIO. Rinaldo, well encounter'd.
RINALDO.   Why? What news?
CLAUDIO. Most sudden and infortunate, Rinaldo.
Cornelio is incens'd so 'gainst his wife
That no man can procure her quiet with him.
I have assay'd him, and made Marc Antonio
With all his gentle rhetoric second me.
Yet all, I fear me, will be cast away.
See, see, they come. Join thy wit, good Rinaldo,
And help to pacify his yellow fury.
RINALDO. With all my heart. I consecrate my wit
To the wish'd comfort of distressed ladies.

Enter Cornelio, Marc Antonio, Valerio, Page.

CORNELIO. Will any man assure me of her good behavior?
VALERIO. Who can assure a jealous spirit? You may be afraid
of the shadow of your ears, and imagine them to be horns. If you
will assure yourself, appoint keepers to watch her.
CORNELIO. And who shall watch the keepers?
MARC ANTONIO. To be sure of that, be you her keeper.
VALERIO. Well said, and share the horns yourself, for that's the
keeper's fee.
CORNELIO. But say I am gone out of town, and must trust
others. How shall I know if those I trust be trusty to me?

RINALDO. Marry, sir, by a singular instinct, given naturally to all you married men, that if your wives play leger-de-heel, though you be a hundred miles off, yet you shall be sure instantly to find it in your foreheads.

CORNELIO. Sound doctrine, I warrant you. I am resolved, i'faith.

PAGE. Then give me leave to speak, sir, that hath all this while been silent. I have heard you with extreme patience. Now, therefore, prick up your ears, and vouchsafe me audience.

CLAUDIO. Good boy, o' mine honor.

CORNELIO. Pray, what are you, sir?

PAGE. I am here, for default of better, of counsel with the fair Gazetta. And though herself had been best able to defend herself if she had been here, and would have pleased to put forth the buckler which Nature hath given all women—
I mean her tongue—

VALERIO. Excellent good boy.

PAGE. Yet since she either vouchsafes it not, or thinks her innocence a sufficient shield against your jealous accusations, I will presume to undertake the defense of that absent and honorable lady, whose sworn knight I am, and in her of all that name (for lady is grown a common name to their whole sex), which sex I have ever loved from my youth, and shall never cease to love, till I want wit to admire.

MARC ANTONIO. An excellent spoken boy.

VALERIO. Give ear, Cornelio. Here is a young Mercurio sent to persuade thee.

CORNELIO. Well, sir, let him say on.

PAGE. It is a heavy case to see how this light sex is tumbled and tossed from post to pillar under the unsavory breath of every humorous peasant. Gazetta, you said, is unchaste, disloyal, and I wot not what. Alas, is it her fault? Is she not a woman? Did she not suck it (as others of her sex do) from her mother's breast? And will you condemn that as her fault which is her nature? Alas, sir, you must consider a woman is an unfinished creature, delivered hastily to the world before Nature had set to that seal which should have made them perfect. Faults they have (no doubt) but are we free? Turn your eye into yourself, good Signor Cornelio, and weigh your own imperfections with hers. If she be wanton abroad, are not you wanting at home? If she be amorous, are not you jealous? If she be high set, are not you taken down? If she be a courtesan, are not you a cuckold?

CORNELIO. Out, you rogue.

RINALDO. On with thy speech, boy.

MARC ANTONIO. You do not well, Cornelio, to discourage the bashful youth.

CLAUDIO. Forth, boy, I warrant thee.

PAGE. But if our own imperfections will not teach us to bear with theirs, yet let their virtues persuade us. Let us endure their bad qualities for their good, allow the prickle for the rose, the brack for the velvet, the paring for the cheese, and so forth. If you say they range abroad, consider it is nothing but to avoid idleness at home. Their nature is still to be doing; keep 'em a-doing at home. Let them practice one good quality or other, either sewing, singing, playing, chiding, dancing, or so, and these will put such idle toys out of their heads into yours. But if you cannot find them variety of business within doors, yet at least imitate the ancient, wise citizens of this city, who used carefully to provide their wives gardens near the town to plant, to graft in, as occasion served, only to keep 'em from idleness.

VALERIO. Everlasting good boy.

CORNELIO. I perceive your knavery, sir, and will yet have patience.

RINALDO. Forth, my brave Curio.

PAGE. As to her unquietness (which some have rudely termed shrewishness), though the fault be in her, yet the cause is in you. What so calm as the sea of its own nature? Art was never able to equal it. Your dicing-tables, nor your bowling alleys, are not comparable to it. Yet if a blast of wind do but cross it, not so turbulent and violent an element in the world. So (Nature in lieu of women's scarcity of wit, having indued them with a large portion of will) if they may (without impeach) enjoy their wills, no quieter creatures under heaven. But if the breath of their husbands' mouths once cross their wills, nothing more tempestuous. Why then, sir, should you husbands cross your wives' wills thus, considering the law allows them no wills at all at their deaths, because it intended they should have their wills while they lived?

VALERIO. Answer him but that, Cornelio.

CORNELIO. All shall not serve her turn. I am thinking of other matters.

MARC ANTONIO. Thou hast half won him, wag. Ply him yet a little further.

PAGE. Now, sir, for these cuckooish songs of yours, of cuckolds, horns, grafting, and such-like, what are they but mere imaginary toys, bred out of your own heads as your own, and so by tradition delivered from man to man, like scarecrows to terrify fools from this earthly paradise of wedlock, coined at first by some spent poets, superannated bachelors, or some that were scarce men of their hands, who, like the fox, having lost his tail, would persuade others to lose theirs for company? Again, for your cuckold, what is it but a mere fiction? Show me any such creature in nature. If there be, I could never see it; neither could I ever find any sensible difference betwixt a cuckold and a Christen creature. To conclude, let poets coin, or fools credit what they list. For mine own part, I am clear of this opinion, that your cuckold is a mere chimera, and that there are no cuckolds in the world—but those that have wives. And so I will leave them.

CORNELIO. 'Tis excellent good, sir. I do take you, sir—d'ye see?—to be as it were bastard to the saucy courtier that would have me father more of your fraternity—d'ye see?—and so are instructed (as we hear) to second that villain with your tongue, which he has acted with his tenure piece—d'ye see?

PAGE. No such matter, o' my credit, sir.

CORNELIO. Well, sir, be as be may, I scorn to set my head against yours—d'ye see?—when in the meantime I will firk your father, whether you see or no.   *Exit drawing his rapier.*

RINALDO. God's my life, Cornelio!   *Exit.*

VALERIO. Have at your father, i'faith, boy, if he can find him.

MARC ANTONIO. See, he comes here. He has missed him.

Enter Dariotto.

DARIOTTO. How now, my hearts. What, not a wench amongst you?
'Tis a sign y'are not in the grace of wenches
That they will let you be thus long alone.

VALERIO. Well, Dariotto, glory not too much
That for thy brisk attire and lips perfum'd,
Thou playest the stallion ever where thou com'st,
And like the husband of the flock, runn'st through

The whole town herd, and no man's bed secure,
No woman's honor unattempted by thee.
Think not to be thus fortunate forever,
But in thy amorous conquests at the last
Some wound will slice your mazer. Mars himself
Fell into Vulcan's snare, and so may you.

    DARIOTTO. Alas, alas. Faith, I have but the name.
I love to court and win, and the consent,
Without the act obtain'd, is all I seek.
I love the victory that draws no blood.

    CLAUDIO. O, 'tis a high desert in any man
To be a secret lecher. I know some
That (like thyself) are true in nothing else.

    MARC ANTONIO. And, methinks, it is nothing if not told.
At least the joy is never full before.

    VALERIO. Well, Dariotto, th' hadst as good confess.
The sun shines broad upon your practices.
Vulcan will wake and intercept you one day.

    DARIOTTO. Why, the more jealous knave and coxcomb he.
What, shall the shaking of his bed a little
Put him in motion? It becomes him not.
Let him be dull'd and stal'd, and then be quiet.
The way to draw my custom to his house
Is to be mad and jealous. 'Tis the sauce
That whets my appetite.

    VALERIO.   Or any man's.
Sine periculo friget lusus.
They that are jealous, use it still of purpose
To draw you to their houses.

    DARIOTTO.   Ay, by heaven,
I am of that opinion. Who would steal
Out of a common orchard? Let me gain
My love with labor, and enjoy't with fear,
Or I am gone.

Enter Rinaldo.

    RINALDO.   What, Dariotto here?
Foot, dar'st thou come near Cornelio's house?

    DARIOTTO. Why? Is the bull run mad? What ails he, trow?

RINALDO. I know not what he ails, but I would wish you
To keep out of the reach of his sharp horns,
For by this hand he'll gore you.
        DARIOTTO.   And why me
More than thyself, or these two other whelps?
You all have basted him as well as I.
I wonder what's the cause.
        RINALDO.   Nay, that he knows,
And swears withal that wheresoe'er he meets you,
He'll mark you for a marker of men's wives.
        VALERIO. Pray heaven he be not jealous by some tales
That have been told him lately. Did you never
Attempt his wife? Hath no love's harbinger,
No looks, no letters, pass'd 'twixt you and her?
        DARIOTTO. For looks I cannot answer. I bestow them
At large and carelessly, much like the sun.
If any be so foolish to apply them
To any private fancy of their own
(As many do), it's not my fault, thou knowest.
        VALERIO. Well, Dariotto, this set face of thine
(If thou be guilty of offense to him)
Comes out of very want of wit and feeling
What danger haunts thee. For Cornelio
Is a tall man, I tell you, and 'twere best
You shunn'd his sight awhile, till we might get
His patience, or his pardon. For past doubt
Thou diest if he but see thee.

Enter Cornelio.

        RINALDO.   Foot, he comes.
        DARIOTTO. Is this the cockatrice that kills with sight?
How dost thou, boy? Ha?
        Cornelio.   Well.
        DARIOTTO.   What, lingering still
About this paltry town? Hadst thou been rul'd
By my advice, thou hadst by this time been
A gallant courtier, and at least a knight.
I would have got thee dubb'd by this time, certain.
        CORNELIO. And why then did you not yourself that honor?

DARIOTTO. Tush, 'tis more honor still to make a knight
Than 'tis to be a knight, to make a cuckold
Than 'tis to be a cuckold.

CORNELIO.   Y'are a villain.

DARIOTTO. God shield, man! Villain?

CORNELIO.   Ay, I'll prove thee one.

DARIOTTO. What, wilt thou prove a villain?
By this light thou deceiv'st me, then.

CORNELIO. Well, sir, thus I prove it.   *Draws.*

OMNES.   Hold, hold. Raise the streets.

[Cornelio *runs at him.*]

CLAUDIO. Cornelio!

RINALDO.   Hold, Dariotto, hold!

VALERIO.   What, are thou hurt?

DARIOTTO. A scratch, a scratch.

VALERIO.   Go, sirrah, fetch a surgeon.
                                                  [*Exit* Page.]

CORNELIO. You'll set a badge on the jealous fool's head, sir.
Now set a coxcomb on your own.

VALERIO. What's the cause of these wars, Dariotto?

DARIOTTO. Foot, I know not.

CORNELIO. Well, sir, know and spare not. I will presently be
divorced, and then take her amongst ye.

RINALDO. Divorc'd? Nay, good Cornelio.

CORNELIO. By this sword, I will. The world shall not dissuade
me.   *Exit.*

VALERIO. Why this has been your fault now, Dariotto.
You youths have fashions, when you have obtain'd
A lady's favor, straight your hat must wear it,
Like a jackdaw that when he lights upon
A dainty morsel caws and makes his brags,
And then some kite doth scoop it from him straight,
Where if he fed without his dawish noise,
He might fare better, and have less disturbance.
Forbear it in this case, and when you prove
Victorious over fair Gazetta's fort,
Do not for pity sound your trump for joy,
But keep your valor close, and 'tis your honor.

Enter Page *and* Pock.

POCK. God save you, Signor Dariotto.

DARIOTTO. I know you not, sir. Your name, I pray?

POCK. My name is Pock, sir, a practitioner in surgery.

DARIOTTO. Pock, the surgeon. Y'are welcome, sir. I know a doctor of your name, Master Pock.

POCK. My name has made many doctors, sir.

RINALDO. Indeed, 'tis a worshipful name.

VALERIO. Marry is it, and of an ancient descent.

POCK. Faith, sir, I could fetch my pedigree far, if I were so disposed.

RINALDO. Out of France, at least.

POCK. And if I stood on my arms, as others do—

DARIOTTO. No, do not, Pock. Let other stand o' their arms, and thou o' thy legs as long as thou canst.

POCK. Though I live by my bare practice, yet I could show good cards for my gentility.

VALERIO. Tush, thou canst not shake off thy gentry, Pock. 'Tis bred i'th' bone. But to the main, Pock. What thinkest thou of this gentleman's wound, Pock? Canst thou cure it, Pock?

POCK. The incision is not deep, nor the orifice exorbitant. The pericranion is not dislocated. I warrant his life for forty crowns, without perishing of any joint.

DARIOTTO. Faith, Pock, 'tis a joint I would be loath to lose for the best joint of mutton in Italy.

RINALDO. Would such a scatch as this hazard a man's head?

POCK. Ay, by'r-lady, sir. I have known some have lost their heads for a less matter, I can tell you. Therefore, sir, you must keep good diet. If you please to come home to my house till you be perfectly cured, I shall have the more care on you.

VALERIO. That's your only course to have it well quickly.

POCK. By what time would he have it well, sir?

DARIOTTO. A very necessary question. Canst thou limit the time?

POCK. O, sir, cures are like causes in law, which may be lengthened or shortened at the discretion of the lawyer. He can either keep it green with replications or rejoinders, or sometimes skin it fair o'th' outside for fashion sake, but so he may be sure 'twill break out again by a writ of error. And then has he his suit new to begin. But I will convenant with you, that by such a time I'll make your head as sound as a bell, I will bring it to suppuration, and after I will make it coagulate and grow to a perfect cicatrice. And all within these ten days, so you keep a good diet.

DARIOTTO. Well, come, Pock. We'll talk farther on't within. It draws near dinner time. What's o'clock, boy?

PAGE. By your clock, sir, it should be almost one, for your head rung noon some half hour ago.

DARIOTTO. Is't true, sir?

VALERIO. Away, let him alone. Though he came in at the window, he sets the gates of your honor open, I can tell you.

DARIOTTO. Come in, Pock. Come, apply, and for this deed I'll give the knave a wound shall never bleed. So, sir, I think this knock rings loud acquittance for my ridiculous—

        Exeunt all but Rinaldo *and* Valerio.

RINALDO. Well, sir, to turn our heads to salve your license.
Since you have us'd the matter so unwisely
That now your father has discern'd your humor
In your too careless usage in his house,
Your wife must come from his house to Antonio's.
And he, to entertain her, must be told
She is not wife to his son, but to you,
Which news will make his simple wit triumph
Over your father. And your father, thinking
He still is gull'd, will still account him simple.
Come, sir, prepare your villainous wit to feign
A kind submission to your father's fury,
And we shall see what hearty policy
He will discover, in his feigned anger,
To blind Antonio's eyes, and make him think
He thinks her heartily to be your wife.

VALERIO. O, I will gull him rarely with my wench
Low kneeling at my heels before his fury,
And injury shall be salv'd with injury.

Finis Actus Tertii.

[*IV. i*]

[Enter] Marc Antonio, Gostanzo.

MARC ANTONIO. You see how too much wisdom evermore
Outshoots the truth. You were so forwards still
To tax my ignorance, my green experience
In these gray hairs, for giving such advantage
To my son's spirit that he durst undertake
A secret match so far short of his worth;
Your son so seasoned with obedience,
Even from his youth, that all his actions relish
Nothing but duty and your anger's fear.
What shall I say to you, if it fall out
That this most precious son of yours has play'd
A part as bad as this, and as rebellious:
Nay, more, has grossly gull'd your wit withal?
What if my son has undergone the blame
That appertain'd to yours, and that this wench
With which my son is charg'd, may call you father?
Shall I then say you want experience?
Y'are green, y'are credulous; easy to be blinded.
    GOSTANZO. Ha, ha, ha.
Good Marc Antonio, when't comes to that,
Laugh at me, call me fool, proclaim me so.
Let all the world take knowledge I am an ass.
    MARC ANTONIO. O, the good God of Gods,
How blind is pride! What eagles we are still
In matters that belong to other men,
What beetles in our own! I tell you, knight,
It is confess'd to be as I have told you,
And Gratiana is by young Rinaldo
And your white son brought to me as his wife.
How think you now, sir?
    GOSTANZO.   Even just as before,
And have more cause to think honest credulity
Is a true lodestone to draw on decrepity.
You have a heart too open to embrace
All that your ear receives. Alas, good man,
All this is but a plot for entertainment
Within your house, for your poor son's young wife

My house, without huge danger, cannot hold.

 MARC ANTONIO. Is't possible? What danger, sir, I pray?

 GOSTANZO. I'll tell you, sir. 'Twas time to take her thence.
My son that last day you saw could not frame
His looks to entertain her, now by'r-lady,
Is grown a courtier. For myself, unseen,
Saw when he courted her, embrac'd and kiss'd her,
And I can tell you left not much undone
That was the proper office of your son.

 MARC ANTONIO. What world is this?

 GOSTANZO.   I told this to Rinaldo,
Advising him to fetch her from my house,
And his young wit not knowing where to lodge her
Unless with you, and saw that could not be
Without some wile, I presently suggested
This quaint device, to say she was my son's.
And all this plot, good Marc Antonio,
Flow'd from this fount only to blind your eyes.

 MARC ANTONIO. Out of how sweet a dream have you awak'd
me!
By heaven, I durst have laid my part in heaven
All had been true; it was so lively handled,
And drawn with such a seeming face of truth.
Your son had cast a perfect veil of grief
Over his face, for his so rash offense
To seal his love with act of marriage
Before his father had subscrib'd his choice.
My son (my circumstance lessening the fact)
Entreating me to break the matter to you,
And, joining my effectual persuasions
With your son's penitent submission,
Appease your fury, I at first assented,
And now expect their coming to that purpose.

 GOSTANZO. 'Twas well. 'Twas well. Seem to believe it still.
Let art end what credulity began.
When they come, suit your words and looks to theirs,
Second my sad son's feign'd submission,
And see in all points how my brain will answer
His disguis'd grief with a set countenance
Of rage and choler. Now observe and learn
To school your son by me.

Intrant Rinaldo, Valerio, Gratiana.

MARC ANTONIO.   On with your mask.
Here come the other maskers, sir.
     RINALDO.   Come on, I say.
Your father with submission will be calm'd.
Come on. Down o' your knees.   [*Valerio kneels.*]
     GOSTANZO.   Villain, durst thou
Presume to gull thy father? Dost thou not
Tremble to see my bent and cloudy brows
Ready to thunder on thy graceless head,
And with the bolt of my displeasure cut
The thread of all my living from thy life,
For taking thus a beggar to thy wife?
     VALERIO. Father, if that part I have in your blood,
If tears, which so abundantly distil
Out of my inward eyes, and for a need
Can drown these outward—[*Aside to* Rinaldo.] Lend me thy
handkercher—
And being indeed as many drops of blood
Issuing from the creator of my heart,
Be able to beget so much compassion
Not on my life, but on this lovely dame,
Whom I hold dearer—
     GOSTANZO.   Out upon thee, villain.
     MARC ANTONIO. Nay, good Gostanzo. Think you are a father.
     GOSTANZO. I will not hear a word. Out, out upon thee.
Wed without my advice, my love, my knowledge,
Ay, and a beggar too, a trull, a blowse!
     RINALDO [*aside to* Gostanzo]. You thought not so last day,
when you offer'd her
A twelvemonths' board for one night's lodging with her.
     GOSTANZO [*aside*]. Go to, no more of that. Peace, good Rinaldo.
It is a fault that only she and you know.
     RINALDO [*aside*]. Well, sir, go on, I pray.
     GOSTANZO.   Have I, fond wretch,
With utmost care and labor brought thee up,
Ever instructing thee, omitting never
The office of a kind and careful father,
To make thee wise and virtuous like thy father,
And hast thou in one act everted all,

Proclaim'd thyself to all the world a fool,
To wed a beggar?

    VALERIO.   Father, say not so.

    GOSTANZO. Nay, she's thy own. Here, rise, fool. Take her to thee;
Live with her still. I know thou count'st thyself
Happy in soul only in winning her.
Be happy still. Here, take her hand, enjoy her.
Would not a son hazard his father's wrath,
His reputation in the world, his birthright,
To have but such a mess of broth as this?

    MARC ANTONIO. Be not so violent, I pray you, good Gostanzo.
Take truce with passion; license your sad son
To speak in his excuse.

    GOSTANZO.   What! What excuse?
Can any orator in this case excuse him?
What can he say? What can be said of any?

    VALERIO. Alas, sir, hear me. All that I can say
In my excuse is but to show love's warrant.

    GOSTANZO [*aside*]. Notable wag.

    VALERIO.   I know I have committed
A great impiety not to move you first
Before the dame I meant to make my wife.
Consider what I am, yet young and green.
Behold what she is. Is there not in her,
Ay, in her very eye, a power to conquer
Even age itself and wisdom? Call to mind,
Sweet father, what yourself being young have been.
Think what you may be, for I do not think
The world so far spent with you but you may
Look back on such a beauty, and I hope
To see you young again, and to live long
With young affections. Wisdom makes a man
Live young for ever, and where is this wisdom
If not in you? Alas, I know not what
Rests in your wisdom to subdue affections,
But I protest it wrought with me so strongly
That I had quite been drown'd in seas of tears,
Had I not taken hold in happy time
Of this sweet hand. My heart had been consum'd
T'a heap of ashes with the flames of love,

Had it not sweetly been assuag'd and cool'd
With the moist kisses of these sugar'd lips.

GOSTANZO [*aside*]. O, puissant wag. What huge large thongs
he cuts
Out of his friend Fortunio's stretching leather.

MARC ANTONIO [*aside*]. He knows he does it but to blind my
eyes.

GOSTANZO [*aside*]. O, excellent! These men will put up
anything.

VALERIO. Had I not had her, I had lost my life,
Which life indeed I would have lost before
I had displeas'd you, had I not receiv'd it
From such a kind, a wise, and honor'd father.

GOSTANZO [*aside*]. Notable boy!

VALERIO.   Yet do I here renounce
Love, life, and all, rather than one hour longer
Endure to have your love eclipsed from me.

GRATIANA. O, I can hold no longer. If thy words
Be us'd in earnest, my Valerio,
Thou wound'st my heart, but I know 'tis in jest.

GOSTANZO [*aside*]. No, I'll be sworn she has her lyripoop too.

GRATIANA. Didst thou not swear to love me spite of father
And all the world, that nought should sever us
But death itself?

VALERIO.   I did, but if my father
Will have his son forsworn, upon his soul
The blood of my black perjury shall lie,
For I will seek his favor though I die.

GOSTANZO. No, no. Live still my son. Thou well shalt know,
I have a father's heart. Come, join your hands.
Still keep thy vows, and live together still,
Till cruel death set foot betwixt you both.

VALERIO. O speak you this in earnest?

GOSTANZO.   Ay, by heaven.

VALERIO. And never to recall it?

GOSTANZO.   Not till death.

RINALDO. Excellent sir, you have done like yourself.
What would you more, Valerio?

VALERIO.   Worshipful father!

RINALDO. Come, sir, come you in, and celebrate your joys.

                              Exeunt all save the old men.

GOSTANZO. O Marc Antonio,
Had I not arm'd you with an expectation,
Would not this make you pawn your very soul
The wench had been my son's wife?

MARC ANTONIO.   Yes, by heaven.
A knavery thus effected might deceive
A wiser man than I, for I, alas,
Am no good politician. Plain believing,
Simple honesty, is my policy still.

GOSTANZO. The visible marks of folly, honesty
And quick credulity, his younger brother.
I tell you, Marc Antonio, there is much
In that young boy, my son.

MARC ANTONIO.   Not much honesty,
If I may speak without offense to his father.

GOSTANZO. O God, you cannot please me better, sir.
H'as honesty enough to serve his turn;
The less honesty ever the more wit.
But go you home, and use your daughter kindly.
Meantime I'll school your son, and do you still
Dissemble what you know. Keep off your son.
The wench at home must still be my son's wife.
Remember that, and be you blinded still.

MARC ANTONIO. You must remember, too, to let your son
Use his accustom'd visitations,
Only to blind my eyes.

GOSTANZO.   He shall not fail.
But still take you heed, have a vigilant eye
On that sly child of mine, for by this light,
He'll be too bold with your son's forehead else.

MARC ANTONIO. Well, sir, let me alone. I'll bear a brain.
                                                    Exeunt.

Enter Valerio, Rinaldo.

VALERIO. Come, they are gone.

RINALDO.   Gone? They were far gone here.

VALERIO. Gull'd I my father, or gull'd he himself?
Thou told'st him Gratiana was my wife,
I have confess'd it, he has pardon'd it.

RINALDO. Nothing more true, enow can witness it.

And therefore when he comes to learn the truth
(As certainly, for all these sly disguises,
Time will strip Truth into her nakedness),
Thou hast good plea against him to confess
The honor'd action, and to claim his pardon.

VALERIO. 'Tis true, for all was done, he deeply swore,
Out of his heart.

RINALDO.   He has much faith the whiles
That swore a thing so quite against his heart.

VALERIO. Why, this is policy.

RINALDO.   Well, see you repair
To Gratiana daily, and enjoy her
In her true kind. And now we must expect
The resolute and ridiculous divorce
Cornelio hath sued against his wedlock.

VALERIO. I think it be not so; the ass dotes on her.

RINALDO. It is too true, and thou shalt answer it
For setting such debate 'twixt man and wife.
See, we shall see the solemn manner of it.

Enter Cornelio, Dariotto, Claudio, Notary, Page, Gazetta,
Bellanora, Gratiana.

BELLANORA. Good Signor Cornelio, let us poor gentlewomen
entreat you to forbear.

CORNELIO. Talk no more to me. I'll not be made cuckold in
my own house. Notary, read me the divorce.

GAZETTA. My dear Cornelio, examine the cause better before
you condemn me.

CORNELIO. Sing to me no more, siren, for I will hear thee no
more. I will take no compassion on thee.

PAGE. Good Signor Cornelio, be not too mankind against your
wife. Say y'are a cuckold (as the best that is may be so at a time)
will you make a trumpet of your own horns?

CORNELIO. Go to, sir, y'are a rascal. I'll give you a fee for
pleading for her one day. Notary, do you your office.

VALERIO. Go to, signor. Look better to your wife, and be better advised before you grow to this extremity.

CORNELIO. Extremity? Go to, I deal but too mercifully with
her. If I should use extremity with her, I might hang her and her
copesmate, my drudge here. How say you, Master Notary, might
I not do it by law?

NOTARY. Not hang 'em, but you may bring them both to a white sheet.

CORNELIO. Nay, by the mass, they have had too much of the sheet already.

NOTARY. And besides you may set capital letters on their foreheads.

CORNELIO. What's that to the capital letter that's written in mind? I say for all your law, Master Notary, that I may hang 'em. May I not hang him that robs me of mine honor as well as he that robs me of my horse?

NOTARY. No, sir. Your horse is a chattel.

CORNELIO. So is honor. A man may buy it with his penny, and if I may hang a man for stealing my horse (as I say), much more for robbing me of my honor. For why? If my horse be stolen, it may be my own fault. For why? Either the stable is not strong enough, or the pasture not well fenced, or watched, or so forth. But for your wife that keeps the stable of your honor, let her be locked in a brazen tower, let Argus himself keep her, yet can you never be secure of your honor. For why? She can run through all with her serpent noddle. Besides, you may hang a lock upon your horse, and so can you not upon your wife.

RINALDO. But I pray you, sir, what are the presumptions on which you would build this divorce?

CORNELIO. Presumption enough, sir. For besides their intercourse, or commerce of glances that passed betwixt this cockerel-drone and her, at my table the last Sunday night at supper, their winks, their becks—*Dieu garde*—their treads o'the toe (as, by heaven, I swear she trod once upon my toe instead of his), this is chiefly to be noted: the same night she would needs lie alone, and the same night her dog barked. Did not you hear him, Valerio?

VALERIO. And understand him too, I'll be sworn of a book.

CORNELIO. Why, very good. If these be not manifest presumptions now, let the world be judge. Therefore without more ceremony, Master Notary, pluck out your instrument.

NOTARY. I will, sir, if there be no remedy.

CORNELIO. Have you made it strong in law, Master Notary? Have you put in words enough?

NOTARY. I hope so, sir; it has taken me a whole skin of parchment, you see.

CORNELIO. Very good, and is egress and regress in?

NOTARY. I'll warrant you, sir, it is *forma juris*.

CORNELIO. Is there no hole to be found in the orthography?

NOTARY. None in the world, sir.

CORNELIO. You have written *Sunt* with an *S,* have you not?

NOTARY. Yes, that I have.

CORNELIO. You have done the better for quietness' sake. And are none of the authentical dashes over the head left out? If there be, Master Notary, an error will lie out.

NOTARY. Not for a dash over head, sir, I warrant you, if I should oversee. I have seen that tried in Butiro and Caseo, in Butler and Cason's case, *decimo sexto* of Duke Anonimo.

RINALDO. Y'ave gotten a learned notary, Signor Cornelio.

CORNELIO. He's a shrewd fellow indeed. I had as lief have his head in a matter of felony or treason as any notary in Florence. Read out, Master Notary. Hearken you, mistress; gentlemen, mark, I beseech you.

OMNES. We will all mark you, sir, I warrant you.

NOTARY. I think it would be something tedious to read all, and therefore, gentlemen, the sum is this: That you, Signor Cornelio, gentleman, for divers and sundry weighty and mature considerations you especially moving, specifying all the particulars of your wife's enormities in a schedule hereunto annexed, the transcript whereof is in your own tenure, custody, occupation, and keeping: That for these, the aforesaid premises, I say, you renounce, disclaim, and discharge Gazetta from being your leeful or your lawful wife: And that you eftsoons divide, disjoin, separate, remove, and finally eloign, sequester, and divorce her, from your bed and your board: That you forbid her all access, repair, egress or regress to your person or persons, mansion or mansions, dwellings, habitations, remanences, or abodes, or to any shop, cellar, sollar, easement's chamber, dormer, and so forth, now in the tenure, custody, occupation, or keeping of the said Cornelio; notwithstanding all former contracts, convenants, bargains, conditions, agreements, compacts, promises, vows, affiances, assurances, bonds, bills, indentures, polldeeds, deeds of gift, defeasances, feoffments, endowments, vouchers, double vouchers, privy entries, actions, declarations, explications, rejoinders, surrejoinders, rights, interests, demands, claims, or titles whatsoever, heretofore betwixt the one and the other party, or parties, being had, made, passed, covenanted, and agreed, from the beginning of the world till the day of the date hereof. Given the seventeenth of November, fifteen hundred and so forth. Here, sir, you must set to your hand.

CORNELIO. What else, Master Notary? I am resolute, i'faith.

GAZETTA. Sweet husband, forbear.

CORNELIO. Avoid, I charge thee in name of this divorce. Thou mightst have looked to it in time, yet this I will do for thee. If thou canst spy out any other man that thou wouldst cuckold, thou shalt have my letter to him. I can do no more. More ink, Master Notary. I write my name at large.

NOTARY. Here is more, sir.

CORNELIO. Ah, ass, that thou could not know thy happiness till thou hadst lost it. How now? My nose bleed? Shall I write in blood? What, only three drops? 'Sfoot, this's ominous. I will not set my hand to't now, certain. Master Notary, I like not this abodement. I will defer the setting to of my hand till the next court day. Keep the divorce, I pray you, and the woman in your house together.

OMNES. Burn the divorce, burn the divorce.

CORNELIO. Not so, sir. It shall not serve her turn. Master Notary, keep it at your peril, and gentlemen, you may be gone, o' God's name. What have you to do to flock about me thus? I am neither howlet nor cuckoo. Gentlewomen, for God's sake, meddle with your own cases. It is not fit you should haunt these public assemblies.

OMNES. Well, farewell, Cornelio.

VALERIO. Use the gentlewoman kindly, Master Notary.

NOTARY. As mine own wife, I assure you, sir.

Exeunt [*all but* Claudio *and* Cornelio].

CLAUDIO. Signor Cornelio, I cannot but in kindness tell you that Valerio, by counsel of Rinaldo, hath whispered all this jealousy into your ears. Not that he knew any just cause in your wife, but only to be revenged on you for the gull you put upon him when you drew him with his glory to touch the theorbo.

CORNELIO. May I believe this?

CLAUDIO. As I am a gentleman. And if this accident of your nose had not fallen out, I would have told you this before you set to your hand.

CORNELIO. It may well be. Yet have I cause enough
To perfect my divorce. But it shall rest
Till I conclude it with a counterbuff
Given to these noble rascals. Claudio, thanks.
What comes of this, watch but my brain a little,
And ye shall see if like two parts in me

I leave not both these gullers' wits imbrier'd.
Now I perceive well where the wild wind sits,
Here's gull for gull and wits at war with wits.   *Exeunt*.

[*Finis Actus Quarti.*]

[*V.i*]

Rinaldo, *solus*.

RINALDO. Fortune, the great commandress of the world,
Hath divers ways to advance her followers.
To some she gives honor without deserving,
To other some, deserving without honor,
Some wit, some wealth, and some wit without wealth,
Some wealth without wit, some, nor wit nor wealth
But good smock-faces, or some qualities
By nature without judgment, with the which
They live in sensual acceptation,
And make show only, without touch of substance.
My fortune is to win renown by gulling
Gostanzo, Dariotto, and Cornelio,
All which suppose, in all their different kinds,
Their wits entire, and in themselves no piece.
All at one blow, my helmet yet unbruis'd,
I have unhors'd, laid flat on earth for gulls.
Now in what taking poor Cornelio is
Betwixt his large divorce and no divorce,
I long to see, and what he will resolve.
I lay my life he cannot chew his meat,
And looks much like an ape had swallowed pills,
And all this comes of bootless jealousy.
And see, where bootless jealousy appears.

Enter Cornelio.

I'll bourd him straight.—How now, Cornelio,
Are you resolv'd on the divorce or no?
    CORNELIO. What's that to you? Look to your own affairs;
The time requires it. Are not you engag'd
In some bonds forfeit for Valerio?

RINALDO. Yes, what of that?

CORNELIO.   Why, so am I myself,
And both our dangers great. He is arrested
On a recognizance by a usuring slave.

RINALDO. Arrested? I am sorry with my heart.
It is a matter may import me much.
May not our bail suffice to free him, think you?

CORNELIO. I think it may, but I must not be seen in't,
Nor would I wish you, for we both are parties,
And liker far to bring ourselves in trouble,
Than bear him out. I have already made
Means to the officers to sequester him
In private for a time till some in secret
Might make his father understand his state,
Who would perhaps take present order for him
Rather than suffer him t'endure the shame
Of his imprisonment. Now, would you but go
And break the matter closely to his father
(As you can wisely do't), and bring him to him,
This were the only way to save his credit,
And to keep off a shrewd blow from ourselves.

RINALDO. I know his father will be mov'd past measure.

CORNELIO. Nay, if you stand on such nice ceremonies,
Farewell our substance. Extreme diseases
Ask extreme remedies. Better he should storm
Some little time than we be beat forever
Under the horrid shelter of a prison.

RINALDO. Where is the place?

CORNELIO.   'Tis at the Half Moon Tavern.
Haste, for the matter will abide no stay.

RINALDO. Heaven send my speed be equal with my haste.
                                                        Exit.

CORNELIO. Go, shallow scholar, you that make all gulls,
You that can out-see clear-eyed jealousy,
Yet make this sleight a millstone, where your brain
Sticks in the midst amaz'd. This gull to him
And to his fellow guller shall become
More bitter than their baiting of my humor.
Here at this tavern shall Gostanzo find
Fortunio, Dariotto, Claudio,
And amongst them, the ringleader, his son,

His husband, and his Saint Valerio—
That knows not of what fashion dice are made,
Nor ever yet look'd towards a red lettice
(Thinks his blind sire), at drinking and at dice—
With all their wenches, and at full discover
His own gross folly and his son's distempers.
And both shall know (although I be no scholar)
Yet I have thus much Latin, as to say
Jam sumus ergo pares.   *Exit.*

[*V.ii*]

Enter Valerio, Fortunio, Claudio, Page, Gratiana, Gazetta,
            Bellanora. *A* Drawer *or two, setting a table.*

VALERIO. Set me the table here. We will shift rooms
To see if Fortune will shift chances with us.
Sit, ladies, sit. Fortunio, place thy wench,
And Claudio, place you Dariotto's mistress.
I wonder where that neat, spruce slave becomes.
I think he was some barber's son, by th' mass.
'Tis such a picked fellow, not a hair
About his whole bulk but it stands in print.
Each pin hath his due place, not any point
But hath his perfect tie, fashion, and grace.
A thing whose soul is specially employ'd
In knowing where best gloves, best stockings, waistcoats
Curiously wrought are sold, sacks milliners' shops
For all new tires and fashions, and can tell ye
What new devices of all sorts there are,
And that there is not in the whole Rialto
But one new-fashion'd waistcoat, or one nightcap,
One pair of gloves pretty or well perfum'd,
And from a pair of gloves of half a crown
To twenty crowns, will to a very scute
Smell out the price. And for these womanly parts
He is esteem'd a witty gentleman.

Enter Dariotto.

FORTUNIO. See where he comes.
DARIOTTO.   God save you, lovely ladies.

VALERIO. Ay, well said, lovely Paris. Your walleye
Must ever first be gloating on men's wives.
You think to come upon us, being half drunk,
And so to part the freshest man among us,
But you shall overtake us, I'll be sworn.

DARIOTTO. Tush, man, where are your dice? Let's fall to them.

CLAUDIO. We have been at 'em. Drawer, call for more.

VALERIO. First let's have wine. Dice have no perfect edge
Without the liquid whetstone of the syrup.

FORTUNIO. True, and to welcome Dariotto's lateness,
He shall (unpledg'd) carouse one crowned cup
To all these ladies' health.

DARIOTTO.   I am well pleas'd.

VALERIO. Come on, let us vary our sweet time
With sundry exercises. Boy! Tobacco.
And, drawer, you must get us music too.
Call's in a cleanly noise, the slaves grow lousy.

DRAWER. You shall have such as we can get you, sir.   *Exit.*

DARIOTTO. Let's have some dice, I pray thee; they are cleanly.

VALERIO. Page, let me see that leaf.

PAGE.   It is not leaf, sir.
'Tis pudding-cane tobacco.

VALERIO.   But I mean
Your linstock, sir. What leaf is that, I pray?

PAGE. I pray you see, sir, for I cannot read.

VALERIO. 'Sfoot, a rank, stinking satire. This had been
Enough to have poison'd every man of us.

DARIOTTO. And now you speak of that, my boy once lighted
A pipe of cane tobacco with a piece
Of a vild ballad, and I'll swear I had
A singing in my head a whole week after.

VALERIO. Well, th'old verse is, *A potibus incipe io-c-um.*

Enter Drawer *with wine and a cup.*

VALERIO. Drawer, fill out this gentleman's carouse,
And harden him for our society.

DARIOTTO. Well, ladies, here is to your honor'd healths.

FORTUNIO. What, Dariotto, without hat or knee?

VALERIO. Well said, Fortunio. O, y'are a rare courtier.
Your knee, good signor, I beseech your knee.

DARIOTTO. Nay, pray you. Let's take it by degrees,

Valerio. On our feet first, for this
Will bring's too soon upon our knees.

    VALERIO.   Sir, there
Are no degrees of order in a tavern.
Here you must, I charg'd ye, run all ahead.
'Slight, courtier, down.
I hope you are no elephant. You have joints?

    DARIOTTO. Well, sir, here's to the ladies, on my knees.

                                      He kneels.

    VALERIO. I'll be their pledge.

    Enter Gostanzo *and* Rinaldo [*unseen by the others*].

    FORTUNIO.   Not yet, Valerio.
This he must drink unpledg'd.

    VALERIO. He shall not. I will give him this advantage.

    GOSTANZO. How now, what's here? Are these the officers?

    RINALDO [*aside*]. 'Slight, I would all were well.

    Enter Cornelio [*unseen by the others*].

    VALERIO.   Here is his pledge.
Here's to our common friend Cornelio's health.

    DARIOTTO. Health to Gazetta, poison to her husband.

    CORNELIO [*aside*]. Excellent guests; these are my daily guests.

    VALERIO. Drawer, make even th'impartial scales of justice.
Give it to Claudio, and from him fill round.
Come, Dariotto, set me. Let the rest
Come in when they have done the ladies right.

    GOSTANZO. Set me! Do you know what belongs to setting?

    RINALDO [*aside*]. What a dull slave was I to be thus gull'd.

    CORNELIO [*aside to* Rinaldo]. Why, Rinald, what meant you
to intrap your friend,
And bring his father to this spectacle?
You are a friend indeed.

    RINALDO.   'Tis very good, sir.
Perhaps my friend, or I, before we part,
May make even with you.

    FORTUNIO.   Come, let's set him round.

    VALERIO. Do so. At all! A plague upon these dice.
Another health. 'Sfoot, I shall have no luck

Till I be drunk. Come on, here's to the comfort
The cavalier, my father, should take in me
If he now saw me, and would do me right.

FORTUNIO. I'll pledge it, and his health, Valerio.

GOSTANZO. Here's a good husband.

RINALDO.   I pray you have patience, sir.

VALERIO. Now have at all, an 'twere a thousand pound.

GOSTANZO [*coming forward*]. Hold sir. I bar the dice.

VALERIO.   What, sir, are you there?
Fill's a fresh pottle. By this light, Sir Knight,
You shall do right.

Enter Marc Antonio.

GOSTANZO.   O, thou ungracious villain.

VALERIO. Come, come, we shall have you now thunder forth
Some of your thrifty sentences, as gravely:
"For as much, Valerius, as everything has time, and a pudding
has two, yet ought not satisfaction to swerve so much from
defalcation of well-disposed people, as that indemnity should
prejudice what security doth insinuate." A trial, yet once again!

MARC ANTONIO. Here's a good sight. Y'are well encounter'd,
sir.
Did not I tell you you'd o'ershoot yourself
With too much wisdom?

VALERIO.   Sir, your wisest do so.
Fill the old man some wine.

GOSTANZO.   Here's a good infant.

MARC ANTONIO. Why, sir? Alas, I'll wager with your wisdom
His consorts drew him to it, for of himself
He is both virtuous, bashful, innocent,
Comes not at city, knows no city art,
But plies your husbandry, dares not view a wench.

VALERIO. Father, he comes upon you.

GOSTANZO.   Here's a son.

MARC ANTONIO. Whose wife is Gratiana now, I pray?

GOSTANZO. Sing your old song no more. Your brain's too
short
To reach into these policies.

MARC ANTONIO.   'Tis true,
Mine eye's soon blinded, and yourself would say so,

If you knew all. Where lodg'd your son last night?
Do you know that with all your policy?

GOSTANZO. You'll say he lodg'd with you. And did not I
Foretell you all this must for color sake
Be brought about, only to blind your eyes?

MARC ANTONIO. By heaven, I chanc'd this morn, I know not
why,
To pass by Gratiana's bedchamber,
And whom saw I fast by her naked side
But your Valerio.

GOSTANZO.   Had you not warning given?
Did not I bid you watch my courtier well,
Or he would set a crest o' your son's head?

MARC ANTONIO. That was not all, for by them on a stool
My son sat laughing to see you so gull'd.

GOSTANZO. 'Tis too, too plain.

MARC ANTONIO.   Why, sir, do you suspect it
The more for that?

GOSTANZO.   Suspect it? Is there any
So gross a wittol as, if 'twere his wife,
Would sit by her so tamely?

MARC ANTONIO.   Why not, sir,
To blind my eyes?

GOSTANZO.   Well, sir, I was deceiv'd,
But I shall make it prove a dear deceit
To the deceiver.

RINALDO.   Nay, sir, let's not have
A new infliction set on an old fault.
He did confess his fault upon his knees.
You pardon'd it, and swore 'twas from your heart.

GOSTANZO. Swore, a great piece of work! The wretch shall
know
I have a daughter here to give my land to.
I'll give my daughter all. The prodigal
Shall not have one poor house to hide his head in.

FORTUNIO. I humbly thank you, sir, and vow all duty
My life can yield you.

GOSTANZO.   Why are you so thankful?

FORTUNIO. For giving to your daughter all your lands,
Who is my wife, and so you gave them me.

GOSTANZO. Better and better!

FORTUNIO.   Pray, sir, be not mov'd.
You drew me kindly to your house, and gave me
Access to woo your daughter, whom I lov'd,
And since (by honor'd marriage) made my wife.

GOSTANZO. Now all my choler fly out in your wits.
Good tricks of youth, i'faith, no indecorum,
Knight's son, knight's daughter. Marc Antonio,
Give me your hand. There is no remedy.
Marriage is ever made by destiny.

RINALDO. Silence, my masters. Now here all are pleas'd,
Only but Cornelio, who lacks but persuasion
To reconcile himself to his fair wife.
Good sir, will you (of all men our best speaker)
Persuade him to receive her into grace?

GOSTANZO. That I will gladly, and he shall be rul'd. Good
Cornelio, I have heard of your wayward jealousy, and I must tell
you plain as a friend, y'are an ass. You must pardon me; I knew
your father.

RINALDO. Then you must pardon him, indeed, sir.

GOSTANZO. Understand me: put case Dariotto loved your wife,
whereby you would seem to refuse her. Would you desire to
have such a wife as no man could love but yourself?

MARC ANTONIO. Answer but that, Cornelio.

GOSTANZO. Understand me: say Dariotto hath kissed your
wife, or performed other offices of that nature, whereby they did
converse together at bed and at board, as friends may seem to
do.—

MARC ANTONIO. Mark but the "now understand me."

GOSTANZO. Yet if there come no proofs but that her actions
were cleanly, or in discreet private, why, 'twas a sign of modesty.
And will you blow the horn yourself, when you may keep it to
yourself? Go to, you are a fool; understand me!

VALERIO. Do understand him, Cornelio.

GOSTANZO. Nay, Cornelio, I tell you again, I knew your father.
He was a wise gentleman, and so was your mother. Methinks I
see her yet, a lusty, stout woman, bore great children. You were
the very scoundrel of 'em all, but let that pass. As for your mother,
she was wise. A most flippant tongue she had, and could set out
her tail with as good grace as any she in Florence, come cut and
long-tail, and she was honest enough too. But yet, by your leave,
she would tickle Dob now and then, as well as the best on 'em.

By Jove, it's true, Cornelio. I speak it not to flatter you. Your
father knew it well enough, and would he do as you do, think
you? Set rascals to undermine her, or look to her water (as they
say)? No, when he saw 'twas but her humor (for his own quietness' sake) he made a back-door to his house for convenience,
got a bell to his fore-door, and had an odd fashion in ringing, by
which she and her maid knew him, and would stand talking to
his next neighbor to prolong time, that all things might be rid
cleanly out o'the way before he came, for the credit of his wife.
This was wisdom now, for a man's own quiet.

MARC ANTONIO. Here was a man, Cornelio.

GOSTANZO. What, I say! Young men think old men are fools,
but old men know young men are fools.

CORNELIO. Why, hark you, you two knights. Do you think I
will forsake Gazetta?

GOSTANZO. And will you not?

CORNELIO. Why, there's your wisdom. Why did I make show
of divorce, think you?

MARC ANTONIO. Pray you why, sir?

CORNELIO. Only to bridle her stout stomach, and how did I
draw on the color for my divorce? I did train the woodcock
Dariotto into the net, drew him to my house, gave him opportunity with my wife (as you say my father dealt with his wife's
friends) only to train him in; let him alone with my wife in her
bedchamber, and sometimes found him abed with her, and went
my way back again softly, only to draw him into the pit.

GOSTANZO. This was well handled indeed, Cornelio.

MARC ANTONIO. Ay marry, sir. Now I commend your wisdom.

CORNELIO. Why, if I had been so minded as you think, I could
have flung his pantable down the stairs, or done him some other
disgrace. But I winked at it, and drew on the good fool more
and more, only to bring him within my compass.

GOSTANZO. Why, this was policy in grain.

CORNELIO. And now shall the world see I am as wise as my
father.

VALERIO. Is't come to this? Then will I make a speech in praise
of this reconcilement, including therein the praise and honor of
the most fashionable and authentical HORN. Stand close, gen-
tles, and be silent.   *He gets into a chair.*

GOSTANZO. Come on. Let's hear his wit in this potable humor.

VALERIO. The course of the world (like the life of man) is said to be divided into several ages. As we into infancy, childhood, youth, and so forward to old age, so the world into the golden age, the silver, the brass, the iron, the leaden, the wooden, and now into this present age, which we term the *horned age*. Not that but former ages have enjoyed this benefit as well as our times, but that in ours it is more common, and nevertheless precious. It is said that in the golden age of the world the use of gold was not then known: an argument of the simplicity of that age. Lest therefore succeeding ages should hereafter impute the same fault to us which we lay upon the first age, that we, living in the horned age of the world, should not understand the use, the virtue, the honor, and the very royalty of the horn, I will in brief sound the praises thereof that they who are already in possession of it may bear their heads aloft as being proud of such lofty accouterments, and they that are but in possibility may be ravished with a desire to be in possession.

A trophy so honorable and unmatchably powerful that it is able to raise any man from a beggar to an emperor's fellow, a duke's fellow, a nobleman's fellow, alderman's fellow; so glorious that it deserves to be worn (by most opinions) in the most conspicuous place about a man. For what worthier crest can you bear than the horn, which if it might be seen with our mortal eyes, what a wonderful spectacle would there be, and how highly they would ravish the beholders? But their substance is incorporal, not falling under sense, nor mixed of the gross concretion of elements, but a quintessence beyond them, a spiritual essence, invisible and everlasting.

And this hath been the cause that many men have called their being in question, whether there be such a thing *in rerum natura,* or not, because they are not to be seen; as though nothing were that were not to be seen! Who ever saw the wind? Yet what wonderful effects are seen of it! It drives the clouds, yet no man sees it. It rocks the house, bears down trees, castles, steeples, yet who sees it? In like sort does your horn. It swells the forehead, yet none sees it. It rocks the cradle, yet none sees it. So that you plainly perceive sense is no judge of essence. The moon to any man's sense seems to be horned, yet who knows not the moon to be ever perfectly round? So likewise your heads seem ever to be round, when indeed they are oftentimes horned. For their original, it is unsearchable. Natural they are not, for where is beast born with horns, more than with teeth? Created they were not, for *ex nihilo nihil fit*. Then will you ask me, how came they into the world? I know not, but I am sure women brought them into this part of the world, howsoever some doctors are of opinion that they came in with the Devil. And not unlike, for as the Devil brought sin into the world, but the woman brought it to the man, so it may very well be that the Devil brought horns into the world, but the woman brought them to the man.

For their power, it is general over the world. No nation so barbarous, no country so proud, but doth equal homage to the horn. Europa, when she was carried through the sea by the Saturnian bull, was said (for fear of falling) to have held by the horn, and what is this but a plain showing to us, that all Europe, which took name from that Europa, should likewise hold by the horn. So that I say it is universal over the face of the world, general over the face of Europe, and common over the face of this country. What city, what town, what village, what street, nay, what house, can quit itself of this prerogative? I have read that the lion once made a proclamation through all the forest, that all horned beasts should depart forthwith upon pain of death. If this proclamation should be made through our forest, Lord, what pressing, what running, what flying would there be even from all the parts of it! He that had but a bunch of flesh in his head would away, and some, foolishly fearful, would imagine the shadow of his ears to be horns. Alas, how desert would this forest be left!

To conclude: for their force it is irrevitable, for were they not irrevitable, then might either properness of person secure a man, or wisdom prevent 'em, or greatness exempt, or riches redeem them. But present experience hath taught us that in this case all these stand in no stead. For we see the properest men take part of them, the best wits cannot avoid them (for then should poets be no cuckolds). Nor can money redeem them, for then would rich men fine for their horns, as they do for offices. But this is held for a maxim, that there are more rich cuckolds than poor. Lastly, for continuance of the horn, it is undeterminable till death. Neither do they determine with the wife's death (howsoever ignorant writers hold opinion they do). For as when a knight dies, his lady still retains the title of lady; when a company is cast, yet the captain still retains the title of captain; so though the wife

die, by whom this title came to her husband, yet by the courtesy
of the City, he shall be a cuckold during life, let all ignorant asses
prate what they list.

GOSTANZO. Notable wag! Come, sir, shake hands with him
In whose high honor you have made this speech.

MARC ANTONIO [*to* Cornelio]. And you, sir, come, join hands.
Y'are one amongst them.

GOSTANZO. Very well done. Now take your several wives,
And spread like wild-geese, though you now grow tame.
Live merrily together and agree,
Horns cannot be kept off with jealousy.

FINIS

EASTWARD HO!

Ben Jonson, George Chapman, and John Marston

[DRAMATIS PERSONAE

WILLIAM TOUCHSTONE, *a goldsmith*
MISTRESS TOUCHSTONE, *his wife*
FRANCIS QUICKSILVER ⎱ *his apprentices*
GOLDING ⎰
GERTRUDE ⎱ *his daughters*
MILDRED ⎰
BETTRICE, *Mildred's maid*
POLDAVY, *a tailor*
SIR PETRONEL FLASH, *a new-made knight*
SECURITY, *an old usurer*
WINIFRED, *his wife*
SINDEFY, *Quicksilver's mistress*
BRAMBLE, *a lawyer*
SEAGULL, *a sea captain*
SCAPETHRIFT ⎱ *adventurers bound for Virginia*
SPENDALL ⎰
HAMLET, *a footman*
POTKIN, *a tankard-bearer*
MISTRESS FOND ⎱ *citizens' wives*
MISTRESS GAZER ⎰
SLITGUT, *a butcher's apprentice*
WOLF ⎱ *Officers of the Counter*
HOLDFAST ⎰

A SCRIVENER, A COACHMAN, SIR PETRONEL'S PAGE, A DRAWER
at the Blue Anchor Tavern, MESSENGER, GENTLEMEN, PRISONERS,
FRIEND]

PROLOGUE

Not out of envy, for there's no effect
Where there's no cause; nor out of imitation,
For we have evermore been imitated;
Nor out of our contention to do better
Than that which is opposed to ours in title,
For that was good; and better cannot be:
And for the title, if it seem affected,
We might as well have called it, 'God you good even'.
Only that eastward, westwards still exceeds—
Honour the sun's fair rising, not his setting.
Nor is our title utterly enforced,
As by the points we touch at, you shall see.
Bear with our willing pains, if dull or witty;
We only dedicate it to the City.

Act I, Scene i

[Goldsmith's Row]

Enter MASTER TOUCHSTONE *and* QUICKSILVER *at several doors;*
QUICKSILVER *with his hat, pumps, short sword and dagger, and a*
racket trussed up under his cloak. At the middle door, enter GOLDING,
discovering a goldsmith's shop, and walking short turns before it

TOUCHSTONE. And whither with you now? What loose action
are you bound for? Come, what comrades are you to meet withal?
Where's the supper? Where's the rendezvous?

QUICKSILVER. Indeed, and in very good sober truth, sir—

TOUCHSTONE. 'Indeed, and in very good sober truth, sir'!
Behind my back thou wilt swear faster than a French foot-boy,
and talk more bawdily than a common midwife; and now, 'indeed,
and in very good sober truth, sir'! But if a privy search should be
made, with what furniture are you rigged now? Sirrah, I tell thee,
I am thy master, William Touchstone, goldsmith; and thou my
prentice, Francis Quicksilver; and I will see whither you are
running. 'Work upon that now'!

QUICKSILVER. Why, sir, I hope a man may use his recreation
with his master's profit.

TOUCHSTONE. Prentices' recreations are seldom with their
master's profit. 'Work upon that now'! You shall give up your
cloak, though you be no alderman. Heyday, Ruffians' Hall!
Sword, pumps, here's a racket indeed!

TOUCHSTONE uncloaks QUICKSILVER

QUICKSILVER. 'Work upon that now'!

TOUCHSTONE. Thou shameless varlet, dost thou jest at thy
lawful master contrary to thy indentures?

QUICKSILVER. Why, 'sblood, sir, my mother's a gentlewoman,
and my father a Justice of Peace, and of Quorum. And though I

am a younger brother and a prentice, yet I hope I am my father's son; and, by God's lid, 'tis for your worship and for your commodity that I keep company. I am entertained among gallants, true! They call me cousin Frank, right! I lend them moneys, good! They spend it, well! But when they are spent, must not they strive to get more? Must not their land fly? And to whom? Shall not your worship ha' the refusal? Well, I am a good member of the City, if I were well considered. How would merchants thrive, if gentlemen would not be unthrifts? How could gentlemen be unthrifts, if their humours were not fed? How should their humours be fed but by white-meat and cunning secondings? Well, the City might consider us. I am going to an ordinary now: the gallants fall to play; I carry light gold with me; the gallants call, 'Cousin Frank, some gold for silver!'; I change, gain by it; the gallants lose the gold, and then call, 'Cousin Frank, lend me some silver!' Why—

TOUCHSTONE. Why? I cannot tell. Seven-score pound art thou out in the cash; but look to it, I will not be gallanted out of my moneys! And as for my rising by other men's fall; God shield me! Did I gain my wealth by ordinaries? No! By exchanging of gold? No! By keeping of gallants' company? No! I hired me a little shop, sought low, took small gain, kept no debt-book, garnished my shop for want of plate, with good wholesome thrifty sentences, as, 'Touchstone, keep thy shop, and thy shop will keep thee'. 'Light gains makes heavy purses'. ''Tis good to be merry and wise'. And when I was wived, having something to stick to, I had the horn of suretyship ever before my eyes. You all know the device of the horn, where the young fellow slips in at the butt-end, and comes squeezed out at the buckle. And I grew up, and, I praise Providence, I bear my brows now as high as the best of my neighbours: but thou—well, look to the accounts; your father's bond lies for you; seven score pound is yet in the rear.

QUICKSILVER. Why, 'slid, sir, I have as good, as proper, gallants' words for it as any are in London; gentlemen of good phrase, perfect language, passingly behaved; gallants that wear socks and clean linen, and call me 'kind Cousin Frank', 'good Cousin Frank'—for they know my father; and, by God's lid, shall not I trust 'em? Not trust?

Enter a PAGE, *as inquiring for* TOUCHSTONE's *shop*

GOLDING. What do ye lack, sir? What is't you'll buy, sir?

TOUCHSTONE. Ay, marry, sir; there's a youth of another piece. There's thy fellow-prentice, as good a gentleman born as thou art; nay, and better miened. But does he pump it, or racket it? Well, if he thrive not, if he outlast not a hundred such crackling bavins as thou art, God and men neglect industry.

GOLDING. It is his shop, and here my master walks.

To the PAGE

TOUCHSTONE. With me, boy?

PAGE. My master, Sir Petronel Flash, recommends his love to you, and will instantly visit you.

TOUCHSTONE. To make up the match with my eldest daughter, my wife's dilling, whom she longs to call madam. He shall find me unwillingly ready, boy.   *Exit* PAGE

There's another affliction too. As I have two prentices, the one of a boundless prodigality, the other of a most hopeful industry; so have I only two daughters: the eldest, of a proud ambition and nice wantonness, the other of a modest humility and comely soberness. The one must be ladyfied, forsooth, and be attired just to the court-cut and long-tail. So far is she ill-natured to the place and means of my preferment and fortune, that she throws all the contempt and despite hatred itself can cast upon it. Well, a piece of land she has, 'twas her grandmother's gift: let her, and her Sir Petronel, flash out that! But as for my substance, she that scorns me, as I am a citizen and tradesman, shall never pamper her pride with my industry; shall never use me as men do foxes: keep themselves warm in the skin, and throw the body that bare it to the dunghill. I must go entertain this Sir Petronel. Golding, my utmost care's for thee, and only trust in thee; look to the shop. As for you, Master Quicksilver, think of husks, for thy course is running directly to the Prodigals' hogs' trough! Husks, sirrah! 'Work upon that now'!   *Exit* TOUCHSTONE

QUICKSILVER. Marry faugh, goodman flat-cap! 'Sfoot! though I am a prentice, I can give arms; and my father's a Justice-o'-Peace by descent; and 'sblood—

GOLDING. Fie, how you swear!

QUICKSILVER. 'Sfoot man, I am a gentleman, and may swear by my pedigree, God's my life. Sirrah Golding, wilt be ruled by a fool? Turn good fellow, turn swaggering gallant, and 'Let the welkin roar, and Erebus also'. Look not westward to the fall of Don Phoebus, but to the East—Eastward Ho!

'Where radiant beams of lusty Sol appear,
And bright Eoüs makes the welkin clear'.

We are both gentlemen, and therefore should be no coxcombs; let's be no longer fools to this flat-cap, Touchstone. Eastward, bully! This satin-belly, and canvas-backed Touchstone—'slife, man, his father was a malt-man, and his mother sold gingerbread in Christ-church!

GOLDING. What would ye ha' me do?

QUICKSILVER. Why, do nothing, be like a gentleman, be idle; the curse of man is labour. Wipe thy bum with testons, and make ducks and drakes with shillings. What, Eastward Ho! Wilt thou cry, 'what is't ye lack?', stand with a bare pate and a dropping nose under a wooden pent-house, and art a gentleman? Wilt thou bear tankards, and may'st bear arms? Be ruled, turn gallant, Eastward Ho! 'Ta ly-re, ly-re ro! Who calls Jeronimo? Speak, here I am!' God's so, how like a sheep thou look'st! O' my conscience some cowherd begot thee, thou Golding of Golding Hall, ha, boy?

GOLDING. Go, ye are a prodigal coxcomb; I a cowherd's son, because I turn not a drunken whore-hunting rake-hell like thyself?

QUICKSILVER. Rake-hell! Rake-hell!

Offers to draw, and GOLDING *trips up his heels and holds him*

GOLDING. Pish, in soft terms ye are a cowardly bragging boy, I'll ha' you whipped.

QUICKSILVER. Whipped? That's good, i'faith. Untruss me?

GOLDING. No, thou wilt undo thyself. Alas, I behold thee with pity, not with anger, thou common shot-clog, gull of all companies! Methinks I see thee already walking in Moorfields without a cloak, with half a hat, without a band, a doublet with three buttons, without a girdle, a hose with one point and no garter, with a cudgel under thine arm, borrowing and begging threepence.

QUICKSILVER. Nay, 'slife, take this and take all! As I am a gentleman born, I'll be drunk, grow valiant, and beat thee.

Exit

GOLDING. Go, thou most madly vain, whom nothing can recover but that which reclaims atheists, and makes great persons sometimes religious: calamity. As for my place and life, thus I have read:

'Whate'er some vainer youth may term disgrace,
The gain of honest pains is never base;
From trades, from arts, from valour, honour springs;
These three are founts of gentry, yea of kings'.

[*Retires*]

[*Act I, Scene ii*

A Room in TOUCHSTONE'S *House*]

Enter GERTRUDE, MILDRED, BETTRICE, *and* POLDAVY, *a tailor;*
POLDAVY *with a fair gown, Scotch farthingale, and French fall in his
arms;* GERTRUDE *in a French head-attire and citizen's gown;*
MILDRED *sewing, and* BETTRICE *leading a monkey after her*

GERTRUDE. For the passion of patience, look if Sir Petronel
approach; that sweet, that fine, that delicate, that—for love's
sake, tell me if he come. O sister Mill, though my father be a
low-capped tradesman, yet I must be a lady; and, I praise God,
my mother must call me Madam. (Does he come?) Off with
this gown for shame's sake, off with this gown! Let not my
knight take me in the city-cut in any hand. Tear't, pax on't—
does he come?—tear't off! [*Sings*] *Thus whilst she sleeps, I sorrow
for her sake,* &c.

MILDRED. Lord, sister, with what an immodest impatiency and
disgraceful scorn do you put off your city tire; I am sorry to think
you imagine to right yourself in wronging that which hath made
both you and us.

GERTRUDE. I tell you I cannot endure it, I must be a lady: do
you wear your coif with a London licket, your stammel petticoat
with two guards, the buffin gown with the tuf-taffety cape, and
the velvet lace. I must be a lady, and I will be a lady. I like some
humours of the city dames well: to eat cherries only at an angel
a pound, good. To dye rich scarlet black, pretty. To line a gro-
gram gown clean through with velvet, tolerable. Their pure linen,
their smocks of three pound a smock, are to be borne withal.
But your mincing niceries, taffeta pipkins, durance petticoats,
and silver bodkins—God's my life, as I shall be a lady, I cannot
endure it! Is he come yet? Lord, what a long knight 'tis! [*Sings*]
And ever she cried, Shoot home!—and yet I knew one longer—*And
ever she cried, Shoot home! Fa, la, ly, re, lo, la!*

MILDRED. Well, sister, those that scorn their nest, oft fly with a sick wing.

GERTRUDE. Bow-bell!

MILDRED. Where titles presume to thrust before fit means to second them, wealth and respect often grow sullen and will not follow. For sure in this, I would for your sake I spoke not truth: 'Where ambition of place goes before fitness of birth, contempt and disgrace follow'. I heard a scholar once say that Ulysses, when he counterfeited himself mad, yoked cats and foxes and dogs together to draw his plough, whilst he followed and sowed salt; but sure I judge them truly mad that yoke citizens and courtiers, tradesmen and soldiers, a goldsmith's daughter and a knight. Well, sister, pray God my father sow not salt too.

GERTRUDE. Alas! Poor Mill, when I am a lady, I'll pray for thee yet, i'faith: nay, and I'll vouchsafe to call thee Sister Mill still; for though thou art not like to be a lady as I am, yet sure thou art a creature of God's making, and mayest peradventure to be saved as soon as I—does he come?

[Sings, and monkey cartwheels]
And ever and anon she doubled in her song.

Now, Lady's my comfort, what a profane ape's here! Tailor, Poldavis, prithee, fit it, fit it! Is this a right Scot? Does it clip close, and bear up round?

POLDAVY. Fine and stiffly, i'faith; 'twill keep your thighs so cool, and make your waist so small; here was a fault in your body, but I have supplied the defect with the effect of my steel instrument, which, though it have but one eye, can see to rectify the imperfection of the proportion.

GERTRUDE. Most edifying tailor! I protest you tailors are most sanctified members, and make many crooked things go upright. How must I bear my hands? Light, light?

POLDAVY. O, ay, now you are in the lady-fashion, you must do all things light. Tread light, light. Ay, and fall so: that's the court-amble.

She trips about the stage

GERTRUDE. Has the Court ne'er a trot?

POLDAVY. No, but a false gallop, lady.

GERTRUDE. *And if she will not go to bed,—*

Cantat

BETTRICE. The knight's come, forsooth.

Enter SIR PETRONEL, MASTER TOUCHSTONE, *and* MISTRESS
TOUCHSTONE

GERTRUDE. Is my knight come? O the Lord, my band? Sister, do my cheeks look well? Give me a little box o' the ear that I may seem to blush; now, now. So, there, there, there! Here he is! O my dearest delight! Lord, Lord, and how does my knight?

TOUCHSTONE. Fie, with more modesty!

GERTRUDE. Modesty! Why, I am no citizen now—modesty! Am I not to be married? Y'are best to keep me modest, now I am to be a lady.

SIR PETRONEL. Boldness is good fashion and courtlike.

GERTRUDE. Ay, in a country lady I hope it is; as I shall be. And how chance ye came no sooner, Knight?

SIR PETRONEL. 'Faith, I was so entertained in the progress with one Count Epernoum, a Welsh knight; we had a match at balloon too with my Lord Whachum, for four crowns.

GERTRUDE. At baboon? Jesu! You and I will play at baboon in the country, Knight?

SIR PETRONEL. O, sweet lady, 'tis a strong play with the arm.

GERTRUDE. With arm or leg or any other member, if it be a court sport. And when shall's be married, my Knight?

SIR PETRONEL. I come now to consummate it, and your father may call a poor knight son-in-law.

TOUCHSTONE. Sir, ye are come. What is not mine to keep, I must not be sorry to forgo. A hundred pound land her grandmother left her, 'tis yours; herself (as her mother's gift) is yours. But if you expect aught from me, know, my hand and mine eyes open together: I do not give blindly. 'Work upon that now'!

SIR PETRONEL. Sir, you mistrust not my means! I am a knight.

TOUCHSTONE. Sir, sir, what I know not, you will give me leave to say I am ignorant of.

MISTRESS TOUCHSTONE. Yes, that he is a knight; I know where he had money to pay the gentlemen-ushers and heralds their fees. Ay, that he is a knight; and so might you have been, too, if you had been aught else than an ass, as well as some of your neighbours. And I thought you would not ha' been knighted (as I am an honest woman), I would ha' dubbed you myself. I praise God I have wherewithal. But as for you, daughter—

GERTRUDE. Ay, mother, I must be a lady tomorrow; and by your leave, mother (I speak it not without my duty, but only in the right of my husband), I must take place of you, mother.

MISTRESS TOUCHSTONE. That you shall, Lady-daughter, and have a coach as well as I too.

GERTRUDE. Yes, mother. But by your leave, mother (I speak it not without my duty, but only in my husband's right), my coach-horses must take the wall of your coach-horses.

TOUCHSTONE. Come, come, the day grows low: 'tis supper-time. Use my house; the wedding solemnity is at my wife's cost; thank me for nothing but my willing blessing, for (I cannot feign) my hopes are faint. And, sir, respect my daughter; she has refused for you wealthy and honest matches, known good men, well-moneyed, better traded, best reputed.

GERTRUDE. Body o' truth, 'chitizens, chitizens'. Sweet Knight, as soon as ever we are married, take me to thy mercy out of this miserable 'chity', presently, carry me out of the scent of Newcastle coal, and the hearing of Bow-bell, I beseech thee, down with me, for God's sake!

TOUCHSTONE. Well, daughter, I have read, that old wit sings:

> 'The greatest rivers flow from little springs.
>
> Though thou art full, scorn not thy means at first;
>
> He that's most drunk may soonest be athirst'.

'Work upon that now'!

All but TOUCHSTONE, MILDRED *and* GOLDING *depart*

No, no! Yond' stand my hopes. Mildred, come hither daughter. And how approve you your sister's fashion? How do you fancy her choice? What dost thou think?

MILDRED. I hope, as a sister, well.

TOUCHSTONE. Nay but, nay but, how dost thou like her behaviour and humour? Speak freely.

MILDRED. I am loath to speak ill; and yet, I am sorry of this, I cannot speak well.

TOUCHSTONE. Well! Very good, as I would wish; a modest answer. Golding, come hither; hither, Golding! How dost thou like the knight, Sir Flash? Does he not look big? How lik'st thou the elephant? He says he has a castle in the country.

GOLDING. Pray heaven, the elephant carry not his castle on his back.

TOUCHSTONE. 'Fore heaven, very well! But, seriously, how dost repute him?

GOLDING. The best I can say of him is, I know him not.

TOUCHSTONE. Ha, Golding! I commend thee, I approve thee, and will make it appear my affection is strong to thee. My wife has her humour, and I will ha' mine. Dost thou see my daughter here? She is not fair, well-favoured or so, indifferent, which modest measure of beauty shall not make it thy only work to watch her, nor sufficient mischance, to suspect her. Thou art towardly, she is modest; thou art provident, she is careful. She's now mine: give me thy hand, she's now thine. 'Work upon that now'!

GOLDING. Sir, as your son, I honour you; and as your servant, obey you.

TOUCHSTONE. Sayest thou so? Come hither, Mildred. Do you see yond' fellow? He is a gentleman, though my prentice, and has somewhat to take to; a youth of good hope, well-friended, well parted. Are you mine? You are his. 'Work you upon that now'!

MILDRED. Sir, I am all yours; your body gave me life; your care and love, happiness of life; let your virtue still direct it, for to your wisdom I wholly dispose myself.

TOUCHSTONE. Sayest thou so? Be you two better acquainted. Lip her, lip her, knave! So, shut up shop, in! We must make holiday!

Exeunt GOLDING *and* MILDRED

'This match shall on, for I intend to prove
Which thrives the best, the mean or lofty love.
Whether fit wedlock vowed 'twixt like and like,
Or prouder hopes, which daringly o'erstrike
Their place and means. 'Tis honest time's expense,
When seeming lightness bears a moral sense'.
'Work upon that now'!

Exit

Act II, Scene i

[*Goldsmith's Row*]

TOUCHSTONE, GOLDING, *and* MILDRED, *sitting
on either side of the stall*

TOUCHSTONE. Quicksilver! Master Francis Quicksilver! Master Quicksilver!

Enter QUICKSILVER

QUICKSILVER. Here, sir—ump!

TOUCHSTONE. So, sir; nothing but flat Master Quicksilver (without any familiar addition) will fetch you! Will you truss my points, sir?

QUICKSILVER. Ay, forsooth—ump!

TOUCHSTONE. How now, sir? The drunken hiccup so soon this morning?

QUICKSILVER. 'Tis but the coldness of my stomach, forsooth.

TOUCHSTONE. What, have you the cause natural for it? Y'are a very learned drunkard; I believe I shall miss some of my silver spoons with your learning. The nuptial night will not moisten your throat sufficiently, but the morning likewise must rain her dews into your gluttonous weasand.

QUICKSILVER. An't please you, sir, we did but drink—ump!—to the coming off of the knightly bridegroom.

TOUCHSTONE. To the coming off on him?

QUICKSILVER. Ay, forsooth! We drunk to his coming on—ump!—when we went to bed; and now we are up, we must drink to his coming off; for that's the chief honour of a soldier, sir; and therefore we must drink so much the more to it, for-sooth—ump!

TOUCHSTONE. A very capital reason! So that you go to bed late, and rise early to commit drunkenness; you fulfil the Scripture very sufficient wickedly, forsooth!

QUICKSILVER. The knight's men, forsooth, be still o' their knees at it—ump!—and because 'tis for your credit, sir, I would be loath to flinch.

TOUCHSTONE. I pray, sir, e'en to 'em again, then; y'are one of the separated crew, one of my wife's faction, and my young lady's, with whom, and with their great match, I will have nothing to do.

QUICKSILVER. So, sir; now I will go keep my—ump!—credit with 'em, an't please you, sir!

TOUCHSTONE. In any case, sir, lay one cup of sack more o' your cold stomach, I beseech you!

QUICKSILVER. Yes, forsooth!

Exit QUICKSILVER

TOUCHSTONE. This is for my credit; servants ever maintain drunkenness in their master's house, for their master's credit; a good idle serving-man's reason. I thank Time the night is past! I ne'er waked to such cost; I think we have stowed more sorts of flesh in our bellies than ever Noah's Ark received; and for wine, why, my house turns giddy with it, and more noise in it than at a conduit. Ay me, even beasts condemn our gluttony! Well, 'tis our City's fault, which, because we commit seldom, we commit the more sinfully; we lose no time in our sensuality, but we make amends for it. O that we would do so in virtue and religious negligences! But see, here are all the sober parcels my house can show. I'll eavesdrop, hear what thoughts they utter this morning.

[*He retires*]

GOLDING [*and* MILDRED *come forward*]

GOLDING. But is it possible, that you, seeing your sister preferred to the bed of a knight, should contain your affections in the arms of a prentice?

MILDRED. I had rather make up the garment of my affections in some of the same piece, than, like a fool, wear gowns of two colours, or mix sackcloth with satin.

GOLDING. And do the costly garments; the title and fame of a lady, the fashion, observation, and reverence proper to such preferment, no more enflame you, than such convenience as my poor means and industry can offer to your virtues?

MILDRED. I have observed that the bridle given to those violent flatteries of fortune is seldom recovered; they bear one headlong in desire from one novelty to another, and where those ranging appetites reign, there is ever more passion than reason; no stay, and so no happiness. These hasty advancements are not natural; Nature hath given us legs to go to our objects, not wings to fly to them.

GOLDING. How dear an object you are to my desires I cannot express; whose fruition would my master's absolute consent and yours vouchsafe me, I should be absolutely happy. And though it were a grace so far beyond my merit, that I should blush with unworthiness to receive it, yet thus far both my love and my means shall assure your requital: you shall want nothing fit for your birth and education; what increase of wealth and advancement the honest and orderly industry and skill of our trade will afford in any, I doubt not will be aspired by me. I will ever make your contentment the end of my endeavours; I will love you above all; and only your grief shall be my misery, and your delight my felicity.

TOUCHSTONE. 'Work upon that now'! By my hopes, he woos honestly and orderly; he shall be anchor of my hopes! Look, see the ill-yoked monster, his fellow!

Enter QUICKSILVER *unlaced, a towel about his neck, in his flat cap, drunk*

QUICKSILVER. Eastward Ho! 'Holla ye pampered jades of Asia!'
TOUCHSTONE. Drunk now downright, o' my fidelity!
QUICKSILVER. Ump!—Pulldo, pulldo! Showse, quoth the caliver.
GOLDING. Fie, fellow Quicksilver, what a pickle are you in!
QUICKSILVER. Pickle? Pickle in thy throat; zounds, pickle! Wa, ha, ho! Good-morrow, Knight Petronel; 'morrow, lady goldsmith; come off, Knight, with a counter-buff, for the honour of knighthood.
GOLDING. Why, how now, sir? Do ye know where you are?
QUICKSILVER. Where I am? Why, 'sblood, you jolthead, where I am?
GOLDING. Go to, go to, for shame, go to bed and sleep out this immodesty: thou sham'st both my master and his house!
QUICKSILVER. Shame? What shame? I thought thou wouldst show thy bringing-up; and thou wert a gentleman as I am, thou wouldst think it no shame to be drunk. Lend me some money, save my credit; I must dine with the serving-men and their wives— and their wives, sirrah!
GOLDING. E'en who you will; I'll not lend thee threepence.
QUICKSILVER. 'Sfoot, lend me some money! 'Hast thou not Hiren here?'

TOUCHSTONE. Why, how now, sirrah, what vein's this, ha?

QUICKSILVER. 'Who cries on murther? Lady, was it you?' How does our master? Pray thee, cry Eastward Ho!

TOUCHSTONE. Sirrah, sirrah, y'are past your hiccup now; I see y'are drunk—

QUICKSILVER. 'Tis for your credit, master.

TOUCHSTONE. And hear you keep a whore in town—

QUICKSILVER. 'Tis for your credit, master.

TOUCHSTONE. And what you are out in cash, I know.

QUICKSILVER. So do I. My father's a gentleman; 'work upon that now'! Eastward Ho!

TOUCHSTONE. Sir, Eastward Ho will make you go Westward Ho. I will no longer dishonest my house, nor endanger my stock with your licence. There, sir, there's your indenture; all your apparel (that I must know) is on your back; and from this time my door is shut to you: from me be free; but for other freedom, and the moneys you have wasted, Eastward Ho shall not serve you.

QUICKSILVER. Am I free o' my fetters? Rent, fly with a duck in thy mouth! And now I tell thee, Touchstone—

TOUCHSTONE. Good sir—

QUICKSILVER. 'When this eternal substance of my soul'—

TOUCHSTONE. Well said; change your gold-ends for your play-ends.

QUICKSILVER. 'Did live imprisoned in my wanton flesh'—

TOUCHSTONE. What then, sir?

QUICKSILVER. 'I was a courtier in the Spanish Court, And Don Andrea was my name'—

TOUCHSTONE. Good master Don Andrea, will you march?

QUICKSILVER. Sweet Touchstone, will you lend me two shillings?

TOUCHSTONE. Not a penny!

QUICKSILVER. Not a penny? I have friends, and I have acquaintance; I will piss at thy shop posts, and throw rotten eggs at thy sign. 'Work upon that now'!

Exit staggering

TOUCHSTONE. Now, sirrah, you, hear you? You shall serve me no more neither; not an hour longer!

GOLDING. What mean you, sir?

TOUCHSTONE. I mean to give thee thy freedom, and with thy freedom my daughter, and with my daughter a father's love. And

with all these such a portion as shall make Knight Petronel himself envy thee! Y'are both agreed, are ye not?

BOTH. With all submission, both of thanks and duty.

TOUCHSTONE. Well, then, the great power of heaven bless and
confirm you. And Golding, that my love to thee may not show
less than my wife's love to my eldest daughter, thy marriage-feast
shall equal the knight's and hers.

GOLDING. Let me beseech you, no, sir; the superfluity and cold
meat left at their nuptials will with bounty furnish ours. The
grossest prodigality is superfluous cost of the belly; nor would I
wish any invitement of states or friends, only your reverent presence and witness shall sufficiently grace and confirm us.

TOUCHSTONE. Son to mine own bosom, take her and my
blessing. The nice fondling, my lady, sir-reverence, that I must
not now presume to call daughter, is so ravished with desire to
hansel her new coach, and see her knight's eastward castle, that
the next morning will sweat with her busy setting-forth. Away
will she and her mother, and while their preparation is making,
ourselves, with some two or three other friends, will consummate
the humble match we have in God's name concluded.

> ''Tis to my wish, for I have often read,
> Fit birth, fit age, keeps long a quiet bed.
> 'Tis to my wish: for tradesmen (well 'tis known)
> Get with more ease than gentry keeps his own'.

Exeunt

[Act II, Scene ii

A Room in SECURITY'S House]

SECURITY SOLUS

SECURITY. My privy guest, lusty Quicksilver, has drunk too
deep of the bride-bowl; but with a little sleep, he is much
recovered; and, I think, is making himself ready to be drunk in
a gallanter likeness. My house is, as 'twere, the cave where the
young outlaw hoards the stolen vails of his occupation; and here,
when he will revel it in his prodigal similitude, he retires to his
trunks, and (I may say softly) his punks: he dares trust me with
the keeping of both; for I am Security itself; my name is Security,
the famous usurer.

Enter QUICKSILVER *in his prentice's coat and cap, his gallant
breeches and stockings, gartering himself;* SECURITY
following

QUICKSILVER. Come, old Security, thou father of destruction!
Th' indented sheepskin is burned wherein I was wrapped; and I
am now loose, to get more children of perdition into thy usurous
bonds. Thou feed'st my lechery, and I thy covetousness; thou art
pander to me for my wench, and I to thee for thy cozenages: 'Ka
me, ka thee', runs through court and country.

SECURITY. Well said, my subtle Quicksilver! These K's ope
the doors to all this world's felicity; the dullest forehead sees it.
Let not master courtier think he carries all the knavery on his
shoulders: I have known poor Hob in the country, that has worn
hob-nails on's shoes, have as much villany in's head as he that
wears gold buttons in's cap.

QUICKSILVER. Why, man, 'tis the London high-way to thrift;
if virtue be used, 'tis but as a scrap to the net of villany. They
that use it simply, thrive simply, I warrant. 'Weight and fashion
makes goldsmiths cuckolds'.

Enter SINDEFY, *with* QUICKSILVER'*s doublet, cloak,
rapier, and dagger*

SINDEFY. Here, sir, put off the other half of your prenticeship.
QUICKSILVER. Well said, sweet Sin! Bring forth my bravery.
Now let my trunks shoot forth their silks concealed,
I now am free, and now will justify
My trunks and punks. Avaunt, dull flat-cap, then!
Via the curtain that shadowed Borgia!
There lie, thou husk of my envassaled state,
I, Samson, now have burst the Philistines' bands,
And in thy lap, my lovely Dalida,
I'll lie, and snore out my enfranchised state.

[*Sings*]

> 'When Samson was a tall young man,
> His power and strength increased then';
> He sold no more nor cup nor can,
> But did them all despise.
> Old Touchstone, now write to thy friends
> For one to sell thy base gold-ends;

> *Quicksilver now no more attends*
> *Thee, Touchstone.*

But, Dad, hast thou seen my running gelding dressed today?

SECURITY. That I have, Frank. The ostler o' th' Cock dressed him for a breakfast.

QUICKSILVER. What, did he eat him?

SECURITY. No, but he eat his breakfast for dressing him; and so dressed him for breakfast.

QUICKSILVER. 'O witty age, where age is young in wit, And all youth's words have gray beards full of it'!

SINDEFY. But alas, Frank, how will all this be maintained now? Your place maintained it before.

QUICKSILVER. Why, and I maintained my place. I'll to the Court, another manner of place for maintenance, I hope, than the silly City! I heard my father say, I heard my mother sing an old song and a true: 'Thou art a she fool, and know'st not what belongs to our male wisdom'. I shall be a merchant, forsooth, trust my estate in a wooden trough as he does! What are these ships but tennis-balls for the winds to play withal? Tossed from one wave to another: now under-line, now over the house; sometimes brick-walled against a rock, so that the guts fly out again; sometimes struck under the wide hazard, and farewell, master merchant!

SINDEFY. Well, Frank, well; the seas, you say, are uncertain; but he that sails in your court seas shall find 'em ten times fuller of hazard; wherein to see what is to be seen is torment more than a free spirit can endure. But when you come to suffer, how many injuries swallow you! What care and devotion must you use to humour an imperious lord: proportion your looks to his looks, [your] smiles to his smiles, fit your sails to the wind of his breath!

QUICKSILVER. Tush, he's no journeyman in his craft that cannot do that!

SINDEFY. But he's worse than a prentice that does it; not only humouring the lord, but every trencher-bearer, every groom that by indulgence and intelligence crept into his favour, and by panderism into his chamber: he rules the roost; and when my honourable lord says, 'it shall be thus', my worshipful rascal, the groom of his close stool, says, 'it shall not be thus', claps the door after him, and who dares enter? A prentice, quoth you? 'Tis but to learn to live; and does that disgrace a man? He that rises hardly, stands firmly; but he that rises with ease, alas, falls as easily!

QUICKSILVER. A pox on you! Who taught you this morality?

SECURITY. 'Tis long of this witty age, Master Francis. But indeed, Mistress Sindefy, all trades complain of inconvenience, and therefore 'tis best to have none. The merchant, he complains and says, 'traffic is subject to much uncertainty and loss'. Let 'em keep their goods on dry land, with a vengeance, and not expose other men's substances to the mercy of the winds, under protection of a wooden wall (as Master Francis says); and all for greedy desire to enrich themselves with unconscionable gain, two for one, or so; where I, and such other honest men as live by lending money, are content with moderate profit—thirty or forty i' th' hundred—so we may have it with quietness, and out of peril of wind and weather, rather than run those dangerous courses of trading as they do.

[SINDEFY *retires*]

QUICKSILVER. Ay, Dad, thou may'st well be called Security, for thou takest the safest course.

SECURITY. Faith, the quieter and the more contented, and, out of doubt, the more godly; for merchants, in their courses, are never pleased, but ever repining against heaven: one prays for a westerly wind to carry his ship forth; another for an easterly to bring his ship home; and at every shaking of a leaf he falls into an agony to think what danger his ship is in on such a coast, and so forth. The farmer, he is ever at odds with the weather: sometimes the clouds have been too barren; sometimes the heavens forget themselves, their harvests answer not their hopes; sometimes the season falls out too fruitful, corn will bear no price, and so forth. Th' artificer, he's all for a stirring world; if his trade be too dull and fall short of his expectation, then falls he out of joint. Where we, that trade nothing but money, are free from all this; we are pleased with all weathers: let it rain or hold up, be calm or windy, let the season be whatsoever, let trade go how it will, we take all in good part, e'en what please the heavens to send us, so the sun stand not still, and the moon keep her usual returns, and make up days, months, and years—

QUICKSILVER. And you have good security?

SECURITY. Ay, marry, Frank, that's the special point.

QUICKSILVER. And yet, forsooth, we must have trades to live withal; for we cannot stand without legs, nor fly without wings (and a number of such scurvy phrases). No, I say still, he that has wit, let him live by his wit; he that has none, let him be a tradesman.

SECURITY. Witty Master Francis! 'Tis pity any trade should dull that quick brain of yours! Do but bring Knight Petronel into my parchment toils once, and you shall never need to toil in any trade, o' my credit! You know his wife's land?

QUICKSILVER. Even to a foot, sir; I have been often there; a pretty fine seat, good land, all entire within itself.

SECURITY. Well wooded?

QUICKSILVER. Two hundred pounds' worth of wood ready to fell; and a fine sweet house that stands just in the midst on't, like a prick in the midst of a circle. Would I were your farmer, for a hundred pound a year!

SECURITY. Excellent Master Francis, how I do long to do thee good! 'How I do hunger and thirst to have the honour to enrich thee'! Ay, even to die that thou mightest inherit my living; 'even hunger and thirst'! For o' my religion, Master Francis—and so tell Knight Petronel—I do it to do him a pleasure.

QUICKSILVER. Marry, Dad, his horses are now coming up to bear down his lady; wilt thou lend him thy stable to set 'em in?

SECURITY. Faith, Master Francis, I would be loath to lend my stable out of doors; in a greater matter I will pleasure him, but not in this.

QUICKSILVER. A pox of your 'hunger and thirst'! Well, Dad, let him have money; all he could any way get is bestowed on a ship now bound for Virginia; the frame of which voyage is so closely conveyed that his new lady nor any of her friends know it. Notwithstanding, as soon as his lady's hand is gotten to the sale of her inheritance, and you have furnished him with money, he will instantly hoist sail and away.

SECURITY. Now, a frank gale of wind go with him, Master Frank! We have too few such knight adventurers. Who would not sell away competent certainties to purchase, with any danger, excellent uncertainties? Your true knight venturer ever does it. Let his wife seal today; he shall have his money today.

QUICKSILVER. Tomorrow, she shall, Dad, before she goes into the country. To work her to which action with the more engines, I purpose presently to prefer my sweet Sin here to the place of her gentlewoman; whom you (for the more credit) shall present as your friend's daughter, a gentlewoman of the country new come up with a will for awhile to learn fashions, forsooth, and be toward some lady; and she shall buzz pretty devices into her lady's ear, feeding her humours so serviceably (as the manner of such as she is, you know)—

SECURITY. True, good Master Francis!

Enter SINDEFY

QUICKSILVER. That she shall keep her port open to anything she commends to her.

SECURITY. O' my religion, a most fashionable project; as good she spoil the lady, as the lady spoil her, for 'tis three to one of one side. Sweet Mistress Sin, how are you bound to Master Francis! I do not doubt to see you shortly wed one of the head men of our City.

SINDEFY. But, sweet Frank, when shall my father Security present me?

QUICKSILVER. With all festination; I have broken the ice to it already; and will presently to the knight's house, whither, my good old Dad, let me pray thee with all formality to man her.

SECURITY. Command me, Master Francis; 'I do hunger and thirst to do thee service'. Come, sweet Mistress Sin, take leave of my Winifred, and we will instantly meet frank Master Francis at your lady's.

Enter WINIFRED *above*

WINIFRED. Where is my Cu there? Cu?

SECURITY. Ay, Winnie.

WINIFRED. Wilt thou come in, sweet Cu?

SECURITY. Ay, Winnie, presently!

Exeunt [*all but* QUICKSILVER]

QUICKSILVER. 'Ay, Winnie', quod he! That's all he can do, poor man, he may well cut off her name at Winnie. O 'tis an egregious pander! What will not an usurous knave be, so he may be rich? O 'tis a notable Jew's trump! I hope to live to see dog's meat made of the old usurer's flesh, dice of his bones, and indentures of his skin; and yet his skin is too thick to make parchment, 'twould make good boots for a peterman to catch salmon in. Your only smooth skin to make fine vellum is your Puritan's skin; they be the smoothest and slickest knaves in a country.

[*Exit*]

[*Act II, Scene iii*

Before Sir Petronel's *Lodging*]

Enter Sir Petronel *in boots, with a riding wand,*
[*followed by* Quicksilver]

Petronel. I'll out of this wicked town as fast as my horse can
trot. Here's now no good action for a man to spend his time in.
Taverns grow dead; ordinaries are blown up; plays are at a stand;
houses of hospitality at a fall; not a feather waving, nor a spur
jingling anywhere. I'll away instantly.

Quicksilver. Y'ad best take some crowns in your purse,
Knight, or else your eastward castle will smoke but miserably.

Petronel. O, Frank! My castle? Alas, all the castles I have are
built with air, thou know'st!

Quicksilver. I know it, Knight, and therefore wonder whither
your lady is going.

Petronel. Faith, to seek her fortune, I think. I said I had a
castle and land eastward, and eastward she will, without contra-
diction. Her coach and the coach of the sun must meet full butt;
and the sun being outshined with her ladyship's glory, she fears
he goes westward to hang himself.

Quicksilver. And I fear, when her enchanted castle becomes
invisible, her ladyship will return and follow his example.

Petronel. O that she would have the grace, for I shall never
be able to pacify her, when she sees herself deceived so.

Quicksilver. As easily as can be. Tell her she mistook your
directions, and that shortly yourself will down with her to approve
it; then clothe but her crupper in a new gown, and you may
drive her any way you list. For these women, sir, are like Essex
calves, you must wriggle 'em on by the tail still, or they will never
drive orderly.

Petronel. But, alas, sweet Frank, thou know'st my hability
will not furnish her blood with those costly humours.

Quicksilver. Cast that cost on me, sir. I have spoken to my
old pander, Security, for money or commodity; and commodity
(if you will) I know he will procure you.

Petronel. Commodity! Alas, what commodity?

Quicksilver. Why, sir, what say you to figs and raisins?

PETRONEL. A plague of figs and raisins, and all such frail commodities! We shall make nothing of 'em.

QUICKSILVER. Why, then, sir, what say you to forty pound in roasted beef?

PETRONEL. Out upon't! I have less stomach to that than to the figs and raisins. I'll out of town, though I sojourn with a friend of mine; for stay here I must not; my creditors have laid to arrest me, and I have no friend under heaven but my sword to bail me.

QUICKSILVER. God's me, Knight, put 'em in sufficient sureties, rather than let your sword bail you! Let 'em take their choice, either the King's Bench or the Fleet, or which of the two Counters they like best, for, by the Lord, I like none of 'em.

PETRONEL. Well, Frank, there is no jesting with my earnest necessity; thou know'st if I make not present money to further my voyage begun, all's lost, and all I have laid out about it.

QUICKSILVER. Why, then, sir, in earnest, if you can get your wise lady to set her hand to the sale of her inheritance, the bloodhound, Security, will smell out ready money for you instantly.

PETRONEL. There spake an angel! To bring her to which conformity, I must feign myself extremely amorous; and alleging urgent excuses for my stay behind, part with her as passionately as she would from her foisting hound.

QUICKSILVER. You have the sow by the right ear, sir. I warrant there was never child longed more to ride a cock-horse or wear his new coat, than she longs to ride in her new coach. She would long for everything when she was a maid; and now she will run mad for 'em. I lay my life, she will have every year four children; and what charge and change of humour you must endure while she is with child; and how she will tie you to your tackling till she be with child, a dog would not endure. Nay, there is no turnspit dog bound to his wheel more servilely than you shall be to her wheel; for as that dog can never climb the top of his wheel but when the top comes under him, so shall you never climb the top of her contentment but when she is under you.

PETRONEL. 'Slight, how thou terrifiest me!

QUICKSILVER. Nay, hark you, sir; what nurses, what midwives, what fools, what physicians, what cunning women must be sought for (fearing sometimes she is bewitched, sometimes in a consumption) to tell her tales, to talk bawdy to her, to make her laugh, to give her glisters, to let her blood under the tongue, and betwixt the toes; how she will revile and kiss you, spit in your face, and lick it off again; how she will vaunt you are her creature; she made you of nothing; how she could have had thousand-mark jointures; she could have been made a lady by a Scotch knight, and never ha' married him; she could have had poynados in her bed every morning; how she set you up, and how she will pull you down: you'll never be able to stand of your legs to ensure it.

PETRONEL. Out of my fortune! What a death is my life bound face to face to! The best is, a large time-fitted conscience is bound to nothing; marriage is but a form in the school of policy, to which scholars sit fastened only with painted chains. Old Security's young wife is ne'er the further off with me.

QUICKSILVER. Thereby lies a tale, sir. The old usurer will be here instantly, with my punk Sindefy, whom you know your lady has promised me to entertain for her gentlewoman; and he (with a purpose to feed on you) invites you most solemnly by me to supper.

PETRONEL. It falls out excellently fitly: I see desire of gain makes jealousy venturous.

Enter GERTRUDE

See, Frank, here comes my lady. Lord, how she views thee! She knows thee not, I think, in this bravery.

GERTRUDE. How now? Who be you, I pray?

QUICKSILVER. One Master Francis Quicksilver, an't please your Ladyship.

GERTRUDE. God's my dignity! As I am a lady, if he did not make me blush so that mine eyes stood a-water, would I were unmarried again! Where's my woman, I pray?

Enter SECURITY *and* SINDEFY

QUICKSILVER. See, Madam, she now comes to attend you.

SECURITY. God save my honourable Knight and his worshipful Lady!

GERTRUDE. Y'are very welcome; you must not put on your hat yet.

SECURITY. No, Madam; till I know your Ladyship's further pleasure, I will not presume.

GERTRUDE. And is this a gentleman's daughter new come out of the country?

SECURITY. She is, Madam; and one that her father hath a special care to bestow in some honourable lady's service, to put her out of her honest humours, forsooth; for she had a great desire to be a nun, an't please you.

GERTRUDE. A nun? What nun? A nun substantive, or a nun adjective?

SECURITY. A nun substantive, Madam, I hope, if a nun be a noun. But I mean, Lady, a vowed maid of that order.

GERTRUDE. I'll teach her to be a maid of the order, I warrant you! And can you do any work belongs to a lady's chamber?

SINDEFY. What I cannot do, Madam, I would be glad to learn.

GERTRUDE. Well said, hold up then; hold up your head, I say! Come hither a little.

SINDEFY. I thank your Ladyship.

GERTRUDE. And hark you—good man, you may put on your hat now; I do not look on you—I must have you of my faction now; not of my knight's, maid!

SINDEFY. No, forsooth, Madam, of yours.

GERTRUDE. And draw all my servants in my bow, and keep my counsel, and tell me tales, and put me riddles, and read on a book sometimes when I am busy, and laugh at country gentlewomen, and command anything in the house for my retainers, and care not what you spend, for it is all mine; and in any case, be still a maid, whatsoever you do, or whatsoever any man can do unto you.

SECURITY. I warrant your Ladyship for that.

GERTRUDE. Very well; you shall ride in my coach with me into the country tomorrow morning. Come, Knight, pray thee, let's make a short supper, and to bed presently.

SECURITY. Nay, good Madam, this night I have a short supper at home waits on his worship's acceptation.

GERTRUDE. By my faith, but he shall not go, sir; I shall swoon and he sup from me.

PETRONEL. Pray thee, forbear; shall he lose his provision?

GERTRUDE. Ay, by'r Lady, sir, rather than I lose my longing. Come in, I say—as I am a lady, you shall not go!

QUICKSILVER. [*Aside to* SECURITY] I told him what a bur he had gotten.

SECURITY. If you will not sup from your knight, Madam, let me entreat your Ladyship to sup at my house with him.

GERTRUDE. No, by my faith, sir; then we cannot be abed soon enough after supper.

PETRONEL. What a medicine is this! Well, Master Security, you are new married as well as I; I hope you are bound as well. We must honour our young wives, you know.

QUICKSILVER. [*Aside to* SECURITY] In policy, Dad, till tomorrow she has sealed.

SECURITY. I hope in the morning, yet, your Knighthood will breakfast with me?

PETRONEL. As early as you will, sir.

SECURITY. Thank your good worship; 'I do hunger and thirst to do you good, sir'.

GERTRUDE. Come, sweet Knight, come, 'I do hunger and thirst to be abed with thee'.

Exeunt

Act III, Scene i

[SECURITY's House]

Enter PETRONEL, QUICKSILVER, SECURITY, BRAMBLE, *and*
WINIFRED

PETRONEL. Thanks for our feast-like breakfast, good Master Security; I am sorry (by reason of my instant haste to so long a voyage as Virginia) I am without means by any kind amends to show how affectionately I take your kindness, and to confirm by some worthy ceremony a perpetual league of friendship betwixt us.

SECURITY. Excellent Knight, let this be a token betwixt us of inviolable friendship: I am new married to this fair gentlewoman, you know, and by my hope to make her fruitful, though I be something in years, I vow faithfully unto you to make you god-father (though in your absence) to the first child I am blessed withal; and henceforth call me Gossip, I beseech you, if you please to accept it.

PETRONEL. In the highest degree of gratitude, my most worthy Gossip; for confirmation of which friendly title, let me entreat my fair Gossip, your wife, here, to accept this diamond, and keep it as my gift to her first child; wheresoever my fortune, in event of my voyage, shall bestow me.

SECURITY. How now, my coy wedlock! Make you strange of so noble a favour? Take it, I charge you, with all affection, and, by way of taking your leave, present boldly your lips to our honourable gossip.

QUICKSILVER. [*Aside*] How venturous he is to him, and how jealous to others!

PETRONEL. Long may this kind touch of our lips print in our hearts all the forms of affection. And now my good Gossip, if the writings be ready to which my wife should seal, let them be brought this morning before she takes coach into the country, and my kindness shall work her to despatch it.

SECURITY. The writings are ready, sir. My learned counsel here, Master Bramble the lawyer, hath perused them; and within this hour, I will bring the scrivener with them to your worshipful lady.

PETRONEL. Good Master Bramble, I will here take my leave of you, then. God send you fortunate pleas, sir, and contentious clients!

BRAMBLE. And you foreright winds, sir, and a fortunate voyage!
Exit

Enter a MESSENGER

MESSENGER. Sir Petronel, here are three or four gentlemen desire to speak with you.

PETRONEL. What are they?

QUICKSILVER. They are your followers in this voyage, Knight, Captain Seagull and his associates; I met them this morning, and told them you would be here.

PETRONEL. Let them enter, I pray you; I know they long to be gone, for their stay is dangerous.

Enter SEAGULL, SCAPETHRIFT, *and* SPENDALL

SEAGULL. God save my honourable Colonel!

PETRONEL. Welcome, good Captain Seagull and worthy gentlemen. If you will meet my friend Frank here, and me, at the Blue Anchor Tavern by Billingsgate this evening, we will there drink to our happy voyage, be merry, and take boat to our ship with all expedition.

SPENDALL. Defer it no longer, I beseech you, sir; but as your voyage is hitherto carried closely, and in another knight's name, so for your own safety and ours, let it be continued—our meeting and speedy purpose of departing known to as few as is possible, lest your ship and goods be attached.

QUICKSILVER. Well advised, Captain! Our colonel shall have money this morning to despatch all our departures. Bring those gentlemen at night to the place appointed, and with our skins full of vintage we'll take occasion by the 'vantage, and away.

SPENDALL. We will not fail but be there, sir.

PETRONEL. Good morrow, good Captain, and my worthy associates. Health and all sovereignty to my beautiful Gossip. For you, sir, we shall see you presently with the writings.

SECURITY. With writings and crowns to my honourable Gossip. 'I do hunger and thirst to do you good, sir'!

Exeunt

Act III, Scene ii

[An Inn-yard]

Enter a COACHMAN *in haste, in's frock, feeding*

COACHMAN. Here's a stir when citizens ride out of town, indeed, as if all the house were afire! 'Slight, they will not give a man leave to eat's breakfast afore he rises!

Enter HAMLET, *a footman, in haste*

HAMLET. What, coachman! My lady's coach, for shame! Her Ladyship's ready to come down.

Enter POTKIN, *a tankard-bearer*

POTKIN. 'Sfoot, Hamlet, are you mad? Whither run you now? You should brush up my old mistress!

[*Exit* HAMLET]

Enter SINDEFY

SINDEFY. What, Potkin? You must put off your tankard, and put on your blue coat and wait upon Mistress Touchstone into the country.   *Exit*

POTKIN. I will, forsooth, presently. *Exit*

Enter MISTRESS POND *and* MISTRESS GAZER

FOND. Come, sweet Mistress Gazer, let's watch here, and see my Lady Flash take coach.

GAZER. O' my word, here's a most fine place to stand in. Did you see the new ship launched last day, Mistress Fond?

FOND. O God, and we citizens should lose such a sight!

GAZER. I warrant here will be double as many people to see her take coach as there were to see it take water.

FOND. O, she's married to a most fine castle i' th' country, they say.

GAZER. But there are no giants in the castle, are there?

FOND. O no; they say her knight killed 'em all, and therefore he was knighted.

GAZER. Would to God her Ladyship would come away!

Enter GERTRUDE, MISTRESS TOUCHSTONE, SINDEFY,
HAMLET, POTKIN

FOND. She comes, she comes, she comes!

GAZER. ⎫
FOND. ⎬ Pray heaven bless your Ladyship!

GERTRUDE. Thank you, good people! My coach! For the love of heaven, my coach! In good truth I shall swoon else.

HAMLET. Coach, coach, my lady's coach! *Exit*

GERTRUDE. As I am a lady, I think I am with child already, I long for a coach so. May one be with child afore they are married, mother?

MISTRESS TOUCHSTONE. Ay, by'r Lady, Madam; a little thing does that. I have seen a little prick no bigger than a pin's head swell bigger and bigger till it has come to an ancome; and e'en so 'tis in these cases.

Enter HAMLET

HAMLET. Your coach is coming, Madam.

GERTRUDE. That's well said. Now, heaven! Methinks I am e'en up to the knees in preferment!

[Sings]

> *But a little higher, but a little higher, but a little higher;*
> *There, there, there lies Cupid's fire!*

MISTRESS TOUCHSTONE. But must this young man, an't please you, Madam, run by your coach all the way a-foot?

GERTRUDE. Ay, by my faith, I warrant him! He gives no other milk, as I have another servant does.

MISTRESS TOUCHSTONE. Alas, 'tis e'en pity, methinks! For God's sake, Madam, buy him but a hobby-horse; let the poor youth have something betwixt his legs to ease 'em. Alas, we must do as we would be done to!

GERTRUDE. Go to, hold your peace, dame; you talk like an old fool, I tell you.

Enter PETRONEL *and* QUICKSILVER

PETRONEL. Wilt thou be gone, sweet honeysuckle, before I can go with thee?

GERTRUDE. I pray thee, sweet Knight, let me; I do so long to dress up thy castle afore thou com'st. But I marle how my modest sister occupies herself this morning, that she cannot wait on me to my coach, as well as her mother!

QUICKSILVER. Marry, Madam, she's married by this time to prentice Golding. Your father, and some one more, stole to church with 'em, in all the haste, that the cold meat left at your wedding might serve to furnish their nuptial table.

GERTRUDE. There's no base fellow, my father, now! But he's e'en fit to father such a daughter: he must call me daughter no more now; but 'Madam', and, 'please you Madam', and, 'please your worship, Madam', indeed. Out upon him! Marry his daughter to a base prentice!

MISTRESS TOUCHSTONE. What should one do? Is there no law for one that marries a woman's daughter against her will? How shall we punish him, Madam?

GERTRUDE. As I am a lady, an't would snow, we'd so pebble 'em with snowballs as they come from church! But sirrah, Frank Quicksilver—

QUICKSILVER. Ay, Madam.

GERTRUDE. Dost remember since thou and I clapped what-d'ye-call'ts in the garret?

QUICKSILVER. I know not what you mean, Madam.

GERTRUDE. [*Sings*]
> *His head as white as milk,*
> *All flaxen was his hair;*
> *But now he is dead,*
> *And laid in his bed,*
> *And never will come again.*

God be at your labour!

Enter TOUCHSTONE, GOLDING, MILDRED *with rosemary*

PETRONEL. [*Aside*] Was there ever such a lady?

QUICKSILVER. See, Madam, the bride and bridegroom!

GERTRUDE. God's my precious! God give you joy, Mistress What-lack-you! Now out upon thee, baggage! My sister married in a taffeta hat! Marry, hang you! Westward with a wanion t' ye! Nay, I have done wi' ye, minion, then, i'faith; never look to have my countenance any more, nor anything I can do for thee. Thou ride in my coach? Or come down to my castle? Fie upon thee! I charge thee in my Ladyship's name, call me sister no more.

TOUCHSTONE. An't please your worship, this is not your sister; this is my daughter, and she calls me father, and so does not your Ladyship, an't please your worship, Madam.

MISTRESS TOUCHSTONE. No, nor she must not call thee father by heraldry, because thou mak'st thy prentice thy son as well as she. Ah, thou misproud prentice, dar'st thou presume to marry a lady's sister?

GOLDING. It pleased my master, forsooth, to embolden me with his favour; and though I confess myself far unworthy so worthy a wife (being in part her servant, as I am your prentice) yet (since I may say it without boasting) I am born a gentleman, and by the trade I have learned of my master (which I trust taints not my blood) able with mine own industry and portion to maintain your daughter, my hope is, heaven will so bless our humble beginning, that in the end I shall be no disgrace to the grace with which my master hath bound me his double prentice.

TOUCHSTONE. Master me no more, son, if thou think'st me worthy to be thy father.

GERTRUDE. Sun? Now, good Lord, how he shines, and you mark him! He's a gentleman?

GOLDING. Ay, indeed, Madam, a gentleman born.

PETRONEL. Never stand o' your gentry, Master Bridegroom; if your legs be no better than your arms, you'll be able to stand upon neither shortly.

TOUCHSTONE. An't please your good worship, sir, there are two sorts of gentleman.

PETRONEL. What mean you, sir?

TOUCHSTONE. Bold to put off my hat to your worship—

[*Doffs his hat*]

PETRONEL. Nay, pray forbear, sir, and then forth with your two sorts of gentlemen.

TOUCHSTONE. If your worship will have it so: I say there are two sorts of gentlemen. There is a gentleman artificial, and a gentleman natural. Now, though your worship be a gentleman natural—'work upon that now'!

QUICKSILVER. Well said old Touchstone; I am proud to hear thee enter a set speech, i'faith! Forth, I beseech thee!

TOUCHSTONE. Cry you mercy, sir, your worship's a gentleman I do not know. If you be one of my acquaintance, y'are very much disguised, sir.

QUICKSILVER. Go to, old quipper! Forth with thy speech, I say!

TOUCHSTONE. What, sir, my speeches were ever in vain to your gracious worship; and therefore, till I speak to you gallantry indeed, I will save my breath for my broth anon. Come, my poor son and daughter, let us hide ourselves in our poor humility, and live safe. Ambition consumes itself with the very show. 'Work upon that now'!

[*Exeunt* TOUCHSTONE, GOLDING *and* MILDRED]

GERTRUDE. Let him go, let him go, for God's sake! Let him make his prentice his son, for God's sake! Give away his daughter, for God's sake! And when they come a-begging to us, for God's sake, let's laugh at their good husbandry, for God's sake! Farewell, sweet Knight, pray thee make haste after.

PETRONEL. What shall I say? I would not have thee go.

QUICKSILVER.   [*Sings*]
>   *Now, O now, I must depart;*
>   *Parting though it absence move—*
This ditty, Knight, do I see in thy looks in capital letters.
>   *What a grief 'tis to depart,*
>   *And leave the flower that has my heart!*

> *My sweet lady, and alack for woe,*
> *Why should we part so?*

Tell truth, Knight, and shame all dissembling lovers; does not your pain lie on that side?

PETRONEL. If it do, canst thou tell me how I may cure it?

QUICKSILVER. Excellent easily! Divide yourself in two halves, just by the girdlestead; send one half with your lady, and keep the tother yourself. Or else do as all true lovers do—part with your heart, and leave your body behind. I have seen't done a hundred times: 'tis as easy a matter for a lover to part without a heart from his sweetheart, and he ne'er the worse, as for a mouse to get from a trap and leave his tail behind him. See, here comes the writings.

Enter SECURITY *with a* SCRIVENER

SECURITY. Good morrow to my worshipful Lady! I present your Ladyship with this writing, to which if you please to set your hand, with your knight's, a velvet gown shall attend your journey, o' my credit.

GERTRUDE. What writing is it, Knight?

PETRONEL. The sale, sweetheart, of the poor tenement I told thee of, only to make a little money to send thee down furniture for my castle, to which my hand shall lead thee.

GERTRUDE. Very well! Now give me your pen, I pray.

QUICKSILVER. [*Aside*] It goes down without chewing, i'faith!

SCRIVENER. Your worships deliver this as your deed?

BOTH. We do.

GERTRUDE. So now, Knight, farewell till I see thee!

PETRONEL. All farewell to my sweetheart!

MISTRESS TOUCHSTONE. Good-bye, son Knight!

PETRONEL. Farewell, my good mother!

GERTRUDE. Farewell, Frank; I would fain take thee down if I could.

QUICKSILVER. I thank your good Ladyship. Farewell, Mistress Sindefy.

Exeunt [GERTRUDE *and her party*]

PETRONEL. O tedious voyage, whereof there is no end! What will they think of me?

QUICKSILVER. Think what they list. They longed for a vagary into the country, and now they are fitted. So a woman marry to ride in a coach, she cares not if she ride to her ruin. 'Tis the great

end of many of their marriages. This is not first time a lady has
rid a false journey in her coach, I hope.

PETRONEL. Nay, 'tis no matter. I care little what they think;
he that weighs men's thoughts has his hands full of nothing. A
man, in the course of this world, should be like a surgeon's instrument: work in the wounds of others, and feel nothing himself—
the sharper and subtler, the better.

QUICKSILVER. As it falls out now, Knight, you shall not need
to devise excuses, or endure her outcries, when she returns. We
shall now be gone before, where they cannot reach us.

PETRONEL. Well, my kind compeer, you have now th'assurance
we both can make you. Let me now entreat you, the money we
agreed on may be brought to the Blue Anchor, near to Billingsgate,
by six o'clock; where I and my chief friends, bound for this voyage, will with feasts attend you.

SECURITY. The money, my most honourable compeer, shall
without fail observe your appointed hour.

PETRONEL. Thanks, my dear Gossip, I must now impart
To your approved love a loving secret,
As one on whom my life doth more rely
In friendly trust than any man alive.
Nor shall you be the chosen secretary
Of my affections for affection only:
For if I protest (if God bless my return)
To make you partner in my actions' gain
As deeply as if you had ventured with me
Half my expenses. Know then, honest Gossip,
I have enjoyed with such divine contentment
A gentlewoman's bed, whom you well know,
That I shall ne'er enjoy this tedious voyage,
Nor live the least part of the time it asketh,
Without her presence; 'so I thirst and hunger'
To taste the dear feast of her company.
And if the hunger and the thirst you vow,
(As my sworn gossip) to my wished good
Be (as I know it is) unfeigned and firm,
Do me an easy favour in your power.

SECURITY. Be sure, brave Gossip, all that I can do,
To my best nerve, is wholly at your service:
Who is the woman, first, that is your friend?

PETRONEL. The woman is your learned counsel's wife,

The lawyer, Master Bramble; whom would you
Bring out this even', in honest neighbourhood,
To take his leave with you, of me your gossip.
I, in the meantime, will send this my friend
Home to his house, to bring his wife disguised,
Before his face, into our company;
For love hath made her look for such a wile
To free her from his tyrannous jealousy.
And I would take this course before another,
In stealing her away to make us sport
And gull his circumspection the more grossly.
And I am sure that no man like yourself
Hath credit with him to entice his jealousy
To so long stay abroad as may give time
To her enlargement in such safe disguise.

    SECURITY. A pretty, pithy, and most pleasant project!
Who would not strain a point of neighbourhood,
For such a point-device, that, as the ship
Of famous Draco went about the world,
Will wind about the lawyer, compassing
The world himself; he hath it in his arms,
And that's enough, for him, without his wife.
A lawyer is ambitious, and his head
Cannot be praised nor raised too high,
With any fork of highest knavery.
I'll go fetch him straight.

Exit SECURITY

    PETRONEL. So, so. Now, Frank, go thou home to his house,
'Stead of his lawyer's, and bring his wife hither,
Who, just like to the lawyer's wife, is prisoned
With his stern usurous jealousy, which could never
Be over-reached thus, but with over-reaching.

Enter SECURITY

    SECURITY. And, Master Francis, watch you th'instant time
To enter with his exit; 'twill be rare,
Two fine horned beasts—a camel and a lawyer!   [*Exit*]

    QUICKSILVER. How the old villain joys in villainy!

Enter SECURITY

SECURITY. And hark you, Gossip, when you have her here,
Have your boat ready; ship her to your ship
With utmost haste, lest Master Bramble stay you.
To o'er-reach that head that out-reacheth all heads,
'Tis a trick rampant! 'Tis a very quiblin!
I hope this harvest to pitch cart with lawyers,
Their heads will be so forked. 'This sly touch
Will get apes to invent a number such'.   *Exit*

QUICKSILVER. Was ever rascal honeyed so with poison?
'He that delights in slavish avarice,
Is apt to joy in every sort of vice'.
Well, I'll go fetch his wife, whilst he the lawyer.

PETRONEL. But stay, Frank, let's think how we may disguise her
Upon this sudden.

QUICKSILVER. God's me, there's the mischief!
But hark you, here's an excellent device;
'Fore God, a rare one! I will carry her
A sailor's gown and cap, and cover her,
And a player's beard.

PETRONEL. And what upon her head?

QUICKSILVER. I tell you; a sailor's cap! 'Slight, God forgive me,
What kind of figent memory have you?

PETRONEL. Nay, then, what kind of figent wit hast thou?
A sailor's cap? How shall she put it off
When thou present'st her to our company?

QUICKSILVER. Tush, man! For that, make her a saucy sailor.

PETRONEL. Tush, tush, 'tis no fit sauce for such sweet mutton!
I know not what t'advise.

Enter SECURITY, *with his wife's gown*

SECURITY. Knight, Knight, a rare device!

PETRONEL. 'Swounds, yet again!

QUICKSILVER. What stratagem have you now?

SECURITY. The best that ever! You talked of disguising?

PETRONEL. Ay, marry, Gossip, that's our present care.

SECURITY. Cast care away then; here's the best device
For plain security (for I am no better),
I think, that ever lived. Here's my wife's gown,
Which you may put upon the lawyer's wife,
And which I brought you, sir, for two great reasons:

One is, that Master Bramble may take hold
Of some suspicion that it is my wife,
And gird me so, perhaps, with his law wit;
The other (which is policy indeed)
Is, that my wife may now be tied at home,
Having no more but her old gown abroad,
And not show me a quirk, while I firk others.
Is not this rare?

    BOTH. The best that ever was!

    SECURITY. Am I not born to furnish gentlemen?

    PETRONEL. O my dear Gossip!

    SECURITY. Well, hold, Master Francis!
Watch when the lawyer's out, and put it in.
And now I will go fetch him.   *Exit*

    QUICKSILVER. O my Dad!
He goes, as 'twere the devil, to fetch the lawyer;
And devil shall he be, if horns will make him.

        [*Re-enter* SECURITY]

    PETRONEL. Why, how now, Gossip? Why stay you there
musing?

    SECURITY. A toy, a toy runs in my head, i'faith!

    QUICKSILVER. A pox of that head! Is there more toys yet?

    PETRONEL. What is it, pray thee, Gossip?

    SECURITY. Why, sir, what if you
Should slip away now with my wife's best gown,
I have no security for it?

    QUICKSILVER. For that, I hope, Dad, you will take our words.

    SECURITY. Ay, by th'mass, your word! That's a proper staff
For wise Security to lean upon!
But 'tis no matter, once I'll trust my name
On your cracked credits; let it take no shame.
Fetch the wench, Frank!   *Exit*

    QUICKSILVER. I'll wait upon you, sir,
And fetch you over, you were ne'er so fetched.
Go to the tavern, Knight; your followers
Dare not be drunk, I think, before their captain.   *Exit*

    PETRONEL. Would I might lead them to no hotter service,
Till our Virginian gold were in our purses!   *Exit*

[*Act III, Scene iii*

Blue Anchor Tavern, Billingsgate]

Enter SEAGULL, SPENDALL, *and* SCAPETHRIFT, *in the tavern,
with a* DRAWER

SEAGULL. Come, drawer, pierce your neatest hogsheads, and
let's have cheer, not fit for your Billingsgate tavern, but for our
Virginian colonel; he will be here instantly.

DRAWER. You shall have all things fit, sir; please you have any
more wine?

SPENDALL. More wine, slave! Whether we drink it or no, spill
it, and draw more.

SCAPETHRIFT. Fill all the pots in your house with all sorts of
liquor, and let 'em wait on us here like soldiers in their pewter
coats; and though we do not employ them now, yet we will
maintain 'em till we do.

DRAWER. Said like an honourable captain! You shall have all
you can command, sir!   *Exit* DRAWER

SEAGULL. Come, boys, Virginia longs till we share the rest of
her maidenhead.

SPENDALL. Why, is she inhabited already with any English?

SEAGULL. A whole country of English is there, man, bred of
those that were left there in '79. They have married with the
Indians, and make 'em bring forth as beautiful faces as any we
have in England; and therefore the Indians are so in love with
'em, that all the treasure they have they lay at their feet.

SCAPETHRIFT. But is there such treasure there, Captain, as I
have heard?

SEAGULL. I tell thee, gold is more plentiful there than copper
is with us; and for as much red copper as I can bring, I'll have
thrice the weight in gold. Why, man, all their dripping-pans and
their chamber-pots are pure gold; and all the chains with which
they chain up their streets are massy gold; all the prisoners they
take are fettered in gold; and for rubies and diamonds, they go
forth on holidays and gather 'em by the seashore to hang on their
children's coats, and stick in their caps, as commonly as our
children wear saffron-gilt brooches, and groats with holes in 'em.

SCAPETHRIFT. And is it a pleasant country withal?

SEAGULL. As ever the sun shined on; temperate and full of all
sorts of excellent viands; wild boar is as common there as our

tamest bacon is here; venison, as mutton. And then you shall live freely there, without sergeants, or courtiers, or lawyers, or intelligencers; only a few industrious Scots, perhaps, who indeed are dispersed over the face of the whole earth. But as for them, there are no greater friends to Englishmen and England, when they are out on't, in the world, than they are. And for my part, I would a hundred thousand of 'em were there; for we are all one countrymen now, ye know; and we should find ten times more comfort of them there than we do here. Then for your means to advancement, there it is simple and not preposterously mixed. You may be an alderman there, and never be scavenger; you may be a nobleman, and never be a slave; you may come to preferment enough, and never be a pander; to riches and fortune enough, and have never the more villainy nor the less wit.

SPENDALL. God's me! And how far is it thither?

SEAGULL. Some six weeks' sail, no more, with any indifferent good wind. And if I get to any part of the coast of Africa, I'll sail thither with any wind; or when I come to Cape Finisterre, there's a foreright wind continually wafts us till we come at Virginia. See, our colonel's come.

Enter SIR PETRONEL *with his followers*

PETRONEL. Well met, good Captain Seagull, and my noble gentlemen! Now the sweet hour of our freedom is at hand. Come, drawer, fill us some carouses, and prepare us for the mirth that will be occasioned presently. Here will be a pretty wench, gentlemen, that will bear us company all our voyage.

SEAGULL. Whatsoever she be, here's to her health, noble Colonel, both with cap and knee.

PETRONEL. Thanks, kind Captain Seagull! She's one I love dearly, and must not be known till we be free from all that know us. And so, gentlemen, here's to her health!

BOTH. Let it come, worthy Colonel; 'we do hunger and thirst for it'!

PETRONEL. Afore heaven, you have hit the phrase of one that her presence will touch from the foot to the forehead, if ye knew it.

SPENDALL. Why, then, we will join his forehead with her health, sir; and, Captain Scapethrift, here's to 'em both!

[*All kneel and drink*]

Enter SECURITY *and* BRAMBLE

SECURITY. See, see, Master Bramble, 'fore heaven, their voyage cannot but prosper: they are o' their knees for success to it.

BRAMBLE. And they pray to god Bacchus.

SECURITY. God save my brave Colonel, with all his tall captains and corporals! See, sir, my worshipful learned counsel, Master Bramble, is come to take his leave of you.

PETRONEL. Worshipful Master Bramble, how far do you draw us into the sweet brier of your kindness! Come, Captain Seagull, another health to this rare Bramble, that hath never a prick about him.

SEAGULL. I pledge his most smooth disposition, sir. Come, Master Security, bend your supporters, and pledge this notorious health here.

SECURITY. Bend you yours likewise, Master Bramble; for it is you shall pledge me.

SEAGULL. Not so, Master Security! He must not pledge his own health!

SECURITY. No, Master Captain?

Enter QUICKSILVER *with* WINIFRED *disguised*

Why then, here's one is fitly come to do him that honour.

QUICKSILVER. Here's the gentlewoman your cousin, sir, whom, with much entreaty, I have brought to take her leave of you in a tavern; ashamed whereof, you must pardon her if she put not off her mask.

PETRONEL. Pardon me, sweet cousin; my kind desire to see you before I went, made me so importunate to entreat your presence here.

SECURITY. How now, Master Francis, have you honoured this presence with a fair gentlewoman?

QUICKSILVER. Pray, sir, take you no notice of her, for she will not be known to you.

SECURITY. But my learned counsel, Master Bramble here, I hope may know her.

QUICKSILVER. No more than you, sir, at this time; his learning must pardon her.

SECURITY. Well, God pardon her for my part, and I do, I'll be sworn; and so, Master Francis, here's to all that are going eastward tonight, towards Cuckold's Haven; and so, to the health of Master Bramble!

QUICKSILVER. [*Kneels*] I pledge it, sir. Hath it gone round, Captains?

SEAGULL. It has, sweet Frank; and the round closes with thee.

QUICKSILVER. Well, sir, here's to all eastward and toward cuckolds, and so to famous Cuckold's Haven, so fatally remembered.

Surgit

PETRONEL. [*To* WINIFRED] Nay, pray thee, coz, weep not. Gossip Security?

SECURITY. Ay, my brave Gossip.

PETRONEL. A word, I beseech you, sir. Our friend, Mistress Bramble here, is so dissolved in tears that she drowns the whole mirth of our meeting. Sweet Gossip, take her aside and comfort her.

SECURITY. [*Aside to* WINIFRED] Pity of all true love, Mistress Bramble! What, weep you to enjoy your love? What's the cause, lady? Is't because your husband is so near, and your heart earns, to have a little abused him? Alas, alas, the offence is too common to be respected. So great a grace hath seldom chanced to so unthankful a woman: to be rid of an old jealous dotard, to enjoy the arms of a loving young knight, that, when your prickless Bramble is withered with grief of your loss, will make you flourish afresh in the bed of a lady.

Enter DRAWER

DRAWER. Sir Petronel, here's one of your watermen come to tell you it will be flood these three hours; and that 'twill be dangerous going against the tide, for the sky is overcast, and there was a porcpisce even now seen at London Bridge, which is always the messenger of tempests, he says.

PETRONEL. A porcpisce! What's that to th' purpose? Charge him, if he love his life, to attend us; can we not reach Blackwall (where my ship lies) against the tide, and in spite of tempests? Captains and gentlemen, we'll begin a new ceremony at the beginning of our voyage, which I believe will be followed of all future adventurers.

SEAGULL. What's that, good Colonel?

PETRONEL. This, Captain Seagull. We'll have our provided supper brought aboard Sir Francis Drake's ship, that hath compassed the world; where, with full cups and banquets, we will do sacrifice for a prosperous voyage. My mind gives me that some good spirits of the waters should haunt the desert ribs of her, and be auspicious to all that honour her memory, and will with like orgies enter their voyages.

SEAGULL. Rarely conceited! One health more to this motion, and aboard to perform it. He that will not this night be drunk, may he never be sober!

They compass in WINIFRED, *dance the drunken round, and drink carouses*

BRAMBLE. Sir Petronel and his honourable Captains, in these young services we old servitors may be spared. We only came to take our leaves, and with one health to you all, I'll be bold to do so. Here, neighbour Security, to the health of Sir Petronel and all his captains!

SECURITY. You must bend, then, Master Bramble. [*They kneel*] So, now I am for you. I have one corner of my brain, I hope, fit to bear one carouse more. Here, lady, to you that are encompassed there, and are ashamed of our company! Ha, ha, ha! By my troth, my learned counsel, Master Bramble, my mind runs so of Cuckold's Haven tonight, that my head runs over with admiration.

BRAMBLE. [*Aside*] But is not that your wife, neighbour?

SECURITY. [*Aside*] No, by my troth, Master Bramble. Ha, ha, ha! A pox of all Cuckold's Havens, I say!

BRAMBLE. [*Aside*] O' my faith, her garments are exceeding like your wife's.

SECURITY. [*Aside*] *Cucullus non facit monachum,* my learned counsel; all are not cuckolds that seem so, nor all seem not that are so. Give me your hand, my learned counsel; you and I will sup somewhere else than at Sir Francis Drake's ship tonight. Adieu, my noble Gossip!

BRAMBLE. Good fortune, brave Captains; fair skies God send ye!

ALL. Farewell, my hearts, farewell!

PETRONEL. Gossip, laugh no more at Cuckold's Haven, Gossip.

SECURITY. I have done, I have done, sir. Will you lead, Master Bramble? Ha, ha, ha!   *Exit* [*with* BRAMBLE]

PETRONEL. Captain Seagull, charge a boat!

ALL. A boat, a boat, a boat!   *Exeunt*

DRAWER. Y'are in a proper taking, indeed, to take a boat, especially at this time of night, and against tide and tempest. They say yet, 'drunken men never take harm'. This night will try the truth of that proverb. *Exit*

[Act III, Scene iv

Outside SECURITY's House]

Enter SECURITY

SECURITY. What, Winnie? Wife, I say? Out of doors at this time! Where should I seek the gad-fly? Billingsgate, Billingsgate, Billingsgate! She's gone with the knight, she's gone with the knight! Woe be to thee, Billingsgate. A boat, a boat, a boat! A full hundred marks for a boat! *Exit*

Act IV, Scene i]

Enter SLITGUT, with a pair of ox-horns, discovering Cuckold's Haven, above [right]

SLITGUT. All hail, fair haven of married men only, for there are none but married men cuckolds! For my part, I presume not to arrive here, but in my master's behalf (a poor butcher of Eastcheap), who sends me to set up (in honour of Saint Luke) these necessary ensigns of his homage. And up I got this morning, thus early, to get up to the top of this famous tree, that is all fruit and no leaves, to advance this crest of my master's occupation. Up then; heaven and Saint Luke bless me, that I be not blown into the Thames as I climb, with this furious tempest. 'Slight, I think the devil be abroad, in likeness of a storm, to rob me of my horns! Hark how he roars! Lord, what a coil the Thames keeps! She bears some unjust burden, I believe, that she kicks and curvets thus to cast it. Heaven bless all honest passengers that are upon her back now; for the bit is out of her mouth, I see, and she will run away with 'em! So, so, I think I have made it look the right way; it runs against London Bridge, as it were, even full butt. And now, let me discover from this lofty prospect, what pranks the rude Thames plays in her desperate lunacy. O me, here's a boat has been cast away hard by! Alas, alas, see one

of her passengers, labouring for his life to land at this haven here!
Pray heaven he may recover it! His next land is even just under
me; hold out yet a little, whatsoever thou art: pray, and take a
good heart to thee. 'Tis a man; take a man's heart to thee; yet a
little further, get up o' thy legs, man; now 'tis shallow enough.
So, so, so! Alas, he's down again! Hold thy wind, father! 'Tis a
man in a night-cap. So! Now he's got up again; now he's past
the worst; yet, thanks be to heaven, he comes toward me pretty
and strongly.

Enter SECURITY *without his hat, in a nightcap, wet band, &c.*
[stage right]

SECURITY. Heaven, I beseech thee, how have I offended thee!
Where am I cast ashore now, that I may go a righter way home
by land? Let me see. O, I am scarce able to look about me! Where
is there any sea-mark that I am acquainted withal?
    SLITGUT. Look up, father; are you acquainted with this mark?
    SECURITY. What! Landed at Cuckold's Haven! Hell and dam-
nation! I will run back and drown myself.

He falls down

SLITGUT. Poor man, how weak he is! The weak water has
washed away his strength.
    SECURITY. Landed at Cuckold's Haven! If it had not been to
die twenty times alive, I should never have 'scaped death! I will
never arise more; I will grovel here and eat dirt till I be choked.
I will make the gentle earth do that which the cruel water has
denied me!
    SLITGUT. Alas, good father, be not so desperate! Rise, man; if
you will, I'll come presently and lead you home.
    SECURITY. Home! Shall I make any know my home, that has
known me thus abroad? How low shall I crouch away, that no
eye may see me? I will creep on the earth while I live, and never
look heaven in the face more.   *Exit creeping*
    SLITGUT. What young planet reigns now, trow, that old men
are so foolish? What desperate young swaggerer would have
been abroad such a weather as this upon the water? Ay me, see
another remnant of this unfortunate shipwreck, or some other!
A woman, i'faith, a woman! Though it be almost at Saint
Katherine's, I discern it to be a woman, for all her body is above
the water, and her clothes swim about her most handsomely.

O, they bear her up most bravely! Has not a woman reason to love the taking up of her clothes the better while she lives, for this? Alas, how busy the rude Thames is about her! A pox o' that wave! It will drown her, i'faith, 'twill drown her! Cry God mercy, she has 'scaped it, I thank heaven she has 'scaped it! O, how she swims like a mermaid! Some vigilant body look out and save her. That's well said; just where the priest fell in, there's one sets down a ladder, and goes to take her up. God's blessing o' thy heart, boy! Now, take her up in thy arms and to bed with her. She's up, she's up! She's a beautiful woman, I warrant her; the billows durst not devour her.

Enter the DRAWER *in the Tavern before, with* WINIFRED
[*stage left*]

DRAWER. How fare you now, lady?

WINIFRED. Much better, my good friend, than I wish; as one desperate of her fame, now my life is preserved.

DRAWER. Comfort yourself: that power that preserved you from death can likewise defend you from infamy, howsoever you deserve it. Were not you one that took boat late this night with a knight and other gentlemen at Billingsgate?

WINIFRED. Unhappy that I am, I was.

DRAWER. I am glad it was my good hap to come down thus far after you, to a house of my friend's here in St. Katherine's; since I am now happily made a mean to your rescue from the ruthless tempest, which (when you took boat) was so extreme, and the gentleman that brought you forth so desperate and unsober, that I feared long ere this I should hear of your shipwreck, and therefore (with little other reason) made thus far this way. And this I must tell you, since perhaps you may make use of it: there was left behind you at our tavern, brought by a porter (hired by the young gentleman that brought you) a gentlewoman's gown, hat, stockings, and shoes; which, if they be yours, and you please to shift you, taking a hard bed here in this house of my friend, I will presently go fetch you.

WINIFRED. Thanks, my good friend, for your more than good news. The gown with all things bound with it are mine; which if you please to fetch as you have promised, I will boldly receive the kind favour you have offered till your return; entreating you, by all the good you have done in preserving me hitherto, to let none take knowledge of what favour you do me, or where such a one as I am bestowed, lest you incur me much more damage in my fame than you have done me pleasure in preserving my life.

DRAWER. Come in, lady, and shift yourself; resolve that nothing but your own pleasure shall be used in your discovery.

WINIFRED. Thank you, good friend. The time may come, I shall requite you.   *Exeunt*

SLITGUT. See, see, see! I hold my life, there's some other a-taking up at Wapping now! Look, what a sort of people cluster about the gallows there! In good troth, it is so. O me, a fine young gentleman! What, and taken up at the gallows? Heaven grant he be not one day taken down there! O' my life, it is ominous! Well, he is delivered for the time. I see the people have all left him; yet will I keep my prospect awhile, to see if any more have been shipwrecked.

Enter QUICKSILVER, *bareheaded*

[*centre*]

QUICKSILVER. Accursed that ever I was saved or born!
How fatal is my sad arrival here!
As if the stars and Providence spake to me,
And said, 'The drift of all unlawful courses
(Whatever end they dare propose themselves
In frame of their licentious policies)
In the firm order of just Destiny,
They are the ready highways to our ruins'.
I know not what to do; my wicked hopes
Are, with this tempest, torn up by the roots!
O, which way shall I bend my desperate steps,
In which unsufferable shame and misery
Will not attend them? I will walk this bank
And see if I can meet the other relics
Of our poor, shipwrecked crew, or hear of them.
The knight—alas—was so far gone with wine,
And th'other three, that I refused their boat,
And took the hapless woman in another,
Who cannot but be sunk, whatever Fortune
Hath wrought upon the others' desperate lives.   *Exit*

Enter PETRONEL *and* SEAGULL, *bareheaded*

[*downstage, right*]

PETRONEL. Zounds, Captain! I tell thee, we are cast up o' the coast of France! 'Sfoot, I am not drunk still, I hope! Dost remember where we were last night?

SEAGULL. No, by my troth, Knight, not I. But methinks we have been a horrible while upon the water, and in the water.

PETRONEL. Ay me, we are undone for ever! Hast any money about thee?

SEAGULL. Not a penny, by heaven!

PETRONEL. Not a penny betwixt us, and cast ashore in France!

SEAGULL. Faith, I cannot tell that; my brains nor mine eyes are not mine own yet.

Enter TWO GENTLEMEN

PETRONEL. 'Sfoot, wilt not believe me? I know't by th'elevation of the pole, and by the altitude and latitude of the climate. See, here comes a couple of French gentlemen; I knew we were in France; dost thou think our Englishmen are so Frenchified that a man knows not whether he be in France or in England when he sees 'em? What shall we do? We must e'en to 'em, and entreat some relief of 'em. Life is sweet, and we have no other means to relieve our lives now, but their charities.

SEAGULL. Pray you, do you beg on 'em then; you can speak French.

PETRONEL. *Monsieur, plaist-il d'avoir pitié de nostre grand infortunes. Je suis un povre chevalier d'Angleterre qui a souffri l'infortune de naufrage.*

1 GENTLEMAN. *Un povre chevalier d'Angleterre?*

PETRONEL. *Oui, monsieur, il est trop vraye; mais vous scavés bien nous sommes toutes subject a fortune.*

2 GENTLEMAN. A poor knight of England? A poor knight of Windsor, are you not? Why speak you this broken French when y'are a whole Englishman? On what coast are you, think you?

PETRONEL. On the coast of France, sir.

1 GENTLEMAN. On the coast of Dogs, sir; y'are i'th' Isle o' Dogs, I tell you! I see y'ave been washed in the Thames here, and I believe ye were drowned in a tavern before, or else you would never have took boat in such a dawning as this was.

Farewell, farewell; we will not know you for shaming of you.—
I ken the man weel; he's one of my thirty-pound knights.

2 GENTLEMAN. No, no, this is he that stole his knighthood o'
the grand day for four pound, giving to a page all the money in's
purse, I wot well.

Exeunt [GENTLEMEN]

SEAGULL. Death, Colonel! I knew you were overshot!

PETRONEL. Sure, I think now, indeed, Captain Seagull, we
were something overshot.

Enter QUICKSILVER

What, my sweet Frank Quicksilver! Dost thou survive to rejoice
me? But what! Nobody at thy heels, Frank? Ay me, what is
become of poor Mistress Security?

QUICKSILVER. Faith, gone quite from her name, as she is from
her fame, I think; I left her to the mercy of the water.

SEAGULL. Let her go, let her go! Let us go to our ship at
Blackwall, and shift us.

PETRONEL. Nay, by my troth, let our clothes rot upon us, and
let us rot in them! Twenty to one our ship is attached by this
time! If we set her not under sail this last tide, I never looked for
any other. Woe, woe is me! What shall become of us? The last
money we could make, the greedy Thames has devoured, and if
our ship be attached, there is no hope can relieve us.

QUICKSILVER. 'Sfoot, Knight, what an unknightly faintness
transports thee! Let our ship sink, and all the world that's without
us be taken from us, I hope I have some tricks in this brain of
mine shall not let us perish.

SEAGULL. Well said, Frank, i' faith. O my nimble-spirited
Quicksilver! 'Fore God, would thou hadst been our colonel!

PETRONEL. I like his spirit rarely; but I see no means he has to
support that spirit.

QUICKSILVER. Go to, Knight! I have more means than thou
art aware of. I have not lived amongst goldsmiths and goldmak-
ers all this while, but I have learned something worthy of my
time with 'em. And not to let thee stink where thou stand'st,
Knight, I'll let thee know some of my skill presently.

SEAGULL. Do, good Frank, I beseech thee!

QUICKSILVER. I will blanch copper so cunningly that it shall
endure all proofs but the test: it shall endure malleation, it shall

have the ponderosity of Luna, and the tenacity of Luna, by no means friable.

PETRONEL. 'Slight, where learn'st thou these terms, trow?

QUICKSILVER. Tush, Knight, the terms of this art every ignorant quacksalver is perfect in. But I'll tell you how yourself shall blanch copper thus cunningly. Take arsenic, otherwise called realgar (which, indeed, is plain ratsbane); sublime 'em three or four times, then take the sublimate of this realgar, and put 'em into a glass, into *chymia,* and let 'em have a convenient decoction natural, four-and-twenty hours, and he will become perfectly fixed; then take this fixed powder, and project him upon well-purged copper, *et habebis magisterium.*

BOTH. Excellent Frank, let us hug thee!

QUICKSILVER. Nay, this I will do besides: I'll take you off twelvepence from every angel, with a kind of *aqua fortis,* and never deface any part of the image.

PETRONEL. But then it will want weight?

QUICKSILVER. You shall restore that thus: take your *sal achyme,* prepared, and your distilled urine, and let your angels lie in it but four-and-twenty hours, and they shall have their perfect weight again. Come on, now, I hope this is enough to put some spirit into the livers of you; I'll infuse more another time. We have saluted the proud air long enough with our bare sconces. Now will I have you to a wench's house of mine at London; there make shift to shift us, and after, take such fortunes as the stars shall assign us.

BOTH. Notable Frank, we will ever adore thee!   *Exeunt*

Enter DRAWER, *with* WINIFRED, *new-attired*
                                        [*stage left*]

WINIFRED. Now, sweet friend, you have brought me near enough your tavern, which I desired that I might with some colour be seen near, inquiring for my husband, who, I must tell you, stole thither last night with my wet gown we have left at your friend's—which, to continue your former honest kindness, let me pray you to keep close from the knowledge of any; and so, with all vow of your requital, let me now entreat you to leave me to my woman's wit, and fortune.

DRAWER. All shall be done you desire; and so, all the fortune you can wish for attend you!   *Exit* DRAWER

Enter SECURITY

SECURITY. I will once more to this unhappy tavern before I shift one rag of me more, that I may there know what is left behind, and what news of their passengers. I have bought me a hat and band with the little money I had about me, and made the streets a little leave staring at my night-cap.

WINIFRED. O my dear husband! Where have you been tonight? All night abroad at taverns? Rob me of my garments, and fare as one run away from me? Alas, is this seemly for a man of your credit, of your age, and affection to your wife?

SECURITY. What should I say? How miraculously sorts this! Was not I at home, and called thee last night?

WINIFRED. Yes, sir, the harmless sleep you broke, and my answer to you, would have witnessed it, if you had had the patience to have stayed and answered me: but your so sudden retreat made me imagine you were gone to Master Bramble's, and so rested patient and hopeful of your coming again, till this your unbelieved absence brought me abroad with no less than wonder, to seek you where the false knight had carried you.

SECURITY. Villain and monster that I was, how have I abused thee! I was suddenly gone indeed; for my sudden jealousy transferred me. I will say no more but this; dear wife, I suspected thee.

WINIFRED. Did you suspect me?

SECURITY. Talk not of it, I beseech thee; I am ashamed to imagine it. I will home, I will home; and every morning on my knees ask thee heartily forgiveness.   *Exeunt*

SLITGUT. Now will I descend my honourable prospect, the farthest seeing sea-mark of the world; no marvel, then, if I could see two miles about me. I hope the red tempest's anger be now overblown, which sure I think heaven sent as a punishment for profaning holy Saint Luke's memory with so ridiculous a custom. Thou dishonest satyr, farewell to honest married men; farewell to all sorts and degrees of thee! Farewell, thou horn of hunger, that call'st th'Inns o' Court to their manger! Farewell, thou horn of abundance, that adornest the headsmen of the commonwealth! Farewell, thou horn of direction, that is the city lanthorn! Farewell, thou horn of pleasure, the ensign of the huntsman! Farewell, thou horn of destiny, th'ensign of the married man! Farewell, thou horn tree, that bearest nothing but stone-fruit!   *Exit*

Act IV, Scene ii

[*A Room in* TOUCHSTONE's *House*]

Enter TOUCHSTONE

TOUCHSTONE. Ha, sirrah! Thinks my Knight adventurer we can no point of our compass? Do we not know north-north-east? north-east-and-by-east? east-and-by-north? nor plain eastward? Ha! Have we never heard of Virginia? Nor the Cavallaria? Nor the Colonaria? Can we discover no discoveries? Well, mine errant Sir Flash and my runagate Quicksilver, you may drink drunk, crack cans, hurl away a brown dozen of Monmouth caps or so, in sea ceremony to your *bon voyage*; but for reaching any coast save the coast of Kent or Essex, with this tide, or with this fleet, I'll be your warrant for a Gravesend toast. There's that gone afore will stay your admiral and vice-admiral and rear-admiral, were they all (as they are) but one pinnace and under sail, as well as a remora, doubt it not, and from this sconce, without either powder or shot. 'Work upon that now'! Nay, and you'll show tricks, we'll vie with you a little. My daughter, his lady, was sent eastward by land to a castle of his i' the air (in what region I know not) and, as I hear, was glad to take up her lodging in her coach, she and her two waiting-women (her maid and her mother), like three snails in a shell, and the coachman a-top on 'em, I think. Since they have all found the way back again by Weeping Cross; but I'll not see 'em. And for two on 'em, madam and her malkin, they are like to bite o' the bridle for William, as the poor horses have done all this while that hurried 'em, or else go graze o' the common. So should my Dame Touchstone, too; but she has been my cross these thirty years, and I'll now keep her, to fright away sprites, i' faith. I wonder I hear no news of my son Golding. He was sent for to the Guildhall this morning betimes, and I marvel at the matter. If I had not laid up comfort and hope in him, I should grow desperate of all.

Enter GOLDING

See, he is come i' my thought! How now, son? What news at the Court of Aldermen?

GOLDING. Troth, sir, an accident somewhat strange, else it hath little in it worth the reporting.

TOUCHSTONE. What? It is not borrowing of money, then?

GOLDING. No, sir; it hath pleased the worshipful commoners of the City to take me one i' their number at presentation of the inquest—

TOUCHSTONE. Ha!

GOLDING. And the alderman of the ward wherein I dwell to appoint me his deputy—

TOUCHSTONE. How!

GOLDING. In which place I have had an oath ministered me, since I went.

TOUCHSTONE. Now, my dear and happy son! Let me kiss thy new worship, and a little boast mine own happiness in thee. What a fortune was it (or rather my judgement, indeed) for me, first to see that in his disposition which a whole city so conspires to second! Ta'en into the livery of his company the first day of his freedom! Now (not a week married) chosen commoner and alderman's deputy in a day! Note but the reward of a thrifty course. The wonder of his time! Well, I will honour Master Alderman for this act (as becomes me) [*doffing his cap*] and shall think the better of the Common Council's wisdom and worship while I live, for thus meeting, or but coming after me, in the opinion of his desert. Forward, my sufficient son, and as this is the first, so esteem it the least step to that high and prime honour that expects thee.

GOLDING. Sir, as I was not ambitious of this, so I covet no higher place; it hath dignity enough, if it will but save me from contempt; and I had rather my bearing in this or any other office should add worth to it, than the place give the least opinion to me.

TOUCHSTONE. Excellently spoken! This modest answer of thine blushes, as if it said, I will wear scarlet shortly. Worshipful son! I cannot contain myself, I must tell thee: I hope to see thee one o' the monuments of our City, and reckoned among her worthies, to be remembered the same day with the Lady Ramsey and grave Gresham, when the famous fable of Whittington and his puss shall be forgotten, and thou and thy acts become the posies for hospitals; when thy name shall be written upon conduits, and thy deeds played i' thy lifetime by the best companies of actors, and be called their get-penny. This I divine; this I prophesy.

GOLDING. Sir, engage not your expectation farther than my abilities will answer. I, that know mine own strengths, fear 'em; and there is so seldom a loss in promising the least, that commonly it brings with it a welcome deceit. I have other news for you, sir.

TOUCHSTONE. None more welcome, I am sure!

GOLDING. They have their degree of welcome, I dare affirm. The colonel, and all his company, this morning putting forth drunk from Billingsgate, had like to have been cast away o' this side Greenwich; and (as I have intelligence, by a false brother) are come dropping to town like so many masterless men, i' their doublets and hose, without hat, or cloak, or any other—

TOUCHSTONE. A miracle! The justice of heaven! Where are they? Let's go presently and lay for 'em.

GOLDING. I have done that already, sir, both by constables, and other officers, who shall take 'em at their old Anchor, and with less tumult or suspicion than if yourself were seen in't, under colour of a great press that is now abroad, and they shall here be brought afore me.

TOUCHSTONE. Prudent and politic son! Disgrace 'em all that ever thou canst; their ship I have already arrested. How to my wish it falls out, that thou hast the place of a justicer upon 'em! I am partly glad of the injury done to me, that thou may'st punish it. Be severe i' thy place, like a new officer o' the first quarter, unreflected. You hear how our lady is come back with her train from the invisible castle?

GOLDING. No; where is she?

TOUCHSTONE. Within; but I ha' not seen her yet, nor her mother, who now begins to wish her daughter undubbed, they say, and that she had walked a foot-pace with her sister. Here they come; stand back.

[*Enter*] MISTRESS TOUCHSTONE, GERTRUDE, MILDRED, SINDEFY

God save your Ladyship, 'save your good Ladyship! Your Ladyship is welcome from your enchanted castle, so are your beauteous retinue. I hear your knight-errant is travelled on strange adventures. Surely, in my mind, your Ladyship 'hath fished fair and caught a frog', as the saying is.

MISTRESS TOUCHSTONE. Speak to your father, Madam, and kneel down.

GERTRUDE. Kneel? I hope I am not brought so low yet! Though my knight be run away, and has sold my land, I am a lady still!

TOUCHSTONE. Your Ladyship says true, Madam; and it is fitter, and a greater decorum, that I should curtsey to you that are a knight's wife, and a lady, than you be brought o' your knees to me, who am a poor cullion, and your father.

GERTRUDE. Law! My father knows his duty.

MISTRESS TOUCHSTONE. O child!

TOUCHSTONE. And therefore I do desire your Ladyship, my good Lady Flash, in all humility, to depart my obscure cottage, and return in quest of your bright and most transparent castle, 'however presently concealed to mortal eyes'. And as for one poor woman of your train here, I will take that order, she shall no longer be a charge unto you, nor help to spend your Ladyship; she shall stay at home with me, and not go abroad; not put you to the pawning of an odd coach-horse or three wheels, but take part with the Touchstone. If we lack, we will not complain to your Ladyship. And so, good Madam, with your damsel here, please you to let us see your straight backs, in equipage; for truly, here is no roost for such chickens as you are, or birds o' your feather, if it like your Ladyship.

GERTRUDE. Marry, fist o' your kindness! I thought as much. Come away, Sin. We shall soon get a fart from a dead man, as a farthing of courtesy here.

MILDRED. O good sister!

GERTRUDE. Sister, sir-reverence? Come away, I say, hunger drops out at his nose.

GOLDING. O Madam, 'fair words never hurt the tongue'.

GERTRUDE. How say you by that? You out with your gold-ends now!

MISTRESS TOUCHSTONE. Stay, Lady-daughter! Good husband!

TOUCHSTONE. Wife, no man loves his fetters, be they made of gold. I list not ha' my head fastened under my child's girdle; as she has brewed, so let her drink, o' God's name! She went wit-less to wedding, now she may go wisely a-begging. It's but hon-eymoon yet with her ladyship; she has coach-horses, apparel, jewels, yet left; she needs care for no friends, nor take knowledge of father, mother, brother, sister, or anybody. When those are pawned or spent, perhaps we shall return into the list of her acquaintance.

GERTRUDE. I scorn it, i'faith! Come, Sin!

MISTRESS TOUCHSTONE. O Madam, why do you provoke your father thus?

Exit GERTRUDE [*with* SINDEFY]

TOUCHSTONE. Nay, nay; e'en let pride go afore, shame will follow after, I warrant you. Come, why dost thou weep now? Thou art not the first good cow hast had an ill calf, I trust.

[*Exit* MISTRESS TOUCHSTONE *and*]

Enter CONSTABLE

What's the news with that fellow?

GOLDING. Sir, the knight and your man Quicksilver are without; will you ha' 'em brought in?

TOUCHSTONE. O, by any means!

[*Exit* CONSTABLE]

And, son, here's a chair; appear terrible unto 'em on the first interview. Let them behold the melancholy of a magistrate, and taste the fury of a citizen in office.

GOLDING. Why, sir, I can do nothing to 'em, except you charge 'em with somewhat.

TOUCHSTONE. I will charge 'em and recharge 'em, rather than authority should want foil to set it off.

[*Offers* GOLDING *a chair*]

GOLDING. No, good sir, I will not.

TOUCHSTONE. Son, it is your place, by any means!

GOLDING. Believe it, I will not, sir.

Enter KNIGHT PETRONEL, QUICKSILVER, CONSTABLE, OFFICERS

PETRONEL. How misfortune pursues us still in our misery!

QUICKSILVER. Would it had been my fortune to have been trussed up at Wapping, rather than ever ha' come here!

PETRONEL. Or mine to have famished in the island!

QUICKSILVER. Must Golding sit upon us?

CONSTABLE. You might carry an M. under your girdle to Master Deputy's worship.

GOLDING. What are those, Master Constable?

CONSTABLE. An't please your worship, a couple of masterless men I pressed for the Low Countries, sir.

GOLDING. Why do you not carry 'em to Bridewell, according to your order, they may be shipped away?

CONSTABLE. An't please your worship, one of 'em says he is a knight; and we thought good to show him to your worship, for our discharge.

GOLDING. Which is he?

CONSTABLE. This, sir!

GOLDING. And what's the other?

CONSTABLE. A knight's fellow, sir, an't please you.

GOLDING. What! A knight and his fellow thus accoutred? Where are their hats and feathers, their rapiers and their cloaks?

QUICKSILVER. O, they mock us!

CONSTABLE. Nay, truly, sir, they had cast both their feathers and hats too, before we see 'em. Here's all their furniture, an't please you, that we found. They say knights are now to be known without feathers, like cockerels by their spurs, sir.

GOLDING. What are their names, say they?

TOUCHSTONE. [*Aside*] Very well, this! He should not take knowledge of 'em in his place, indeed.

CONSTABLE. This is Sir Petronel Flash.

TOUCHSTONE. How!

CONSTABLE. And this, Francis Quicksilver.

TOUCHSTONE. Is't possible? I thought your worship had been gone for Virginia, sir. You are welcome home, sir. Your worship has made a quick return, it seems, and no doubt a good voyage. Nay, pray you be covered, sir. How did your biscuit hold out, sir? Methought I had seen this gentleman afore. Good Master Quicksilver, how a degree to the southward has changed you!

GOLDING. Do you know 'em, father?—forbear your offers a little, you shall be heard anon.

TOUCHSTONE. Yes, Master Deputy; I had a small venture with them in the voyage—a thing called a son-in-law, or so. Officers, you may let 'em stand alone, they will not run away; I'll give my word for them. A couple of very honest gentlemen! One of 'em was my prentice, Master Quicksilver here; and when he had two year to serve, kept his whore and his hunting nag, would play his hundred pound at gresco, or primero, as familiarly (and all o' my purse) as any bright piece of crimson on 'em all; had his changeable trunks of apparel standing at livery, with his mare, his chest of perfumed linen, and his bathing-tubs: which when I told him of, why he—he was a gentleman, and I a poor Cheapside groom! The remedy was, we must part. Since when, he hath had the gift of gathering up some small parcels of mine, to the value of five hundred pound, dispersed among my customers, to furnish this his Virginian venture; wherein this knight was the chief, Sir Flash—one that married a daughter of mine, ladyfied her, turned two thousand pounds' worth of good land of hers into cash within the first week, bought her a new gown and a coach, sent her to seek her fortune by land, whilst himself prepared for his fortune by sea; took in fresh flesh at Billingsgate, for his own diet, to serve him the whole voyage—the wife of a certain usurer, called Security, who hath been the broker for 'em in all this business. Please, Master Deputy, 'work upon that now'!

GOLDING. If my worshipful father have ended.

TOUCHSTONE. I have, it shall please Master Deputy.

GOLDING. Well then, under correction—

TOUCHSTONE. Now, son, come over 'em with some fine gird, as, thus: 'Knight, you shall be encountered', that is, had to the Counter, or, 'Quicksilver, I will put you in a crucible', or so—

GOLDING. Sir Petronel Flash, I am sorry to see such flashes as these proceed from a gentleman of your quality and rank; for mine own part, I could wish I could say I could not see them; but such is the misery of magistrates and men in place, that they must not wink at offenders. Take him aside: I will hear you anon, sir.

TOUCHSTONE. I like this well, yet; there's some grace i' the knight left—he cries!

GOLDING. Francis Quicksilver, would God thou hadst turned quacksalver, rather than run into these dissolute and lewd courses! It is great pity; thou art a proper young man, of an honest and clean face, somewhat near a good one (God hath done his part in thee); but thou hast made too much and been too proud of that face, with the rest of thy body; for maintenance of which in neat and garish attire (only to be looked upon by some light housewives) thou hast prodigally consumed much of thy master's estate; and being by him gently admonished, at several times, hast returned thyself haughty and rebellious in thine answers, thundering out uncivil comparisons, requiting all his kindness with a coarse and harsh behaviour, never returning thanks for any one benefit, but receiving all, as if they had been debts to thee and no courtesies. I must tell thee, Francis, these are manifest signs of an ill nature; and God doth often punish such pride and *outrecuidance* with scorn and infamy, which is the worst of misfortune. My worshipful father, what do you please to charge them withal? From the press I will free 'em, Master Constable.

CONSTABLE. Then I'll leave your worship, sir.

GOLDING. No, you may stay; there will be other matters against 'em.

TOUCHSTONE. Sir, I do charge this gallant, Master Quicksilver, on suspicion of felony; and the knight as being accessory in the receipt of my goods.

QUICKSILVER. O God, sir!

TOUCHSTONE. Hold thy peace, impudent varlet, hold thy peace! With what forehead or face dost thou offer to chop logic with me, having run such a race of riot as thou hast done? Does not the sight of this worshipful man's fortune and temper confound thee, that was thy younger fellow in household, and now come to have the place of a judge upon thee? Dost not observe this? Which of all thy gallants and gamesters, thy swearers and thy swaggerers, will come now to moan thy misfortune, or pity thy penury? They'll look out at a window, as thou rid'st in triumph to Tyburn, and cry, 'Yonder goes honest Frank, mad Quicksilver'! 'He was a free boon companion, when he had money', says one; 'Hang him, fool'! says another, 'he could not keep it when he had it'! 'A pox o' the cullion, his master', says a third, 'he has brought him to this'; when their pox of pleasure, and their piles of perdition, would have been better bestowed upon thee, that hast ventured for 'em with the best, and by the clew of thy knavery, brought thyself weeping to the cart of calamity.

QUICKSILVER. Worshipful master!

TOUCHSTONE. Offer not to speak, crocodile; I will not hear a sound come from thee. Thou hast learnt to whine at the play yonder. Master Deputy, pray you commit 'em both to safe custody, till I be able farther to charge 'em.

QUICKSILVER. O me, what an infortunate thing am I!

PETRONEL. Will you not take security, sir?

TOUCHSTONE. Yes, marry, will I, Sir Flash, if I can find him, and charge him as deep as the best on you. He has been the plotter of all this; he is your engineer, I hear. Master Deputy, you'll dispose of these? In the meantime, I'll to my Lord Mayor, and get his warrant to seize that serpent Security into my hands, and seal up both house and goods to the King's use or my satisfaction.

GOLDING. Officers, take 'em to the Counter.

QUICKSILVER. } O God!
PETRONEL.

TOUCHSTONE. Nay, on, on! You see the issue of your sloth. Of sloth cometh pleasure, of pleasure cometh riot, of riot comes whoring, of whoring comes spending, of spending comes want, of want comes theft, of theft comes hanging; and there is my Quicksilver fixed. *Exeunt*

Act V, Scene i

[GERTRUDE's Lodging]

GERTRUDE, SINDEFY

GERTRUDE. Ah, Sin! hast thou ever read i'the chronicle of any lady and her waiting-woman driven to that extremity that we are, Sin?

SINDEFY. Not I, truly, Madam; and if I had, it were but cold comfort should come out of books now.

GERTRUDE. Why, good faith, Sin, I could dine with a lamentable story now. *O hone, hone, o no nera,* &c. Canst thou tell ne'er a one, Sin?

SINDEFY. None but mine own, Madam, which is lamentable enough: first to be stolen from my friends, which were worshipful and of good accompt, by a prentice in the habit and disguise of a gentleman, and here brought up to London and promised marriage, and now likely to be forsaken, for he is in possibility to be hanged!

GERTRUDE. Nay, weep not, good Sin; my Petronel is in as good possibility as he. Thy miseries are nothing to mine, Sin; I was more than promised marriage, Sin; I had it, Sin, and was made a lady; and by a knight, Sin; which is now as good as no knight, Sin. And I was born in London, which is more than brought up, Sin; and already forsaken, which is past likelihood, Sin; and instead of land i' the country, all my knight's living lies i' the Counter, Sin; there's his castle now!

SINDEFY. Which he cannot be forced out of, Madam.

GERTRUDE. Yes, if he would live hungry a week or two. 'Hunger', they say, 'breaks stone walls'! But he is e'en well enough served, Sin, that so soon as ever he had got my hand to the sale of my inheritance, run away from me, and I had been his punk, God bless us! Would the Knight o' the Sun, or Palmerin of England, have used their ladies so, Sin? or Sir Lancelot? or Sir Tristram?

SINDEFY. I do not know, Madam.

GERTRUDE. Then thou know'st nothing, Sin. Thou art a fool, Sin. The knighthood nowadays are nothing like the knighthood of old time. They rid a-horseback; ours go a-foot. They were attended by their squires; ours by their lackeys. They went buckled in their armour; ours muffled in their cloaks. They travelled wildernesses and deserts; ours dare scarce walk the streets. They were still pressed to engage their honour; ours still ready to pawn their clothes. They would gallop on at sight of a monster; ours run away at sight of a sergeant. They would help poor ladies; ours make poor ladies.

SINDEFY. Ay, Madam, they were Knights of the Round Table at Winchester, that sought adventures; but these of the Square Table at ordinaries, that sit at hazard—

GERTRUDE. True, Sin, let him vanish. And tell me, what shall we pawn next?

SINDEFY. Ay, marry, Madam, a timely consideration; for our hostess (profane woman!) has sworn by bread and salt, she will not trust us another meal.

GERTRUDE. Let it stink in her hand then! I'll not be beholding to her. Let me see: my jewels be gone, and my gowns, and my red velvet petticoat that I was married in, and my wedding silk stockings, and all thy best apparel, poor Sin! Good faith, rather than thou shouldst pawn a rag more, I'd lay my Ladyship in lavender—if I knew where.

SINDEFY. Alas, Madam, your Ladyship?

GERTRUDE. Ay, why? You do not scorn my Ladyship, though it is in a waistcoat? God's my life, you are a peat indeed! Do I offer to mortgage my Ladyship, for you and for your avail, and do you turn the lip and the alas to my Ladyship?

SINDEFY. No, Madam; but I make question who will lend anything upon it?

GERTRUDE. Who? Marry, enow, I warrant you, if you'll seek 'em out. I'm sure I remember the time when I would ha' given a thousand pound (if I had had it) to have been a lady; and I hope I was not bred and born with that appetite alone: some other gentleborn o' the City have the same longing, I trust. And for my part, I would afford 'em a penny'rth; my Ladyship is little the worse for the wearing, and yet I would bate a good deal of the sum. I would lend it (let me see) for forty pound in hand, Sin— that would apparel us—and ten pound a year. That would keep

me and you, Sin (with our needles)—and we should never need
to be beholding to our scurvy parents! Good Lord, that there are
no fairies nowadays, Sin!

SINDEFY. Why, Madam?

GERTRUDE. To do miracles, and bring ladies money. Sure, if
we lay in a cleanly house, they would haunt it, Sin? I'll try. I'll
sweep the chamber soon at night, and set a dish of water o' the
hearth. A fairy may come, and bring a pearl or a diamond. We
do not know, Sin? Or, there may be a pot of gold hid o' the
backside, if we had tools to dig for't? Why may not we two rise
early i' the morning, Sin, afore anybody is up, and find a jewel
i' the streets worth a hundred pound? May not some great
court-lady, as she comes from revels at midnight, look out of
her coach as 'tis running, and lose such a jewel, and we find
it? Ha?

SINDEFY. They are pretty waking dreams, these.

GERTRUDE. Or may not some old usurer be drunk overnight,
with a bag of money, and leave it behind him on a stall? For
God-sake, Sin, let's rise tomorrow by break of day, and see! I
protest, law! if I had as much money as an alderman, I would
scatter some of it i' the streets for poor ladies to find, when their
knights were laid up. And now I remember my song o' the
Golden Shower, why may not I have such a fortune? I'll sing it,
and try what luck I shall have after it.

[*Sings*]

> Fond fables tell of old
> How Jove in Danaë's lap
> Fell in a shower of gold,
> By which she caught a clap;
> O had it been my hap
>
> (*How e'er the blow doth threaten*)
> So well I like the play,
> That I could wish all day
> And night to be so beaten.

Enter MISTRESS TOUCHSTONE

O here's my mother! Good luck, I hope. Ha' you brought any
money, mother? Pray you, mother, your blessing. Nay, sweet
mother, do not weep.

MISTRESS TOUCHSTONE. God bless you! I would I were in my grave!

GERTRUDE. Nay, dear mother, can you steal no more money from my father? Dry your eyes, and comfort me. Alas, it is my knight's fault, and not mine, that I am in a waistcoat, and attired thus simply.

MISTRESS TOUCHSTONE. Simply? 'Tis better than thou deserv'st. Never whimper for the matter. 'Thou shouldst have looked before thou hadst leaped'. Thou wert afire to be lady, and now your Ladyship and you may both blow at the coal, for aught I know. 'Self do, self have'. 'The hasty person never wants woe', they say.

GERTRUDE. Nay, then, mother, you should ha' looked to it. A body would think you were the older; I did but my kind, I. He was a knight, and I was fit to be a lady. 'Tis not lack of liking, but lack of living, that severs us. And you talk like yourself and a cittiner in this, i' faith. You show what husband you come on, I wis: you smell o'the Touchstone—he that will do more for his daughter that he has married [to] a scurvy gold-end man, and his prentice, than he will for his tother daughter, that has wedded a knight, and his customer. By this light, I think he is not my legitimate father.

SINDEFY. O good Madam, do not take up your mother so!

MISTRESS TOUCHSTONE. Nay, nay, let her e'en alone! Let her Ladyship grieve me still, with her bitter taunts and terms. I have not dole enough to see her in this miserable case, I, without her velvet gowns, without ribands, without jewels, without French wires, or cheat-bread, or quails, or a little dog, or a gentleman-usher, or anything, indeed, that's fit for a lady—

SINDEFY. [*Aside*] Except her tongue.

MISTRESS TOUCHSTONE. And I not able to relieve her, neither, being kept so short by my husband. Well, God knows my heart. I did little think that ever she should have had need of her sister Golding.

GERTRUDE. Why, mother, I ha' not yet. Alas, good mother, be not intoxicate for me; I am well enough. I would not change husbands with my sister, I. 'The leg of a lark is better than the body of a kite'.

MISTRESS TOUCHSTONE. I know that, but—

GERTRUDE. What, sweet mother, what?

MISTRESS TOUCHSTONE. It's but ill food when nothing's left but the claw.

GERTRUDE. That's true, mother. Ay me!

MISTRESS TOUCHSTONE. Nay, sweet lady-bird, sigh not! Child, Madam, why do you weep thus? Be of good cheer; I shall die, if you cry and mar your complexion thus.

GERTRUDE. Alas, mother, what should I do?

MISTRESS TOUCHSTONE. Go to thy sister's, child; she'll be proud thy Ladyship will come under her roof. She'll win thy father to release thy knight, and redeem thy gowns and thy coach and thy horses, and set thee up again.

GERTRUDE. But will she get him to set my knight up too?

MISTRESS TOUCHSTONE. That she will, or anything else thou'lt ask her.

GERTRUDE. I will begin to love her, if I thought she would do this.

MISTRESS TOUCHSTONE. Try her, good chuck, I warrant thee.

GERTRUDE. Dost thou think she'll do't?

SINDEFY. Ay, Madam, and be glad you will receive it.

MISTRESS TOUCHSTONE. That's a good maiden; she tells you true. Come, I'll take order for your debts i' the ale-house.

GERTRUDE. Go, Sin, and pray for thy Frank, as I will for my Pet.   [*Exeunt*]

[*Act V, Scene ii*

Goldsmith's Row]

Enter TOUCHSTONE, GOLDING, WOLF

TOUCHSTONE. I will receive no letters, Master Wolf; you shall pardon me.

GOLDING. Good father, let me entreat you.

TOUCHSTONE. Son Golding, I will not be tempted; I find mine own easy nature, and I know not what a well-penned subtle letter may work upon it; there may be tricks, packing, do you see? Return with your packet, sir.

WOLF. Believe it, sir, you need fear no packing here; these are but letters of submission, all.

TOUCHSTONE. Sir, I do look for no submission. I will bear myself in this like blind Justice. 'Work upon that now'! When the Sessions come, they shall hear from me.

GOLDING. From whom come your letters, Master Wolf?

WOLF. An't please you, sir, one from Sir Petronel, another from Francis Quicksilver, and a third from old Security, who is almost mad in prison. There are two to your worship; one from Master Francis, sir, another from the knight.

TOUCHSTONE. I do wonder, Master Wolf, why you should travail thus in a business so contrary to kind or the nature o' your place! That you, being the keeper of a prison, should labour the release of your prisoners! Whereas, methinks, it were far more natural and kindly in you to be ranging about for more, and not let these 'scape you have already under the tooth. But they say, you wolves, when you ha' sucked the blood once, that they are dry, you ha' done.

WOLF. Sir, your worship may descant as you please o' my name; but I protest I was never so mortified with any men's discourse or behaviour in prison; yet I have had of all sorts of men i' the kingdom under my keys, and almost of all religions i' the land, as: Papist, Protestant, Puritan, Brownist, Anabaptist, Millenary, Family-o'-Love, Jew, Turk, Infidel, Atheist, Good Fellow, &c.

GOLDING. And which of all these, thinks Master Wolf, was the best religion?

WOLF. Troth, Master Deputy, they that pay fees best: we never examine their consciences farder.

GOLDING. I believe you, Master Wolf. Good faith, sir, here's a great deal of humility i' these letters.

WOLF. Humility, sir? Ay, were your worship an eye-witness of it, you would say so. The knight will i' the Knight's Ward, do what we can sir; and Master Quicksilver would be i' the Hole if we would let him. I never knew or saw prisoners more penitent, or more devout. They will sit you up all night singing of psalms and edifying the whole prison. Only Security sings a note too high sometimes, because he lies i' the two-penny ward, far off, and cannot take his tune. The neighbours cannot rest for him, but come every morning to ask what godly prisoners we have.

TOUCHSTONE. Which on 'em is't is so devout—the knight, or the tother?

WOLF. Both, sir; but the young man especially! I never heard his like! He has cut his hair too. He is so well given, and has such good gifts. He can tell you almost all the stories of the Book of Martyrs, and speak you all the Sick Man's Salve, without book.

TOUCHSTONE. Ay, if he had had grace—he was brought up where it grew, I wis. On, Master Wolf!

WOLF. And he has converted one Fangs, a sergeant, a fellow could neither write nor read, he was called the Bandog o' the Counter; and he has brought him already to pare his nails, and say his prayers; and 'tis hoped he will sell his place shortly, and become an intelligencer.

TOUCHSTONE. No more; I am coming already. If I should give any farther ear, I were taken. Adieu, good Master Wolf! Son, I do feel mine own weaknesses; do not importune me. Pity is a rheum that I am subject to; but I will resist it. Master Wolf, 'fish is cast away that is cast in dry pools'. Tell Hypocrisy it will not do; I have touched and tried too often; I am yet proof, and I will remain so; when the Sessions come, they shall hear from me. In the meantime, to all suits, to all entreaties, to all letters, to all tricks, I will be deaf as an adder, and blind as a beetle, lay mine ear to the ground, and lock mine eyes i' my hand against all temptations. *Exit*

GOLDING. You see, Master Wolf, how inexorable he is. There is no hope to recover him. Pray you commend me to my brother knight, and to my fellow Francis; present 'em with this small token of my love [*Giving money*]. Tell 'em, I wish I could do 'em any worthier office; but in this, 'tis desperate; yet I will not fail to try the uttermost of my power for 'em. And, sir, as far as I have any credit with you, pray you let 'em want nothing; though I am not ambitious, they should know so much.

WOLF. Sir, both your actions and words speak you to be a true gentleman. They shall know only what is fit, and no more.

Exeunt

[*Act V, Scene iii*

The Counter]

HOLDFAST, BRAMBLE

HOLDFAST. Who would you speak with, sir?

BRAMBLE. I would speak with one Security, that is prisoner here.

HOLDFAST. You are welcome, sir! Stay there, I'll call him to you. Master Security!

SECURITY. [*At the grate*] Who calls?

HOLDFAST. Here's a gentleman would speak with you.

SECURITY. What is he? Is't one that grafts my forehead now I am in prison, and comes to see how the horns shoot up and prosper?

HOLDFAST. You must pardon him, sir; the old man is a little crazed with his imprisonment.

SECURITY. What say you to me, sir? Look you here. My learned counsel, Master Bramble! Cry you mercy, sir! When saw you my wife?

BRAMBLE. She is now at my house, sir; and desired me that I would come to visit you, and inquire of you your case, that we might work some means to get you forth.

SECURITY. My case, Master Bramble, is stone walls and iron grates; you see it, this is the weakest part on't. And, for getting me forth, no means but hang myself, and so to be carried forth, from which they have here bound me in intolerable bands.

BRAMBLE. Why, but what is't you are in for, sir?

SECURITY. For my sins, for my sins, sir, whereof marriage is the greatest! O, had I never married, I had never known this purgatory, to which hell is a kind of cool bath in respect. My wife's confederacy, sir, with old Touchstone, that she might keep her jubilee and the feast of her new moon. Do you understand me, sir?

Enter QUICKSILVER

QUICKSILVER. Good sir, go in and talk with him. The light does him harm, and his example will be hurtful to the weak prisoners. Fie, Father Security, that you'll be still so profane! Will nothing humble you? [*Exeunt*]

Enter TWO PRISONERS *with a* FRIEND

FRIEND. What's he?

1 PRISONER. O, he is a rare young man! Do you not know him?

FRIEND. Not I! I never saw him, I can remember.

2 PRISONER. Why, it is he that was the gallant prentice of London—Master Touchstone's man.

FRIEND. Who, Quicksilver?

1 PRISONER. Ay, this is he.

FRIEND. Is this he? They say he has been a gallant indeed.

1 PRISONER. O' the royalest fellow that ever was bred up i' the city! He would play you his thousand pound a night at dice; keep knights and lords company; go with them to bawdy-houses; and his six men in a livery; kept a stable of hunting-horses, and his wench in her velvet gown and her cloth of silver. Here's one knight with him here in prison.

FRIEND. And how miserably he is changed!

1 PRISONER. O, that's voluntary in him: he gave away all his rich clothes as soon as ever he came in here among the prisoners; and will eat o' the basket, for humility.

FRIEND. Why will he do so?

1 PRISONER. Alas, he has no hope of life! He mortifies himself. He does but linger on till the Sessions.

2 PRISONER. O, he has penned the best thing, that he calls his 'Repentance' or his 'Last Farewell', that ever you heard. He is a pretty poet, and for prose—you would wonder how many prisoners he has helped out, with penning petitions for 'em, and not take a penny. Look! This is the knight, in the rug gown. Stand by!

Enter PETRONEL, BRAMBLE, QUICKSILVER

BRAMBLE. Sir, for Security's case, I have told him. Say he should be condemned to be carted or whipped for a bawd, or so; why, I'll lay an execution on him o' two hundred pound; let him acknowledge a judgement, he shall do it in half an hour; they shall not all fetch him out without paying the execution, o' my word.

PETRONEL. But can we not be bailed, Master Bramble?

BRAMBLE. Hardly; there are none of the judges in town, else you should remove yourself (in spite of him) with a *habeas corpus*. But if you have a friend to deliver your tale sensibly to some justice o' the town, that he may have feeling of it (do you see) you may be bailed; for as I understand the case, 'tis only done *in terrorem*; and you shall have an action of false imprisonment against him when you come out, and perhaps a thousand pound costs.

Enter MASTER WOLF

QUICKSILVER. How now, Master Wolf? What news? What return?

WOLF. Faith, bad all! Yonder will be no letters received. He says the Sessions shall determine it. Only Master Deputy Golding commends him to you, and with this token wishes he could do you other good.

[*Gives money*]

QUICKSILVER. I thank him. Good Master Bramble, trouble our quiet no more; do not molest us in prison thus with your winding devices. Pray you, depart. For my part, I commit my cause to him that can succour me; let God work his will. Master Wolf, I pray you let this be distributed among the prisoners, and desire 'em to pray for us.

WOLF. It shall be done, Master Francis.

[*Exit* QUICKSILVER]

1 PRISONER. An excellent temper!

2 PRISONER. Now God send him good luck!

Exeunt [BRAMBLE, TWO PRISONERS, *and* FRIEND]

PETRONEL. But what said my father-in-law, Master Wolf?

Enter HOLDFAST

HOLDFAST. Here's one would speak with you, sir.

WOLF. I'll tell you anon, Sir Petronel. Who is't?

HOLDFAST. A gentleman, sir, that will not be seen.

Enter GOLDING

WOLF. Where is he? Master Deputy! Your worship is welcome—

GOLDING. Peace!

WOLF. Away, sirrah!

[*Exit* HOLDFAST *with* SIR PETRONEL]

GOLDING. Good faith, Master Wolf, the estate of these gentlemen, for whom you were so late and willing a suitor, doth much affect me; and because I am desirous to do them some fair office, and find there is no means to make my father relent so likely as to bring him to be a spectator of their miseries, I have ventured on a device, which is, to make myself your prisoner, entreating you will presently go report it to my father, and (feigning an action, at suit of some third person) pray him by this token [*Giving a ring*], that he will presently, and with all secrecy, come hither for my bail; which train, if any, I know will bring him abroad; and then, having him here, I doubt not but we shall be all fortunate in the event.

WOLF. Sir, I will put on my best speed to effect it. Please you, come in.

GOLDING. Yes; and let me rest concealed, I pray you.

WOLF. See here a benefit truly done, when it is done timely, freely, and to no ambition.   *Exit* [*with* GOLDING]

[*Act V, Scene iv*

A Room in TOUCHSTONE'S House]

Enter TOUCHSTONE, WIFE, DAUGHTERS, SINDEFY, WINIFRED

TOUCHSTONE. I will sail by you and not hear you, like the wise Ulysses.

MILDRED. Dear father!

MISTRESS TOUCHSTONE. Husband!

GERTRUDE. Father!

WINIFRED. }
SINDEFY.   } Master Touchstone!

TOUCHSTONE. Away, sirens, I will immure myself against your cries, and lock myself up to your lamentations.

MISTRESS TOUCHSTONE. Gentle husband, hear me!

GERTRUDE. Father, it is I, father, my Lady Flash. My sister and I am friends.

MILDRED. Good father!

WINIFRED. Be not hardened, good Master Touchstone!

SINDEFY. I pray you, sir, be merciful!

TOUCHSTONE. I am deaf, I do not hear you. I have stopped mine ears with shoemakers' wax, and drunk Lethe and mandragora to forget you. All you speak to me I commit to the air.

Enter WOLF

MILDRED. How now, Master Wolf?

WOLF. Where's Master Touchstone? I must speak with him presently—I have lost my breath for haste.

MILDRED. What's the matter, sir? Pray all be well!

WOLF. Master Deputy Golding is arrested upon an execution, and desires him presently to come to him, forthwith.

MILDRED. Ay me! Do you hear, father?

TOUCHSTONE. Tricks, tricks, confederacy, tricks! I have 'em in my nose—I scent 'em!

WOLF. Who's that? Master Touchstone?

MISTRESS TOUCHSTONE. Why, it is Master Wolf himself, husband.

MILDRED. Father!

TOUCHSTONE. I am deaf still, I say. I will neither yield to the song of the siren, nor the voice of the hyena, the tears of the crocodile, nor the howling o' the wolf. Avoid my habitation, monsters!

WOLF. Why, you are not mad, sir? I pray you, look forth, and see the token I have brought you, sir.

TOUCHSTONE. Ha! What token is it?

WOLF. Do you know it, sir?

TOUCHSTONE. My son Golding's ring! Are you in earnest, Master Wolf?

WOLF. Ay, by my faith, sir! He is in prison, and required me to use all speed and secrecy to you.

TOUCHSTONE. My cloak, there! Pray you be patient. I am plagued for my austerity. My cloak! At whose suit, Master Wolf?

WOLF. I'll tell you as we go, sir.   *Exeunt*

[*Act V, Scene v*

The Counter]

Enter FRIEND, PRISONERS

FRIEND. Why, but is his offence such as he cannot hope of life?

1 PRISONER. Troth, it should seem so; and 'tis great pity, for he is exceeding penitent.

FRIEND. They say he is charged but on suspicion of felony, yet.

2 PRISONER. Ay, but his master is a shrewd fellow; he'll prove great matter against him.

FRIEND. I'd as lief as anything I could see his 'Farewell'.

1 PRISONER. O, 'tis rarely written; why, Toby may get him to sing it to you; he's not curious to anybody.

2 PRISONER. O no! He would that all the world should take knowledge of his 'Repentance', and thinks he merits in't, the more shame he suffers.

1 PRISONER. Pray thee, try what thou canst do.

2 PRISONER. I warrant you, he will not deny it, if he be not hoarse with the often repeating of it.   *Exit*

1 PRISONER. You never saw a more courteous creature than he is, and the knight too: the poorest prisoner of the house may command 'em. You shall hear a thing admirably penned.

FRIEND. Is the knight any scholar too?

1 PRISONER. No, but he will speak very well, and discourse admirably of running horses, and Whitefriars, and against bawds, and of cocks; and talk as loud as a hunter, but is none.

Enter WOLF *and* TOUCHSTONE

WOLF. Please you, stay here, sir: I'll call his worship down to you.   [*Exit*]

Enter [2ND PRISONER *with*] QUICKSILVER, PETRONEL [*and* SECURITY; GOLDING *with* WOLF, *who stands aside*]

1 PRISONER. See, he has brought him, and the knight too. Salute him, I pray. Sir, this gentleman, upon our report, is very desirous to hear some piece of your 'Repentance'.

QUICKSILVER. Sir, with all my heart; and, as I told Master Toby, I shall be glad to have any man a witness of it. And the more openly I profess it, I hope it will appear the heartier and the more unfeigned.

TOUCHSTONE. [*Aside*] Who is this? My man Francis, and my son-in-law?

QUICKSILVER. Sir, it is all the testimony I shall leave behind me to the world, and my master, that I have so offended.

FRIEND. Good sir!

QUICKSILVER. I writ it when my spirits were oppressed.

PETRONEL. Ay, I'll be sworn for you, Francis!

QUICKSILVER. It is in imitation of Mannington's: he that was hanged at Cambridge, that cut off the horse's head at a blow.

FRIEND. So, sir!

QUICKSILVER. To the tune of, 'I wail in woe, I plunge in pain'.

PETRONEL. An excellent ditty it is, and worthy of a new tune.

QUICKSILVER.

> *In Cheapside, famous for gold and plate,*
> *Quicksilver, I did dwell of late.*
> *I had a master good and kind,*
> *That would have wrought me to his mind.*
> *He bade me still, 'Work upon that',*
> *But, alas, I wrought I knew not what!*
> *He was a Touchstone black, but true,*
> *And told me still what would ensue;*
> *Yet, woe is me! I would not learn;*
> *I saw, alas, but could not discern!*

FRIEND. Excellent, excellent well!

GOLDING. [*Aside to* WOLF] O, let him alone; he is taken already.

QUICKSILVER.

> *I cast my coat and cap away,*
> *I went in silks and satins gay;*
> *False metal of good manners, I*
> *Did daily coin unlawfully.*
> *I scorned my master, being drunk;*
> *I kept my gelding and my punk;*
> *And with a knight, Sir Flash by name,*
> *(Who now is sorry for the same)—*

PETRONEL. I thank you, Francis!

QUICKSILVER.

> *I thought by sea to run away,*
> *But Thames and tempest did me stay.*

TOUCHSTONE. [*Aside*] This cannot be feigned, sure. Heaven pardon my severity! The ragged colt may prove a good horse.

GOLDING. [*Aside*] How he listens, and is transported! He has forgot me.

QUICKSILVER.

> Still Eastward Ho was all my word;
> But westward I had no regard,
> Nor never thought what would come after,
> As did, alas, his youngest daughter!
> At last the black ox trod o' my foot,
> And I saw then what 'longed unto't.
> Now cry I, 'Touchstone, touch me still,
> And make me current by thy skill'.

TOUCHSTONE. [*Aside*] And I will do it, Francis.

WOLF. [*Aside to* GOLDING] Stay him, Master Deputy; now is [not] the time; we shall lose the song else.

FRIEND. I protest, it is the best that ever I heard.

QUICKSILVER. How like you it, gentlemen?

ALL. O, admirable, sir!

QUICKSILVER. This stanze now following alludes to the story of Mannington, from whence I took my project for my invention.

FRIEND. Pray you, go on, sir.

QUICKSILVER.

> O Mannington, thy stories show,
> Thou cut'st a horse-head off at a blow!
> But I confess, I have not the force
> For to cut off the head of a horse;
> Yet I desire this grace to win,
> That I may cut off the horse-head of Sin,
> And leave his body in the dust
> Of Sin's highway and bogs of Lust,
> Whereby I may take Virtue's purse,
> And live with her for better, for worse.

FRIEND. Admirable, sir, and excellently conceited!

QUICKSILVER. Alas, sir!

TOUCHSTONE. [*Coming to* GOLDING *and* WOLF] Son Golding and Master Wolf, I thank you: the deceit is welcome, especially from thee, whose charitable soul in this hath shown a high point of wisdom and honesty. Listen! I am ravished with his 'Repentance', and could stand here a whole prenticeship to hear him.

FRIEND. Forth, good sir!

QUICKSILVER. This is the last, and the 'Farewell'.

> Farewell, Cheapside, farewell, sweet trade
> Of goldsmiths all, that never shall fade!

> *Farewell, dear fellow prentices all,*
> *And be you warned by my fall:*
> *Shun usurers, bawds, and dice, and drabs;*
> *Avoid them as you would French scabs.*
> *Seek not to go beyond your tether,*
> *But cut your thongs unto your leather;*
> *So shall you thrive by little and little,*
> *'Scape Tyburn, Counters, and the Spital!*

TOUCHSTONE. And scape them shalt thou, my penitent and dear Francis!

QUICKSILVER. Master!

PETRONEL. Father!

TOUCHSTONE. I can no longer forbear to do your humility right. Arise, and let me honour your 'Repentance' with the hearty and joyful embraces of a father and friend's love. Quicksilver, thou hast eat into my breast, Quicksilver, with the drops of thy sorrow, and killed the desperate opinion I had of thy reclaim.

QUICKSILVER. O, sir, I am not worthy to see your worshipful face!

PETRONEL. Forgive me, father!

TOUCHSTONE. Speak no more! All former passages are forgotten, and here my word shall release you. Thank this worthy brother and kind friend, Francis.—Master Wolf, I am their bail.

A shout in the prison

[SECURITY *appears at the grate*]

SECURITY. Master Touchstone! Master Touchstone!

TOUCHSTONE. Who's that?

WOLF. Security, sir.

SECURITY. Pray you, sir, if you'll be won with a song, hear my lamentable tune, too!

SONG

> *O Master Touchstone,*
> *My heart is full of woe!*
> *Alas, I am a cuckold;*
> *And why should it be so?*
> *Because I was a usurer,*
> *And bawd, as all you know,*

> *For which, again I tell you,*
> *My heart is full of woe.*

TOUCHSTONE. Bring him forth, Master Wolf, and release his bands. This day shall be sacred to Mercy and the mirth of this encounter in the Counter—see, we are encountered with more suitors!

Enter MISTRESS TOUCHSTONE, GERTRUDE, MILDRED, SINDEFY, WINIFRED, &c.

Save your breath, save your breath! All things have succeeded to your wishes, and we are heartily satisfied in their events.

GERTRUDE. Ah, runaway, runaway! Have I caught you? And how has my poor Knight done all this while?

PETRONEL. Dear Lady-wife, forgive me.

GERTRUDE. As heartily as I would be forgiven, Knight. Dear father, give me your blessing, and forgive me too. I ha' been proud and lascivious, father, and a fool, father; and being raised to the state of a wanton coy thing, called a lady, father, have scorned you, father, and my sister, and my sister's velvet cap, too; and would make a mouth at the City as I rid through it; and stop mine ears at Bow-bell. I have said your beard was a base one, father; and that you looked like Twierpipe the taborer; and that my mother was but my midwife.

MISTRESS TOUCHSTONE. Now God forgi' you, Child Madam!

TOUCHSTONE. No more repetitions! What is else wanting to make our harmony full?

GOLDING. Only this, sir: that my fellow Francis make amends to Mistress Sindefy with marriage.

QUICKSILVER. With all my heart!

GOLDING. And Security give her a dower, which shall be all the restitution he shall make of that huge mass he hath so unlawfully gotten.

TOUCHSTONE. Excellently devised! A good motion! What says Master Security?

SECURITY. I say anything, sir, what you'll ha' me say. Would I were no cuckold!

WINIFRED. Cuckold, husband? Why, I think this wearing of yellow has infected you.

TOUCHSTONE. Why, Master Security, that should rather be a comfort to you than a corrosive. If you be a cuckold, it's an argument you have a beautiful woman to your wife; then, you shall be much made of; you shall have store of friends; never want money; you shall be eased of much o' your wedlock pain: others will take it for you. Besides, you being a usurer, and likely to go to hell, the devils will never torment you; they'll take you for one o' their own race. Again, if you be a cuckold, and know it not, you are an innocent; if you know it and endure it, a true martyr.

SECURITY. I am resolved, sir. Come hither, Winny!

TOUCHSTONE. Well, then, all are pleased; or shall be anon. Master Wolf, you look hungry, methinks; have you no apparel to lend Francis to shift him?

QUICKSILVER. No, sir, nor I desire none; but here make it my suit, that I may go home through the streets in these, as a spectacle, or rather an example, to the children of Cheapside.

TOUCHSTONE. Thou hast thy wish. Now, London, look about,
And in this moral see thy glass run out:
Behold the careful father, thrifty son,
The solemn deeds which each of us have done;
The usurer punished, and from fall so steep
The prodigal child reclaimed, and the lost sheep.

EPILOGUE

[QUICKSILVER]. Stay, sir, I perceive the multitude are gathered together to view our coming out at the Counter. See, if the streets and the fronts of the houses be not stuck with people, and the windows filled with ladies, as on the solemn day of the Pageant!

O may you find in this our pageant, here,
The same contentment which you came to seek,
And as that show but draws you once a year,
May this attract you hither once a week.

[*Exeunt*]

FINIS

EPILOGUE

A TRICK TO CATCH
THE OLD ONE

Thomas Middleton

[DRAMATIS PERSONAE

THEODORUS WITGOOD
PECUNIOUS LUCRE, *his uncle, an old usurer*
WALKADINE HOARD, *another usurer*
ONESIPHORUS, *Walkadine's brother*
LIMBER ⎫
KIX ⎪
LAMPREY ⎬ *Hoard's friends*
SPITCHCOCK ⎭
HARRY DAMPIT ⎫
GULF ⎬ *usurers*
SAM FREEDOM, *Lucre's stepson*
MONEYLOVE
HOST
SIR LANCELOT
GEORGE, *Lucre's servant*
ARTHUR, *Hoard's servant*

COURTESAN, *Witgood's former mistress*
MISTRESS LUCRE
JOYCE, *Walkadine's* NIECE
LADY FOXSTONE
AUDREY, *Dampit's servant*

Creditors; Gentlemen; Servants; Drawers; Vintner; Sergeants;
Scrivener; Tailor; Barber; Perfumer; Huntsman; Falconer; Boy.

Scene: Leicestershire and London.]

[ACT ONE]

[*scene 1*]

Enter WITGOOD, *a gentleman, solus.*

WITGOOD. All's gone! Still thou'rt a gentleman, that's all; but a poor one, that's nothing. What milk brings thy meadows forth now? Where are thy goodly uplands and thy downlands? All sunk into that little pit, lechery. Why should a gallant pay but two shillings for his ord'nary that nourishes him, and twenty times two for his brothel that consumes him? But where's Long-acre? In my uncle's conscience, which is three years' voyage about. He that sets out upon his conscience ne'er finds the way home again; he is either swallowed in the quicksands of law-quillets or splits upon the piles of a *praemunire;* yet these old fox-brain'd and ox-brow'd uncles have still defences for their avarice and apologies for their practices and will thus greet our follies:

> He that doth his youth expose
> To brothel, drink, and danger,
> Let him that is his nearest kin
> Cheat him before a stranger.

And that's his uncle, 'tis a principle in usury. I dare not visit the City; there I should be too soon visited by that horrible plague, my debts, and by that means I lose a virgin's love, her portion, and her virtues. Well, how should a man live now that has no living? Hum? Why, are there not a million of men in the world that only sojourn upon their brain and make their wits their

279

mercers? And am I but one amongst that million and cannot thrive upon't? Any trick out of the compass of law now would come happily to me.

Enter COURTESAN.

COURTESAN. My love.

WITGOOD. My loathing! Hast thou been the secret consumption of my purse, and now com'st to undo my last means, my wits? Wilt leave no virtue in me, and yet thou ne'er the better? Hence, Courtesan, round-webb'd tarantula,
That driest the roses in the cheeks of youth.

COURTESAN. I have been true unto your pleasure, and all your lands thrice rack'd was never worth the jewel which I prodigally gave you, my virginity:
Lands mortgag'd may return, and more esteem'd,
But honesty once pawn'd is ne'er redeem'd.

WITGOOD. Forgive; I do thee wrong
To make thee sin and then to chide thee for't.

COURTESAN. I know I am your loathing now; farewell.

WITGOOD. Stay, best invention, stay.

COURTESAN. I that have been the secret consumption of your purse, shall I stay now to undo your last means, your wits? Hence, Courtesan, away!

WITGOOD. I prithee make me not mad at my own weapon; stay—a thing few women can do, I know that, and therefore they had need wear stays—be not contrary. Dost love me? Fate has so cast it that all my means I must derive from thee.

COURTESAN. From me? Be happy then;
What lies within the power of my performance
Shall be commanded of thee.

WITGOOD. Spoke like an honest drab, i'faith; it may prove something. What trick is not an embryon at first, until a perfect shape come over it?

COURTESAN. Come, I must help you. Whereabouts left you? I'll proceed.
Though you beget, 'tis I must help to breed.
Speak, what is't? I'd fain conceive it.

WITGOOD. So, so, so; thou shalt presently take the name and form upon thee of a rich country widow, four hundred a year valiant, in woods, in bullocks, in barns and in rye stacks. We'll to London and to my covetous uncle.

COURTESAN. I begin to applaud thee; our states being both desperate, they're soon resolute. But how for horses?

WITGOOD. Mass, that's true; the jest will be of some continuance. Let me see; horses now, a bots on 'em! Stay, I have acquaintance with a mad host, never yet bawd to thee; I have rins'd the whoreson's gums in mull-sack many a time and often; put but a good tale into his ear now so it come off cleanly, and there's horse and man for us, I dare warrant thee.

COURTESAN. Arm your wits then speedily; there shall want nothing in me, either in behaviour, discourse, or fashion, that shall discredit your intended purpose.
I will so artfully disguise my wants
And set so good a courage on my state
That I will be believed.

WITGOOD. Why, then, all's furnish'd; I shall go nigh to catch that old fox mine uncle. Though he make but some amends for my undoing, yet there's some comfort in't—he cannot otherwise choose, though it be but in hope to cozen me again, but supply any hasty want that I bring to town with me. The device well and cunningly carried, the name of a rich widow and four hundred a year in good earth will so conjure up a kind of usurer's love in him to me that he will not only desire my presence, which at first shall scarce be granted him—I'll keep off a' purpose—but I shall find him so officious to deserve, so ready to supply! I know the state of an old man's affection so well: if his nephew be poor indeed, why, he lets God alone with him; but if he be once rich, then he'll be the first man that helps him.

COURTESAN. 'Tis right the world; for in these days an old man's love to his kindred is like his kindness to his wife, 'tis always done before he comes at it.

WITGOOD. I owe thee for that jest. Begone; here's all my wealth. [*Gives money.*] Prepare thyself. Away! I'll to mine host with all possible haste, and, with the best art and most profitable form, pour the sweet circumstance into his ear, which shall have the gift to turn all the wax to honey.

[*Exit* COURTESAN.]

How now? O the right worshipful seniors of our country.

[*Enter* ONESIPHORUS, LIMBER *and* KIX.]

ONESIPHORUS. Who's that?

LIMBER. O the common rioter; take no note of him.

WITGOOD [*Aside*.]. You will not see me now; the comfort is
ere it be long you will scarce see yourselves.

[*Exit*.]

ONESIPHORUS. I wonder how he breathes; h'as consum'd all
upon that courtesan.

LIMBER. We have heard so much.

ONESIPHORUS. You have heard all truth. His uncle and my
brother have been these three years mortal adversaries. Two old
tough spirits, they seldom meet but fight, or quarrel when 'tis
calmest: I think their anger be the very fire that keeps their age
alive.

LIMBER. What was the quarrel, sir?

ONESIPHORUS. Faith, about a purchase, fetching over a young
heir. Master Hoard, my brother, having wasted much time in
beating the bargain, what did me old Lucre, but as his conscience
mov'd him, knowing the poor gentleman, stepp'd in between
'em and cozen'd him himself.

LIMBER. And was this all, sir?

ONESIPHORUS. This was e'en it, sir. Yet for all this, I know no
reason but the match might go forward betwixt his wife's son
and my niece. What though there be a dissension between the
two old men, I see no reason it should put a difference between
the two younger: 'tis as natural for old folks to fall out as for
young to fall in! A scholar comes a-wooing to my niece: well,
he's wise, but he's poor. Her son comes a-wooing to my niece:
well, he's a fool, but he's rich.

LIMBER. Ay, marry, sir.

ONESIPHORUS. Pray now, is not a rich fool better than a poor
philosopher?

LIMBER. One would think so, i'faith!

ONESIPHORUS. She now remains at London with my brother,
her second uncle, to learn fashions, practise music; the voice
between her lips, and the viol between her legs, she'll be fit for
a consort very speedily. A thousand good pound is her portion;
if she marry, we'll ride up and be merry.

KIX. A match, if it be a match!

Exeunt.

[scene 2]

Enter at one door, WITGOOD; *at the other,* HOST.

WITGOOD. Mine host?

HOST. Young Master Witgood.

WITGOOD. I have been laying all the town for thee.

HOST. Why, what's the news, Bully Had–land?

WITGOOD. What geldings are in the house, of thine own? Answer me to that first.

HOST. Why, man, why?

WITGOOD. Mark me what I say: I'll tell thee such a tale in thine ear that thou shalt trust me spite of thy teeth, furnish me with some money, willy-nilly, and ride up with me thyself *contra voluntatem et professionem.*

HOST. How? Let me see this trick, and I'll say thou hast more art than a conjurer.

WITGOOD. Dost thou joy in my advancement?

HOST. Do I love sack and ginger?

WITGOOD. Comes my prosperity desiredly to thee?

HOST. Come forfeitures to a usurer, fees to an officer, punks to an host, and pigs to a parson desiredly? Why, then, la!

WITGOOD. Will the report of a widow of four hundred a year, boy, make thee leap and sing and dance and come to thy place again?

HOST. Wilt thou command me now? I am thy spirit; conjure me into any shape.

WITGOOD. I ha' brought her from her friends, turn'd back the horses by a sleight; not so much as one amongst her six men, goodly large, yeomanly fellows, will she trust with this her purpose; by this light, all unmann'd, regardless of her state, neglectful of vainglorious ceremony, all for my love. O 'tis a fine little voluble tongue, mine host, that wins a widow.

HOST. No, 'tis a tongue with a great T, my boy, that wins a widow.

WITGOOD. Now, sir, the case stands thus: good mine host, if thou lov'st my happiness, assist me.

HOST. Command all my beasts i'th'house.

WITGOOD. Nay, that's not all neither; prithee, take truce with thy joy and listen to me. Thou know'st I have a wealthy uncle i'th'City, somewhat the wealthier by my follies; the report of this

fortune, well and cunningly carried, might be a means to draw
some goodness from the usuring rascal; for I have put her in hope
already of some estate that I have, either in land or money. Now
if I be found true in neither, what may I expect but a sudden
breach of our love, utter dissolution of the match, and confusion
of my fortunes for ever?

HOST. Wilt thou but trust the managing of thy business with
me?

WITGOOD. With thee? Why, will I desire to thrive in my
purpose? Will I hug four hundred a year? I that know the misery
of nothing? Will that man wish a rich widow, that has ne'er a
hole to put his head in? With thee, mine host? Why, believe it,
sooner with thee than with a covey of counsellors!

HOST. Thank you for your good report, i'faith, sir, and if I
stand you not in stead, why then let an host come off *hic et haec
hostis,* a deadly enemy to dice, drink, and venery. Come, where's
this widow?

WITGOOD. Hard at Park End.

HOST. I'll be her serving-man for once.

WITGOOD. Why, there we let off together, keep full time; my
thoughts were striking then just the same number.

HOST. I knew't. Shall we then see our merry days again?

WITGOOD. Our merry nights—which ne'er shall be more seen.

Exeunt.

[*scene 3*]

Enter at several doors old LUCRE *and old* [WALKADINE] HOARD,
Gentlemen [LAMPREY, SPITCHCOCK, SAM FREEDOM, *and*
MONEYLOVE] *coming between them to pacify 'em.*

LAMPREY. Nay, good Master Lucre, and you, Master Hoard,
anger is the wind which you're both too much troubled withal.

HOARD. Shall my adversary thus daily affront me, ripping up
the old wound of our malice, which three summers could not
close up? Into which wound the very sight of him drops scalding
lead instead of balsamum?

LUCRE. Why, Hoard, Hoard, Hoard, Hoard, Hoard! May I
not pass in the state of quietness to mine own house? Answer me
to that, before witness, and why? I'll refer the cause to honest,
even-minded gentlemen, or require the mere indifferences of the

law to decide this matter. I got the purchase, true; was't not any man's case? Yes. Will a wise man stand as a bawd, whilst another wipes his nose of the bargain? No, I answer, no, in that case.

LAMPREY. Nay, sweet Master Lucre.

HOARD. Was it the part of a friend? No, rather of a Jew. Mark what I say: when I had beaten the bush to the last bird, or, as I may term it, the price to a pound, then like a cunning usurer to come in the evening of the bargain and glean all my hopes in a minute; to enter, as it were, at the back door of the purchase, for thou ne'er cam'st the right way by it!

LUCRE. Hast thou the conscience to tell me so, without any impeachment to thyself?

HOARD. Thou that canst defeat thy own nephew, Lucre, lap his lands into bonds, and take the extremity of thy kindred's forfeitures because he's a rioter, a wastethrift, a brothel-master, and so forth—what may a stranger expect from thee but *vulnera dilacerata,* as the poet says, dilacerate dealing?

LUCRE. Upbraid'st thou me with 'nephew'? Is all imputation laid upon me? What acquaintance have I with his follies? If he riot, 'tis he must want it; if he surfeit, 'tis he must feel it; if he drab it, 'tis he must lie by't. What's this to me?

HOARD. What's all to thee? Nothing, nothing; such is the gulf of thy desire and the wolf of thy conscience; but be assured, old Pecunious Lucre, if ever fortune so bless me that I may be at leisure to vex thee, or any means so favour me that I may have opportunity to mad thee, I will pursue it with that flame of hate, that spirit of malice, unrepressed wrath, that I will blast thy comforts.

LUCRE. Ha, ha, ha!

LAMPREY. Nay, Master Hoard, you're a wise gentleman.

HOARD. I will so cross thee—

LUCRE. And I thee.

HOARD. So without mercy fret thee—

LUCRE. So monstrously oppose thee—

HOARD. Dost scoff at my just anger? O that I had as much power as usury has over thee!

LUCRE. Then thou wouldst have as much power as the Devil has over thee!

HOARD. Toad!

LUCRE. Aspic!

HOARD. Serpent!

LUCRE. Viper!

SPITCHCOCK. Nay, gentlemen, then we must divide you perforce.

LAMPREY. When the fire grows too unreasonable hot, there's no better way than to take off the wood.

> *Exeunt* [LAMPREY, SPITCHCOCK, LUCRE *and* HOARD].
> *Mane*[*n*]*t* SAM [FREEDOM] *and* MONEYLOVE.

SAM. A word, good signior.

MONEYLOVE. How now, what's the news?

SAM. 'Tis given me to understand that you are a rival of mine in the love of Mistress Joyce, Master Hoard's niece: say me ay, say me no.

MONEYLOVE. Yes, 'tis so.

SAM. Then look to yourself; you cannot live long. I'm practising every morning; a month hence I'll challenge you.

MONEYLOVE. Give me your hand upon't; there's my pledge I'll meet you!

> *Strikes him. Exit.*

SAM. O! O! What reason had you for that, sir, to strike before the month? You knew I was not ready for you, and that made you so crank. I am not such a coward to strike again, I warrant you; my ear has the law of her side, for it burns horribly. I will teach him to strike a naked face, the longest day of his life. 'Slid, it shall cost me some money, but I'll bring this box into the Chancery.

> *Exit.*

[scene 4]

> *Enter* WITGOOD *and the* HOST.

HOST. Fear you nothing, sir, I have lodg'd her in a house of credit, I warrant you.

WITGOOD. Hast thou the writings?

HOST. Firm, sir.

> [*Enter* DAMPIT *and* GULF, *who talk apart.*]

WITGOOD. Prithee, stay, and behold two the most prodigious rascals that ever slipp'd into the shape of men: Dampit, sirrah, and young Gulf, his fellow caterpillar.

Host. Dampit? Sure, I have heard of that Dampit.

Witgood. Heard of him? Why, man, he that has lost both his ears may hear of him; a famous infamous trampler of time; his own phrase. Note him well: that Dampit, sirrah, he in the uneven beard and the serge cloak, is the most notorious, usuring, blasphemous, atheistical, brothel-vomiting rascal that we have in these latter times now extant, whose first beginning was the stealing of a mastie dog from a farmer's house.

Host. He look'd as if he would obey the commandment well, when he began first with stealing.

Witgood. True. The next town he came at, he set the dogs together by th'ears.

Host. A sign he should follow the law, by my faith.

Witgood. So it followed, indeed; and being destitute of all fortunes, stak'd his mastie against a noble, and by great fortune his dog had the day. How he made it up ten shillings I know not, but his own boast is that he came to town with but ten shillings in his purse, and now is credibly worth ten thousand pound.

Host. How the Devil came he by it?

Witgood. How the Devil came he not by it? If you put in the Devil once, riches come with a vengeance. H'as been a trampler of the law, sir, and the Devil has a care of his footmen. The rogue has spied me now; he nibbled me finely once too; a pox search you.—O Master Dampit! [*Aside.*] The very loins of thee!—Cry you mercy, Master Gulf; you walk so low I promise you I saw you not, sir.

Gulf. He that walks low walks safe, the poets tell us.

Witgood [*Aside.*]. And nigher hell by a foot and a half than the rest of his fellows. [*To* Dampit.] But my old Harry!

Dampit. My sweet Theodorus!

Witgood. 'Twas a merry world when thou cam'st to town with ten shillings in thy purse.

Dampit. And now worth ten thousand pound, my boy. Report it: Harry Dampit, a trampler of time; say he would be up in a morning and be here with his serge gown, dash'd up to the hams in a cause, have his feet stink about Westminster Hall, and come home again; see the galleons, the galleasses, the great armadas of the law; then there be hoys and petty vessels, oars and scullers of the time; there be picklocks of the time too. Then would I be here, I would trample up and down like a mule: now to the judges, 'May it please your reverend, honourable fatherhoods';

then to my counsellor, 'May it please your worshipful patience';
then to the examiner's office, 'May it please your mastership's
gentleness'; then to one of the clerks, 'May it please your worshipful lousiness', for I find him scrubbing in his codpiece; then
to the hall again; then to the chamber again—

WITGOOD. And when to the cellar again?

DAMPIT. E'en when thou wilt again. Tramplers of time, motions
of Fleet Street, and visions of Holborn; here I have fees of one,
there I have fees of another; my clients come about me, the
fooliaminy and coxcombry of the country. I still trash'd and trot-
ted for other men's causes; thus was poor Harry Dampit made
rich by others' laziness, who, though they would not follow their
own suits, I made 'em follow me with their purses.

WITGOOD. Didst thou so, old Harry?

DAMPIT. Ay, and I sous'd 'em with bills of charges, i'faith;
twenty pound a year have I brought in for boat-hire, and I ne'er
stepp'd into boat in my life.

WITGOOD. Tramplers of time!

DAMPIT. Ay, tramplers of time, rascals of time, bull-beggars.

WITGOOD. Ah, thou'rt a mad old Harry! Kind Master Gulf, I
am bold to renew my acquaintance.

GULF. I embrace it, sir.

Music.

Exeunt.

ACT TWO

[scene 1]

Enter LUCRE.

LUCRE. My adversary ever more twits me with my nephew,
forsooth, my nephew; why may not a virtuous uncle have a
dissolute nephew? What though he be a brotheller, a wastethrift,
a common surfeiter, and, to conclude, a beggar? Must sin in
him call up shame in me? Since we have no part in their follies,
why should we have part in their infamies? For my strict hand
towards his mortgage, that I deny not; I confess I had an uncle's

pen'worth. Let me see, half in half, true. I saw neither hope of his reclaiming nor comfort in his being, and was it not then better bestow'd upon his uncle than upon one of his aunts? I need not say 'bawd', for everyone knows what 'aunt' stands for in the last translation.

[*Enter* Servant.]

Now, sir?

SERVANT. There's a country serving-man, sir, attends to speak with your worship.

LUCRE. I'm at best leisure now; send him in to me.

[*Exit* Servant.]

Enter HOST, *like a serving-man.*

HOST. Bless your venerable worship.

LUCRE. Welcome, good fellow.

HOST [*Aside*.]. He calls me thief at first sight, yet he little thinks I am an host.

LUCRE. What's thy business with me?

HOST. Faith, sir, I am sent from my mistress to any sufficient gentleman indeed, to ask advice upon a doubtful point. 'Tis indifferent, sir, to whom I come, for I know none, nor did my mistress direct me to any particular man, for she's as mere a stranger here as myself; only I found your worship within, and 'tis a thing I ever lov'd, sir, to be dispatch'd as soon as I can.

LUCRE [*Aside*.]. A good blunt honesty; I like him well.—What is thy mistress?

HOST. Faith, a country gentlewoman, and a widow, sir. Yesterday was the first flight of us, but now she intends to stay until a little Term business be ended.

LUCRE. Her name, I prithee.

HOST. It runs there in the writings, sir, among her lands: Widow Medler.

LUCRE. Medler? Mass, have I ne'er heard of that widow?

HOST. Yes, I warrant you, have you, sir; not the rich widow in Staffordshire?

LUCRE. Cuds me, there 'tis indeed. Thou hast put me into memory; there's a widow indeed! Ah, that I were a bachelor again!

HOST. No doubt your worship might do much then, but she's fairly promis'd to a bachelor already.

LUCRE. Ah, what is he, I prithee?

HOST. A country gentleman too, one whom your worship knows not, I'm sure; h'as spent some few follies in his youth, but marriage, by my faith, begins to call him home; my mistress loves him, sir, and love covers faults, you know. One Master Witgood, if ever you have heard of the gentleman.

LUCRE. Ha? Witgood, say'st thou?

HOST. That's his name indeed, sir. My mistress is like to bring him to a goodly seat yonder; four hundred a year, by my faith.

LUCRE. But, I pray, take me with you.

HOST. Ay, sir.

LUCRE. What countryman might this young Witgood be?

HOST. A Leicestershire gentleman, sir.

LUCRE [*Aside.*]. My nephew, by th'mass, my nephew! I'll fetch out more of this, i'faith; a simple country fellow, I'll work't out of him. [*To* HOST.] And is that gentleman, say'st thou, presently to marry her?

HOST. Faith, he brought her up to town, sir; h'as the best card in all the bunch for't, her heart; and I know my mistress will be married ere she go down. Nay, I'll swear that, for she's none of those widows that will go down first and be married after; she hates that, I can tell you, sir.

LUCRE. By my faith, sir, she is like to have a proper gentleman and a comely; I'll give her that gift!

HOST. Why, does your worship know him, sir?

LUCRE. I know him! Does not all the world know him? Can a man of such exquisite qualities be hid under a bushel?

HOST. Then your worship may save me a labour, for I had charge given me to inquire after him.

LUCRE. Inquire of him? If I might counsel thee, thou shouldst ne'er trouble thyself further; inquire of him of no more but of me; I'll fit thee! I grant he has been youthful, but is he not now reclaim'd? Mark you that, sir; has not your mistress, think you, been wanton in her youth? If men be wags, are there no women wagtails?

HOST. No doubt, sir.

LUCRE. Does not he return wisest, that comes home whipp'd with his own follies?

HOST. Why, very true, sir.

LUCRE. The worst report you can hear of him, I can tell you, is that he has been a kind gentleman, a liberal, and a worthy; who but lusty Witgood, thrice-noble Witgood!

HOST. Since your worship has so much knowledge in him, can you resolve me, sir, what his living might be? My duty binds me, sir, to have a care of my mistress' estate; she has been ever a good mistress to me, though I say it. Many wealthy suitors has she nonsuited for his sake; yet, though her love be so fix'd, a man cannot tell whether his nonperformance may help to remove it, sir. He makes us believe he has lands and living.

LUCRE. Who, young Master Witgood? Why believe it, he has as goodly a fine living out yonder—what do you call the place?

HOST. Nay, I know not, i'faith.

LUCRE. Hum—see, like a beast, if I have not forgot the name— puh! And out yonder again, goodly grown woods and fair meadows—pax on't, I can ne'er hit of that place neither. He? Why, he's Witgood of Witgood Hall; he, an unknown thing?

HOST. Is he so, sir? To see how rumour will alter! Trust me, sir, we heard once he had no lands, but all lay mortgag'd to an uncle he has in town here.

LUCRE. Push! 'Tis a tale, 'tis a tale.

HOST. I can assure you, sir, 'twas credibly reported to my mistress.

LUCRE. Why, do you think, i'faith, he was ever so simple to mortgage his lands to his uncle, or his uncle so unnatural to take the extremity of such a mortgage?

HOST. That was my saying still, sir.

LUCRE. Puh! Ne'er think it.

HOST. Yet that report goes current.

LUCRE. Nay, then you urge me; cannot I tell that best that am his uncle.

HOST. How, sir? What have I done!

LUCRE. Why, how now? In a swoon, man?

HOST. Is your worship his uncle, sir?

LUCRE. Can that be any harm to you, sir?

HOST. I do beseech you, sir, do me the favour to conceal it. What a beast was I to utter so much! Pray, sir, do me the kindness to keep it in; I shall have my coat pull'd o'er my ears an't should be known; for the truth is, an't please your worship, to prevent much rumour and many suitors, they intend to be married very suddenly and privately.

LUCRE. And dost thou think it stands with my judgment to do them injury? Must I needs say the knowledge of this marriage comes from thee? Am I a fool at fifty-four? Do I lack subtlety now, that have got all my wealth by it? There's a leash of angels for thee: come, let me woo thee. Speak; where lie they?

HOST. So I might have no anger, sir,—

LUCRE. Passion of me, not a jot. Prithee, come.

HOST. I would not have it known it came by my means.

LUCRE. Why, am I a man of wisdom?

HOST. I dare trust your worship, sir, but I'm a stranger to your house, and to avoid all intelligencers I desire your worship's ear.

LUCRE [*Aside*.]. This fellow's worth a matter of trust. [*To* HOST.] Come, sir. [HOST *whispers*.] Why now, thou'rt an honest lad. [*Aside*.] Ah, sirrah nephew!

HOST. Please you, sir, now I have begun with your worship, when shall I attend for your advice upon that doubtful point? I must come warily now.

LUCRE. Tut, fear thou nothing; tomorrow's evening shall resolve the doubt.

HOST. The time shall cause my attendance.

Exit.

LUCRE. Fare thee well.—There's more true honesty in such a country serving-man than in a hundred of our cloak companions; I may well call 'em companions, for since blue coats have been turn'd into cloaks, we can scarce know the man from the master.—George!

[*Enter* GEORGE.]

GEORGE. Anon, sir.

LUCRE. List hither. [*Whispers*.] Keep the place secret. Commend me to my nephew; I know no cause, tell him, but he might see his uncle.

GEORGE. I will, sir.

LUCRE. And, do you hear, sir, take heed you use him with respect and duty.

GEORGE [*Aside*.]. Here's a strange alteration; one day he must be turn'd out like a beggar, and now he must be call'd in like a knight.

Exit.

LUCRE. Ah, sirrah, that rich widow! Four hundred a year! Beside, I hear she lays claim to a title of a hundred more. This falls unhappily that he should bear a grudge to me now, being likely to prove so rich. What is't, trow, that he makes me a stranger for? Hum, I hope he has not so much wit to apprehend that I cozened him; he deceives me then. Good heaven, who would have thought it would ever have come to this pass! Yet he's a proper gentleman, i'faith, give him his due. Marry, that's his mortgage, but that I ne'er mean to give him. I'll make him rich enough in words, if that be good; and if it come to a piece of money, I will not greatly stick for't: there may be hope some of the widow's lands too may one day fall upon me if things be carried wisely.

[*Enter* GEORGE.]

Now, sir, where is he?

GEORGE. He desires your worship to hold him excused; he has such weighty business it commands him wholly from all men.

LUCRE. Were those my nephew's words?

GEORGE. Yes, indeed, sir.

LUCRE [*Aside.*]. When men grow rich they grow proud too, I perceive that. He would not have sent me such an answer once within this twelvemonth; see what 'tis when a man's come to his lands. [*To* GEORGE.] Return to him again, sir; tell him his uncle desires his company for an hour; I'll trouble him but an hour, say; 'tis for his own good, tell him; and, do you hear, sir, put 'worship' upon him. Go to, do as I bid you; he's like to be a gentleman of worship very shortly.

GEORGE [*Aside.*]. This is good sport, i'faith.

Exit.

LUCRE. Troth, he uses his uncle discourteously now. Can he tell what I may do for him? Goodness may come from me in a minute that comes not in seven year again. He knows my humour; I am not so usually good; 'tis no small thing that draws kindness from me; he may know that, and he will. The chief cause that invites me to do him most good is the sudden astonishing of old Hoard, my adversary. How pale his malice will look at my nephew's advancement! With what a dejected spirit he will behold his fortunes, whom but last day he proclaimed rioter, penurious

makeshift, despised brothel-master! Ha, ha! 'Twill do me more
secret joy than my last purchase, more precious comfort than all
these widows' revenues.

Enter [GEORGE *and*] WITGOOD.

Now, sir.

GEORGE. With much entreaty he's at length come, sir.

[*Exit.*]

LUCRE. O nephew, let me salute you, sir; you're welcome,
nephew.

WITGOOD. Uncle, I thank you.

LUCRE. Y'ave a fault, nephew; you're a stranger here. Well,
heaven give you joy!

WITGOOD. Of what, sir?

LUCRE. Ha, we can hear. You might have known your uncle's
house, i'faith, you and your widow; go to, you were too blame,
if I may tell you so without offence.

WITGOOD. How could you hear of that, sir?

LUCRE. O pardon me! It was your will to have it kept from
me, I perceive now.

WITGOOD. Not for any defect of love, I protest, uncle.

LUCRE. O 'twas unkindness, nephew. Fie, fie, fie!

WITGOOD. I am sorry you take it in that sense, sir.

LUCRE. Puh! You cannot colour it, i'faith, nephew.

WITGOOD. Will you but hear what I can say in my just excuse,
sir?

LUCRE. Yes, faith, will I, and welcome.

WITGOOD. You that know my danger i'th'City, sir, so well,
how great my debts are, and how extreme my creditors, could
not out of your pure judgment, sir, have wish'd us hither.

LUCRE. Mass, a firm reason indeed.

WITGOOD. Else my uncle's house, why, 't'ad been the only
make-match.

LUCRE. Nay, and thy credit.

WITGOOD. My credit? Nay, my countenance! Push! Nay, I
know, uncle, you would have wrought it so; by your wit you
would have made her believe in time the whole house had been
mine.

LUCRE. Ay, and most of the goods too.

WITGOOD. La, you there; well, let 'em all prate what they will, there's nothing like the bringing of a widow to one's uncle's house.

LUCRE. Nay, let nephews be ruled as they list, they shall find their uncle's house the most natural place when all's done.

WITGOOD. There they may be bold.

LUCRE. Life, they may do anything there, man, and fear neither beadle nor sum'ner. An uncle's house! A very Cole Harbour! Sirrah, I'll touch thee near now: hast thou so much interest in thy widow that by a token thou couldst presently send for her?

WITGOOD. Troth, I think I can, uncle.

LUCRE. Go to, let me see that.

WITGOOD. Pray, command one of your men hither, uncle.

LUCRE. George!

[Enter GEORGE.*]*

GEORGE. Here, sir.

LUCRE. Attend my nephew.

                         *[*WITGOOD *and* GEORGE *speak apart]*
[Aside.] I love a' life to prattle with a rich widow; 'tis pretty, methinks, when our tongues go together, and then to promise much and perform little. I love that sport a' life, i'faith, yet I am in the mood now to do my nephew some good, if he take me handsomely.

                                          [Exit GEORGE.*]*
What, have you dispatch'd?

WITGOOD. I ha' sent, sir.

LUCRE. Yet I must condemn you of unkindness, nephew.

WITGOOD. Heaven forbid, uncle!

LUCRE. Yes, faith, must I; say your debts be many, your creditors importunate, yet the kindness of a thing is all, nephew; you might have sent me close word on't, without the least danger or prejudice to your fortunes.

WITGOOD. Troth, I confess it, uncle, I was too blame there; but indeed my intent was to have clapp'd it up suddenly, and so have broke forth like a joy to my friends and a wonder to the world. Beside, there's a trifle of a forty-pound matter towards the setting of me forth; my friends should ne'er have known on't; I meant to make shift for that myself.

LUCRE. How, nephew! Let me not hear such a word again, I beseech you. Shall I be beholding to you?

WITGOOD. To me? Alas, what do you mean, uncle?

LUCRE. I charge you, upon my love: you trouble nobody but myself.

WITGOOD. Y'ave no reason for that, uncle.

LUCRE. Troth, I'll ne'er be friends with you while you live and you do.

WITGOOD. Nay, an you say so, uncle, here's my hand; I will not do't.

LUCRE. Why, well said! There's some hope in thee when thou wilt be ruled; I'll make it up fifty, faith, because I see thee so reclaimed. Peace, here comes my wife with Sam, her tother husband's son.

[*Enter* WIFE *and* SAM FREEDOM.]

WITGOOD. Good aunt—

SAM. Cousin Witgood! I rejoice in my salute; you're most welcome to this noble City, govern'd with the sword in the scabbard.

WITGOOD [*Aside*.]. And the wit in the pommel! [*To* SAM FREEDOM.] Good Master Sam Freedom, I return the salute.

LUCRE. By the mass, she's coming; wife, let me see now how thou wilt entertain her.

WIFE. I hope I am not to learn, sir, to entertain a widow; 'tis not so long ago since I was one myself.

[*Enter* COURTESAN.]

WITGOOD. Uncle—

LUCRE. She's come indeed.

WITGOOD. My uncle was desirous to see you, widow, and I presum'd to invite you.

COURTESAN. The presumption was nothing, Master Witgood; is this your uncle, sir?

LUCRE. Marry am I, sweet widow, and his good uncle he shall find me: ay, by this smack that I give thee, thou'rt welcome. [*Kisses her*.] Wife, bid the widow welcome the same way again.

SAM [*Aside*.]. I am a gentleman now too, by my father's occupation, and I see no reason but I may kiss a widow by my father's copy; truly, I think the charter is not against it; surely these are the words: 'The son, once a gentleman, may revel it, though his father were a dauber'; 'tis about the fifteenth page. I'll to her.

[*Attempts to kiss the* Courtesan.]

Lucre. Y'are not very busy now; a word with thee, sweet widow—

Sam [*Aside.*]. Coad's nigs! I was never so disgrac'd since the hour my mother whipp'd me!

Lucre. Beside, I have no child of mine own to care for; she's my second wife, old, past bearing; clap sure to him, widow; he's like to be my heir, I can tell you.

Courtesan. Is he so, sir?

Lucre. He knows it already, and the knave's proud on't; jolly rich widows have been offer'd him here i'th'City, great merchants' wives, and do you think he would once look upon 'em? Forsooth, he'll none. You are beholding to him i' th' country then, ere we could be; nay, I'll hold a wager, widow, if he were once known to be in town, he would be presently sought after; nay, and happy were they that could catch him first.

Courtesan. I think so.

Lucre. O there would be such running to and fro, widow, he should not pass the streets for 'em; he'd be took up in one great house or other presently. Fah! They know he has it and must have it. You see this house here, widow? This house and all comes to him, goodly rooms ready furnish'd, ceil'd with plaster of Paris, and all hung about with cloth of Arras. Nephew!

Witgood. Sir?

Lucre. Show the widow your house; carry her into all the rooms and bid her welcome. You shall see, widow. [*Aside.*] Nephew, strike all sure above an thou be'st a good boy, ah.

Witgood. Alas, sir, I know not how she would take it.

Lucre. The right way, I warrant 'ee. A pox, art an ass? Would I were in thy stead. Get you up! I am asham'd of you.

[*Exeunt* Witgood *and* Courtesan.]

[*Aside.*] So, let 'em agree as they will now; many a match has been struck up in my house a' this fashion: let 'em try all manner of ways, still there's nothing like an uncle's house to strike the stroke in. I'll hold my wife in talk a little. [*To her.*] Now, Ginny, your son there goes a-wooing to a poor gentlewoman but of a thousand portion; see my nephew, a lad of less hope, strikes at four hundred a year in good rubbish.

WIFE. Well, we must do as we may, sir.

LUCRE. I'll have his money ready told for him again he come down. Let me see too—by th'mass, I must present the widow with some jewel, a good piece of plate, or such a device; 'twill hearten her on well. I have a very fair standing cup, and a good high standing cup will please a widow above all other pieces.

Exit.

WIFE. Do you mock us with your nephew? I have a plot in my head, son; i'faith, husband, to cross you.

SAM. Is it a tragedy plot or a comedy plot, good mother?

WIFE. 'Tis a plot shall vex him. I charge you, of my blessing, son Sam, that you presently withdraw the action of your love from Master Hoard's niece.

SAM. How, mother?

WIFE. Nay, I have a plot in my head, i'faith, Here, take this chain of gold and this fair diamond; dog me the widow home to her lodging, and at thy best opportunity fasten 'em both upon her. Nay, I have a reach I can tell you. Thou art known what thou art, son, among the right worshipful, all the twelve companies.

SAM. Truly, I thank 'em for it.

WIFE. He? He's a scab to thee! And so certify her thou hast two hundred a year of thyself, beside thy good parts—a proper person and a lovely. If I were a widow I could find it in my heart to have thee myself, son, ay, from 'em all.

SAM. Thank you for your good will, mother, but indeed I had rather have a stranger; and if I woo her not in that violent fashion, that I will make her be glad to take these gifts ere I leave her, let me never be called the heir of your body.

WIFE. Nay, I know there's enough in you, son, if you once come to put it forth.

SAM. I'll quickly make a bolt or a shaft on't.

Exeunt.

[scene 2]

Enter HOARD *and* MONEYLOVE.

MONEYLOVE. Faith, Master Hoard, I have bestowed many months in the suit of your niece, such was the dear love I ever bore to her virtues, but since she hath so extremely denied me, I am to lay out for my fortunes elsewhere.

HOARD. Heaven forbid but you should, sir; I ever told you my niece stood otherwise affected.

MONEYLOVE. I must confess you did, sir; yet in regard of my great loss of time and the zeal with which I sought your niece, shall I desire one favour of your worship?

HOARD. In regard of those two, 'tis hard, but you shall, sir.

MONEYLOVE. I shall rest grateful. 'Tis not full three hours, sir, since the happy rumour of a rich country widow came to my hearing.

HOARD. How? A rich country widow?

MONEYLOVE. Four hundred a year, landed.

HOARD. Yea?

MONEYLOVE. Most firm, sir, and I have learn'd her lodging; here my suit begins, sir: if I might but entreat your worship to be a countenance for me and speak a good word—for your words will pass—I nothing doubt but I might set fair for the widow; nor shall your labour, sir, end altogether in thanks, two hundred angels—

HOARD. So, so, what suitors has she?

MONEYLOVE. There lies the comfort, sir; the report of her is yet but a whisper, and only solicited by young riotous Witgood, nephew to your mortal adversary.

HOARD. Ha! Art certain he's her suitor?

MONEYLOVE. Most certain, sir, and his uncle very industrious to beguile the widow and make up the match.

HOARD. So! Very good.

MONEYLOVE. Now, sir, you know this young Witgood is a spendthrift, dissolute fellow.

HOARD. A very rascal.

MONEYLOVE. A midnight surfeiter.

HOARD. The spume of a brothel-house.

MONEYLOVE. True, sir! Which being well told in your worship's phrase may both heave him out of her mind, and drive a fair way for me to the widow's affections.

HOARD. Attend me about five.

MONEYLOVE. With my best care, sir.

Exit.

HOARD. Fool, thou hast left thy treasure with a thief, to trust a widower with a suit in love! Happy revenge, I hug thee! I have not only the means laid before me extremely to cross my adversary and confound the last hopes of his nephew, but thereby to

enrich my state, augment my revenues, and build mine own
fortunes greater, ha, ha!
I'll mar your phrase, o'erturn your flatteries,
Undo your windings, policies, and plots,
Fall like a secret and dispatchful plague
On your secured comforts. Why, I am able
To buy three of Lucre, thrice outbid him,
Let my out-monies be reckon'd and all.

Enter three Creditors.

CREDITOR 1. I am glad of this news.

CREDITOR 2. So are we, by my faith.

CREDITOR 3. Young Witgood will be a gallant again now.

HOARD [*Aside*.]. Peace!

CREDITOR 1. I promise you, Master Cockpit, she's a mighty
rich widow.

CREDITOR 2. Why, have you ever heard of her?

CREDITOR 1. Who? Widow Medler? She lies open to much
rumour.

CREDITOR 3. Four hundred a year, they say, in very good land.

CREDITOR 1. Nay, tak't of my word, if you believe that, you
believe the least.

CREDITOR 2. And to see how close he keeps it!

CREDITOR 1. O sir, there's policy in that, to prevent better
suitors.

CREDITOR 3. He owes me a hundred pound, and I protest I
ne'er look'd for a penny.

CREDITOR 1. He little dreams of our coming; he'll wonder to
see his creditors upon him.

Exeunt [Creditors].

HOARD. Good, his creditors; I'll follow. This makes for me:
all know the widow's wealth, and 'tis well known I can estate
her fairly, ay, and will.
In this one chance shines a twice-happy fate;
I both deject my foe and raise my state.

Music. Exit.

ACT THREE

[scene 1]

[Enter] WITGOOD with his Creditors.

WITGOOD. Why, alas, my creditors, could you find no other time to undo me but now? Rather your malice appears in this than the justness of the debt.

CREDITOR 1. Master Witgood, I have forborne my money long.

WITGOOD. I pray, speak low, sir; what do you mean?

CREDITOR 2. We hear you are to be married suddenly to a rich country widow.

WITGOOD. What can be kept so close but you creditors hear on't? Well, 'tis a lamentable state that our chiefest afflicters should first hear of our fortunes. Why, this is no good course, i'faith, sirs; if ever you have hope to be satisfied, why do you seek to confound the means that should work it? There's neither piety, no, nor policy in that. Shine favourably now, why, I may rise and spread again, to your great comforts.

CREDITOR 1. He says true, i'faith.

WITGOOD. Remove me now, and I consume for ever.

CREDITOR 2. Sweet gentleman!

WITGOOD. How can it thrive which from the sun you sever?

CREDITOR 3. It cannot indeed.

WITGOOD. O then, show patience! I shall have enough to satisfy you all.

CREDITOR 1. Ay, if we could be content, a shame take us.

WITGOOD. For, look you, I am but newly sure yet to the widow, and what a rend might this discredit make! Within these three days will I bind you lands for your securities.

CREDITOR 1. No, good Master Witgood; would 'twere as much as we dare trust you with.

WITGOOD. I know you have been kind; however, now either by wrong report or false incitement, your gentleness is injur'd; in such a state as this a man cannot want foes. If on the sudden he begin to rise, no man that lives can count his enemies. You had some intelligence, I warrant ye, from an ill-willer.

CREDITOR 2. Faith, we heard you brought up a rich widow, sir, and were suddenly to marry her.

WITGOOD. Ay, why, there it was, I knew 'twas so: but since you are so well resolv'd of my faith towards you, let me be so much favour'd of you, I beseech you all—

ALL. O it shall not need, i'faith, sir,—

WITGOOD. As to lie still awhile and bury my debts in silence, till I be fully possessed of the widow; for the truth is, I may tell you as my friends—

ALL. O, o, o—

WITGOOD. I am to raise a little money in the City towards the setting forth of myself, for mine own credit and your comfort. Now if my former debts should be divulg'd, all hope of my proceedings were quite extinguish'd.

CREDITOR 1 [*To* WITGOOD.]. Do you hear, sir? I may deserve your custom hereafter; pray, let my money be accepted before a stranger's: Here's forty pound I receiv'd as I came to you; if that may stand you in any stead, make use on't. Nay, pray, sir, 'tis at your service.

WITGOOD [*To* CREDITOR 1.]. You do so ravish me with kindness that I'm constrain'd to play the maid and take it!

CREDITOR 1 [*To* WITGOOD.]. Let none of them see it, I beseech you.

WITGOOD [*Aside*.]. Fah!

CREDITOR 1 [*To* WITGOOD.]. I hope I shall be first in your remembrance after the marriage rites.

WITGOOD [*To* CREDITOR 1.]. Believe it firmly.

CREDITOR 1. So. [*To* CREDITORS 2 *and* 3.] What, do you walk, sirs?

CREDITOR 2. I go. [*To* WITGOOD.] Take no care, sir, for money to furnish you; within this hour I'll send you sufficient. [*To* CREDITOR 3.] Come, Master Cockpit, we both stay for you.

CREDITOR 3. I ha' lost a ring, i'faith, I'll follow you presently.
[*Exeunt* Creditors 1 *and* 2.]
But you shall find it, sir; I know your youth and expenses have disfurnish'd you of all jewels; there's a ruby of twenty pound price, sir; bestow it upon your widow. What, man! 'Twill call up her blood to you; beside, if I might so much work with you, I would not have you beholding to those blood-suckers for any money.

WITGOOD. Not I, believe it.

CREDITOR 3. Th'are a brace of cut-throats.

WITGOOD. I know 'em.

CREDITOR 3. Send a note of all your wants to my shop, and I'll supply you instantly.

WITGOOD. Say you so? Why, here's my hand then; no man living shall do't but thyself.

CREDITOR 3. Shall I carry it away from 'em both then?

WITGOOD. I'faith, shalt thou!

CREDITOR 3. Troth, then, I thank you, sir.

WITGOOD. Welcome, good Master Cockpit.

Exit [Creditor 3].

Ha, ha, ha! Why, is not this better now than lying abed? I perceive there's nothing conjures up wit sooner than poverty, and nothing lays it down sooner than wealth and lechery. This has some savour yet. O that I had the mortgage from mine uncle as sure in possession as these trifles, I would forswear brothel at noonday and muscadine and eggs at midnight!

Enter COURTESAN.

COURTESAN. Master Witgood, where are you?

WITGOOD. Holla!

COURTESAN. Rich news!

WITGOOD. Would 'twere all in plate!

COURTESAN. There's some in chains and jewels. I am so haunted with suitors, Master Witgood, I know not which to dispatch first.

WITGOOD. You have the better Term, by my faith!

COURTESAN. Among the number, one Master Hoard, an ancient gentleman.

WITGOOD. Upon my life, my uncle's adversary!

COURTESAN. It may well hold so, for he rails on you,
Speaks shamefully of him.

WITGOOD.   As I could wish it.

COURTESAN. I first denied him, but so cunningly
It rather promis'd him assured hopes
Than any loss of labour.

WITGOOD.   Excellent.

COURTESAN. I expect him every hour, with gentlemen
With whom he labours to make good his words,
To approve you riotous, your state consum'd,
Your uncle—

WITGOOD. Wench, make up thy own fortunes now; do thyself a good turn once in thy days. He's rich in money, movables, and lands. Marry him, he's an old doting fool, and that's worth all; marry him, 'twould be a great comfort to me to see thee do well, i'faith. Marry him, 'twould ease my conscience well to see thee well bestow'd; I have a care of thee, i'faith.

COURTESAN. Thanks, sweet Master Witgood.

WITGOOD. I reach at farder happiness: first, I am sure it can be no harm to thee, and there may happen goodness to me by it. Prosecute it well: let's send up for our wits, now we require their best and most pregnant assistance.

COURTESAN. Step in. I think I hear 'em.

Exit [with WITGOOD].

Enter HOARD *and* Gentlemen, *with the* HOST [*as*] *serving-man.*

HOARD. Art thou the widow's man? By my faith, sh'as a company of proper men then.

HOST. I am the worst of six, sir, good enough for blue-coats.

HOARD. Hark hither: I hear say thou art in most credit with her.

HOST. Not so, sir.

HOARD. Come, come, thou'rt modest. There's a brace of royals; prithee, help me to th'speech of her.

HOST. I'll do what I may, sir, always saving myself harmless.

HOARD. Go to, do't, I say; thou shalt hear better from me.

HOST [*Aside*.]. Is not this a better place than five mark a year standing wages? Say a man had but three such clients in a day, methinks he might make a poor living on't; beside, I was never brought up with so little honesty to refuse any man's money: never. What gulls there are a' this side the world! Now know I the widow's mind, none but my young master comes in her clutches. Ha, ha, ha!

Exit.

HOARD. Now, my dear gentlemen, stand firmly to me. You know his follies and my worth.

GENTLEMAN 1. We do, sir.

GENTLEMAN 2. But, Master Hoard, are you sure he is not i'th'house now?

HOARD. Upon my honesty, I chose this time
A' purpose, fit; the spendthrift is abroad.

Assist me; here she comes.

[*Enter* COURTESAN.]

                    Now, my sweet widow.
COURTESAN. Y'are welcome, Master Hoard.
    HOARD. Dispatch, sweet gentlemen, dispatch.
I am come, widow, to prove those my words
Neither of envy sprung nor of false tongues,
But such as their deserts and actions
Do merit and bring forth; all which these gentlemen,
Well known and better reputed, will confess.
    COURTESAN. I cannot tell
How my affections may dispose of me,
But surely if they find him so desertless
They'll have that reason to withdraw themselves.
And therefore, gentlemen, I do entreat you,
As you are fair in reputation
And in appearing form, so shine in truth.
I am a widow, and, alas, you know
Soon overthrown; 'tis a very small thing
That we withstand, our weakness is so great.
Be partial unto neither, but deliver,
Without affection, your opinion.
    HOARD. And that will drive it home.
    COURTESAN. Nay, I beseech your silence, Master Hoard;
You are a party.
    HOARD.   Widow, not a word!
    GENTLEMAN 1. The better first to work you to belief,
Know neither of us owe him flattery,
Nor tother malice, but unbribed censure,
So help us our best fortunes.
    COURTESAN.   It suffices.
    GENTLEMAN 1. That Witgood is a riotous, undone man,
Imperfect both in fame and in estate,
His debts wealthier than he, and executions
In wait for his due body, we'll maintain
With our best credit and our dearest blood.
    COURTESAN. Nor land nor living, say you? Pray, take heed
you do not wrong the gentleman.
    GENTLEMAN 1. What we speak

Our lives and means are ready to make good.

COURTESAN. Alas, how soon are we poor souls beguil'd!

GENTLEMAN 2. And for his uncle—

HOARD.   Let that come to me.
His uncle, a severe extortioner,
A tyrant at a forfeiture, greedy of others'
Miseries, one that would undo his brother,
Nay, swallow up his father if he can,
Within the fathoms of his conscience.

GENTLEMAN 1. Nay, believe it, widow,
You had not only match'd yourself to wants,
But in an evil and unnatural stock.

HOARD [*To* Gentlemen.]. Follow hard, gentlemen, follow hard!

COURTESAN. Is my love so deceiv'd? Before you all
I do renounce him; on my knees I vow
He ne'er shall marry me.

[WITGOOD *enters apart.*]

WITGOOD [*Aside.*]. Heaven knows he never meant it!

HOARD [*To* Gentlemen.]. There, take her at the bound.

GENTLEMAN 1. Then, with a new and pure affection,
Behold yon gentleman, grave, kind, and rich,
A match worthy yourself; esteeming him,
You do regard your state.

HOARD [*To* GENTLEMAN 1.]. I'll make her a jointure, say.

GENTLEMAN 1. He can join land to land and will possess you
of what you can desire.

GENTLEMAN 2. Come, widow, come.

COURTESAN. The world is so deceitful.

GENTLEMAN 1.   There, 'tis deceitful,
Where flattery, want, and imperfection lies.
But none of these in him. Push!

COURTESAN.   Pray, sir,—

GENTLEMAN 1. Come, you widows are ever most backward
when you should do yourselves most good; but were it to marry
a chin not worth a hair now, then you would be forward enough.
[*Joins their hands.*] Come, clap hands, a match!

HOARD. With all my heart, widow. Thanks, gentlemen;
I will deserve your labour, and thy love.

COURTESAN. Alas, you love not widows but for wealth.
I promise you I ha' nothing, sir.

HOARD. Well said, widow, well said; thy love is all I seek,
before these gentlemen.

COURTESAN. Now I must hope the best.

HOARD. My joys are such they want to be express'd.

COURTESAN. But, Master Hoard, one thing I must remember
you of before these gentlemen, your friends: how shall I suddenly
avoid the loathed soliciting of that perjur'd Witgood and his
tedious, dissembling uncle, who this very, very day hath appointed
a meeting for the same purpose too, where, had not truth come
forth, I had been undone, utterly undone?

HOARD. What think you of that, gentlemen?

GENTLEMAN 1. 'Twas well devis'd.

HOARD. Hark thee, widow: train out young Witgood single;
hasten him thither with thee, somewhat before the hour, where,
at the place appointed, these gentlemen and myself will wait the
opportunity, when by some sleight, removing him from thee,
we'll suddenly enter and surprise thee, carry thee away by boat
to Cole Harbour, have a priest ready, and there clap it up instantly.
How lik'st it, widow?

COURTESAN. In that it pleaseth you, it likes me well.

HOARD. I'll kiss thee for those words. Come, gentlemen;
Still must I live a suitor to your favours,
Still to your aid beholding.

GENTLEMAN 1.   We're engag'd, sir;
'Tis for our credits now to see't well ended.

HOARD. 'Tis for your honours, gentlemen; nay, look to't:
Not only in joy, but I in wealth excel.
No more sweet widow, but sweet wife, farewell.

COURTESAN. Farewell, sir.

Exeunt [HOARD *and* Gentlemen].

Enter WITGOOD.

WITGOOD. O for more scope! I could laugh eternally. Give
you joy, Mistress Hoard! I promise your fortune was good,
forsooth; y'ave fell upon wealth enough, and there's young
gentlemen enow can help you to the rest. Now it requires our
wits; carry thyself but heedfully now, and we are both—

[*Enter* HOST.]

HOST. Master Witgood, your uncle—

WITGOOD. Cuds me! [*To* COURTESAN.] Remove thyself awhile;
I'll serve for him.

[*Exeunt* COURTESAN *and* HOST.]

Enter LUCRE.

LUCRE. Nephew, good morrow, nephew.

WITGOOD. The same to you, kind uncle.

LUCRE. How fares the widow? Does the meeting hold?

WITGOOD. O no question of that, sir.

LUCRE. I'll strike the stroke, then, for thee; no more days.

WITGOOD. The sooner the better, uncle. O she's mightily
followed.

LUCRE. And yet so little rumour'd.

WITGOOD. Mightily! Here comes one old gentleman, and he'll
make her a jointure of three hundred a year, forsooth; another
wealthy suitor will estate his son in his lifetime and make him
weigh down the widow; here's a merchant's son will possess her
with no less than three goodly lordships at once, which were all
pawns to his father.

LUCRE. Peace, nephew, let me hear no more of 'em; it mads
me. Thou shalt prevent 'em all. No words to the widow of my
coming hither. Let me see, 'tis now upon nine; before twelve,
nephew, we will have the bargain struck, we will, faith, boy.

WITGOOD. O, my precious uncle!

Exit [*with* LUCRE].

[scene 2]

Enter HOARD *and his* NIECE.

HOARD. Niece, sweet niece, prithee have a care to my house;
I leave all to thy discretion. Be content to dream awhile; I'll have
a husband for thee shortly; put that care upon me, wench, for in
choosing wives and husbands I am only fortunate: I have that gift
given me.

Exit.

NIECE. But 'tis not likely you should choose for me,

Since nephew to your chiefest enemy
Is he whom I affect; but, o forgetful,
Why dost thou flatter thy affections so,
With name of him that for a widow's bed
Neglects thy purer love? Can it be so,
Or does report dissemble?

[*Enter* GEORGE.]

How now, sir?

GEORGE. A letter, with which came a private charge.

NIECE. Therein I thank your care.

[*Exit* GEORGE.]

I know this hand.

Reads.

'Dearer than sight, what the world reports of me, yet believe not;
rumour will alter shortly. Be thou constant; I am still the same
that I was in love, and I hope to be the same in fortunes.

Theodorus Witgood.'

I am resolv'd; no more shall fear or doubt
Raise their pale powers to keep affection out.

Exit.

[*scene 3*]

Enter, with a Drawer, HOARD *and two* Gentlemen.

DRAWER. You're very welcome, gentlemen. Dick, show these
gentlemen the Pom'granate there.

HOARD. Hist!

DRAWER. Up those stairs, gentlemen.

HOARD. Pist! Drawer—

DRAWER. Anon, sir.

HOARD. Prithee, ask at the bar if a gentlewoman came not in
lately.

DRAWER. William, at the bar, did you see any gentlewoman
come in lately? Speak you ay, speak you no?

WILLIAM [*Within.*]. No, none came in yet but Mistress Florence.

DRAWER. He says none came in yet, sir, but one Mistress
Florence.

HOARD. What is that Florence? A widow?

DRAWER. Yes, a Dutch widow.

HOARD. How!

DRAWER. That's an English drab, sir; give your worship good
morrow.

                                                                    [*Exit.*]

HOARD. A merry knave, i'faith! I shall remember 'a Dutch
widow' the longest day of my life.

GENTLEMAN 1. Did not I use most art to win the widow?

GENTLEMAN 2. You shall pardon me for that, sir; Master Hoard
knows I took her at best 'vantage.

HOARD. What's that, sweet gentlemen, what's that?

GENTLEMAN 2. He will needs bear me down that his art only
wrought with the widow most.

HOARD. O you did both well, gentlemen, you did both well,
I thank you.

GENTLEMAN 1. I was the first that mov'd her.

HOARD.   You were, i'faith.

GENTLEMAN 2. But it was I that took her at the bound.

HOARD. Ay, that was you; faith, gentlemen, 'tis right.

GENTLEMAN 1. I boasted least, but 'twas I join'd their hands.

HOARD. By th' mass, I think he did. You did all well, gentlemen, you did all well. Contend no more.

GENTLEMAN 1. Come, yon room's fittest.

HOARD.   True, 'tis next the door.

                                            Exit [*with* Gentlemen.]

        Enter WITGOOD, COURTESAN, [Drawer,] *and* HOST.

Drawer. You're very welcome; please you to walk upstairs;
cloth's laid, sir.

COURTESAN. Upstairs? Troth, I am weary, Master Witgood.

WITGOOD. Rest yourself here awhile, widow; we'll have a cup
of muscadine in this little room.

DRAWER. A cup of muscadine? You shall have the best, sir.

WITGOOD. But, do you hear, sirrah?

DRAWER. Do you call? Anon, sir.

WITGOOD. What is there provided for dinner?

DRAWER. I cannot readily tell you, sir; if you please, you may
go into the kitchen and see yourself, sir; many gentlemen of
worship do use to do it, I assure you, sir.

                                                                    [*Exit.*]

HOST. A pretty familiar, priggin' rascal, he has his part without book.

WITGOOD. Against you are ready to drink to me, widow, I'll be present to pledge you.

COURTESAN. Nay, I commend your care; 'tis done well of you.

[*Exit* WITGOOD.]

'Las, what have I forgot!

HOST. What, mistress?

COURTESAN. I slipp'd my wedding ring off when I wash'd and left it at my lodging; prithee, run, I shall be sad without it.

[*Exit* HOST.]

So, he's gone. Boy!

[*Enter* Boy.]

BOY. Anon, forsooth.

COURTESAN. Come hither, sirrah: learn secretly if one Master Hoard, an ancient gentleman, be about house.

BOY. I heard such a one nam'd.

COURTESAN. Commend me to him.

Enter HOARD *with* Gentlemen.

HOARD. I'll do thy commendations.

COURTESAN. O you come well. Away! To boat! Begone!

HOARD. Thus wise men are reveng'd, give two for one.

Exeunt.

Enter WITGOOD *and* Vintner.

WITGOOD. I must request you, sir, to show extraordinary care; my uncle comes with gentlemen, his friends, and 'tis upon a making.

VINTNER. Is it so? I'll give a special charge, good Master Witgood. May I be bold to see her?

WITGOOD. Who, the widow? With all my heart, i'faith. I'll bring you to her!

VINTNER. If she be a Staffordshire gentlewoman, 'tis much if I know her not.

WITGOOD. How now? Boy! Drawer!

VINTNER. Hie!

[*Enter* Boy.]

Boy. Do you call, sir?

Witgood. Went the gentlewoman up that was here?

Boy. Up, sir? She went out, sir.

Witgood. Out, sir?

Boy. Out, sir. One Master Hoard, with a guard of gentlemen, carried her out at back door a pretty while since, sir.

[*Exit* Boy.]

Witgood. Hoard? Death and darkness, Hoard?

Enter Host.

Host. The devil of ring I can find!

Witgood. How now, what news? Where's the widow?

Host. My mistress? Is she not here, sir?

Witgood. More madness yet!

Host. She sent me for a ring.

Witgood. A plot, a plot! To boat! She's stole away!

Host. What?

Enter Lucre *with* Gentlemen.

Witgood. Follow! Enquire, old Hoard, my uncle's adversary—

[*Exit* Host.]

Lucre. Nephew, what's that?

Witgood. Thrice-miserable wretch!

Lucre. Why, what's the matter?

Vintner. The widow's borne away, sir.

Lucre. Ha! Passion of me! A heavy welcome, gentlemen.

Gentleman 1. The widow gone?

Lucre. Who durst attempt it?

Witgood. Who but old Hoard, my uncle's adversary!

Lucre. How!

Witgood. With his confederates.

Lucre. Hoard, my deadly enemy! Gentlemen, stand to me.
I will not bear it. 'Tis in hate of me;
That villain seeks my shame, nay, thirsts my blood;
He owes me mortal malice.
I'll spend my wealth on this despiteful plot,
Ere he shall cross me and my nephew thus.

Witgood. So maliciously!

Enter HOST.

LUCRE. How now, you treacherous rascal?

HOST. That's none of my name, sir.

WITGOOD. Poor soul, he knew not on't.

LUCRE. I'm sorry. I see then 'twas a mere plot.

HOST. I trac'd 'em nearly—

LUCRE. Well?

HOST. And hear for certain they have took Cole Harbour.

LUCRE. The devil's sanctuary!
They shall not rest. I'll pluck her from his arms.
Kind and dear gentlemen,
If ever I had seat within your breasts—

GENTLEMAN 1. No more, good sir. It is a wrong to us
To see you injur'd; in a cause so just
We'll spend our lives, but we will right our friends.

LUCRE. Honest and kind! Come, we have delay'd too long:
Nephew, take comfort; a just cause is strong.

WITGOOD. That's all my comfort, uncle.

Exeunt [LUCRE, Gentlemen *and* HOST].
Ha, ha, ha!
Now may events fall luckily and well;
He that ne'er strives, says wit, shall ne'er excel.

Exit.

[scene 4]

Enter DAMPIT, *the usurer, drunk.*

DAMPIT. When did I say my prayers? In anno '88, when the great armada was coming; and in anno '99, when the great thund'ring and lightning was, I pray'd heartily then, i'faith, to overthrow Poovies' new buildings; I kneel'd by my great iron chest, I remember.

[*Enter* AUDREY.]

AUDREY. Master Dampit, one may hear you before they see you. You keep sweet hours, Master Dampit; we were all abed three hours ago.

DAMPIT. Audrey?

AUDREY. O y'are a fine gentleman.

DAMPIT. So I am, i'faith, and a fine scholar. Do you use to go to bed so early, Audrey?

AUDREY. Call you this early, Master Dampit?

DAMPIT. Why, is't not one of clock i'th'morning? Is not that early enough? Fetch me a glass of fresh beer.

AUDREY. Here, I have warm'd your nightcap for you, Master Dampit.

DAMPIT. Draw it on then. I am very weak truly; I have not eaten so much as the bulk of an egg these three days.

AUDREY. You have drunk the more, Master Dampit.

DAMPIT. What's that?

AUDREY. You mought and you would, Master Dampit.

DAMPIT. I answer you, I cannot. Hold your prating; you prate too much and understand too little. Are you answered? Give me a glass of beer.

AUDREY. May I ask you how you do, Master Dampit?

DAMPIT. How do I? I'faith, naught.

AUDREY. I ne'er knew you do otherwise.

DAMPIT. I eat not one penn'ort' of bread these two years. Give me a glass of fresh beer, I am not sick, nor I am not well.

AUDREY. Take this warm napkin about your neck, sir, whilst I help you make you unready.

DAMPIT. How now, Audrey-prater, with your scurvy devices, what say you now?

AUDREY. What say I, Master Dampit? I say nothing but that you are very weak.

DAMPIT. Faith, thou hast more cony-catching devices than all London!

AUDREY. Why, Master Dampit, I never deceiv'd you in all my life!

DAMPIT. Why was that? Because I never did trust thee.

AUDREY. I care not what you say, Master Dampit.

DAMPIT. Hold thy prating. I answer thee, thou art a beggar, a quean, and a bawd. Are you answer'd?

AUDREY. Fie, Master Dampit! A gentleman, and have such words!

DAMPIT. Why, thou base drudge of infortunity, thou kitchen-stuff drab of beggary, roguery, and coxcombry, thou cavernesed quean of foolery, knavery, and bawdreaminy, I'll tell thee what, I will not give a louse for thy fortunes.

AUDREY. No, Master Dampit? And there's a gentleman comes a-wooing to me, and he doubts nothing but that you will get me from him.

DAMPIT. I? If I would either have thee or lie with thee for two thousand pound, would I might be damn'd! Why, thou base, impudent quean of foolery, flattery, and coxcombry, are you answer'd?

AUDREY. Come, will you rise and go to bed, sir?

DAMPIT. Rise, and go to bed too, Audrey? How does Mistress Proserpine?

AUDREY. Fooh!

DAMPIT. She's as fine a philosopher of a stinkard's wife as any within the liberties.—Fah, fah, Audrey!

AUDREY. How now, Master Dampit?

DAMPIT. Fie upon't, what a choice of stinks here is! What hast thou done, Audrey? Fie upon't, here's a choice of stinks indeed! Give me a glass of fresh beer and then I will to bed.

AUDREY. It waits for you above, sir.

DAMPIT. Foh, I think they burn horns in Barnard's Inn; if ever I smell'd such an abominable stink, usury forsake me.

[*Exit.*]

AUDREY. They be the stinking nails of his trampling feet, and he talks of burning of horns.

Exit.

ACT FOUR

[*scene 1*]

Enter at Cole Harbour, HOARD, *the* WIDOW, *and Gentlemen* [*including* LAMPREY *and* SPITCHCOCK], *he married now.*

GENTLEMAN 1. Join hearts, join hands,
In wedlock's bands,
Never to part,
Till death cleave your heart;
   [*To* HOARD.] You shall forsake all other women;

[*To* COURTESAN.] You, lords, knights, gentlemen, and yeomen.
What my tongue slips
Make up with your lips.

HOARD. Give you joy, Mistress Hoard; let the kiss come about.
                                                    [*Knocking.*]
Who knocks? Convey my little pig-eater out.

LUCRE [*Within.*]. Hoard!

HOARD. Upon my life, my adversary, gentlemen!

LUCRE [*Within.*]. Hoard, open the door or we will force it ope.
Give us the widow.

HOARD. Gentlemen, keep 'em out.

LAMPREY. He comes upon his death that enters here.

LUCRE [*Within.*]. My friends, assist me.

HOARD. He has assistants, gentlemen.

LAMPREY. Tut! Nor him nor them, we in this action fear.

LUCRE [*Within.*]. Shall I in peace speak one word with the
widow?

COURTESAN. Husband and gentlemen, hear me but a word.

HOARD. Freely, sweet wife.

COURTESAN. Let him in peaceably; you know we're sure from
any act of his.

HOARD. Most true.

COURTESAN. You may stand by and smile at his old weakness;
let me alone to answer him.

HOARD. Content. 'Twill be good mirth, i'faith; how think
you, gentle men?

LAMPREY. Good gullery!

HOARD. Upon calm conditions, let him in.

LUCRE [*Within.*]. All spite and malice—

LAMPREY.   Hear me, Master Lucre:
So you will vow a peaceful entrance
With those your friends, and only exercise
Calm conference with the widow, without fury,
The passage shall receive you.

LUCRE [*Within.*].   I do vow it.

LAMPREY. Then enter and talk freely; here she stands.

Enter LUCRE [*Gentlemen and* HOST].

LUCRE. O Master Hoard, your spite has watch'd the hour.
You're excellent at vengeance, Master Hoard.

HOARD. Ha, ha, ha!

LUCRE. I am the fool you laugh at.
You are wise, sir, and know the seasons. Well,
Come hither, widow.

                                        [*They speak apart.*]

                    Why, is it thus?
O you have done me infinite disgrace
And your own credit no small injury.
Suffer mine enemy so despitefully
To bear you from my nephew! O I had
Rather half my substance had been forfeit
And begg'd by some starv'd rascal!

    COURTESAN. Why, what would you wish me do, sir?
I must not overthrow my state for love,
We have too many precedents for that.
From thousands of our wealthy undone widows
One may derive some wit. I do confess
I lov'd your nephew; nay, I did affect him
Against the mind and liking of my friends,
Believ'd his promises, lay here in hope
Of flatter'd living and the boast of lands:
Coming to touch his wealth and state indeed,
It appears dross. I find him not the man;
Imperfect, mean, scarce furnish'd of his needs;
In words, fair lordships; in performance, hovels:
Can any woman love the thing that is not?

    LUCRE. Broke you for this?

    COURTESAN.   Was it not cause too much?
Send to inquire his state. Most part of it
Lay two years mortgag'd in his uncle's hands.

    LUCRE. Why, say it did. You might have known my mind;
I could have soon restor'd it.

    COURTESAN. Ay, had I but seen any such thing perform'd,
why, 'twould have tied my affection and contain'd me in my first
desires: do you think, i'faith, that I could twine such a dry oak
as this, had promise in your nephew took effect?

    LUCRE. Why, and there's no time pass'd, and rather than
My adversary should thus thwart my hopes,
I would—

    COURTESAN. Tut, y'ave been ever full of golden speech.
If words were lands, your nephew would be rich.

LUCRE. Widow, believe it, I vow by my best bliss,
Before these gentlemen, I will give in
The mortgage to my nephew instantly,
Before I sleep or eat.

GENTLEMAN 2. We'll pawn our credits, widow, what he speaks
shall be perform'd in fullness.

LUCRE. Nay, more. I will estate him
In farder blessings: he shall be my heir.
I have no son.
I'll bind myself to that condition.

COURTESAN. When I shall hear this done I shall soon yield to
reasonable terms.

LUCRE. In the mean season,
Will you protest, before these gentlemen,
To keep yourself as you are now at this present?

COURTESAN. I do protest, before these gentlemen,
I will be as clear then as I am now.

LUCRE. I do believe you. Here's your own honest servant;
I'll take him along with me.

COURTESAN.   Ay, with all my heart.

LUCRE. He shall see all perform'd, and bring you word.

COURTESAN. That's all I wait for.

HOARD. What, have you finish'd, Master Lucre? Ha, ha, ha,
ha!

LUCRE. So, laugh, Hoard, laugh at your poor enemy, do;
The wind may turn; you may be laugh'd at too.
Yes, marry, may you, sir. Ha, ha, ha!

Exeunt [LUCRE, Gentlemen, *and* HOST].

HOARD. Ha, ha, ha! If every man that swells in malice
Could be reveng'd as happily as I,
He would choose hate and forswear amity.
What did he say, wife, prithee?

COURTESAN. Faith, spoke to ease his mind.

HOARD. O, o, o!

COURTESAN. You know now, little to any purpose.

HOARD. True, true, true.

COURTESAN. He would do mountains now.

HOARD. Ay, ay, ay, ay.

LAMPREY. Y'ave struck him dead, Master Hoard.

SPITCHCOCK. Ay, and his nephew desperate.

HOARD. I know't, sirs, ay.
Never did man so crush his enemy.

Exeunt.

[*scene 2*]

Enter LUCRE *with* Gentlemen [*and* HOST],
meeting SAM FREEDOM.

LUCRE. My son-in-law, Sam Freedom, where's my nephew?

SAM. O man in lamentation, father!

LUCRE. How!

SAM. He thumps his breast like a gallant dicer that has lost his doublet, and stands in's shirt to do penance.

LUCRE. Alas, poor gentleman.

SAM. I warrant you may hear him sigh in a still evening to your house at Highgate.

LUCRE. I prithee, send him in.

SAM. Were it to do a greater matter, I will not stick with you, sir, in regard you married my mother.

[*Exit.*]

LUCRE. Sweet gentlemen, cheer him up; I will but fetch the mortgage and return to you instantly.

Exit.

GENTLEMAN 1. We'll do our best, sir. See where he comes,
E'en joyless and regardless of all form.

[*Enter* WITGOOD.]

GENTLEMAN 2. Why, how, Master Witgood? Fie, you a firm scholar and an understanding gentleman, and give your best parts to passion?

GENTLEMAN 1. Come, fie!

WITGOOD. O gentlemen,—

GENTLEMAN 1. Sorrow of me, what a sigh was there, sir! Nine such widows are not worth it.

WITGOOD. To be borne from me by that lecher, Hoard!

GENTLEMAN 1. That vengeance is your uncle's, being done
More in despite to him than wrong to you,
But we bring comfort now.

WITGOOD. I beseech you, gentlemen,—

GENTLEMAN 2. Cheer thyself, man; there's hope of her, i'faith.

WITGOOD. Too gladsome to be true.

Enter LUCRE.

LUCRE. Nephew, what cheer? Alas, poor gentleman, how art thou chang'd! Call thy fresh blood into thy cheeks again: she comes—

WITGOOD. Nothing afflicts me so much
But that it is your adversary, uncle,
And merely plotted in despite of you.

LUCRE. Ay, that's it mads me, spites me! I'll spend my wealth ere he shall carry her so, because I know 'tis only to spite me. Ay, this is it. Here, nephew, before these kind gentlemen, I deliver in your mortgage, my promise to the widow. [*Gives a paper.*] See, 'tis done. Be wise, you're once more master of your own; the widow shall perceive now you are not altogether such a beggar as the world reputes you: you can make shift to bring her to three hundred a year, sir.

GENTLEMAN 1. Berlady, and that's no toy, sir.

LUCRE. A word, nephew.

GENTLEMAN 1 [*To* HOST.]. Now you may certify the widow.

LUCRE. You must conceive it aright, nephew, now; to do you good, I am content to do this.

WITGOOD. I know it, sir.

LUCRE. But your own conscience can tell I had it dearly enough of you.

WITGOOD. Ay, that's most certain.

LUCRE. Much money laid out, beside many a journey to fetch the rent; I hope you'll think on't, nephew.

WITGOOD. I were worse than a beast else, i'faith.

LUCRE. Although to blind the widow and the world, I out of policy do't, yet there's a conscience, nephew.

WITGOOD. Heaven forbid else!

LUCRE. When you are full possess'd, 'tis nothing to return it.

WITGOOD. Alas, a thing quickly done, uncle.

LUCRE. Well said! You know I give it you but in trust.

WITGOOD. Pray let me understand you rightly, uncle: you give it me but in trust?

LUCRE. No.

WITGOOD. That is, you trust me with it.

LUCRE. True, true.

WITGOOD [*Aside.*]. But if ever I trust you with it again, would I might be truss'd up for my labour!

LUCRE. You can all witness, gentlemen, and you, sir yeoman?

HOST. My life for yours, sir, now; I know my mistress's mind to well towards your nephew; let things be in preparation and I'll train her hither in most excellent fashion.

Exit.

LUCRE. A good old boy.—Wife! Ginny!

Enter WIFE.

WIFE. What's the news, sir?

LUCRE. The wedding day's at hand: prithee, sweet wife, express thy housewifery; thou'rt a fine cook, I know't; thy first husband married thee out of an alderman's kitchen. [WIFE *protests.*] Go to! He rais'd thee for raising of paste. What! Here's none but friends; most of our beginnings must be wink'd at. Gentlemen, I invite you all to my nephew's wedding against Thursday morning.

GENTLEMAN 1. With all our hearts, and we shall joy to see your enemy so mock'd.

LUCRE. He laugh'd at me, gentlemen; ha, ha, ha!

Exeunt [all but WITGOOD].

WITGOOD. He has no conscience, faith, would laugh at them.
They laugh at one another!
Who then can be so cruel? Troth, not I;
I rather pity now than aught envy.
I do conceive such joy in mine own happiness,
I have no leisure yet to laugh at their follies.

[*Kisses mortgage.*]

Thou soul of my estate, I kiss thee,
I miss life's comfort when I miss thee.
O never will we part again,
Until I leave the sight of men.
We'll ne'er trust conscience of our kin,
Since cozenage brings that title in.

[*Exit.*]

[*scene 3*]

Enter Three Creditors.

CREDITOR 1. I'll wait these seven hours but I'll see him caught.
CREDITOR 2. Faith, so will I.
CREDITOR 3. Hang him, prodigal, he's stripp'd of the widow.
CREDITOR 1. A' my troth, she's the wiser; she has made the happier choice, and I wonder of what stuff those widows' hearts are made of, that will marry unfledg'd boys before comely thrum-chinn'd gentlemen.

Enter a Boy.

BOY. News, news, news!
CREDITOR 1. What, boy?
BOY. The rioter is caught.
CREDITOR 1. So, so, so, so. It warms me at the heart; I love a' life to see dogs upon men. O here he comes.

Enter WITGOOD *with* Sergeants.

WITGOOD. My last joy was so great it took away the sense of all future afflictions. What a day is here o'ercast! How soon a black tempest rises!
CREDITOR 1. O we may speak with you now, sir! What's become of your rich widow? I think you may cast your cap at the widow, may you not, sir?
CREDITOR 2. He, a rich widow? Who, a prodigal, a daily rioter, and a nightly vomiter? He, a widow of account? He, a hole i'th'Counter!
WITGOOD. You do well, my masters, to tyrannize over misery, to afflict the afflicted; 'tis a custom you have here amongst you. I would wish you never leave it, and I hope you'll do as I bid you.
CREDITOR 1. Come, come, sir; what say you extempore now to your bill of a hundred pound? A sweet debt for frotting your doublets.
CREDITOR 2. Here's mine of forty.
CREDITOR 3. Here's mine of fifty.

WITGOOD. Pray, sirs, you'll give me breath?

CREDITOR: No, sir, we'll keep you out of breath still; then we shall be sure you will not run away from us.

WITGOOD. Will you but hear me speak?

CREDITOR 2. You shall pardon us for that, sir; we know you have too fair a tongue of your own; you overcame us too lately, a shame take you! We are like to lose all that for want of witnesses; we dealt in policy then: always when we strive to be most politic we prove most coxcombs, *non plus ultra*. I perceive by us we're not ordain'd to thrive by wisdom, and therefore we must be content to be tradesmen.

WITGOOD. Give me but reasonable time and I protest I'll make you ample satisfaction.

CREDITOR 1. Do you talk of reasonable time to us?

WITGOOD. 'Tis true, beasts know no reasonable time.

CREDITOR 2. We must have either money or carcass.

WITGOOD. Alas, what good will my carcass do you?

CREDITOR 3. O 'tis a secret delight we have amongst us. We that are used to keep birds in cages have the heart to keep men in prison, I warrant you.

WITGOOD [*Aside.*]. I perceive I must crave a little more aid from my wits: do but make shift for me this once, and I'll forswear ever to trouble you in the like fashion hereafter; I'll have better employment for you an I live. [*To* Creditors.] You'll give me leave, my masters, to make trial of my friends, and raise all means I can?

CREDITOR 1. That's our desires, sir.

Enter HOST.

HOST. Master Witgood.

WITGOOD. O art thou come?

HOST. May I speak one word with you in private, sir?

WITGOOD. No, by my faith, canst thou. I am in hell here, and the devils will not let me come to thee.

CREDITORS. Do you call us devils? You shall find us puritans! [*To* Sergeants.] Bear him away; let 'em talk as they go; we'll not stand to hear 'em. [*To* WITGOOD.] Ah, sir, am I a devil? I shall think the better of myself as long as I live: a devil, i'faith!

Exeunt.

[scene 4]

Enter HOARD.

HOARD. What a sweet blessing hast thou, Master Hoard, above
a multitude! Wilt thou never be thankful? How dost thou think
to be blest another time? Or dost thou count this the full measure
of thy happiness? By my troth, I think thou dost: not only a wife
large in possessions, but spacious in content: she's rich, she's
young, she's fair, she's wise. When I wake, I think of her lands;
that revives me: when I go to bed, I dream of her beauty, and
that's enough for me; she's worth four hundred a year in her very
smock, if a man knew how to use it. But the journey will be all,
in troth, into the country; to ride to her lands in state and order
following my brother and other worshipful gentlemen, whose
companies I ha' sent down for already, to ride along with us in
their goodly decorum beards, their broad velvet cassocks, and
chains of gold twice or thrice double; against which time I'll
entertain some ten men of mine own into liveries, all of occupations
or qualities. I will not keep an idle man about me. The sight of
which will so vex my adversary Lucre, for we'll pass by his door
of purpose, make a little stand for nonce, and have our horses
curvet before the window—certainly he will never endure it,
but run up and hang himself presently.

[*Enter* Servant.]

How now, sirrah what news? Any that offer their service to me
yet?
    SERVANT. Yes, sir, there are some i'th'hall that wait for your
worship's liking and desire to be entertain'd.
    HOARD. Are they of occupation?
    SERVANT. They are men fit for your worship, sir.
    HOARD. Say'st so? Send 'em all in.

[*Exit* Servant.]
To see ten men ride after me in watchet liveries with orange-
tawny capes, 'twill cut his comb, i'faith.

Enter [Tailor, Barber, Perfumer, Falconer, *and* Huntsman].

How now? Of what occupation are you, sir?

TAILOR. A tailor, an't please your worship.

HOARD. A tailor? O very good: you shall serve to make all the liveries.—What are you, sir?

BARBER. A barber, sir.

HOARD. A barber? Very needful: you shall have all the house, and if need require, stand for a reaper i'th'summer time.— You, sir?

PERFUMER. A perfumer.

HOARD. I smell'd you before. Perfumers, of all men, had need carry themselves uprightly, for if they were once knaves they would be smelt out quickly.—To you, sir?

FALCONER. A falc'ner, an't please your worship.

HOARD. Sa ho, sa ho, sa ho!—And you, sir?

HUNTSMAN. A huntsman, sir.

HOARD. There, boy, there, boy, there, boy! I am not so old but I have pleasant days to come. I promise you, my masters, I take such a good liking to you that I entertain you all: I put you already into my countenance, and you shall be shortly in my livery! But especially you two, my jolly falc'ner and my bonny huntsman, we shall have most need of you at my wife's manor houses i'th'country; there's goodly parks and champion grounds for you; we shall have all our sports within ourselves; all the gentlemen a'th'country shall be beholding to us and our pastimes.

FALCONER. And we'll make your worship admire, sir.

HOARD. Say'st thou so? Do but make me admire, and thou shalt want for nothing.—My tailor!

TAILOR. Anon, sir.

HOARD. Go presently in hand with the liveries.

TAILOR. I will, sir.

HOARD. My barber!

BARBER. Here, sir.

HOARD. Make 'em all trim fellows, louse 'em well, especially my huntsman, and cut all their beards of the Polonian fashion.— My perfumer!

PERFUMER. Under your nose, sir.

HOARD. Cast a better savour upon the knaves, to take away the scent of my tailor's feet and my barber's lotium water.

PERFUMER. It shall be carefully perform'd, sir.

HOARD. But you, my falc'ner and huntsman, the welcom'st men alive, i'faith!

HUNTSMAN. And we'll show you that, sir, shall deserve your worship's favour.

HOARD. I prithee, show me that. Go, you knaves all, and wash your lungs i'th'buttery, go.

[*Exeunt* Tailor, Barber, Perfumer, Falconer, *and* Huntsman.]
By th'mass, and well rememb'red, I'll ask my wife that question. Wife! Mistress Jane Hoard!

Enter COURTESAN, *alter'd in apparel.*

COURTESAN. Sir, would you with me?

HOARD. I would but know, sweet wife, which might stand best to thy liking, to have the wedding dinner kept here or i'th'country?

COURTESAN. Hum. Faith, sir, 'twould like me better here; here you were married, here let all rites be ended.

HOARD. Could a marquess give a better answer? Hoard, bear thy head aloft, thou'st a wife will advance it.

[*Enter* HOST *with a letter.*]

What haste comes here now? Yea, a letter? Some dreg of my adversary's malice. Come hither; what the news?

HOST. A thing that concerns my mistress, sir.

[*Gives letter to* COURTESAN.]

HOARD. Why, then it concerns me, knave.

HOST. Ay, and you, knave, too—cry your worship mercy. You are both like to come into trouble, I promise you, sir: a precontract.

HOARD. How! A precontract, say'st thou?

HOST. I fear they have too much proof on't, sir. Old Lucre, he runs mad up and down, and will to law as fast as he can; young Witgood, laid hold on by his creditors, he exclaims upon you a' tother side, says you have wrought his undoing by the injurious detaining of his contract.

HOARD. Body a' me!

HOST. He will have utmost satisfaction.
The law shall give him recompense he says.

COURTESAN [*Aside.*]: Alas, his creditors so merciless! My state being yet uncertain, I deem it not unconscionable to further him.

Host. True, sir,—

Hoard. Wife, what says that letter? Let me construe it.

Courtesan. Curs'd be my rash and unadvised words!
I'll set my foot upon my tongue
And tread my inconsiderate grant to dust.

[*Stamps on the letter.*]

Hoard. Wife—

Host [*Aside.*]. A pretty shift, i'faith. I commend a woman
when she can make away a letter from her husband handsomely,
and this was cleanly done, by my troth.

Courtesan. I did, sir.
Some foolish words I must confess did pass,
Which now litigiously he fastens on me.

Hoard. Of what force? Let me examine 'em.

Courtesan. Too strong, I fear: would I were well freed of
him.

Hoard. Shall I compound?

Courtesan. No, sir, I'd have it done some nobler way
Of your side; I'd have you come off with honour;
Let baseness keep with them. Why, have you not
The means, sir? The occasion's offer'd you.

Hoard. Where? How, dear wife?

Courtesan. He is now caught by his creditors; the slave's
needy, his debts petty; he'll rather bind himself to all inconve-
niences than rot in prison; by this only means you may get a
release from him. 'Tis not yet come to his uncle's hearing; send
speedily for the creditors; by this time he's desperate, he'll set his
hand to anything. Take order for his debts or discharge 'em quite.
A pax on him, let's be rid of a rascal!

Hoard. Excellent! Thou dost astonish me. [*To* Host.] Go,
run, make haste: bring both the creditors and Witgood hither.

Host [*Aside.*]. This will be some revenge yet.

[*Exit.*]

Hoard. In the mean space I'll have a release drawn.—Within
there!

[*Enter* Servant.]

Servant. Sir?

Hoard. Sirrah, come take directions; go to my scrivener.

[*Speaks aside with* Servant.]

COURTESAN [*Aside*.]. I'm yet like those whose riches lie in dreams;
If I be wak'd, they're false; such is my fate,
Who ventures deeper than the desperate state.
Though I have sinn'd, yet could I become new,
For where I once vow, I am ever true.

HOARD. Away! Dispatch! On my displeasure, quickly.

[*Exit* Servant.]

Happy occasion! Pray heaven he be in the right vein now to set his hand to't, that nothing alter him; grant that all his follies may meet in him at once, to besot him enough.
I pray for him, i'faith, and here he comes.

[*Enter* WITGOOD *with* Creditors.]

WITGOOD. What would you with me now, my uncle's spiteful adversary?

HOARD. Nay, I am friends.

WITGOOD. Ay, when your mischief's spent.

HOARD. I heard you were arrested.

WITGOOD. Well, what then? You will pay none of my debts I am sure.

HOARD. A wise man cannot tell.
There may be those conditions 'greed upon
May move me to do much.

WITGOOD.   Ay, when?
'Tis thou, perjured woman! O no name
Is vild enough to match thy treachery,
That art the cause of my confusion.

COURTESAN. Out, you penurious slave!

HOARD. Nay, wife, you are too froward,
Let him alone; give losers leave to talk.

WITGOOD. Shall I remember thee of another promise far stronger than the first?

COURTESAN. I'd fain know that.

WITGOOD. 'Twould call shame to thy cheeks.

COURTESAN. Shame?

WITGOOD. Hark in your ear. [*They talk apart*.] Will he come off, think'st thou, and pay my debts roundly?

COURTESAN. Doubt nothing; there's a release a-drawing and all, to which you must set your hand.

WITGOOD. Excellent!

COURTESAN. But methinks, i'faith, you might have made some shift to discharge this yourself, having in the mortgage, and never have burden'd my conscience with it.

WITGOOD. A' my troth, I could not, for my creditors' cruelties extend to the present.

COURTESAN. No more. [*Aloud.*] Why, do your worst for that, I defy you.

WITGOOD. Y'are impudent! I'll call up witnesses.

COURTESAN. Call up thy wits, for thou hast been devoted to follies a long time.

HOARD. Wife, y'are too bitter. Master Witgood, and you, my masters, you shall hear a mild speech come from me now, and this it is: 't'as been my fortune, gentlemen, to have an extraordinary blessing pour'd upon me a' late, and here she stands; I have wedded her and bedded her, and yet she is little the worse. Some foolish words she hath pass'd to you in the country, and some peevish debts you owe here in the City; set the hare's head to the goose-giblet: release you her of her words, and I'll release you of your debts, sir.

WITGOOD. Would you so? I thank you for that, sir; I cannot blame you, i'faith.

HOARD. Why, are not debts better than words, sir?

WITGOOD. Are not words promises, and are not promises debts, sir?

HOARD [*Aside.*]. He plays at back-racket with me.

CREDITOR 1. Come hither, Master Witgood, come hither; be rul'd by fools once.

CREDITOR 2. We are citizens and know what belong to't.

CREDITOR 1. Take hold of his offer. Pax on her, let her go. If your debts were once discharg'd, I would help you to a widow myself worth ten of her.

CREDITOR 3. Mass, partner, and now you remember me on't, there's Master Mulligrub's sister newly fall'n a widow.

CREDITOR 1. Cuds me, as pat as can be! There's a widow left for you, ten thousand in money, beside plate, jewels, *et cetera;* I warrant it a match; we can do all in all with her. Prithee, dispatch; we'll carry thee to her presently.

WITGOOD. My uncle will ne'er endure me when he shall hear I set my hand to a release.

CREDITOR 2. Hark, I'll tell thee a trick for that. I have spent five hundred pound in suits in my time, I should be wise. Thou'rt now a prisoner; make a release; take't of my word, whatsoever a man makes as long as he is in durance, 'tis nothing in law, not thus much.

[*Snaps his fingers.*]

WITGOOD. Say you so, sir?

CREDITOR 3. I have paid for't, I know't.

WITGOOD. Proceed then: I consent.

CREDITOR 3. Why, well said.

HOARD. How now, my masters, what have you done with him?

CREDITOR 1. With much ado, sir, we have got him to consent.

HOARD. Ah-a-a! And what came his debts to now?

CREDITOR 1. Some eight score odd pounds, sir.

HOARD. Naw, naw, naw, naw, naw! Tell me the second time; give me a lighter sum. They are but desperate debts, you know, ne'er call'd in but upon such an accident; a poor, needy knave, he would starve and rot in prison. Come, come, you shall have ten shillings in the pound, and the sum down roundly.

CREDITOR 1. You must make it a mark, sir.

HOARD. Go to, then; tell your money in the meantime; you shall find little less there. [*Gives them money.*] Come, Master Witgood, you are so unwilling to do yourself good now.

[*Enter* Scrivener.]

Welcome, honest scrivener. Now you shall hear the release read.

SCRIVENER. 'Be it known to all men by these presents that I, Theodorus Witgood, gentleman, sole nephew to Pecunious Lucre, having unjustly made title and claim to one Jane Medler, late widow of Anthony Medler, and now wife to Walkadine Hoard, in consideration of a competent sum of money to discharge my debts, do for ever hereafter disclaim any title, right, estate, or interest in or to the said widow, late in the occupation of the said Anthony Medler and now in the occupation of Walkadine Hoard; as also neither to lay claim by virtue of any former contract, grant, promise or demise, to any of her manor, manor houses, parks, groves, meadow-grounds, arable lands, barns, stacks, stables, dove holes, and cony burrows, together with all her cattell, money, plate, jewels, borders, chains, bracelets, furnitures, hangings, movables, or immovables. In witness whereof, I, the said Theodorus Witgood, have interchangeably set to my hand and seal before these presents, the day and date above written.'

WITGOOD. What a precious fortune hast thou slipp'd here, like a beast as thou art!

HOARD. Come, unwilling heart, come.

WITGOOD. Well, Master Hoard, give me the pen; I see 'Tis vain to quarrel with our destiny.

HOARD. O as vain a thing as can be; you cannot commit a greater absurdity, sir. So, so, give me that hand now: before all these presents, I am friends for ever with thee.

WITGOOD. Troth, and it were pity of my heart now if I should bear you any grudge, i'faith.

HOARD. Content. I'll send for thy uncle against the wedding dinner; we will be friends once again.

WITGOOD. I hope to bring it to pass myself, sir.

HOARD [To Creditors.]. How now? Is't right, my masters?

CREDITOR 1. 'Tis something wanting, sir, yet it shall be sufficient.

HOARD. Why, well said; a good conscience makes a fine show nowadays. Come, my masters, you shall all taste of my wine ere you depart.

ALL: We follow you, sir.

[Exeunt HOARD, Scrivener, and COURTESAN.]

WITGOOD [Aside.]. I'll try these fellows now. [To Creditors.] A word, sir: what, will you carry me to that widow now?

CREDITOR 1. Why, do you think we were in earnest, i'faith? Carry you to a rich widow? We should get much credit by that! A noted rioter, a contemptible prodigal! 'Twas a trick we have amongst us to get in our money. Fare you well, sir.

Exeunt [Creditors].

WITGOOD. Farewell and be hang'd, you short pig-hair'd, ram-headed rascals! He that believes in you shall ne'er be sav'd, I warrant him. By this new league I shall have some access unto my love.

She is above.

NIECE. Master Witgood!

WITGOOD. My life!

NIECE. Meet me presently; that note directs you. [*Throws a paper.*] I would not be suspected. Our happiness attends us. Farewell.

[*Exit.*]

WITGOOD. A word's enough.

[*Exit.*]

[scene 5]

DAMPIT *the usurer in his bed,* AUDREY *spinning by and* Boy.

THE SONG [*sung by* AUDREY].
> *Let the usurer cram him, in interest that excel,*
> *There's pits enow to damn him, before he comes to hell;*
> *In Holborn some, in Fleet Street some,*
> *Where'er he come, there's some, there's some.*

DAMPIT. *Trahe, traheto,* draw the curtain, give me a sip of sack more.

Enter Gentlemen [LAMPREY *and* SPITCHCOCK].

LAMPREY. Look you, did not I tell you he lay like the devil in chains, when he was bound for a thousand year?

SPITCHCOCK. But I think the devil had no steel bedstaffs; he goes beyond him for that.

LAMPREY. Nay, do but mark the conceit of his drinking; one must wipe his mouth for him with a muckinder, do you see, sir?

SPITCHCOCK. Is this the sick trampler? Why, he is only bed-rid with drinking.

LAMPREY. True, sir. He spies us.

DAMPIT. What, Sir Tristram? You come and see a weak man here, a very weak man.

LAMPREY. If you be weak in body, you should be strong in prayer, sir.

DAMPIT. O I have pray'd too much, poor man.

LAMPREY [*To* SPITCHCOCK.]. There's a taste of his soul for you.

SPITCHCOCK [*To* LAMPREY.]. Fah, loathsome!

LAMPREY. I come to borrow a hundred pound of you, sir.

DAMPIT. Alas, you come at an ill time. I cannot spare it, i'faith; I ha' but two thousand i'th'house.

AUDREY. Ha, ha, ha!

DAMPIT. Out, you gernative quean, the mullipood of villainy, the spinner of concupiscency!

Enter other Gentleman [SIR LANCELOT].

SIR LANCELOT. Yea, gentlemen, are you here before us? How is he now?

LAMPREY. Faith, the same man still: the tavern bitch has bit him i'th'head.

SIR LANCELOT. We shall have the better sport with him. Peace.—And how cheers Master Dampit now?

DAMPIT. O my bosom Sir Lancelot, how cheer I? Thy presence is restorative.

SIR LANCELOT. But I hear a great complaint of you, Master Dampit, among gallants.

DAMPIT. I am glad of that, i'faith; prithee, what?

SIR LANCELOT. They say you are wax'd proud a' late, and if a friend visit you in the afternoon, you'll scarce know him.

DAMPIT. Fie, fie! Proud? I cannot remember any such thing; sure, I was drunk then.

SIR LANCELOT. Think you so, sir?

DAMPIT. There 'twas, i'faith, nothing but the pride of the sack, and so certify 'em. [*To* Boy.] Fetch sack, sirrah.

BOY [*Aside*.]. A vengeance sack you once!

AUDREY. Why, Master Dampit, if you hold on as you begin and lie a little longer, you need not take care how to dispose your wealth; you'll make the vintner your heir.

DAMPIT. Out, you babliaminy, you unfeather'd cremitoried quean, you cullisance of scabiosity!

AUDREY. Good words, Master Dampit, to speak before a maid and a virgin.

DAMPIT. Hang thy virginity upon the pole of carnality!

AUDREY. Sweet terms! My mistress shall know 'em.

LAMPREY [*Aside*.]. Note but the misery of this usuring slave: here he lies, like a noisome dunghill, full of the poison of his drunken blasphemies, and they to whom he bequeaths all grudge him the very meat that feeds him, the very pillow that eases him.

Here may a usurer behold his end. What profits it to be a slave
in this world and a devil i'th'next?

DAMPIT. Sir Lancelot, let me buss thee, Sir Lancelot; thou art
the only friend that I honour and respect.

SIR LANCELOT. I thank you for that, Master Dampit.

DAMPIT. Farewell, my bosom Sir Lancelot.

SIR LANCELOT [*To* LAMPREY *and* SPITCHCOCK.]. Gentlemen,
and you love me, let me step behind you, and one of you fall
a-talking of me to him.

LAMPREY. Content.—Master Dampit.

DAMPIT. So, sir?

LAMPREY. Here came Sir Lancelot to see you e'en now.

DAMPIT. Hang him, rascal!

LAMPREY. Who, Sir Lancelot?

DAMPIT. Pythagorical rascal!

LAMPREY. Pythagorical?

DAMPIT. Ay, he changes his cloak when he meets a sergeant.

SIR LANCELOT [*Aside*.]. What a rogue's this!

LAMPREY. I wonder you can rail at him, sir; he comes in love
to see you.

DAMPIT. A louse for his love! His father was a combmaker; I
have no need of his crawling love. He comes to have longer day,
the superlative rascal.

SIR LANCELOT [*Aside*.]. 'Sfoot, I can no longer endure the
rogue.—Master Dampit, I come to take my leave once again, sir.

DAMPIT. Who? My dear and kind Sir Lancelot, the only gentleman of England? Let me hug thee; farewell, and a thousand.

LAMPREY [*Aside*.]. Compos'd of wrongs and slavish flatteries.

SIR LANCELOT [*Aside*.]. Nay, gentlemen, he shall show you
more tricks yet; I'll give you another taste of him.

LAMPREY [*Aside*.]. Is't possible?

SIR LANCELOT [*Aside*.]. His memory is upon departing.

DAMPIT. Another cup of sack!

SIR LANCELOT [*Aside*.]. Mass, then 'twill be quite gone! Before
he drink that, tell him there's a country client come up and here
attends for his learned advice.

LAMPREY [*Aside*.]. Enough.

DAMPIT. One cup more, and then let the bell toll; I hope I
shall be weak enough by that time.

LAMPREY. Master Dampit.

DAMPIT. Is the sack spouting?

LAMPREY. 'Tis coming forward, sir. Here's a countryman, a client of yours, waits for your deep and profound advice, sir.

DAMPIT. A coxcombry? Where is he? Let him approach: set me up a peg higher.

LAMPREY. You must draw near, sir.

DAMPIT. Now, goodman fooliaminy, what say you to me now?

SIR LANCELOT [*Disguising his voice*.]. Please your good worship, I am a poor man, sir—

DAMPIT. What make you in my chamber then?

SIR LANCELOT. I would entreat your worship's device in a just and honest cause, sir.

DAMPIT. I meddle with no such matters; I refer 'em to Master No-man's office.

SIR LANCELOT. I had but one house left me in all the world, sir, which was my father's, my grandfather's, my great-grandfather's, and now a villain has unjustly wrung me out and took possession on't.

DAMPIT. Has he such feats? Thy best course is to bring thy *ejectione firmae,* and in seven year thou mayst shove him out by the law.

SIR LANCELOT. Alas, an't please your worship, I have small friends and less money.

DAMPIT. Hoyday! This gear will fadge well! Hast no money? Why, then, my advice is thou must set fire a'th'house and so get him out.

LAMPREY. That will break strife indeed.

SIR LANCELOT. I thank your worship for your hot counsel, sir. [*Aside*.] Altering but my voice a little, you see he knew me not; you may observe by this that a drunkard's memory holds longer in the voice than in the person. But, gentlemen, shall I show you a sight? Behold the little dive-dapper of damnation, Gulf the usurer, for his time worse than tother.

Enter HOARD *with* GULF.

LAMPREY. What's he comes with him?

SIR LANCELOT. Why, Hoard, that married lately the widow Medler.

LAMPREY. O I cry you mercy, sir.

HOARD. Now, gentlemen visitants, how does Master Dampit?

SIR LANCELOT. Faith, here he lies, e'en drawing in, sir, good canary as fast as he can, sir; a very weak creature, truly, he is almost past memory.

HOARD. Fie, Master Dampit, you lie lazing abed here and I come to invite you to my wedding dinner: up, up, up!

DAMPIT. Who's this? Master Hoard? Who hast thou married, in the name of foolery?

HOARD. A rich widow.

DAMPIT. A Dutch widow!

HOARD. A rich widow, one widow Medler.

DAMPIT. Medler? She keeps open house.

HOARD. She did, I can tell you, in her tother husband's days, open house for all comers: horse and man was welcome, and room enough for 'em all.

DAMPIT. There's too much for thee then; thou mayst let out some to thy neighbours.

GULF. What, hung alive in chains? O spectacle! Bedstaffs of steel? *O monstrum horrendum, informe, ingens cui lumen ademptum!* O Dampit, Dampit, here's a just judgment shown upon usury, extortion, and trampling villainy!

SIR LANCELOT [*Aside*.]. 'Tis ex'llent, thief rails upon the thief!

GULF. Is this the end of cut-throat usury, brothel, and blasphemy? Now mayst thou see what race a usurer runs.

DAMPIT. Why, thou rogue of universality, do not I know thee? Thy sound is like the cuckoo, the Welsh ambassador; thou cowardly slave, that offers to fight with a sick man when his weapon's down! Rail upon me in my naked bed? Why, thou great Lucifer's little vicar, I am not so weak but I know a knave at first sight. Thou inconscionable rascal! Thou that goest upon Middlesex juries and will make haste to give up thy verdict because thou wilt not lose thy dinner, are you answered?

GULF. An't were not for shame—

Draws his dagger.

DAMPIT. Thou wouldst be hang'd then.

SIR LANCELOT. Nay, you must exercise patience, Master Gulf, always in a sick man's chamber.

SIR LANCELOT [*To* DAMPIT.]. He'll quarrel with none, I warrant you, but those that are bed-rid.

DAMPIT. Let him come, gentlemen, I am arm'd: reach my close-stool hither.

SIR LANCELOT. Here will be a sweet fray anon. I'll leave you, gentlemen.

LAMPREY. Nay, we'll along with you. Master Gulf—

GULF. Hang him, usuring rascal!

SIR LANCELOT. Push! Set your strength to his, your wit to his.

AUDREY. Pray, gentlemen, depart, his hour's come upon him. [*Embracing* DAMPIT.] Sleep in my bosom, sleep.

SIR LANCELOT. Nay, we have enough of him, i'faith; Keep him for the house. Now make your best; For thrice his wealth, I would not have his breast.

GULF. A little thing would make me beat him, now he's asleep.

SIR LANCELOT. Mass, then 'twill be a pitiful day when he wakes. I would be loath to see that day.

GULF. You overrule me, gentlemen, i'faith.

Exeunt.

ACT FIVE

[*scene 1*]

Enter LUCRE *and* WITGOOD.

WITGOOD. Nay, uncle, let me prevail with you so much. I'faith, go, now he has invited you.

LUCRE. I shall have great joy there when he has borne away the widow.

WITGOOD. Why, la, I thought where I should find you presently; uncle, a' my troth, 'tis nothing so.

LUCRE. What's nothing so, sir? Is not he married to the widow?

WITGOOD. No, by my troth, is he not, uncle.

LUCRE. How?

WITGOOD. Will you have the truth on't? He is married to a whore, i'faith.

LUCRE. I should laugh at that.

WITGOOD. Uncle, let me perish in your favour if you find it not so, and that 'tis I that have married the honest woman.

LUCRE. Ha! I'd walk ten mile afoot to see that, i'faith.

WITGOOD. And see't you shall, or I'll ne'er see you again.

LUCRE. A quean, i'faith? Ha, ha, ha!

Exeunt.

[*scene 2*]

Enter HOARD, *tasting wine, the* HOST *following in a livery cloak.*

HOARD. Pup, pup, pup, pup! I like not this wine; is there never a better tierce in the house?

HOST. Yes, sir, there are as good tierce in the house as any are in England.

HOARD. Desire your mistress, you knave, to taste 'em all over; she has better skill.

HOST [*Aside.*]. Has she so? The better for her and the worse for you.

Exit.

HOARD. Arthur!

[*Enter* Servant.]

Is the cupboard of plate set out?

ARTHUR. All's in order, sir.

[*Exit.*]

HOARD. I am in love with my liveries every time I think on 'em. They make a gallant show, by my troth.—Niece!

[*Enter* NIECE.]

NIECE. Do you call, sir?

HOARD. Prithee, show a little diligence and overlook the knaves a little; they'll filch and steal today and send whole pasties home to their wives; and thou be'st a good niece, do not see me purloin'd.

NIECE. Fear it not, sir. [*Aside.*] I have cause: though the feast be prepared for you, yet it serves fit for my wedding dinner too.

[*Exit.*]

Enter two Gentleman [LAMPREY *and* SPITCHCOCK].

HOARD. Master Lamprey, and Master Spitchcock, two the most welcome gentlemen alive! Your fathers and mine were all free o'th'fishmongers.

LAMPREY. They were indeed, sir. You see bold guests, sir, soon
entreated.

HOARD. And that's best, sir.

[Enter Servant]

How now, sirrah?

SERVANT. There's a coach come to th'door, sir.

[Exit.]

HOARD. My Lady Foxstone, a' my life!—Mistress Jane Hoard!
Wife!—Mass, 'tis her ladyship indeed.

[Enter LADY FOXSTONE.]

Madam, you are welcome to an unfurnish'd house, dearth of
cheer, scarcity of attendance.

LADY FOXSTONE. You are pleas'd to make the worst, sir.

HOARD. Wife!

[Enter COURTESAN.]

LADY FOXSTONE. Is this your bride?

HOARD. Yes, madam. [To COURTESAN.] Salute my Lady
Foxstone.

COURTESAN. Please you, madam, a while to taste the air in the
garden?

LADY FOXSTONE. 'Twill please us well.

Exeunt [LADY FOXSTONE and COURTESAN].

HOARD. Who would not wed? The most delicious life!
No joys are like the comforts of a wife.

LAMPREY [Aside.]. So we bachelors think, that are not troubled
with them.

[Enter Servant.]

SERVANT. Your worship's brother with another ancient
gentleman are newly alighted, sir.

[Exit.]

HOARD. Master Onesiphorus Hoard! Why, now our company
begins to come in.

[Enter ONESIPHORUS HOARD, LIMBER, and KIX.]

My dear and kind brother, welcome, i'faith.

ONESIPHORUS. You see we are men at an hour, brother.

HOARD. Ay, I'll say that for you, brother; you keep as good an hour to come to a feast as any gentleman in the shire. What, old Master Limber and Master Kix! Do we meet, i'faith, jolly gentlemen?

LIMBER. We hope you lack guests, sir.

HOARD. O welcome, welcome! We lack still such guests as your worships.

ONESIPHORUS. Ah, sirrah brother, have you catch'd up widow Medler?

HOARD. From 'em all, brother; and, I may tell you, I had mighty enemies, those that stuck sore: old Lucre is a sore fox, I can tell you, brother.

ONESIPHORUS. Where is she? I'll go seek her out; I long to have a smack at her lips.

HOARD. And most wishfully, brother. See where she comes.

[*Enter* COURTESAN.]

Give her a smack now we may hear it all the house over.

COURTESAN. O heaven, I am betray'd! I know that face.

Both [COURTESAN *and* ONESIPHORUS] *turn back.*

HOARD. Ha, ha, ha! Why, how now? Are you both asham'd? Come, gentlemen, we'll look another way.

ONESIPHORUS. Nay, brother, hark you; come, y'are dispos'd to be merry.

HOARD. Why do we meet else, man?

ONESIPHORUS. That's another matter. I was ne'er so 'fraid in my life but that you had been in earnest.

HOARD. How mean you, brother?

ONESIPHORUS. You said she was your wife.

HOARD. Did I so? By my troth, and so she is.

ONESIPHORUS. By your troth, brother?

HOARD. What reason have I to dissemble with my friends, brother? If marriage can make her mine, she is mine. Why?

ONESIPHORUS. Troth, I am not well of a sudden. I must crave pardon, brother; I came to see you but I cannot stay dinner, i'faith.

HOARD. I hope you will not serve me so, brother.

LIMBER. By your leave, Master Hoard—

HOARD. What now? What now? Pray, gentlemen, you were wont to show yourselves wise men.

LIMBER. But you have shown your folly too much here.

HOARD. How?

KIX. Fie, fie! A man of your repute and name! You'll feast your friends, but cloy 'em first with shame.

HOARD. This grows too deep; pray, let us reach the sense.

LIMBER. In your old age dote on a courtesan!

HOARD. Ha!

KIX. Marry a strumpet!

HOARD. Gentlemen!

ONESIPHORUS. And Witgood's quean!

HOARD. O! Nor lands nor living?

ONESIPHORUS. Living?

HOARD [*To* COURTESAN.]. Speak!

COURTESAN. Alas, you know, at first, sir. I told you I had nothing.

HOARD. Out, out! I am cheated, infinitely cozen'd!

LIMBER. Nay, Master Hoard—

HOARD. A Dutch widow, a Dutch widow, a Dutch widow!

Enter WITGOOD *and* LUCRE.

LUCRE. Why, nephew, shall I trace thee still a liar? Wilt make me mad? Is not yon thing the widow?

WITGOOD. Why, la, you are so hard a' belief, uncle! By my troth, she's a whore.

LUCRE. Then thou'rt a knave.

WITGOOD. *Negatur argumentum,* uncle.

LUCRE. *Probo tibi,* nephew: he that knows a woman to be a quean must needs be a knave; thou say'st thou know'st her to be one; *ergo,* if she be a quean, thou'rt a knave.

WITGOOD. *Negatur sequela maioris,* uncle: he that knows a woman to be a quean must needs be a knave, I deny that.

HOARD. Lucre and Witgood, y'are both villains; get you out of my house!

LUCRE. Why, didst not invite me to thy wedding dinner?

WITGOOD. And are not you and I sworn perpetual friends, before witness, sir, and were both drunk upon't?

HOARD. Daintily abused! Y'ave put a junt upon me.

LUCRE. Ha, ha, ha!

HOARD. A common strumpet!

WITGOOD. Nay, now you wrong her, sir. If I were she, I'd have the law on you for that; I durst depose for her she ne'er had common use nor common thought.

COURTESAN. Despise me, publish me, I am your wife;
What shame can I have now but you'll have part?
If in disgrace you share, I sought not you;
You pursued me, nay, forc'd me;
Had I friends would follow it,
Less than your action has been prov'd a rape.

ONESIPHORUS. Brother?

COURTESAN. Nor did I ever boast of lands unto you,
Money, or goods; I took a plainer course,
And told you true I'd nothing.
If error were committed, 'twas by you;
Thank your own folly. Nor has my sin been
So odious but worse has been forgiven;
Nor am I so deform'd but I may challenge
The utmost power of any old man's love.
She that tastes not sin before, twenty to one but she'll taste it after; most of you old men are content to marry young virgins and take that which follows; where, marrying one of us, you both save a sinner and are quit from a cuckold for ever.
And more, in brief, let this your best thoughts win,
She that knows sin, knows best how to hate sin.

HOARD. Curs'd be all malice! Black are the fruits of spite
And poison first their owners. O my friends,
I must embrace shame to be rid of shame.
Conceal'd disgrace prevents a public name.
Ah, Witgood, ah, Theodorus!

WITGOOD. Alas, sir, I was prick'd in conscience to see her well bestow'd, and where could I bestow her better than upon your pitiful worship? Excepting but myself, I dare swear she's a virgin; and now by marrying your niece I have banish'd myself for ever from her. She's mine aunt now, by my faith, and there's no meddling with mine aunt, you know, a sin against my nuncle.

COURTESAN. Lo, gentlemen, before you all
In true reclaimed form I fall.

[*Kneels.*]

Henceforth for ever I defy
The glances of a sinful eye,

Waving of fans, which some suppose
Tricks of fancy, treading of toes,
Wringing of fingers, biting the lip,
The wanton gait, th'alluring trip,
All secret friends and private meetings,
Close-borne letters and bawds' greetings,
Feigning excuse to women's labours
When we are sent for to th' next neighbours,
Taking false physic and ne'er start
To be let blood, though sign be at heart,
Removing chambers, shifting beds,
To welcome friends in husbands' steads,
Them to enjoy and you to marry,
They first serv'd while you must tarry,
They to spend and you to gather,
They to get and you to father.
These and thousand thousand more,
New reclaim'd, I now abhor.

    LUCRE. Ah, here's a lesson, rioter, for you!
    WITGOOD. I must confess my follies; I'll down too.

                                                          [Kneels.]

And here for ever I disclaim
The cause of youth's undoing: game,
Chiefly dice, those true outlanders
That shake out beggars, thieves, and panders,
Soul-wasting surfeits, sinful riots,
Queans' evils, doctors' diets,
'Pothecaries' drugs, surgeons' glisters,
Stabbing of arms for a common mistress,
Riband favours, ribald speeches,
Dear perfum'd jackets, penniless breeches,
Dutch flapdragons, healths in urine,
Drabs that keep a man too sure in—
I do defy you all.
Lend me each honest hand, for here I rise
A reclaim'd man, loathing the general vice.

    HOARD. So, so, all friends. The wedding dinner cools.
Who seem most crafty prove oft-times most fools.

                                                          [Exeunt.]

FINIS

EVERY MAN IN HIS HUMOUR

Ben Jonson

SIR,

There are, no doubt, a supercilious race in the world who will esteem all office done you in this kind an injury, so solemn a vice it is with them to use the authority of their ignorance to the crying down of poetry or the professors; but my gratitude must not leave to correct their error, since I am none of those that can suffer the benefits conferr'd upon my youth to perish with my age. It is a frail memory that remembers but present things; and, had the favor of the times so conspir'd with my disposition as it could have brought forth other or better, you had had the same proportion and number of the fruits the first. Now, I pray you to accept this; such wherein neither the confession of my manners shall make you blush, nor of my studies repent you to have been the instructor; and for the profession of my thankfulness, I am sure it will with good men find either praise or excuse.

Your true lover,
BEN. JONSON

PROLOGUE

Though need make many poets, and some such
As art and nature have not better'd much,
Yet ours for want hath not so lov'd the stage
As he dare serve th'ill customs of the age,
Or purchase your delight at such a rate
As, for it, he himself must justly hate:
To make a child now swaddled to proceed
Man, and then shoot up in one beard and weed
Past threescore years; or, with three rusty swords,
And help of some few foot and half-foot words,
Fight over York and Lancaster's long jars,
And in the tiring-house bring wounds to scars.
He rather prays you will be pleas'd to see
One such today as other plays should be:
Where neither Chorus wafts you o'er the seas,
Nor creaking throne comes down, the boys to please,
Nor nimble squib is seen, to make afear'd
The gentlewomen, nor roll'd bullet heard
To say, it thunders, nor tempestuous drum
Rumbles, to tell you when the storm doth come;
But deeds and language such as men do use,
And persons such as Comedy would choose
When she would show an image of the times,
And sport with human follies, not with crimes:
Except we make 'em such by loving still
Our popular errors, when we know they're ill.
I mean, such errors as you'll all confess
By laughing at them, they deserve no less:
Which, when you heartily do, there's hope left then
You that have so grac'd monsters may like men.

THE PERSONS OF THE PLAY

KNO'WELL, *an old gentleman*
ED[WARD] KNO'WELL, *his son*
BRAINWORM, *the father's man*
MASTER STEPHEN, *a country gull*
DOWNRIGHT, *a plain squire*
WELLBRED, *his half-brother*
JUSTICE CLEMENT, *an old merry magistrate*
ROGER FORMAL, *his clerk*
[THOMAS] KITELY, *a merchant*
DAME KITELY, *his wife*
MISTRESS BRIDGET, *his sister*
MASTER MATTHEW, *the town gull*
[THOMAS] CASH, *Kitely's man*
COB, *a water-bearer*
TIB, *his wife*
CAP[TAIN] BOBADILL, *a Paul's man*

[SERVANTS AND ATTENDANTS]

The Scene, *London*

Haud tamen invidias vati, quem pulpita pascunt.
                                                    —Juvenal

[I.i]

[*Enter*] Kno'well [*and*] Brainworm.

KNO'WELL. A goodly day toward, and a fresh morning!
Brainworm,
Call up your young master: bid him rise, sir.
Tell him, I have some business to employ him.
    BRAINWORM. I will, sir, presently.
    KNO'WELL.   But hear you, sirrah:
If he be't his book, disturb him not.
    BRAINWORM.   Well, sir.   [*Exit.*]
    KNO'WELL. How happy yet should I esteem myself
Could I by any practice wean the boy
From one vain course of study he affects.
He is a scholar, if a man may trust
The liberal voice of fame in her report,
Of good account in both our universities,
Either of which hath favor'd him with graces.
But their indulgence must not spring in me
A fond opinion that he cannot err.
Myself was once a student, and indeed
Fed with the self-same humour he is now,
Dreaming on nought but idle poetry,
That fruitless and unprofitable art,
Good unto none, but least to the professors,
Which then I thought the mistress of all knowledge:
But since, time and the truth have wak'd my judgment,
And reason taught me better to distinguish
The vain from th'useful learnings.

[*Enter* Stephen.]

                                        Cousin Stephen!
What news with you, that you are here so early?

STEPHEN. Nothing, but e'en come to see how you do, uncle.

KNO'WELL. That's kindly done; you are welcome, coz.

STEPHEN. Ay, I know that, sir, I would not ha' come else. How
do my cousin Edward, uncle?

KNO'WELL. Oh, well, coz; go in and see; I doubt he be scarce
stirring yet.

STEPHEN. Uncle, afore I go in, can you tell me an' he have e'er
a book of the sciences of hawking and hunting? I would fain
borrow it.

KNO'WELL. Why, I hope you will not a-hawking now, will
you?

STEPHEN. No, wusse; but I'll practice against next year, uncle.
I have bought me a hawk, and a hood and bells and all; I lack
nothing but a book to keep it by.

KNO'WELL. Oh, most ridiculous.

STEPHEN. Nay, look you now, you are angry, uncle. Why, you
know, an' a man have not skill in the hawking and hunting
languages nowadays, I'll not give a rush for him. They are more
studied than the Greek or the Latin. He is for no gallant's company without 'em; and by gad's lid I scorn it, ay, so I do, to be
a consort for every humdrum; hang 'em, scroyles, there's nothing in 'em, i'the world. What do you talk on it? Because I dwell
at Hogsden, I shall keep company with none but the archers of
Finsbury? Or the citizens, that come a-ducking to Islington Ponds?
A fine jest i'faith! 'Slid, a gentleman mun show himself like a
gentleman. Uncle, I pray you be not angry; I know what I have
to do, I trow, I am no novice.

KNO'WELL. You are a prodigal absurb coxcomb; go to.
Nay, never look at me, it's I that speak;
Take't as you will, sir, I'll not flatter you.
Ha' you not yet found means enow to waste
That which your friends have left you, but you must
Go cast away your money on a kite,
And know not how to keep it when you ha' done?
Oh, it's comely: this will make you a gentleman!
Well, cousin, well, I see you are e'en past hope
Of all reclaim. Ay, so, now you are told on it

You look another way.

STEPHEN.   What would you ha' me do?

KNO'WELL. What would I have you do? I'll tell you, kinsman.
Learn to be wise, and practice how to thrive;
That would I have you do; and not to spend
Your coin on every bauble that you fancy,
Or every foolish brain that humours you.
I would not have you to invade each place,
Nor thrust yourself on all societies,
Till men's affections or your own desert
Should worthily invite you to your rank.
He that is so respectless in his courses
Oft sells his reputation at cheap market.
Nor would I you should melt away yourself
In flashing bravery, lest, while you affect
To make a blaze of gentry to the world,
A little puff of scorn extinguish it,
And you be left like an unsavory snuff
Whose property is only to offend.
I'd ha' you sober and contain yourself;
Not that your sail be bigger than your boat;
But moderate your expenses now at first,
As you may keep the same proportion still;
Nor stand so much on your gentility,
Which is an aery and mere borrow'd thing
From dead men's dust and bones, and none of yours
Except you make or hold it. Who comes here?

[*Enter*] Servant.

SERVANT. Save you, gentlemen.

STEPHEN. Nay, we don't stand much on our gentility, friend;
yet you are welcome, and I assure you mine uncle here is a man
of a thousand a year, Middlesex land; he has but one son in all
the world; I am his next heir at the common law, Master Stephen,
as simple as I stand here, if my cousin die, as there's hope he will;
I have a pretty living o' mine own, too, beside, hard by here.

SERVANT. In good time, sir.

STEPHEN. "In good time, sir"? Why, and in very good time,
sir. You do not flout, friend, do you?

SERVANT. Not I, sir.

STEPHEN. Not you, sir? You were not best, sir; an' you should, here be them can perceive it, and that quickly, too; go to. And they can give it again soundly, too, an' need be.

SERVANT. Why, sir, let this satisfy you. Good faith, I had no such intent.

STEPHEN. Sir, an' I thought you had, I would talk with you, and that presently.

SERVANT. Good Master Stephen, so you may, sir, at your pleasure.

STEPHEN. And so I would, sir, good my saucy companion, an' you were out o' mine uncle's ground, I can tell you; though I do not stand upon my gentility, neither, in't.

KNO'WELL. Cousin, cousin! Will this ne'er be left?

STEPHEN. Whoreson base fellow! A mechanical serving man! By this cudgel, an't were not for shame, I would—

KNO'WELL. What would you do, you peremptory gull?
If you cannot be quiet, get you hence.
You see, the honest man demeans himself
Modestly t'wards you, giving no reply
To your unseason'd, quarreling, rude fashion;
And still you huff it with a kind of carriage
As void of wit as of humanity.
Go, get you in; fore heaven, I am asham'd
Thou hast a kinsman's interest in me.   [*Exit* Stephen.]

SERVANT. I pray you, sir, is this Master Kno'well's house?

KNO'WELL. Yes, marry, is it, sir.

SERVANT. I should enquire for a gentleman here, one Master Edward Kno'well; do you know any such, sir, I pray you?

KNO'WELL. I should forget myself else, sir.

SERVANT. Are you the gentleman? Cry you mercy, sir; I was requir'd by a gentleman i'the city, as I rode out at this end o'the town, to deliver you this letter, sir.

KNO'WELL. To me, sir? What do you mean? Pray you remember your court'sy. [*Reads.*] *To his most selected friend, Master Edward Kno'well.* What might the gentleman's name be, sir, that sent it? Nay, pray you be cover'd.

SERVANT. One Master Wellbred, sir.

KNO'WELL. Master Wellbred? A young gentleman, is he not?

SERVANT. The same, sir; Master Kitely married his sister: the rich merchant i'the Old Jewry.

KNO'WELL. You say very true. Brainworm!

[*Enter* Brainworm.]

BRAINWORM. Sir?

KNO'WELL. Make this honest friend drink here. Pray you,
go in.

[*Exeunt* Brainworm *and* Servant.]

This letter is directed to my son;
Yet I am Edward Kno'well too, and may
With the safe conscience of good manners use
The fellow's error to my satisfaction.
Well, I will break it ope—old men are curious—
Be it but for the style's sake and the phrase,
To see if both do answer my son's praises,
Who is almost grown the idolater
Of this young Wellbred.   [*Opens letter.*]
                    What have we here? What's this?
[*Reads.*] *Why, Ned, I beseech thee: hast thou forsworn all thy friends
i'the Old Jewry, or dost thou think us all Jews that inhabit there yet? If
thou dost, come over and but see our frippery: change an old shirt for a
whole smock with us. Do not conceive that antipathy between us and
Hogsden as was between Jews and hogs' flesh. Leave thy vigilant father
alone, to number over his green apricots evening and morning, o'the
northwest wall. An' I had been his son, I had sav'd him the labor long
since, if taking in all the young wenches that pass by at the back door, and
coddling every kernel of the fruit for 'em, would ha' served. But pr'ythee
come over to me, quickly, this morning: I have such a present for thee, our
Turkey Company never sent the like to the Grand Signior. One is a
rhymer, sir, o' your own batch, your own leaven, but doth think himself
Poet Mayor o'the town; willing to be shown, and worthy to be seen. The
other—I will not venture his description with you till you come, because
I would ha' you make hither with an appetite. If the worst of 'em be not
worth your journey, draw your bill of charges as unconscionable as any
Guildhall verdict will give it you, and you shall be allow'd your viaticum.*
                                            From The Windmill

From the Bordello it might come as well;
The Spital, or Pict-hatch. Is this the man
My son hath sung so for the happiest wit,
The choicest brain the times hath sent us forth?

I know not what he may be in the arts,
Nor what in schools, but surely for his manners
I judge him a profane and dissolute wretch;
Worse by possession of such great good gifts,
Being the master of so loose a spirit.
Why, what unhallow'd ruffian would have writ
In such a scurrilous manner to a friend?
Why should he think I tell my apricots,
Or play th' Hesperian dragon with my fruit,
To watch it? Well, my son, I'd thought
You'd had more judgment, t'have made election
Of your companions, than t'have ta'en on trust
Such petulant jeering gamesters, that can spare
No argument or subject from their jest.
But I perceive affection makes a fool
Of any man too much the father. Brainworm!

[*Enter* Brainworm.]

BRAINWORM. Sir?
KNO'WELL. Is the fellow gone that brought this letter?
BRAINWORM. Yes, sir, a pretty while since.
KNO'WELL. And where's your young master?
BRAINWORM. In his chamber, sir.
KNO'WELL. He spake not with the fellow, did he?
BRAINWORM. No, sir, he saw him not.
KNO'WELL. Take you this letter, and deliver it my son,
But with no notice that I have open'd it, on your life.
BRAINWORM. Oh Lord, sir, that were a jest indeed!   [*Exit.*]
KNO'WELL. I am resolv'd I will not stop his journey,
Nor practice any violent mean to stay
The unbridled course of youth in him; for that
Restrain'd, grows more impatient, and in kind
Like to the eager but the generous greyhound,
Who, ne'er so little from his game withheld,
Turns head and leaps up at his holder's throat.
There is a way of winning more by love
And urging of the modesty, than fear:
Force works on servile natures, not the free.
He that's compell'd to goodness may be good,
But 'tis but for that fit, where others drawn

By softness and example get a habit.
Then, if they stray, but warn 'em, and the same
They should for virtue've done, they'll do for shame.

[*Exit.*]

[*I.ii*]

[*Enter*] Edward Kno'well [*and*] Brainworm.

EDWARD KNO'WELL. Did he open it, sayest thou?

BRAINWORM. Yes, o' my word, sir, and read the contents.

EDWARD KNO'WELL. That scarce contents me. What countenance, prithee, made he i'the reading of it? Was he angry or
pleas'd?

BRAINWORM. Nay, sir, I saw him not read it, nor open it, I
assure your worship.

EDWARD KNO'WELL. No? How know'st thou, then, that he
did either?

BRAINWORM. Marry, sir, because he charg'd me on my life to
tell nobody that he open'd it; which, unless he had done, he
would never fear to have it reveal'd.

EDWARD KNO'WELL. That's true. Well, I thank thee, Brainworm.

[*He reads the letter.*]

[*Enter* Master Stephen.]

STEPHEN. Oh Brainworm, didst thou not see a fellow here in
a what-sha'-call-him doublet? He brought mine uncle a letter
e'en now.

BRAINWORM. Yes, Master Stephen; what of him?

STEPHEN. Oh, I ha' such a mind to beat him.—Where is he?
Canst thou tell?

BRAINWORM [*aside*]. Faith, he is not of that mind.—He is gone,
Master Stephen.

STEPHEN. Gone? Which way? When went he? How long since?

BRAINWORM. He is rid hence. He took horse at the street door.

STEPHEN. And I stay'd i'the fields! Whoreson Scanderbag rogue!
Oh, that I had but a horse to fetch him back again.

BRAINWORM. Why, you may ha' my mistress' gelding, to save
your longing, sir.

STEPHEN. But I ha' no boots, that's the spite on't.

BRAINWORM. Why, a fine wisp of hay roll'd hard, Master Stephen—

STEPHEN. No, faith, it's no boot to follow him now; let him e'en go and hang. 'Pray thee, help to truss me a little. He does so vex me—

BRAINWORM. You'll be worse vex'd when you are truss'd, Master Stephen. Best keep unbrac'd, and walk yourself till you be cold: your choler may founder you else.

STEPHEN. By my faith, and so I will, now thou tell'st me on't. How dost thou like my leg, Brainworm?

BRAINWORM. A very good leg, Master Stephen; but the woollen stocking does not commend it so well.

STEPHEN. Foh, the stockings be good enough, now summer is coming on, for the dust. I'll have a pair of silk again winter, that I go to dwell i'the town. I think my leg would show in a silk hose.

BRAINWORM. Believe me, Master Stephen, rarely well.

STEPHEN. In sadness, I think it would: I have a reasonable good leg.

BRAINWORM. You have an excellent good leg, Master Stephen, but I cannot stay to praise it longer now, and I am very sorry for't.

STEPHEN. Another time will serve, Brainworm; gramercy for this.

[*Exit* Brainworm.]

[Edward] Kno'well *laughs having read the letter.*

EDWARD KNO'WELL. Ha, ha, ha!

STEPHEN. 'Slid, I hope he laughs not at me; an' he do—

EDWARD KNO'WELL [*aside*]. Here was a letter, indeed, to be intercepted by a man's father, and do him good with him! He cannot but think most virtuously both of me and the sender, sure, that make the careful costermonger of him in our "Familiar Epistles"! Well, if he read this with patience, I'll be gelt, and troll ballads for Master John Trundle yonder, the rest of my mortality. It is true and likely my father may have as much patience as another man, for he takes much physic, and oft taking physic makes a man very patient. But would your packet, Master Wellbred, had arriv'd at him in such a minute of his patience; then we had known the end of it, which now is doubtful, and threatens—[*Notices* Stephen.] What, my wise cousin! Nay, then, I'll furnish our feast with one gull more t'ward the mess. He writes to me of a brace, and here's one, that's three. Oh, for a fourth! Fortune, if ever thou'lt use thine eyes, I entreat thee—[*Laughs.*]

STEPHEN [*aside*]. Oh, now I see who he laugh'd at. He laugh'd at somebody in that letter. By this good light, an' he had laugh'd at me—

EDWARD KNO'WELL. How now, cousin Stephen, melanch'ly?

STEPHEN. Yes, a little. I thought you had laugh'd at me, cousin.

EDWARD KNO'WELL. Why, what an' I had, coz, what would you ha' done?

STEPHEN. By this light, I would ha' told mine uncle.

EDWARD KNO'WELL. Nay, if you would ha' told your uncle, I did laugh at you, coz.

STEPHEN. Did you indeed?

EDWARD KNO'WELL. Yes indeed.

STEPHEN. Why, then—

EDWARD KNO'WELL. What then?

STEPHEN. I am satisfied; it is sufficient.

EDWARD KNO'WELL. Why, be so, gentle coz. And I pray you, let me entreat a courtesy of you. I am sent for this morning by a friend i'the Old Jewry to come to him; it's but crossing over the fields to Moorgate: will you bear me company? I protest, it is not to draw you into bond, or any plot against the state, coz.

STEPHEN. Sir, that's all one an't were; you shall command me twice so far as Moorgate to do you good in such a matter. Do you think I would leave you? I protest—

EDWARD KNO'WELL. No, no, you shall not protest, coz.

STEPHEN. By my fackins, but I will, by your leave; I'll protest more to my friend than I'll speak of at this time.

EDWARD KNO'WELL. You speak very well, coz.

STEPHEN. Nay, not so, neither, you shall pardon me; but I speak to serve my turn.

EDWARD KNO'WELL. Your turn, coz? Do you know what you say? A gentleman of your sort, parts, carriage, and estimation, to talk o' your turn i' this company, and to me alone, like a tankard-bearer at a conduit: fie! A wight that hitherto his every step hath left the stamp of a great foot behind him, as every word the savor of a strong spirit! And he, this man, so grac'd, gilded, or, to use a more fit metaphor, so tin-foil'd by nature, as not ten housewives'

pewter, again a good time, shows more bright to the world than
he; and he—as I said last, so I say again, and still shall say it—this
man, to conceal such real ornaments as these, and shadow their
glory as a milliner's wife does her wrought stomacher, with a
smoky lawn or a black cyprus? Oh coz, it cannot be answer'd;
go not about it; Drake's old ship at Deptford may sooner circle
the world again. Come, wrong not the quality of your desert
with looking downward, coz; but hold up your head, so; and let
the idea of what you are be portray'd i' your face, that men may
read i' your physnomy: "Here, within this place, is to be seen
the true, rare, and accomplish'd monster, or miracle of nature"—
which is all one. What think you of this, coz?

STEPHEN. Why, I do think of it; and I will be more proud, and
melancholy, and gentlemanlike than I have been; I'll ensure you.

EDWARD KNO'WELL. Why, that's resolute, Master Stephen!
[*Aside.*] Now, if I can but hold him up to his height, as it is
happily begun, it will do well for a suburb-humour: we may
hap have a match with the city, and play him for forty pound.—
Come, coz.

STEPHEN. I'll follow you.

EDWARD KNO'WELL. Follow me? You must go before.

STEPHEN. Nay, an' I must, I will. Pray you, show me, good
cousin.

[*Exeunt.*]

[I. iii]

[*Enter*] Master Matthew.

MATTHEW [*knocks at the door*]. I think this be the house: what
ho!

COB [*opens the door*]. Who's there? Oh, Master Matthew! Gi'
your worship good morrow.

[*Enter* Cob.]

MATTHEW. What, Cob! How dost thou, good Cob? Dost thou
inhabit here, Cob?

COB. Ay, sir, I and my lineage ha' kept a poor house here in
our days.

MATTHEW. Thy lineage, Monsieur Cob? What lineage, what lineage?

COB. Why, sir, an ancient lineage, and a princely. Mine ance'try came from a king's belly, no worse man; and yet no man neither—by your worship's leave, I did lie in that—but Herring, the King of fish—from his belly I proceed—one o'the monarchs o'the world, I assure you. The first red herring that was broil'd in Adam and Eve's kitchen do I fetch my pedigree from, by the harrots' books. His cob was my great, great, mighty-great grandfather.

MATTHEW. Why mighty? Why mighty, I pray thee?

COB. Oh, it was a mighty while ago, sir, and a mighty great cob.

MATTHEW. How know'st thou that?

COB. How know I? Why, I smell his ghost ever and anon.

MATTHEW. Smell a ghost? Oh, unsavory jest! And the ghost of a herring cob!

COB. Ay, sir; with favor of your worship's nose, Master Matthew, why not the ghost of a herring cob as well as the ghost of rasher bacon?

MATTHEW. Roger Bacon, thou wouldst say?

COB. I say rasher bacon. They were both broil'd o'the coals? And a man may smell broil'd meat, I hope? You are a scholar, upsolve me that, now.

MATTHEW. Oh, raw ignorance! Cob, canst thou show me of a gentleman, one Captain Bobadill, where his lodging is?

COB. Oh, my guest, sir, you mean?

MATTHEW. Thy guest! Alas! Ha, ha!

COB. Why do you laugh, sir? Do you not mean Captain Bobadill?

MATTHEW. Cob, 'pray thee, advise thyself well: do not wrong the gentleman, and thyself too. I dare be sworn he scorns thy house. He! He lodge in such a base, obscure place as thy house? Tut, I know his disposition so well; he would not lie in thy bed, if thou'ldst gi' it him.

COB. I will not give it him, though, sir. Mass, I thought somewhat was in't, we could not get him to bed all night. Well, sir, though he lie not o' my bed, he lies o' my bench; an't please you to go up, sir, you shall find him with two cushions under his head, and his cloak wrapp'd about him, as though he had neither won nor lost; and yet I warrant he ne'er cast better in his life than he has done tonight.

MATTHEW. Why, was he drunk?

COB. Drunk, sir? You hear not me say so. Perhaps he swallow'd a tavern token, or some such device, sir; I have nothing to do withal. I deal with water, and not with wine. [*Calls within.*] Gi' me my tankard there, ho!—God b'w'you, sir. It's six o'clock: I should ha' carried two turns by this.—What ho! My stopple! Come.

MATTHEW. Lie in a water-bearer's house, a gentleman of his havings! Well, I'll tell him my mind.

[Tib *appears at the door with a tankard.*]

COB. What, Tib, show this gentleman up to the Captain.

[*Exit* Matthew *with* Tib.]

Oh, an' my house were the Brazen Head now! Faith, it would e'en speak, "Moe fools yet." You should ha' some, now, would take this Master Matthew to be a gentleman, at the least. His father's an honest man, a worshipful fishmonger, and so forth; and now does he creep and wriggle into acquaintance with all the brave gallants about the town, such as my guest is—oh, my guest is a fine man—and they flout him invincibly. He useth every day to a merchant's house, where I serve water, one Master Kitely's, i'the Old Jewry; and here's the jest, he is in love with my master's sister, Mistress Bridget, and calls her "mistress"; and there he will sit you a whole afternoon some-times, reading o' these same abominable, vile—a pox on 'em, I cannot abide them—rascally verses, poyetry, poyetry, and speaking of interludes, 'twill make a man burst to hear him. And the wenches, they do so jeer and tee-hee at him—well, should they do so much to me, I'd forswear them all, by the foot of Pharaoh. There's an oath! How many water-bearers shall you hear swear such an oath? Oh, I have a guest, he teaches me, he does swear the legiblest of any man christen'd: "By Saint George, the foot of Pharaoh, the body of me, as I am gentleman and a soldier"—such dainty oaths! And withal, he does take this same filthy roguish tobacco, the finest and cleanliest! It would do a man good to see the fume come forth at's tunnels! Well, he owes me forty shillings—my wife lent him out of her purse, by sixpence a time—besides his lodging: I would I had it. I shall ha' it, he says, the next action. [*Takes up his tankard.*] Helter skelter, hang sorrow, care'll kill a cat, up-tails all, and a louse for the hangman.   [*Exit.*]

Bobadill *is discovered lying on his bench.*

BOBADILL. Hostess, hostess.

[*Enter* Tib *and goes to him.*]

TIB. What say you, sir?

BOBADILL. A cup o' thy small beer, sweet hostess.

TIB. Sir, there's a gentleman below would speak with you.

BOBADILL. A gentleman! 'Ods so, I am not within.

TIB. My husband told him you were, sir.

BOBADILL. What a plague—what meant he?

MATTHEW [*within*]. Captain Bobadill!

BOBADILL. Who's there?—Take away the basin, good hostess.—Come up, sir.

TIB [*calling*]. He would desire you to come up, sir.

[*Enter* Matthew.]

You come into a cleanly house here.

MATTHEW. 'Save you, sir. 'Save you, Captain.

BOBADILL. Gentle Master Matthew, is it you, sir? Please you sit down.

MATTHEW. Thank you, good Captain; you may see, I am somewhat audacious.

BOBADILL. Not so, sir. I was requested to supper last night by a sort of gallants, where you were wished for, and drunk to, I assure you.

MATTHEW. Vouchsafe me by whom, good Captain.

BOBADILL. Marry, by young Wellbred and others.—Why, hostess, a stool here for this gentleman.

MATTHEW. No haste, sir; 'tis very well.

BOBADILL. Body of me! It was so late ere we parted last night, I can scarce open my eyes yet; I was but new risen as you came. How passes the day abroad, sir? You can tell.

MATTHEW. Faith, some half hour to seven. Now trust me, you have an exceeding fine lodging here, very neat and private!

BOBADILL. Ay, sir; sit down, I pray you. Master Matthew, in any case, possess no gentlemen of our acquaintance with notice of my lodging.

MATTHEW. Who? I, sir? No.

BOBADILL. Not that I need to care who know it, for the cabin is convenient; but in regard I would not be too popular and generally visited, as some are.

MATTHEW. True, Captain; I conceive you.

BOBADILL. For do you see, sir, by the heart of valor in me, except it be to some peculiar and choice spirits, to whom I am extraordinarily engaged, as yourself or so, I could not extend thus far.

MATTHEW. Oh Lord, sir, I resolve so.

BOBADILL. I confess, I love a cleanly and quiet privacy above all the tumult and roar of fortune. What new book ha' you there? What! *Go by, Hieronymo!*

MATTHEW. Ay, did you ever see it acted? Is't not well penn'd?

BOBADILL. Well penn'd? I would fain see all the poets of these times pen such another play as that was! They'll prate and swagger, and keep a stir of art and devices, when, as I am a gentleman, read 'em, they are the most shallow, pitiful, barren fellows that live upon the face of the earth again.

MATTHEW. Indeed, here are a number of fine speeches in this book.—*Oh eyes, no eyes, but fountains fraught with tears!*—There's a conceit! Fountains fraught with tears!—*Oh life, no life, but lively form of death!*—Another! *Oh world, no world, but mass of public wrongs!*—A third!—*Confus'd and fill'd with murder and misdeeds!*—A fourth! Oh, the Muses! Is't not excellent?
Is't not simply the best that ever you heard, Captain? Ha? How do you like it?

BOBADILL. 'Tis good.

MATTHEW [*recites*].

> To thee, the purest object to my sense,
> The most refined essence heaven covers,
> Send I these lines, wherein I do commence
> The happy state of turtle-billing lovers.
> > If they prove rough, unpolish'd, harsh and rude,
> > Haste made the waste; thus mildly I conclude.

Bobadill *is making him ready all this while.*

BOBADILL. Nay, proceed, proceed. Where's this?

MATTHEW. This, sir? A toy o' mine own, in my nonage, the infancy of my Muses. But when will you come and see my study? Good faith, I can show you some very good things I have done of late.—That boot becomes your leg passing well, Captain, methinks.

BOBADILL. So, so; it's the fashion gentlemen now use.

MATTHEW. Troth, Captain, an' now you speak o' the fashion, Master Wellbred's elder brother and I are fall'n out exceedingly. This other day I happen'd to enter into some discourse of a hanger, which I assure you, both for fashion and workmanship, was most peremptory beautiful and gentlemanlike; yet he condemn'd and cried it down for the most pied and ridiculous that ever he saw.

BOBADILL. Squire Downright, the half-brother, was 't not?

MATTHEW. Ay, sir, he.

BOBADILL. Hang him, rook, he! Why, he has no more judgment than a malt-horse. By Saint George, I wonder you'd lose a thought upon such an animal: the most peremptory absurd clown of Christendom this day he is holden. I protest to you, as I am a gentleman and a soldier, I ne'er chang'd words with his like. By his discourse he should eat nothing but hay. He was born for the manger, pannier, or pack-saddle. He has not so much as a good phrase in his belly, but all old iron and rusty proverbs: a good commodity for some smith to make hobnails of.

MATTHEW. Ay, and he thinks to carry it away with his manhood still, where he comes. He brags he will gi' me the *bastinado,* as I hear.

BOBADILL. How, he the *bastinado*! How came he by that word, trow?

MATTHEW. Nay, indeed, he said cudgel me; I term'd it so for my more grace.

BOBADILL. That may be; for I was sure it was none of his word. But when, when said he so?

MATTHEW. Faith, yesterday, they say: a young gallant, a friend of mine, told me so.

BOBADILL. By the foot of Pharaoh, an't were my case now, I should send him a *chartel* presently. The *bastinado*! A most proper and sufficient *dependence,* warranted by the great Carranza. Come hither: you shall *chartel* him. I'll show you a trick or two you shall kill him with at pleasure: the first *stoccata,* if you will, by this air.

MATTHEW. Indeed, you have absolute knowledge i'the mystery. I have heard, sir.

BOBADILL. Of whom? Of whom ha' you heard it, I beseech you?

MATTHEW. Troth, I have heard it spoken of divers, that you have very rare and un-in-one-breath-utterable skill, sir.

BOBADILL. By heaven, no, not I; no skill i'the earth: some small rudiments i'the science, as to know my time, distance, or so. I have profess'd it more for noblemen and gentlemen's use than mine own practice, I assure you. Hostess, accommodate us with another bedstaff here, quickly—lend us another bedstaff.

[*Exit* Tib.]

The woman does not understand the words of action.—Look you, sir, exalt not your point above this state at any hand, and let your poniard maintain your defense, thus.—

[Tib *appears at the door with a bedstaff.*]

Give it the gentleman, and leave us.   [Tib *withdraws.*]

So, sir. Come on; oh, twine your body more about, that you may fall to a more sweet, comely, gentlemanlike guard. So, indifferent. Hollow your body more, sir, thus. Now, stand fast o' your left leg, note your distance, keep your due proportion of time— oh, you disorder your point most irregularly!

MATTHEW. How is the bearing of it now, sir?

BOBADILL. Oh, out of measure ill! A well-experienc'd hand would pass upon you at pleasure.

MATTHEW. How mean you, sir, pass upon me?

BOBADILL. Why, thus, sir: make a thrust at me: come in upon the answer, control your point, and make a full career at the body. The best-practic'd gallants of the time name it the *passada;* a most desperate thrust, believe it!

MATTHEW [*about to thrust*]. Well, come, sir.

BOBADILL. Why, you do not manage your weapon with any facility or grace to invite me; I have no spirit to play with you. Your dearth of judgment renders you tedious.

MATTHEW. But one *venue,* sir.

BOBADILL. "*Venue,*" fie! Most gross denomination as ever I heard. Oh, the *stoccata,* while you live, sir. Note that. Come, put on your cloak, and we'll go to some private place where you are acquainted, some tavern or so, and have a bit. I'll send for one of these fencers, and he shall breathe you by my direction; and then I will teach you your trick. You shall kill him with it at the first, if you please. Why, I will learn you, by the true judgment of the eye, hand, and foot, to control any enemy's point i'the world. Should your adversary confront you with a pistol, 'twere nothing, by this hand; you should, by the same rule, control his bullet in a line: except it were hailshot, and spread. What money ha' you about you, Master Matthew?

MATTHEW. Faith, I ha' not past a two shillings or so.

BOBADILL. 'Tis somewhat with the least: but come. We will have a bunch of radish and salt, to taste our wine, and a pipe of tobacco, to close the orifice of the stomach; and then we'll call upon young Wellbred. Perhaps we shall meet the Corydon his brother there, and put him to the question.

[Exeunt.]

[II.i]

[Enter] Kitely, Cash, [and] Downright.

KITELY. Thomas, come hither:
There lies a note within, upon my desk;
Here, take my key: it is no matter, neither.
Where is the boy?

CASH.   Within, sir, i'the warehouse.

KITELY. Let him tell over straight that Spanish gold,
And weigh it, with th' pieces of eight. Do you
See the delivery of those silver stuffs
To Master Lucar. Tell him, if he will,
He shall ha' the grograns at the rate I told him,
And I will meet him on the Exchange anon.

CASH. Good, sir.   [Exit.]

KITELY. Do you see that fellow, brother Downright?

DOWNRIGHT. Ay, what of him?

KITELY.   He is a jewel, brother.
I took him of a child, up at my door,
And christen'd him, gave him mine own name, Thomas;
Since bred him at the Hospital; where proving
A toward imp, I call'd him home and taught him

So much, as I have made him my cashier,
And giv'n him who had none, a surname, Cash;
And find him in his place so full of faith
That I durst trust my life into his hands.

DOWNRIGHT. So would not I in any bastards, brother,
As it is like he is; although I knew
Myself his father. But you said you'd somewhat
To tell me, gentle brother; what is't? What is't?

KITELY. Faith, I am very loath to utter it,
As fearing it may hurt your patience;
But that I know your judgment is of strength
Against the nearness of affection—

DOWNRIGHT. What need this circumstance? Pray you, be direct.

KITELY. I will not say how much I do ascribe
Unto your friendship; nor in what regard
I hold your love; but let my past behavior
And usage of your sister but confirm
How well I've been affected to your—

DOWNRIGHT. You are too tedious; come to the matter, the matter.

KITELY. Then, without further ceremony, thus.
My brother Wellbred, sir, I know not how,
Of late is much declin'd in what he was,
And greatly alter'd in his disposition.
When he came first to lodge here in my house,
Ne'er trust me, if I were not proud of him.
Methought he bare himself in such a fashion,
So full of man and sweetness in his carriage,
And, what was chief, it show'd not borrow'd in him,
But all he did became him as his own,
And seem'd as perfect, proper and possess'd
As breath with life, or color with the blood.
But now, his course is so irregular,
So loose, affected, and depriv'd of grace,
And he himself withal so far fall'n off
From that first place, as scarce no note remains
To tell men's judgments where he lately stood.
He's grown a stranger to all due respect,
Forgetful of his friends, and, not content
To stale himself in all societies,
He makes my house here common as a mart,

A theater, a public receptacle
For giddy humour and diseased riot:
And here, as in a tavern or a stews,
He and his wild associates spend their hours
In repetition of lascivious jests,
Swear, leap, drink, dance, and revel night by night,
Control my servants; and indeed, what not?

DOWNRIGHT. 'Sdeynes, I know not what I should say to him,
i'the whole world. He values me at a crack'd three-farthings, for
aught I see. It will never out o'the flesh, that's bred i'the bone.
I have told him enough, one would think, if that would serve;
but counsel to him is as good as a shoulder of mutton to a sick
horse. Well, he knows what to trust to, for George. Let him
spend, and spend, and domineer till his heart ache; an' he think
to be reliev'd by me when he is got into one o' your city pounds,
the Counters, he has the wrong sow by the ear, i'faith, and claps
his dish at the wrong man's door. I'll lay my hand o' my halfpenny
ere I part with't to fetch him out, I'll assure him.

KITELY. Nay, good brother, let it not trouble you thus.

DOWNRIGHT. 'Sdeath, he mads me, I could eat my very spur-
leathers for anger! But why are you so tame? Why do not you
speak to him, and tell him how he disquiets your house?

KITELY. Oh, there are divers reasons to dissuade, brother.
But, would yourself vouchsafe to travail in it,
Though but with plain and easy circumstance,
It would both come much better to his sense,
And savor less of stomach or of passion.
You are his elder brother, and that title
Both gives and warrants you authority,
Which, by your presence seconded, must breed
A kind of duty in him and regard;
Whereas, if I should intimate the least,
It would but add contempt to his neglect,
Heap worse on ill, make up a pile of hatred,
That in the rearing would come tott'ring down,
And in the ruin bury all our love.
Nay, more than this, brother; if I should speak,
He would be ready from his heat of humour
And overflowing of the vapor in him
To blow the ears of his familiars
With the false breath of telling, what disgraces

And low disparagements I had put upon him;
Whilst they, sir, to relieve him in the fable,
Make their loose comments upon every word,
Gesture, or look I use; mock me all over,
From my flat cap unto my shining shoes;
And out of their impetuous rioting fant'sies
Beget some slander that shall dwell with me.
And what would that be, think you? Marry, this.
They would give out, because my wife is fair,
Myself but lately married, and my sister
Here sojourning a virgin in my house,
That I were jealous! Nay, as sure as death,
That they would say; and how that I had quarrel'd
My brother purposely, thereby to find
An apt pretext to banish them my house.
    DOWNRIGHT. Mass, perhaps so; they're like enough to do it.
    KITELY. Brother, they would, believe it: so should I,
Like one of these penurious quacksalvers,
But set the bills up to mine own disgrace,
And try experiments upon myself;
Lend scorn and envy opportunity
To stab my reputation and good name—

[*Enter*] Matthew [*and*] Bobadill.

    MATTHEW. I will speak to him—
    BOBADILL. Speak to him? Away, by the foot of Pharaoh, you shall not; you shall not do him that grace.—The time of day to you, gentleman o'the house. Is Master Wellbred stirring?
    DOWNRIGHT. How then? What should he do?
    BOBADILL [*to* Kitely]. Gentleman of the house, it is to you. Is he within, sir?
    KITELY. He came not to his lodging tonight, sir, I assure you.
    DOWNRIGHT [*to* Bobadill]. Why, do you hear? You!
    BOBADILL. The gentleman citizen hath satisfied me, I'll talk to no scavenger.   [*Exeunt* Matthew *and* Bobadill.]
    DOWNRIGHT. How, scavenger? Stay, sir, stay!
    KITELY. Nay, brother Downright.
    DOWNRIGHT. 'Heart! Stand you away, an' you love me.
    KITELY. You shall not follow him now, I pray you, brother. Good faith, you shall not: I will overrule you.

DOWNRIGHT. Ha, scavenger? Well, go to, I say little: but by this good day—God forgive me I should swear—if I put it up so, say I am the rankest cow that ever piss'd. 'Sdeynes, an' I swallow this, I'll ne'er draw my sword in the sight of Fleet Street again, while I live; I'll sit in a barn with Madge Howlet, and catch mice first. Scavenger? 'Heart, and I'll go near to fill that huge tumbrel slop of yours with somewhat, an' I have good luck; your Garagantua breech cannot carry it away so.

KITELY. Oh, do not fret yourself thus; never think on't.

DOWNRIGHT. These are my brother's consorts, these! These are his *cam'rades,* his walking mates! He's a gallant, a *cavaliero* too, right hangman cut! Let me not live, an' I could not find in my heart to swinge the whole ging of 'em, one after another, and begin with him first. I am griev'd it should be said he is my brother, and take these courses. Well, as he brews, so he shall drink, for George, again. Yet he shall hear on't, and that tightly too, an' I live, i'faith.

KITELY. But brother, let your reprehension, then,
Run in an easy current, not o'er-high
Carried with rashness or devouring choler;
But rather use the soft, persuading way,
Whose powers will work more gently, and compose
Th'imperfect thoughts you labor to reclaim;
More winning than enforcing the consent.

DOWNRIGHT. Ay, ay, let me alone for that, I warrant you.

Bell rings.

KITELY. How now? Oh, the bell rings to breakfast.
Brother, I pray you, go in and bear my wife
Company till I come; I'll but give order
For some dispatch of business to my servants.

[*Exit* Downright.]

[*Cob*] *passes by with his tankard.*

What, Cob? Our maids will have you by the back, i'faith, for coming so late this morning.

COB. Perhaps so, sir; take heed somebody have not them by the belly for walking so late in the evening.   [*Exit.*]

KITELY. Well, yet my troubled spirit's somewhat eas'd,

Though not repos'd in that security
As I could wish; but I must be content.
Howe'er I set a face on't to the world,
Would I had lost this finger at a venture,
So Wellbred had ne'er lodg'd within my house.
Why, 't cannot be, where there is such resort
Of wanton gallants and young revelers,
That any woman should be honest long.
Is't like that factious beauty will preserve
The public weal of chastity unshaken,
When such strong motives muster and make head
Against her single peace? No, no. Beware
When mutual appetite doth meet to treat,
And spirits of one kind and quality
Come once to parley in the pride of blood:
It is no slow conspiracy that follows.
Well, to be plain, if I but thought the time
Had answer'd their affections, all the world
Should not persuade me but I were a cuckold.
Marry, I hope they ha' not got that start;
For opportunity hath balk'd 'em yet,
And shall do still, while I have eyes and ears
To attend the impositions of my heart.
My presence shall be as an iron bar
'Twixt the conspiring motions of desire;
Yea, every look or glance mine eye ejects
Shall check occasion, as one doth his slave
When he forgets the limits of prescription.

[*Enter* Dame Kitely *with* Bridget.]

DAME KITELY. Sister Bridget, pray you fetch down the rosewater above in the closet.   [*Exit* Bridget.]
Sweetheart, will you come in to breakfast?
   KITELY [aside]. An' she have overheard me now!
   DAME KITELY. I pray thee, good muss, we stay for you.
   KITELY [*aside*]. By heaven, I would not for a thousand angels!
   DAME KITELY. What ail you, sweetheart? Are you not well? Speak, good muss.
   KITELY. Troth, my head aches extremely, on a sudden.

DAME KITELY. Oh, the Lord!

[*She puts her hand to his forehead.*]

KITELY. How now? What?

DAME KITELY. Alas, how it burns! Muss, keep you warm; good truth, it is this new disease: there's a number are troubled withal. For love's sake, sweetheart, come in out of the air.

KITELY [*aside*]. How simple, and how subtle, are her answers! A new disease, and many troubled with it: Why, true; she heard me, all the world to nothing.

DAME KITELY. I pray thee, good sweetheart, come in; the air will do you harm, in troth.

KITELY [*aside*]. The air: she has me i'the wind.—Sweetheart, I'll come to you presently; 'twill away, I hope.

DAME KITELY. Pray heaven it do.   [*Exit.*]

KITELY. A new disease? I know not, new or old,
But it may well be call'd poor mortals' plague;
For like a pestilence it doth infect
The houses of the brain. First, it begins
Solely to work upon the fantasy,
Filling her seat with such pestiferous air
As soon corrupts the judgment; and from thence
Sends like contagion to the memory,
Still each to other giving the infection,
Which as a subtle vapor spreads itself
Confusedly through every sensive part,
Till not a thought or motion in the mind
Be free from the black poison of suspect.
Ah, but what mis'ry is it to know this,
Or, knowing it, to want the mind's erection
In such extremes! Well, I will once more strive,
In spite of this black cloud, myself to be,
And shake the fever off that thus shakes me.   [*Exit.*]

[II.ii]

[*Enter*] Brainworm [*disguised as a wounded soldier*].

BRAINWORM. 'Slid, I cannot choose but laugh to see myself translated thus, from a poor creature to a creator; for now must I create an intolerable sort of lies, or my present profession loses the grace: and yet the lie to a man of my coat is as ominous a fruit as the *fico.* Oh, sir, it holds for good polity ever, to have that outwardly in vilest estimation that inwardly is most dear to us. So much for my borrowed shape. Well, the troth is, my old master intends to follow my young, dryfoot over Moorfields to London this morning. Now I, knowing of this hunting-match, or rather conspiracy, and to insinuate with my young master—for so must we that are blue-waiters, and men of hope and service, do, or perhaps we may wear motley at the year's end, and "who wears motley," you know—have got me afore in this disguise, determining here to lie in ambuscado, and intercept him in the mid-way. If I can but get his cloak, his purse, his hat, nay, anything to cut him off, that is, to stay his journey, *veni, vidi, vici,* I may say with Captain Caesar; I am made forever, i'faith. Well, now must I practice to get the true garb of one of these lance-knights; my arm here, and my—young master! And his cousin Master Stephen, as I am true counterfeit man of war, and no soldier!

[*Walks apart.*]

[*Enter* Edward Kno'well *and* Stephen.]

EDWARD KNO'WELL. So, sir, and how then, coz?

STEPHEN. 'Sfoot, I have lost my purse, I think.

EDWARD KNO'WELL. How, lost your purse? Where? When had you it?

STEPHEN. I cannot tell.—Stay!

BRAINWORM [*aside*]. 'Slid, I am afeard they will know me; would I could get by them! [*Stands at a distance.*]

EDWARD KNO'WELL. What, ha' you it?

STEPHEN. No; I think I was bewitch'd, I— [*Weeps.*]

EDWARD KNO'WELL. Nay, do not weep the loss; hang it, let it go.

STEPHEN. Oh, it's here. No, an' it had been lost, I had not cared, but for a jet ring Mistress Mary sent me.

EDWARD KNO'WELL. A jet ring? Oh, the poesy, the poesy?

STEPHEN. Fine, i'faith:

> *Though fancy sleep,*
> *My love is deep.*

Meaning that, though I did not fancy her, yet she loved me dearly.

EDWARD KNO'WELL. Most excellent!

STEPHEN. And then I sent her another, and my poesy was:

The deeper, the sweeter,
I'll be judg'd by Saint Peter.

EDWARD KNO'WELL. How, by Saint Peter? I do not conceive
that.

STEPHEN. Marry, Saint Peter, to make up the meter.

EDWARD KNO'WELL. Well, there the saint was your good
patron, he help'd you at your need; thank him, thank him.

BRAINWORM [*aside*]. I cannot take leave on 'em so; I will
venture, come what will. (*Comes back.*)—Gentlemen, please
you change a few crowns for a very excellent good blade here?
I am a poor gentleman, a soldier, one that in the better state of
my fortunes scorn'd so mean a refuge, but now it is the humour
of necessity to have it so. You seem to be gentlemen well
affected to martial men, else I should rather die with silence
than live with shame; however, vouchsafe to remember it is
my want speaks, not myself. This condition agrees not with
my spirit—

EDWARD KNO'WELL. Where hast thou serv'd?

BRAINWORM. May it please you, sir, in all the late wars of
Bohemia, Hungaria, Dalmatia, Poland, where not, sir? I have
been a poor servitor by sea and land, any time this fourteen years,
and follow'd the fortunes of the best commanders in Christendom.
I was twice shot at the taking of Aleppo, once at the relief of
Vienna; I have been at Marseilles, Naples, and the Adriatic Gulf;
a gentleman slave in the galleys thrice, where I was most danger-
ously shot in the head, through both the thighs, and yet, being
thus maim'd, I am void of maintenance, nothing left me but my
scars, the noted marks of my resolution.

STEPHEN. How will you sell this rapier, friend?

BRAINWORM. Generous sir, I refer it to your own judgment;
you are a gentleman, give me what you please.

STEPHEN. True, I am a gentleman, I know that, friend: but
what though? I pray you say, what would you ask?

BRAINWORM. I assure you, the blade may become the side, or
thigh, of the best prince in Europe.

EDWARD KNO'WELL. Ay, with a velvet scabbard, I think!

STEPHEN. Nay, an't be mine, it shall have a velvet scabbard,
coz, that's flat: I'd not wear it as 'tis, an' you would give me an
angel.

BRAINWORM. At your worship's pleasure, sir; nay, 'tis a most
pure Toledo.

STEPHEN. I had rather it were a Spaniard. But tell me, what shall I give you for it? An' it had a silver hilt—

EDWARD KNO'WELL. Come, come, you shall not buy it; hold, there's a shilling, fellow; take thy rapier.

STEPHEN. Why, but I will buy it now, because you say so, and there's another shilling, fellow: I scorn to be out-bidden. What, shall I walk with a cudgel like Higginbottom? And may have a rapier for money?

EDWARD KNO'WELL. You may buy one in the city.

STEPHEN. Tut, I'll buy this i'the field, so I will; I have a mind to't, because 'tis a field rapier. Tell me your lowest price.

EDWARD KNO'WELL. You shall not buy it, I say.

STEPHEN. By this money, but I will, though I give more than 'tis worth.

EDWARD KNO'WELL. Come away, you are a fool.

STEPHEN. Friend, I am a fool, that's granted; but I'll have it for that word's sake. [*To Brainworm.*] Follow me for your money.

BRAINWORM. At your service, sir.   [*Exeunt.*]

[II.iii]

[Enter] Kno'well.

KNO'WELL. I cannot lose the thought yet of this letter
Sent to my son, nor leave t'admire the change
Of manners and the breeding of our youth
Within the kingdom, since myself was one.
When I was young, he liv'd not in the stews
Durst have conceiv'd a scorn and utter'd it
On a grey head; age was authority
Against a buffoon, and a man had then
A certain reverence paid unto his years
That had none due unto his life; so much
The sanctity of some prevail'd for others.
But now we all are fall'n; youth from their fear,
And age from that which bred it, good example.
Nay, would ourselves were not the first, even parents,
That did destroy the hopes in our own children,
Or they not learn'd our vices in their cradles,
And suck'd in our ill customs with their milk.
Ere all their teeth be born, or they can speak,

We make their palates cunning. The first words
We form their tongues with are licentious jests.
Can it call "whore"? Cry "bastard"? Oh, then, kiss it;
A witty child! Can 't swear? The father's dearling!
Give it two plums. Nay, rather than 't shall learn
No bawdy song, the mother 'self will teach it.
But this is in the infancy; the days
Of the long coat; when it puts on the breeches
It will put off all this. Ay, it is like,
When it is gone into the bone already.
No, no; this dye goes deeper than the coat,
Or shirt, or skin. It stains unto the liver
And heart in some. And, rather than it should not,
Note what we fathers do: look how we live:
What mistresses we keep: at what expense
In our sons' eyes, where they may handle our gifts,
Hear our lascivious courtships, see our dalliance,
Taste of the same provoking meats with us,
To ruin of our states. Nay, when our own
Portion is fled, to prey on their remainder
We call them into fellowship of vice,
Bait 'em with the young chambermaid, to seal,
And teach 'em all bad ways, to buy affection.
This is one path; but there are millions more
In which we spoil our own with leading them.
Well, I thank heaven I never yet was he
That travel'd with my son, before sixteen,
To show him the Venetian courtesans;
Nor read the grammar of cheating I had made
To my sharp boy at twelve, repeating still
The rule: "Get money"; still, "Get money, boy;
No matter by what means; money will do
More, boy, than my lord's letter." Neither have I
Dress'd snails or mushrooms curiously before him,
Perfum'd my sauces, and taught him to make 'em;
Preceding still with my grey gluttony
At all the ordinaries; and only fear'd
His palate should degenerate, not his manners.
These are the trade of fathers now; however,
My son, I hope, hath met within my threshold
None of these household precedents, which are strong

And swift to rape youth to their precipice.
But, let the house at home be ne'er so clean-
Swept, or kept sweet from filth, nay, dust and cobwebs,
If he will live abroad with his companions
In dung and leystalls, it is worth a fear;
Nor is the danger of conversing less
Than all that I have mention'd of example.

[*Enter* Brainworm, *disguised.*]

BRAINWORM [*aside*]. My master! Nay, faith, have at you: I am
flesh'd now, I have sped so well.—Worshipful sir, I beseech you,
respect the estate of a poor soldier. I am asham'd of this base
course of life, God's my comfort; but extremity provokes me
to't; what remedy?

KNO'WELL. I have not for you now.

BRAINWORM. By the faith I bear unto truth, gentleman, it is
no ordinary custom in me, but only to preserve manhood. I
protest to you, a man I have been, a man I may be, by your sweet
bounty.

KNO'WELL. 'Pray thee, good friend, be satisfied.

BRAINWORM. Good sir, by that hand, you may do the part of
a kind gentleman, in lending a poor soldier the price of two cans
of beer; a matter of small value; the King of Heaven shall pay
you, and I shall rest thankful: sweet worship—

KNO'WELL. Nay, an' you be so importunate—

BRAINWORM. Oh, tender sir, need will have his course: I was
not made to this vile use. Well, the edge of the enemy could not
have abated me so much. It's hard when a man hath serv'd in his
prince's cause, and be thus—   (*He weeps.*)   Honorable worship,
let me derive a small piece of silver from you; it shall not be given
in the course of time, by this good ground, I was fain to pawn
my rapier last night for a poor supper, I had suck'd the hilts long
before, I am a pagan else: sweet honor.

KNO'WELL. Believe me, I am taken with some wonder,
To think a fellow of thy outward presence
Should, in the frame and fashion of his mind,
Be so degenerate and sordid base.
Art thou a man? And sham'st thou not to beg?
To practice such a servile kind of life?
Why, were thy education ne'er so mean,

Having thy limbs, a thousand fairer courses
Offer themselves to thy election.
Either the wars might still supply thy wants
Or service of some virtuous gentleman,
Or honest labor: nay, what can I name,
But would become thee better than to beg?
But men of thy condition feed on sloth,
As doth the beetle on the dung she breeds in,
Not caring how the mettle of your minds
Is eaten with the rust of idleness.
Now, afore me, whate'er he be that should
Relieve a person of thy quality,
While thou insists in this loose desperate course
I would esteem the sin not thine, but his.

BRAINWORM. Faith, sir, I would gladly find some other course, if so—

KNO'WELL. Ay, you'd gladly find it, but you will not seek it.

BRAINWORM. Alas, sir, where should a man seek? In the wars there's no ascent by desert in these days, but—and for service, would it were as soon purchas'd as wish'd for; the air's my comfort; I know what I would say—

KNO'WELL. What's thy name?

BRAINWORM. Please you, Fitzsword, sir.

KNO'WELL. Fitzsword?
Say that a man should entertain thee now,
Wouldst thou be honest, humble, just and true?

BRAINWORM. Sir, by the place and honor of a soldier—

KNO'WELL. Nay, nay, I like not those affected oaths;
Speak plainly, man: what think'st thou of my words?

BRAINWORM. Nothing, sir, but wish my fortunes were as happy as my service should be honest.

KNO'WELL. Well, follow me; I'll prove thee, if thy deeds
Will carry a proportion to thy words.

BRAINWORM. Yes, sir, straight; I'll but garter my hose.

[*Exit* Kno'well.]
Oh, that my belly were hoop'd now, for I am ready to burst with laughing! Never was bottle or bagpipe fuller. 'Slid, was there ever seen a fox in years to betray himself thus? Now shall I be possess'd of all his counsels, and by that conduit, my young master. Well, he is resolv'd to prove my honesty; faith, and I am resolv'd to prove his patience: oh, I shall abuse him intolerably. This small

piece of service will bring him clean out of love with the soldier forever. He will never come within the sign of it, the sight of a cassock or a musket-rest, again. He will hate the musters at Mile End for it, to his dying day. It's no matter, let the world think me a bad counterfeit, if I cannot give him the slip at an instant; why, this is better than to have stay'd his journey! Well, I'll follow him; oh, how I long to be employed!   [*Exit.*]

[*III.i*]

[*Enter*] Matthew, Wellbred, [*and*] Bobadill.

MATTHEW. Yes, faith, sir, we were at your lodging to seek you, too.

WELLBRED. Oh, I came not there tonight.

BOBADILL. Your brother delivered us as much.

WELLBRED. Who? My brother Downright?

BOBADILL. He. Master Wellbred, I know not in what kind you hold me, but let me say to you this. As sure as honor, I esteem it so much out of the sunshine of reputation to throw the least beam of regard upon such a—

WELLBRED. Sir, I must hear no ill words of my brother.

BOBADILL. I protest to you, as I have a thing to be sav'd about me, I never saw any gentlemanlike part—

WELLBRED. Good captain, faces about: to some other discourse.

BOBADILL. With your leave, sir, an' there were no more men living upon the face of the earth, I should not fancy him, by Saint George.

MATTHEW. Troth, nor I; he is of a rustical cut, I know not how; he doth not carry himself like a gentleman of fashion.

WELLBRED. Oh, Master Matthew, that's a grace peculiar but to a few: *quos aequus amavit Jupiter.*

MATTHEW. I understand you, sir.

WELLBRED. No question you do or you do not, sir.

Young Kno'well *enters* [*and* Stephen].

Ned Kno'well! By my soul, welcome; how dost thou, sweet spirit, my genius? 'Slid, I shall love Apollo and the mad Thespian girls the better, while I live, for this. My dear fury, now I see there's some love in thee! Sirrah, these be the two I writ to thee of.—Nay, what a drowsy humour is this now! Why dost thou not speak?

EDWARD KNO'WELL. Oh, you are a fine gallant; you sent me a rare letter.

WELLBRED. Why, was't not rare?

EDWARD KNO'WELL. Yes, I'll be sworn, I was ne'er guilty of reading the like; match it in all Pliny or Symmachus' Epistles, and I'll have my judgment burn'd in the ear for a rogue: make much of thy vein, for it is inimitable. But I mar'el what camel it was that had the carriage of it? For doubtless, he was no ordinary beast that brought it.

WELLBRED. Why?

EDWARD KNO'WELL. Why, sayest thou? Why, dost thou think that any reasonable creature, especially in the morning—the sober time of the day, too—could have mista'en my father for me?

WELLBRED. 'Slid, you jest, I hope?

EDWARD KNO'WELL. Indeed, the best use we can turn it to is to make a jest on't now; but I'll assure you, my father had the full view o' your flourishing style some hour before I saw it.

WELLBRED. What a dull slave was this! But, sirrah, what said he to it, i'faith?

EDWARD KNO'WELL. Nay, I know not what he said; but I have a shrewd guess what he thought.

WELLBRED. What? What?

EDWARD KNO'WELL. Marry, that thou art some strange, dissolute young fellow, and I a grain or two better, for keeping thee company.

WELLBRED. Tut, that thought is like the moon in her last quarter, 't will change shortly. But, sirrah, I pray thee be acquainted with my two hang-bys here; thou wilt take exceeding pleasure in 'em if thou hear'st 'em once go; my wind-instruments. I'll wind 'em up—but what strange piece of silence is this? The sign of the Dumb Man?

EDWARD KNO'WELL. Oh, sir, a kinsman of mine; one that may make your music the fuller, an' he please; he has his humour, sir.

WELLBRED. Oh, what is't? What is't?

EDWARD KNO'WELL. Nay, I'll neither do your judgment nor his folly that wrong, as to prepare your apprehension. I'll leave him to the mercy o' your search; if you can take him, so.

WELLBRED. Well, Captain Bobadill, Master Matthew, pray you know this gentleman here; he is a friend of mine, and one that will deserve your affection. (*To* Master Stephen.) I know not your name, sir, but I shall be glad of any occasion to render me more familiar to you.

STEPHEN. My name is Master Stephen, sir; I am this gentleman's own cousin, sir, his father is mine uncle; sir, I am somewhat melancholy, but you shall command me, sir, in whatsoever is incident to a gentleman.

BOBADILL (*to* Kno'well). Sir, I must tell you this, I am no general man; but for Master Wellbred's sake—you may embrace it at what height of favor you please—I do communicate with you, and conceive you to be a gentleman of some parts: I love few words.

EDWARD KNO'WELL. And I fewer, sir. I have scarce enow to thank you.

MATTHEW (*to* Master Stephen). But are you indeed, sir, so given to it?

STEPHEN. Ay, truly, sir, I am mightily given to melancholy.

MATTHEW. Oh, it's your only fine humour, sir; your true melancholy breeds your perfect fine wit, sir. I am melancholy myself divers times, sir, and then do I no more but take pen and paper presently, and overflow you half a score or a dozen of sonnets at a sitting.

EDWARD KNO'WELL [*aside*]. Sure, he utters them, then, by the gross.

STEPHEN. Truly, sir, and I love such things out of measure.

EDWARD KNO'WELL [*aside*]. I'faith, better than in measure, I'll undertake.

MATTHEW. Why, I pray you, sir, make use of my study; it's at your service.

STEPHEN. I thank you, sir; I shall be bold, I warrant you; have you a stool there, to be melanch'ly upon?

MATTHEW. That I have, sir, and some papers there of mine own doing at idle hours, that you'll say there's some sparks of wit in 'em when you see them.

WELLBRED [*aside*]. Would the sparks would kindle once, and become a fire amongst 'em; I might see self-love burnt for her heresy!

STEPHEN [*to* Edward Kno'well]. Cousin, is it well? Am I melancholy enough?

EDWARD KNO'WELL. Oh, ay, excellent!

WELLBRED. Captain Bobadill, why muse you so?

EDWARD KNO'WELL [*aside*]. He is melancholy, too.

BOBADILL. Faith, sir, I was thinking of a most honorable piece of service was perform'd tomorrow, being Saint Mark's day: shall be some ten years now.

EDWARD KNO'WELL. In what place, Captain?

BOBADILL. Why, at the beleag'ring of Strigonium; where, in less than two hours, seven hundred resolute gentlemen as any were in Europe lost their lives upon the breach. I'll tell you, gentlemen, it was the first, but the best, leaguer that ever I beheld with these eyes, except the taking in of—what do you call it?—last year by the Genoways; but that of all other was the most fatal and dangerous exploit that ever I was rang'd in, since I first bore arms before the face of the enemy, as I am a gentleman and soldier.

STEPHEN [*aside*]. 'So, I had as lief as an angel I could swear as well as that gentleman!

EDWARD KNO'WELL. Then you were a servitor at both, it seems: at Strigonium, and What-do-you-call't?

BOBADILL. Oh Lord, sir! By Saint George, I was the first man that enter'd the breach; and had I not effected it with resolution, I had been slain if I had had a million of lives.

EDWARD KNO'WELL [*aside*]. 'Twas pity you had not ten; a cat's and your own, i'faith.
—But was it possible?

MATTHEW [*to* Stephen]. 'Pray you, mark this discourse, sir.

STEPHEN. So I do.

BOBADILL. I assure you, upon my reputation, 'tis true, and yourself shall confess.

EDWARD KNO'WELL [*aside*]. You must bring me to the rack first.

BOBADILL. Observe me judicially, sweet sir; they had planted me three demi-culverins just in the mouth of the breach; now, sir, as we were to give on, their master gunner—a man of no mean skill and mark, you must think—confronts me with his linstock ready to give fire; I, spying his intendment, discharg'd my petronel in his bosom, and with these single arms, my poor rapier, ran violently upon the Moors that guarded the ordnance, and put 'em pell-mell to the sword.

WELLBRED. To the sword? To the rapier, Captain.

EDWARD KNO'WELL. Oh, it was a good figure observ'd, sir. But did you all this, Captain, without hurting your blade?

BOBADILL. Without any impeach o'the earth; you shall perceive, sir. [*Shows his rapier.*] It is the most fortunate weapon that ever rid on poor gentleman's thigh: shall I tell you, sir? You talk of Morglay, Excalibur, Durindana or so. Tut, I lend no credit to that is fabled of 'em; I know the virtue of mine own, and therefore I dare the boldlier maintain it.

STEPHEN. I mar'el whether it be a Toledo or no.

BOBADILL. A most perfect Toledo, I assure you, sir.

STEPHEN. I have a countryman of his, here.

[*Shows his rapier.*]

MATTHEW. Pray you, let's see, sir. Yes, faith, it is!

BOBADILL. This a Toledo? Pish!

STEPHEN. Why do you "pish," Captain?

BOBADILL. A Fleming, by heaven; I'll buy them for a guilder a piece, an' I would have a thousand of them.

EDWARD KNO'WELL. How say you, cousin? I told you thus much.

WELLBRED. Where bought you it, Master Stephen?

STEPHEN. Of a scurvy rogue soldier; a hundred of lice go with him; he swore it was a Toledo.

BOBADILL. A poor provant rapier, no better.

MATTHEW. Mass, I think it be, indeed, now I look on't better.

EDWARD KNO'WELL. Nay, the longer you look on't, the worse. Put it up, put it up.

STEPHEN. Well, I will put it up; but by—[*aside*] I ha' forgot the Captain's oath, I thought to ha' sworn by it—an' e'er I meet him—

WELLBRED. Oh, it is past help now, sir; you must have patience.

STEPHEN. Whoreson coney-catching rascal! I could eat the very hilts for anger!

EDWARD KNO'WELL. A sign of good digestion; you have an ostrich stomach, cousin.

STEPHEN. A stomach? Would I had him here, you should see an' I had a stomach.

WELLBRED. It's better as 'tis; come, gentlemen, shall we go?

[*Enter*] Brainworm [*disguised*].

EDWARD KNO'WELL. A miracle, cousin; look here! Look here!

STEPHEN. Oh, God's lid, by your leave, do you know me, sir?

BRAINWORM. Ay, sir, I know you by sight.

STEPHEN. You sold me a rapier, did you not?

BRAINWORM. Yes, marry, did I, sir.

STEPHEN. You said it was a Toledo, ha?

BRAINWORM. True, I did so.

STEPHEN. But it is none?

BRAINWORM. No, sir, I confess it, it is none.

STEPHEN. Do you confess it? Gentlemen, bear witness, he has confess'd it. By God's will, an' you had not confess'd it—

EDWARD KNO'WELL. Oh, cousin, forbear, forbear.

STEPHEN. Nay, I have done, cousin.

WELLBRED. Why, you have done like a gentleman; he has confess'd it, what would you more?

STEPHEN. Yet, by his leave, he is a rascal; under his favor, do you see?

EDWARD KNO'WELL [*aside to* Wellbred]. Ay, by his leave, he is, and under favor; a pretty piece of civility! Sirrah, how dost thou like him?

WELLBRED. Oh, it's a most precious fool, make much on him. I can compare him to nothing more happily than a drum; for everyone may play upon him.

EDWARD KNO'WELL. No, no, a child's whistle were far the fitter.

BRAINWORM [*to* Edward Kno'well]. Sir, shall I entreat a word with you?

EDWARD KNO'WELL. With me, sir? You have not another Toledo to sell, ha' you?

[*They walk apart.*]

BRAINWORM. You are conceited, sir; your name is Master Kno'well, as I take it?

EDWARD KNO'WELL. You are i'the right. You mean not to proceed in the catechism, do you?

BRAINWORM. No, sir, I am none of that coat.

EDWARD KNO'WELL. Of as bare a coat, though. Well, say, sir.

BRAINWORM. Faith, sir, I am but servant to the drum extraordinary; and indeed, this smoky varnish being wash'd off, and three or four patches remov'd, I appear your worship's in reversion, after the decease of your good father—Brainworm.

EDWARD KNO'WELL. Brainworm! 'Slight, what breath of a conjurer hath blown thee hither in this shape?

BRAINWORM. The breath o' your letter, sir, this morning: the same that blew you to the Windmill, and your father after you.

EDWARD KNO'WELL. My father?

BRAINWORM. Nay, never start, 'tis true; he has follow'd you over the fields, by the foot, as you would do a hare i'the snow.

EDWARD KNO'WELL. Sirrah Wellbred, what shall we do, sirrah? My father is come over after me.

WELLBRED. Thy father? Where is he?

BRAINWORM. At Justice Clement's house here, in Coleman Street, where he but stays my return; and then—

WELLBRED. Who's this? Brainworm?

BRAINWORM. The same, sir.

WELLBRED. Why, how i'the name of wit com'st thou transmuted thus?

BRAINWORM. Faith, a device, a device: nay, for the love of reason, gentlemen, and avoiding the danger, stand not here; withdraw, and I'll tell you all.

WELLBRED. But art thou sure he will stay thy return?

BRAINWORM. Do I live, sir? What a question is that?

WELLBRED. We'll prorogue his expectation, then, a little. Brainworm, thou shalt go with us. Come on, gentlemen; nay, I pray thee, sweet Ned, droop not: 'heart, an' our wits be so wretchedly dull that one old plodding brain can outstrip us all, would we were e'en press'd, to make porters of; and serve out the remnant of our days in Thames Street or at Custom House quay, in a civil war against the carmen.

BRAINWORM. Amen, amen, amen, say I!   [*Exeunt.*]

[*III.ii*]

[*Enter*] Kitely [*and*] Cash.

KITELY. What says he, Thomas? Did you speak with him?

CASH. He will expect you, sir, within this half-hour.

KITELY. Has he the money ready, can you tell?

CASH. Yes, sir, the money was brought in last night.

KITELY. Oh, that's well: fetch me my cloak, my cloak.

[*Exit* Cash.]

Stay, let me see; an hour to go and come;
Ay, that will be the least: and then 'twill be
An hour before I can dispatch with him,
Or very near: well, I will say two hours.
Two hours, ha? Things never dream'd of yet

May be contriv'd, ay, and effected too,
In two hours' absence: well, I will not go.
Two hours; no, fleering opportunity,
I will not give your subtlety that scope.
Who will not judge him worthy to be robb'd,
That sets his doors wide open to a thief,
And shows the felon where his treasure lies?
Again, what earthy spirit but will attempt
To taste the fruit of beauty's golden tree,
When leaden sleep seels up the dragon's eyes?
I will not go. Business, go by for once.
No, beauty, no; you are of too good caract
To be left so, without a guard, or open.
Your luster too'll inflame at any distance,
Draw courtship to you as a jet doth straws,
Put motion in a stone, strike fire from ice,
Nay, make a porter leap you with his burden!
You must be then kept up, close and well-watch'd,
For, give you opportunity, no quicksand
Devours or swallows swifter. He that lends
His wife, if she be fair, or time or place,
Compels her to be false. I will not go;
The dangers are too many. And then the dressing
Is a most main attractive; our great heads
Within the city never were in safety
Since our wives wore these little caps: I'll change 'em,
I'll change 'em straight, in mine. Mine shall no more
Wear three-pil'd acorns, to make my horns ache.
Nor will I go: I am resolv'd for that.

[Enter Cash with cloak.]

Carry in my cloak again. Yet, stay. Yet do, too.
I will defer going on all occasions.
    CASH. Sir, Snare your scrivener will be there with th' bonds.
    KITELY. That's true; fool on me, I had clean forgot it;
I must go. What's o'clock?
CASH.   Exchange time, sir.
    KITELY [aside]. 'Heart, then will Wellbred presently be here,
too,
With one or other of his loose consorts.

I am a knave if I know what to say,
What course to take, or which way to resolve.
My brain, methinks, is like an hourglass,
Wherein my 'maginations run like sands,
Filling up time, but then are turn'd, and turn'd,
So that I know not what to stay upon,
And less, to put in act. It shall be so.
Nay, I dare build upon his secrecy;
He knows not to deceive me.—Thomas!

    CASH.   Sir.

    KITELY [*aside*]. Yet, now I have bethought me, too, I will
not.—
Thomas, is Cob within?

    CASH.   I think he be, sir.

    KITELY [*aside*]. But he'll prate, too; there's no speech of him.
No, there were no man o'the earth to Thomas,
If I durst trust him; there is all the doubt.
But should he have a chink in him, I were gone,
Lost i' my fame forever; talk for th'Exchange.
The manner he hath stood with till this present
Doth promise no such change: what should I fear, then?
Well, come what will, I'll tempt my fortune once.—
Thomas—you may deceive me, but I hope—
Your love to me is more—

    CASH.   Sir, if a servant's
Duty with faith may be call'd love, you are
More than in hope; you are possess'd of it.

    KITELY. I thank you heartily, Thomas; gi' me your hand;
With all my heart, good Thomas. I have, Thomas,
A secret to impart unto you—but
When once you have it, I must seal your lips up.
So far I tell you, Thomas.

    CASH.   Sir, for that—

    KITELY. Nay, hear me out. Think I esteem you, Thomas,
When I will let you in thus to my private.
It is a thing sits nearer to my crest
Than thou art ware of, Thomas. If thou shouldst
Reveal it, but—

    CASH.   How, I reveal it?

    KITELY.   Nay,
I do not think thou wouldst; but if thou shouldst,

'Twere a great weakness.

CASH.   A great treachery:
Give it no other name.

KITELY.   Thou wilt not do't, then?

CASH. Sir, if I do, mankind disclaim me ever.

KITELY [aside]. He will not swear; he has some reservation,
Some conceal'd purpose and close meaning, sure;
Else, being urg'd so much, how should he choose
But lend an oath to all this protestation?
He's no precisian, that I am certain of,
Nor rigid Roman Catholic. He'll play
At fayles and tick-tack, I have heard him swear.
What should I think of it? Urge him again,
And by some other way? I will do so.—
Well, Thomas, thou hast sworn not to disclose;
Yes, you did swear?

CASH.   Not yet, sir, but I will,
Please you—

KITELY.   No, Thomas, I dare take thy word.
But if thou wilt swear, do; as thou think'st good;
I am resolv'd without it; at thy pleasure.

CASH. By my soul's safety, then, sir, I protest.
My tongue shall ne'er take knowledge of a word
Deliver'd me in nature of your trust.

KITELY. It's too much; these ceremonies need not;
I know thy faith to be as firm as rock.
Thomas, come hither, near: we cannot be
Too private in this business. So it is—
[Aside.] Now he has sworn, I dare the safelier venture—
I have of late by divers observations—
[Aside.] But whether his oath can bind him, yea or no,
Being not taken lawfully, ha, say you?
I will ask counsel ere I do proceed.—
Thomas, it will be now too long to stay;
I'll spy some fitter time, soon, or tomorrow.

CASH. Sir, at your pleasure.

KITELY.   I will think; and, Thomas,
I pray you search the books 'gainst my return
For the receipts 'twixt me and Traps.

CASH.   I will, sir.

KITELY. And hear you: if your mistress' brother Wellbred

Chance to bring hither any gentlemen
Ere I come back, let one straight bring me word.
    CASH. Very well, sir.
    KITELY.   To the Exchange, do you hear?
Or here, in Coleman Street, to Justice Clement's.
Forget it not, nor be not out of the way.
    CASH. I will not, sir.
    KITELY.   I pray you have a care on't.
Or whether he come or no, if any other,
Stranger or else, fail not to send me word.
    CASH. I shall not, sir.
    KITELY.   Be't your special business
Now, to remember it.
    CASH.   Sir, I warrant you.
    KITELY. But, Thomas, this is not the secret, Thomas,
I told you of.
    CASH.   No, sir, I do suppose it.
    KITELY. Believe me, it is not.
    CASH.   Sir, I do believe you.
    KITELY. By heaven, it is not; that's enough. But, Thomas,
I would not you should utter it, do you see,
To any creature living; yet I care not.
Well, I must hence. Thomas, conceive thus much:
It was a trial of you when I meant
So deep a secret to you; I mean not this,
But that I have to tell you; this is nothing, this.
But, Thomas, keep this from my wife, I charge you,
Lock'd up in silence, midnight, buried here.
[*Aside*]. No greater hell, than to be slave to fear.

                                   [*Exit.*]

    CASH. "Lock'd up in silence, midnight, buried here."
Whence should this flood of passion, trow, take head, ha?
Best dream no longer of this running humour,
For fear I sink! The violence of the stream
Already hath transported me so far
That I can feel no ground at all. But soft:

[*Enter* Cob.]

Oh, 'tis our water-bearer: somewhat has cross'd him now.

COB. Fasting days? What tell you me of fasting days? 'Slid, would they were all on a light fire for me! They say the whole world shall be consum'd with fire one day; but would I had these ember-weeks and villainous Fridays burnt in the meantime, and then—

CASH. Why, how now, Cob, what moves thee to this choler, ha?

COB. Collar, Master Thomas? I scorn your collar; I, sir, I am none o' your cart-horse, though I carry and draw water. An' you offer to ride me with your collar, or halter either, I may hap show you a jade's trick, sir.

CASH. Oh, you'll slip your head out of the collar? Why, Goodman Cob, you mistake me.

COB. Nay, I have my rheum, and I can be angry as well as another, sir.

CASH. Thy rheum, Cob? Thy humour, thy humour; thou mistak'st.

COB. Humour? Mack, I think it be so, indeed. What is that humour? Some rare thing, I warrant.

CASH. Marry, I'll tell thee, Cob: it is a gentlemanlike monster, bred in the special gallantry of our time by affectation, and fed by folly.

COB. How? Must it be fed?

CASH. Oh, ay, humour is nothing if it be not fed. Didst thou never hear that? It's a common phrase, "Feed my humour."

COB. I'll none on it. Humour, avaunt, I know you not, be gone. Let who will make hungry meals for your monstership; it shall not be I. Feed you, quoth he? 'Slid, I ha' much ado to feed myself; especially on these lean rascally days, too; an't had been any other day but a fasting day—a plague on them all, for me!— by this light, one might have done the commonwealth good service, and have drown'd them all i'the flood, two or three hundred thousand years ago. Oh, I do stomach them hugely! I have a maw now, an't were for Sir Bevis his horse, against 'em.

CASH. I pray thee, good Cob, what makes thee so out of love with fasting days?

COB. Marry, that which will make any man out of love with 'em, I think: their bad conditions, an' you will needs know. First, they are of a Flemish breed, I am sure on't, for they raven up more butter than all the days of the week beside; next, they stink of fish and leek porridge miserably; thirdly, they'll keep a man devoutly hungry all day, and at night send him supperless to bed.

CASH. Indeed, these are faults, Cob.

COB. Nay, an' this were all, 'twere something; but they are the only known enemies to my generation. A fasting day no sooner comes, but my lineage goes to rack; poor cobs, they smoke for it, they are made martyrs o'the grid-iron, they melt in passion; and your maids, too, know this, and yet would have me turn Hannibal, and eat my own fish and blood.   (*He pulls out a red herring.*)   My princely coz, fear nothing; I have not the heart to devour you, an' I might be made as rich as King Cophetua. Oh, that I had room for my tears; I could weep salt water enough now to preserve the lives of ten thousand of my kin. But I may curse none but these filthy almanacs, for an't were not for them, these days of persecution would ne'er be known. I'll be hang'd an' some fishmonger's son do not make of 'em, and puts in more fasting days than he should do, because he would utter his father's dried stockfish and stinking conger.

CASH. 'Slight, peace, thou'lt be beaten like a stockfish else. Here is Master Matthew. Now must I look out for a messenger to my master.

[*Exeunt* Cash *and* Cob.]

[*Enter*] Wellbred, Edward Kno'well,
Brainworm, Bobadill, Matthew, [*and*] Stephen.

WELLBRED. Beshrew me, but it was an absolute good jest, and exceedingly well carried!

EDWARD KNO'WELL. Ay, and our ignorance maintain'd it as well, did it not?

WELLBRED. Yes, faith; but was't possible thou shouldst not know him? I forgive Master Stephen, for he is stupidity itself.

EDWARD KNO'WELL. 'Fore God, not I, an' I might have been join'd patten with one of the seven wise masters for knowing him. He had so writhen himself into the habit of one of your poor infantry, your decay'd, ruinous, worm-eaten gentlemen of the round; such as have vowed to sit on the skirts of the city, let your provost and his half-dozen of halberdiers do what they can; and have translated begging out of the old hackney pace to a fine, easy amble, and made it run as smooth of the tongue as a shove-groat shilling. Into the likeness of one of these *refor-mados* had he moulded himself so perfectly, observing every trick of their action, as varying the accent, swearing with an emphasis, indeed all, with so special and exquisite a grace that, hadst thou seen him, thou wouldst have sworn he might have been sergeant-major, if not lieutenant-colonel, to the regiment.

WELLBRED. Why, Brainworm, who would have thought thou hadst been such an artificer?

EDWARD KNO'WELL. An artificer? An architect! Except a man had studied begging all his lifetime, and been a weaver of language from his infancy, for the clothing of it, I never saw his rival!

WELLBRED. Where got'st thou this coat, I mar'el?

BRAINWORM. Of a Houndsditch man, sir; one of the devil's near kinsmen, a broker.

WELLBRED. That cannot be, if the proverb hold; for "a crafty knave needs no broker."

BRAINWORM. True, sir, but I did need a broker; *ergo*—

WELLBRED [*aside*]. Well put off.—No crafty knave, you'll say.

EDWARD KNO'WELL. Tut, he has more of these shifts.

BRAINWORM. And yet where I have one, the broker has ten, sir.

[*Enter* Cash.]

CASH [*calling*]. Francis! Martin! Ne'er a one to be found now? What a spite's this?

WELLBRED. How now, Thomas? Is my brother Kitely within?

CASH. No, sir, my master went forth e'en now; but Master Downright is within. Cob! What, Cob! Is he gone, too?

WELLBRED. Whither went your master? Thomas, canst thou tell?

CASH. I know not; to Justice Clement's, I think, sir. Cob!

[*Exit* Cash.]

EDWARD KNO'WELL. Justice Clement, what's he?

WELLBRED. Why, dost thou not know him? He is a city mag-istrate, a justice here, an excellent good lawyer and a great scholar; but the only mad, merry old fellow in Europe! I show'd him you the other day.

EDWARD KNO'WELL. Oh, is that he? I remember him now. Good faith, and he has a very strange presence, methinks; it shows as if he stood out of the rank from other men. I have heard many of his jests i'the university. They say he will commit a man for taking the wall of his horse.

WELLBRED. Ay, or wearing his cloak of one shoulder, or serving of God; anything indeed, if it come in the way of his humour.

Cash goes in and out calling.

CASH. Gaspar, Martin, Cob! 'Heart, where should they be, trow?

BOBADILL. Master Kitely's man, 'pray thee vouchsafe us the lighting of this match.

CASH. Fire on your match, no time but now to vouchsafe? Francis! Cob!   [*Exit.*]

BOBADILL. Body of me! Here's the remainder of seven pound, since yesterday was seven-night. 'Tis your right Trinidado. Did you never take any, Master Stephen?

STEPHEN. No, truly, sir. But I'll learn to take it now, since you commend it so.

BOBADILL. Sir, believe me, upon my relation; for what I tell you, the world shall not reprove. I have been in the Indies, where this herb grows, where neither myself nor a dozen gentlemen more, of my knowledge, have received the taste of any other nutriment in the world for the space of one and twenty weeks, but the fume of this simple only. Therefore it cannot be but 'tis most divine. Further, take it in the nature, in the true kind so, it makes an antidote that, had you taken the most deadly poisonous plant in all Italy, it should expel it, and clarify you with as much ease as I speak. And for your green wound, your balsamum and your Saint John's wort are all mere gulleries and trash to it, especially your Trinidado; your Nicotian is good, too. I could say what I know of the virtue of it for the expulsion of rheums, raw humours, crudities, obstructions, with a thousand of this kind; but I profess myself no quacksalver. Only thus much: by Hercules, I do hold it and will affirm it, before any prince in Europe, to be the most sovereign and precious weed that ever the earth tender'd to the use of man.

EDWARD KNO'WELL [*aside*]. This speech would ha' done decently in a tobacco trader's mouth!

[*Enter* Cash *and* Cob.]

CASH. At Justice Clement's he is: in the middle of Coleman Street.

COB. Oh, oh!

BOBADILL. Where's the match I gave thee, Master Kitely's man?

CASH [aside]. Would his match, and he, and pipe and all, were at Sancto Domingo! I had forgot it.   [Exit.]

COB. By God's me, I mar'el what pleasure or felicity they have in taking this roguish tobacco! It's good for nothing but to choke a man, and fill him full of smoke and embers: there were four died out of one house last week with taking of it, and two more the bell went for yesternight; one of them, they say, will ne'er scape it: he voided a bushel of soot yesterday, upward and downward. By the stocks, an' there were no wiser man than I, I'd have it present whipping, man or woman, that should but deal with a tobacco pipe; why, it will stifle them all in the end, as many as use it; it's little better than rat's-bane or rosaker.

Bobadill *beats him with a cudgel.*

ALL. Oh, good Captain, hold, hold!

BOBADILL [*beating* Cob]. You base cullion, you!

[*Enter* Cash.]

CASH. Sir, here's your match; come, thou must needs be talking, too; th'art well enough serv'd.

COB. Nay, he will not meddle with his match, I warrant you. Well, it shall be a dear beating, an' I live.

BOBADILL [*to* Cob]. Do you prate? Do you murmur?

EDWARD KNO'WELL. Nay, good Captain, will you regard the humour of a fool? Away, knave.

WELLBRED. Thomas, get him away.   [*Exit* Cash *with* Cob.]

BOBADILL. A whoreson filthy slave, a dung-worm, an excrement! Body o' Caesar, but that I scorn to let forth so mean a spirit, I'd ha' stabb'd him to the earth.

WELLBRED. Marry, the law forbid, sir.

BOBADILL. By Pharaoh's foot, I would have done it.

STEPHEN [*aside*]. Oh, he swears admirably! "By Pharaoh's foot!" "Body of Caesar!" I shall never do it, sure. "Upon mine honor, and by Saint George"—no, I ha' not the right grace.

MATTHEW [*offering tobacco*]. Master Stephen, will you any? By this air, the most divine tobacco that ever I drunk!

STEPHEN. None, I thank you, sir. [*Aside.*] Oh, this gentleman does it rarely, too, but nothing like the other.—By this air; as I am a gentleman; by—(*Master* Stephen *is practicing to the post.*)

[*Exeunt* Bobadill *and* Matthew.]

BRAINWORM. Master, glance, glance! Master Wellbred!

STEPHEN [*to the post*]. As I have somewhat to be saved, I protest—

WELLBRED. You are a fool: it needs no affidavit.

EDWARD KNO'WELL. Cousin, will you any tobacco?

STEPHEN. Ay, sir.   [*To the post.*]   Upon my reputation—

EDWARD KNO'WELL. How now, cousin?

STEPHEN. I protest, as I am a gentleman, but no soldier indeed—

WELLBRED. No, Master Stephen? As I remember, your name is enter'd in the Artillery Garden.

STEPHEN. Ay, sir, that's true; cousin, may I swear "as I am a soldier" by that?

EDWARD KNO'WELL. Oh, yes, that you may. It's all you have for your money.

STEPHEN. Then, as I am a gentleman and a soldier, it is divine tobacco.

WELLBRED. But soft, where's Master Matthew? Gone?

BRAINWORM. No, sir, they went in here.

WELLBRED. Oh, let's follow them. Master Matthew is gone to salute his mistress in verse. We shall ha' the happiness to hear some of his poetry now. He never comes unfurnish'd. Brainworm!

STEPHEN. Brainworm! Where? Is this Brainworm?

EDWARD KNO'WELL. Ay, cousin; no words of it, upon your gentility.

STEPHEN. Not I, body of me, by this air, Saint George, and the foot of Pharaoh.

WELLBRED. Rare! Your cousin's discourse is simply drawn out with oaths.

EDWARD KNO'WELL. 'Tis larded with 'em. A kind of French dressing, if you love it.

[*Exeunt.*]

[III.iii]

[Enter] Kitely *[and]* Cob.

KITELY. Ha? How many are there, sayest thou?

COB. Marry, sir, your brother, Master Wellbred—

KITELY. Tut, beside him: what strangers are there, man?

COB. Strangers? Let me see; one, two; mass, I know not well,
there are so many.

KITELY. How? So many?

COB. Ay, there's some five or six of them, at the most.

KITELY *[aside]*. A swarm, a swarm;
Spite of the devil, how they sting my head
With forked stings, thus wide and large!—But Cob,
How long hast thou been coming hither, Cob?

COB. A little while, sir.

KITELY. Didst thou come running?

COB. No, sir.

KITELY *[aside]*. Nay, then, I am familiar with thy haste.
Bane to my fortunes: what meant I to marry?
I that before was rank'd in such content,
My mind at rest, too, in so soft a peace,
Being free master of mine own free thoughts,
And now become a slave? What, never sigh;
Be of good cheer, man; for thou art a cuckold;
'Tis done, 'tis done! Nay, when such flowing store,
Plenty itself, falls in my wife's lap,
The *cornucopiae* will be mine, I know.—But Cob,
What entertainment had they? I am sure
My sister and my wife would bid them welcome, ha?

COB. Like enough, sir; yet I heard not a word of it.

KITELY *[aside]*. No: their lips were seal'd with kisses, and the
voice,
Drown'd in a flood of joy at their arrival,
Had lost her motion, state, and faculty.—
Cob, which of them was't that first kiss'd my wife?
My sister, I should say. My wife, alas,
I fear not her. Ha, who was it, say'st thou?

COB. By my troth, sir, will you have the truth of it?

KITELY. Oh, ay, good Cob; I pray thee heartily.

COB. Then, I am a vagabond, and fitter for Bridewell than your worship's company, if I saw anybody to be kiss'd, unless they would have kiss'd the post in the middle of the warehouse; for there I left them all, at their tobacco, with a pox.

KITELY. How? Were they not gone in, then, ere thou cam'st?

COB. Oh no, sir.

KITELY. Spite of the devil! What do I stay here, then? Cob, follow me.

COB. Nay, soft and fair, I have eggs on the spit; I cannot go yet, sir.   [*Exit* Kitely.]

Now am I for some five and fifty reasons hammering, hammering revenge; oh, for three or four gallons of vinegar to sharpen my wits. Revenge: vinegar revenge: vinegar and mustard revenge: nay, an' he had not lien in my house, 'twould never have griev'd me; but being my guest, one that, I'll be sworn, my wife has lent him her smock off her back while his one shirt has been at washing; pawn'd her neckerchers for clean bands for him; sold almost all my platters to buy him tobacco; and he to turn monster of ingratitude, and strike his lawful host! Well, I hope to raise up an host of fury for't. Here comes Justice Clement.

[*Enter*] Clement, Kno'well, [*and*] Formal.

CLEMENT. What, 's Master Kitely gone? Roger!

FORMAL. Ay, sir.

CLEMENT. Heart of me! What made him leave us so abruptly? [*To* Cob.] How now, sirrah? What make you here? What would you have, ha?

COB. An't please your worship, I am a poor neighbor of your worship's—

CLEMENT. A poor neighbor of mine? Why, speak, poor neighbor.

COB. I dwell, sir, at the sign of the Water Tankard, hard by the Green Lattice. I have paid scot and lot there any time this eighteen years.

CLEMENT. To the Green Lattice?

COB. No, sir, to the parish: marry, I have seldom scap'd scot-free at the Lattice.

CLEMENT. Oh, well; what business has my poor neighbor with me?

COB. An't like your worship, I am come to crave the peace of your worship.

CLEMENT. Of me, knave? Peace of me, knave? Did I e'er hurt thee? Or threaten thee? Or wrong thee, ha?

COB. No, sir; but your worship's warrant for one that has wrong'd me, sir. His arms are at too much liberty; I would fain have them bound to a treaty of peace, an' my credit could compass it with your worship.

CLEMENT. Thou goest far enough about for't, I'm sure.

KNO'WELL. Why, dost thou go in danger of thy life for him, friend?

COB. No, sir; but I go in danger of my death every hour, by his means: an' I die within a twelvemonth and a day, I may swear by the law of the land that he kill'd me.

CLEMENT. How, how, knave? Swear he kill'd thee? And by the law? What pretense, what color hast thou for that?

COB. Marry, an't please your worship, both black and blue; color enough, I warrant you. I have it here to show your worship.

[Shows his bruises.]

CLEMENT. What is he that gave you this, sirrah?

COB. A gentleman and a soldier he says he is, o'the city here.

CLEMENT. A soldier o'the city? What call you him?

COB. Captain Bobadill.

CLEMENT. Bobadill? And why did he bob and beat you, sirrah? How began the quarrel betwixt you, ha? Speak truly, knave, I advise you.

COB. Marry indeed, an' please your worship, only because I spake against their vagrant tobacco, as I came by 'em when they were taking on't; for nothing else.

CLEMENT. Ha? You speak against tobacco? Formal, his name.

FORMAL. What's your name, sirrah?

COB. Oliver, sir; Oliver Cob, sir.

CLEMENT. Tell Oliver Cob he shall go to the jail, Formal.

FORMAL. Oliver Cob: my master, Justice Clement, says you shall go to the jail.

COB. Oh, I beseech your worship, for God's sake, dear Master Justice.

CLEMENT. Nay, God's precious: an' such drunkards, and tankards, as you are come to dispute of tobacco once, I have done! Away with him!

COB. Oh, good Master Justice; sweet old gentleman!

KNO'WELL. Sweet Oliver, would I could do thee any good. Justice Clement, let me entreat you, sir.

CLEMENT. What? A threadbare rascal, a beggar, a slave that never drunk out of better than pisspot metal in his life! And he to deprave and abuse the virtue of an herb so generally receiv'd in the courts of princes, the chambers of nobles, the bowers of sweet ladies, the cabins of soldiers! Roger, away with him, by God's precious; I say, go to.

COB. Dear Master Justice, let me be beaten again, I have deserv'd it; but not the prison, I beseech you.

KNO'WELL. Alas, poor Oliver!

CLEMENT. Roger, make him a warrant.   [*Aside.*]   He shall not go: I but fear the knave.

FORMAL. Do not stink, sweet Oliver; you shall not go; my master will give you a warrant.

COB. Oh, the Lord maintain his worship, his worthy worship!

CLEMENT. Away, dispatch him.

[*Exit* Formal *with* Cob.]

How now, Master Kno'well! In dumps, in dumps? Come, this becomes not.

KNO'WELL. Sir, would I could not feel my cares—

CLEMENT. Your cares are nothing: they are like my cap, soon put on, and as soon put off. What, your son is old enough to govern himself: let him run his course; it's the only way to make him a staid man. If he were an unthrift, a ruffian, a drunkard, or a licentious liver, then you had reason, you had reason to take care; but being none of these, mirth's my witness, an' I had twice so many cares as you have, I'd drown them all in a cup of sack. Come, come, let's try it; I muse your parcel of a soldier returns not all this while.

[*Exeunt.*]

[IV.i]

[*Enter*] Downright [*and*] Dame Kitely.

DOWNRIGHT. Well, sister, I tell you true; and you'll find it so in the end.

DAME KITELY. Alas, brother, what would you have me to do? I cannot help it; you see, my brother brings 'em in here; they are his friends.

DOWNRIGHT. His friends? His fiends. 'Slud, they do nothing but haunt him up and down like a sort of unlucky sprites, and tempt him to all manner of villainy that can be thought of. Well, by this light, a little thing would make me play the devil with some of 'em; an't were not more for your husband's sake than anything else, I'd make the house too hot for the best on 'em: they should say and swear hell were broken loose ere they went hence. But, by God's will, 'tis nobody's fault but yours; for, an' you had done as you might have done, they should have been parboil'd, and bak'd too, every mother's son, ere they should ha' come in, e'er a one of 'em.

DAME KITELY. God's my life! Did you ever hear the like? What a strange man is this! Could I keep out all them, think you? I should put myself against half a dozen men, should I? Good faith, you'd mad the patient'st body in the world, to hear you talk so, without any sense or reason!

[*Enter*] *Mistress* Bridget, *Master* Matthew, [*and*] Bobadill,
[*followed at a distance by*] Wellbred, Edward Kno'well,
Stephen, [*and*] Brainworm.

BRIDGET. Servant, in troth you are too prodigal
Of your wit's treasure, thus to pour it forth
Upon so mean a subject as my worth.

MATTHEW. You say well, mistress; and I mean as well.

DOWNRIGHT. Hoy-day, here is stuff!

WELLBRED. Oh, now stand close: pray heaven she can get him to read.
He should do it of his own natural impudency.

BRIDGET. Servant, what is this same, I pray you?

MATTHEW. Marry, an elegy, an elegy, an odd toy—

DOWNRIGHT. To mock an ape withal. Oh, I could sew up his mouth now.

DAME KITELY. Sister, I pray you, let's hear it.

DOWNRIGHT. Are you rhyme-given, too?

MATTHEW. Mistress, I'll read it, if you please.

BRIDGET. Pray you do, servant.

DOWNRIGHT. Oh, here's no foppery! Death, I can endure the stocks better.

[*Exit.*]

EDWARD KNO'WELL. What ails thy brother? Can he not hold his water at reading of a ballad?

WELLBRED. Oh no; a rhyme to him is worse than cheese or a bagpipe. But mark: you lose the protestation.

MATTHEW. Faith, I did it in an humour; I know not how it is; but please you come near, sir. This gentleman has judgment, he knows how to censure of a——pray you, sir, you can judge.

STEPHEN. Not I, sir; upon my reputation, and by the foot of Pharaoh.

WELLBRED. Oh, chide your cousin for swearing.

EDWARD KNO'WELL. Not I, so long as he does not forswear himself.

BOBADILL. Master Matthew, you abuse the expectation of your dear mistress and her fair sister. Fie, while you live, avoid this prolixity.

MATTHEW. I shall, sir: well, *incipere dulce*.

EDWARD KNO'WELL. How, *insipere dulce?* A sweet thing to be a fool, indeed.

WELLBRED. What, do you take *incipere* in that sense?

EDWARD KNO'WELL. You do not? You? This was your villainy, to gull him with a *mot*.

WELLBRED. Oh, the benchers' phrase: *pauca verba, pauca verba*.

MATTHEW [*recites*].

> *Rare creature, let me speak without offense,*
> *Would God my rude words had the influence*
> *To rule thy thoughts, as thy fair looks do mine,*
> *Then shouldst thou be his prisoner, who is thine.*

EDWARD KNO'WELL. This is in *Hero and Leander*!

WELLBRED. Oh, ay. Peace, we shall have more of this.

MATTHEW [recites].

> *Be not unkind and fair; misshapen stuff*
> *Is of behavior boisterous and rough—*

WELLBRED [*to* Stephen]. How like you that, sir?

Master Stephen *answers with shaking his head.*

EDWARD KNO'WELL. 'Slight, he shakes his head like a bottle, to feel an' there be any brain in it.

MATTHEW. But observe the catastrophe now:

> *And I in duty will exceed all other,*
> *As you in beauty do excel Love's mother.*

EDWARD KNO'WELL. Well, I'll have him free of the wit-brokers, for he utters nothing but stol'n remnants.

WELLBRED. Oh, forgive it him.

EDWARD KNO'WELL. A filching rogue, hang him! And from the dead; it's worse than sacrilege.

WELLBRED. Sister, what ha' you here? Verses? 'Pray you, let's see.

[Bridget *gives the verses to* Wellbred.]

Who made these verses? They are excellent good!

MATTHEW. Oh, Master Wellbred, 'tis your disposition to say so, sir. They were good i'the morning; I made 'em *extempore* this morning.

WELLBRED. How, *extempore*?

MATTHEW. I would I might be hang'd else: ask Captain Bobadill. He saw me write them at the—pox on it!—the Star, yonder.

BRAINWORM [*aside*]. Can he find in his heart to curse the stars so?

EDWARD KNO'WELL [*aside*]. Faith, his are even with him: they ha' curs'd him enough already.

STEPHEN. Cousin, how do you like this gentleman's verses?

EDWARD KNO'WELL. Oh, admirable! The best that ever I heard, coz!

STEPHEN. Body o'Caesar, they are admirable! The best that ever I heard, as I am a soldier!

[*Enter* Downright.]

DOWNRIGHT. I am vex'd, I can hold ne'er a bone of me still. 'Heart, I think they mean to build and breed here!

WELLBRED. Sister, you have a simple servant here, that crowns your beauty with such encomions and devices. You may see what it is to be the mistress of a wit; that can make your perfections so transparent that every blear eye may look through them, and see him drown'd over head and ears in the deep well of desire. Sister Kitely, I marvel you get you not a servant that can rhyme, and do tricks, too.

DOWNRIGHT. Oh, monster! Impudence itself! Tricks?

DAME KITELY. Tricks, brother? What tricks?

BRIDGET. Nay, speak, I pray you; what tricks?

DAME KITELY. Ay, never spare anybody here; but say, what tricks?

BRIDGET. Passion of my heart! Do tricks?

WELLBRED. 'Slight, here's a trick vied and revied! Why, you monkeys you, what a caterwauling do you keep! Has he not given you rhymes, and verses, and tricks?

DOWNRIGHT. Oh, the fiend!

WELLBRED. Nay, you——lamp of virginity, that take it in snuff so! Come and cherish this tame poetical fury in your "servant"; you'll be begg'd else, shortly, for a concealment. Go to, reward his muse. You cannot give him less than a shilling, in conscience, for the book he had it out of cost him a teston at least. How now, gallants? Master Matthew? Captain? What, all sons of silence? No spirit?

DOWNRIGHT. Come, you might practice your ruffian tricks somewhere else, and not here, I wuss: this is no tavern nor drinking school, to vent your exploits in.

WELLBRED. How now! Whose cow has calv'd?

DOWNRIGHT. Marry, that has mine, sir. Nay, boy, never look askance at me for the matter; I'll tell you of it, I, sir; you and your companions, mend yourselves when I ha' done.

WELLBRED. My companions?

DOWNRIGHT. Yes, sir, your companions, so I say; I am not afraid of you, nor them neither, your hang-bys here. You must have your poets and your potlings, your *soldados* and *foolados,* to follow you up and down the city, and here they must come to domineer and swagger? Sirrah, you ballad-singer, and Slops, your fellow there, get you out; get you home; or by this steel, I'll cut off your ears, and that presently.

WELLBRED. 'Slight, stay, let's see what he dare do. Cut off his ears? Cut a whetstone. You are an ass, do you see? Touch any man here, and by this hand, I'll run my rapier to the hilts in you.

DOWNRIGHT. Yea, that would I fain see, boy.

They all draw, and they of the house make out to part them.

DAME KITELY. Oh, Jesu! Murder! Thomas, Gaspar!
BRIDGET. Help, help, Thomas!
EDWARD KNO'WELL. Gentlemen, forbear, I pray you.

[*Enter* Cash *and servants.*]

BOBADILL. Well, sirrah, you Holofernes: by my hand, I will pink your flesh full of holes with my rapier for this; I will, by this good heaven.

They offer to fight again, and are parted.

Nay, let him come, let him come, gentlemen; by the body of
Saint George, I'll not kill him.

CASH. Hold, hold, good gentlemen.

DOWNRIGHT. You whoreson bragging coistrel!

[*Enter*] Kitely.

KITELY. Why, how now? What's the matter? What's the stir
here?

Whence springs the quarrel? Thomas, where is he?

Put up your weapons, and put off this rage.

My wife and sister, they are cause of this.

What, Thomas? Where is this knave?

CASH. Here, sir.

WELLBRED. Come, let's go; this is one of my brother's ancient
humours, this.

STEPHEN. I am glad nobody was hurt by his ancient humour.

[*Exeunt* Wellbred, Edward Kno'well,
Stephen, Matthew, Bobadill, *and* Brainworm.]

KITELY. Why, how now, brother, who enforc'd this brawl?

DOWNRIGHT. A sort of lewd rakehells, that care neither for
God nor the devil. And they must come here to read ballads, and
roguery, and trash. I'll mar the knot of 'em ere I sleep, perhaps;
especially Bob there, he that's all manner of shapes; and Songs-
and-Sonnets, his fellow.

BRIDGET. Brother, indeed you are too violent,

Too sudden in your humour; and you know

My brother Wellbred's temper will not bear

Any reproof, chiefly in such a presence,

Where every slight disgrace he should receive

Might wound him in opinion and respect.

DOWNRIGHT. Respect? What talk you of respect 'mong such

As ha' nor spark of manhood nor good manners?

'Sdeynes, I am asham'd to hear you! Respect!   [*Exit.*]

BRIDGET. Yes, there was one, a civil gentleman,

And very worthily demean'd himself.

KITELY. Oh, that was some love of yours, sister.

BRIDGET. A love of mine? I would it were no worse, brother.
You'd pay my portion sooner than you think for.

DAME KITELY. Indeed, he seem'd to be a gentleman of an
exceeding fair disposition, and of very excellent good parts.

                              [*Exeunt* Dame Kitely *and* Bridget.]

KITELY. Her love, by heaven! My wife's minion!
Fair disposition? Excellent good parts?
Death, these phrases are intolerable!
Good parts? How should she know his parts?
His parts? Well, well, well, well, well, well!
It is too plain, too clear.—Thomas, come hither.
What, are they gone?
CASH.   Ay, sir, they went in.
My mistress and your sister—
    KITELY. Are any of the gallants within?
    CASH. No, sir, they are all gone.
    KITELY. Art thou sure of it?
    CASH. I can assure you, sir.
    KITELY. What gentleman was that they prais'd so, Thomas?
    CASH. One, they call him Master Kno'well, a handsome young
gentleman, sir.
    KITELY. Ay, I thought so: my mind gave me as much.
I'll die, but they have hid him i'the house
Somewhere; I'll go and search. Go with me, Thomas.
Be true to me, and thou shalt find me a master.

                                                [*Exeunt.*]

[*IV. ii*]

[*Enter*] Cob.

COB [*knocking*]. What, Tib, Tib, I say!
TIB [*within*]. How now, what cuckold is that knocks so hard?

[*Enter* Tib.]

Oh, husband, is't you? What's the news?
    COB. Nay, you have stunn'd me, i'faith! You ha' giv'n me a
knock o'the forehead, will stick by me! Cuckold! 'Slid, cuckold?
    TIB. Away, you fool, did I know it was you that knock'd?
Come, come, you may call me as bad when you list.
    COB. May I? Tib, you are a whore.
    TIB. You lie in your throat, husband.

COB. How, the lie? And in my throat, too? Do you long to be stabb'd, ha?

TIB. Why, you are no soldier, I hope.

COB. Oh, must you be stabb'd by a soldier? Mass, that's true! When was Bobadill here, your Captain? That rogue, that foist, that fencing Burgullian? I'll tickle him, i'faith.

TIB. Why, what's the matter, trow?

COB. Oh, he has basted me rarely, sumptuously! But I have it here in black and white, for his black and blue: shall pay him. Oh, the Justice! The honestest old brave Trojan in London! I do honor the very flea of his dog. A plague on him, though; he put me once in a villainous filthy fear; marry, it vanish'd away, like the smoke of tobacco; but I was smok'd soundly first. I thank the devil, and his good angel, my guest. Well, wife, or Tib, which you will, get you in, and lock the door, I charge you; let no body in to you; wife, no body in to you: those are my words. Not Captain Bob himself, nor the fiend in his like-ness; you are a woman; you have flesh and blood enough in you to be tempted; therefore, keep the door shut upon all comers.

TIB. I warrant you, there shall no body enter here, without my consent.

COB. Nor with your consent, sweet Tib; and so I leave you.

TIB. It's more than you know, whether you leave me so.

COB. How?

TIB. Why, sweet.

COB. Tut, sweet or sour, thou art a flower;
Keep close thy door, I ask no more.   [*Exeunt severally.*]

[*IV.iii*]

[*Enter*] Edward Kno'well, Wellbred,
Stephen, [*and*] Brainworm [*disguised*].

EDWARD KNO'WELL. Well, Brainworm, perform this business happily, and thou makest a purchase of my love forever.

WELLBRED. I'faith, now let thy spirits use their best faculties. But, at any hand, remember the message to my brother; for there's no other means to start him.

BRAINWORM. I warrant you, sir, fear nothing: I have a nimble soul, has wak'd all forces of my fant'sy by this time, and put 'em

in true motion. What you have possess'd me withal, I'll discharge
it amply, sir. Make it no question.

WELLBRED. Forth and prosper, Brainworm.

                                                    [*Exit* Brainworm.]

Faith, Ned, how dost thou approve of my abilities in this device?

EDWARD KNO'WELL. Troth, well, howsoever; but it will come
excellent, if it take.

WELLBRED. Take, man? Why, it cannot choose but take, if the
circumstances miscarry not; but tell me ingenuously, dost thou
affect my sister Bridget, as thou pretend'st?

EDWARD KNO'WELL. Friend, am I worth belief?

WELLBRED. Come, do not protest. In faith, she is a maid of
good ornament and much modesty; and, except I conceiv'd very
worthily of her, thou shouldst not have her.

EDWARD KNO'WELL. Nay, that, I am afraid, will be a question
yet, whether I shall have her or no.

WELLBRED. 'Slid, thou shalt have her; by this light, thou shalt.

EDWARD KNO'WELL. Nay, do not swear.

WELLBRED. By this hand, thou shalt have her: I'll go fetch her
presently. Point but where to meet, and as I am an honest man,
I'll bring her.

EDWARD KNO'WELL. Hold, hold, be temperate.

WELLBRED. Why, by—what shall I swear by? Thou shalt have
her, as I am—

EDWARD KNO'WELL. 'Pray thee, be at peace, I am satisfied,
and do believe thou wilt omit no offered occasion to make my
desires complete.

WELLBRED. Thou shalt see and know, I will not.   [*Exeunt.*]

[*IV. iv*]

[*Enter*] Formal [*and*] Kno'well, [*meeting*]
Brainworm [*disguised*].

FORMAL. Was your man a soldier, sir?

KNO'WELL. Ay, a knave; I took him begging o'the way,
This morning, as I came over Moorfields.
Oh, here he is! You've made fair speed, believe me:
Where, i'the name of sloth, could you be thus—

BRAINWORM. Marry, peace be my comfort, where I thought
I should have had little comfort of your worship's service.

KNO'WELL. How so?

BRAINWORM. Oh, sir! Your coming to the city, your entertainment of me, and your sending me to watch—indeed, all the circumstances, either of your charge or my employment, are as open to your son as to yourself!

KNO'WELL. How should that be? Unless that villain Brainworm
Have told him of the letter, and discover'd
All that I strictly charg'd him to conceal?—'Tis so!

BRAINWORM. I am partly o'the faith 'tis so indeed.

KNO'WELL. But how should he know thee to be my man?

BRAINWORM. Nay, sir, I cannot tell; unless it be by the black art. Is not your son a scholar, sir?

KNO'WELL. Yes, but I hope his soul is not allied
Unto such hellish practice: if it were,
I had just cause to weep my part in him,
And curse the time of his creation.
But where didst thou find them, Fitzsword?

BRAINWORM. You should rather ask where they found me, sir, for I'll be sworn I was going along in the street, thinking nothing, when of a sudden a voice calls, "Master Kno'well's man"; another cries, "Soldier"; and thus half a dozen of 'em, till they had call'd me within a house; where I no sooner came, but they seem'd men, and out flew all their rapiers at my bosom, with some three or four score oaths to accompany 'em, and all to tell me I was but a dead man, if I did not confess where you were, and how I was employed, and about what; which, when they could not get out of me—as I protest, they must ha' dissected and made an anatomy of me first, and so I told 'em—they lock'd me up into a room i'the top of a high house, whence by great miracle, having a light heart, I slid down by a bottom of pack-thread into the street, and so scap'd. But, sir, thus much I can assure you, for I heard it while I was lock'd up: there were a great many rich merchants and brave citizens' wives with 'em at a feast, and your son, Master Edward, withdrew with one of 'em, and has pointed to meet her anon at one Cob's house, a water-bearer that dwells by the wall. Now there your worship shall be sure to take him, for there he preys, and fail he will not.

KNO'WELL. Nor will I fail to break his match, I doubt not.
Go thou along with Justice Clement's man,
And stay there for me. At one Cob's house, say'st thou?

BRAINWORM. Ay, sir, there you shall have him.

[*Exit* Kno'well.]

[*Aside.*] Yes? Invisible? Much wench, or much son! 'Slight, when he has stay'd there three or four hours, travailing with the expectation of wonders, and at length be deliver'd of air: oh, the sport that I should then take to look on him, if I durst! But now I mean to appear no more afore him in this shape. I have another trick to act yet. Oh, that I were so happy as to light on a nupson now of this Justice's novice.—Sir, I make you stay somewhat long.

FORMAL. Not a whit, sir. 'Pray you, what do you mean, sir?

BRAINWORM. I was putting up some papers.

FORMAL. You ha' been lately in the wars, sir, it seems.

BRAINWORM. Marry, have I, sir; to my loss, and expense of all, almost.

FORMAL. Troth, sir, I would be glad to bestow a pottle of wine o'you, if it please you to accept it—

BRAINWORM. Oh, sir!

FORMAL. But to hear the manner of your services and your devices in the wars; they say they be very strange, and not like those a man reads in the Roman histories, or sees at Mile End.

BRAINWORM. No, I assure you, sir; why, at any time when it please you I shall be ready to discourse to you all I know.   [*Aside.*] And more too, somewhat.

FORMAL. No better time than now, sir; we'll go to the Windmill; there we shall have a cup of neat grist, we call it. I pray you, sir, let me request you to the Windmill.

BRAINWORM. I'll follow you, sir.   [*Aside.*]   And make grist o'you, if I have good luck.   [*Exeunt.*]

[IV. v]

[*Enter*] Matthew, Edward Kno'well, Bobadill, *and* Stephen.

MATTHEW. Sir, did your eyes ever taste the like clown of him where we were today, Master Wellbred's half-brother? I think the whole earth cannot show his parallel, by this daylight.

EDWARD KNO'WELL. We were now speaking of him: Captain Bobadill tells me he is fall'n foul o' you, too.

MATTHEW. Oh ay, sir, he threaten'd me with the *bastinado*.

BOBADILL. Ay, but I think I taught you prevention this morning for that. You shall kill him, beyond question, if you be so generously minded.

MATTHEW. Indeed, it is a most excellent trick!   [*Fences.*]

BOBADILL. Oh, you do not give spirit enough to your motion; you are too tardy, too heavy. Oh, it must be done like lightning, *hay!*   *He practices at a post.*

MATTHEW. Rare Captain!

BOBADILL. Tut, 'tis nothing, an't be not done in a—*punto!*

EDWARD KNO'WELL. Captain, did you ever prove yourself upon any of our masters of defense here?

MATTHEW. Oh, good sir! Yes, I hope, he has.

BOBADILL. I will tell you, sir. Upon my first coming to the city, after my long travel, for knowledge in that mystery only there came three or four of 'em to me at a gentleman's house, where it was my chance to be resident at that time, to entreat my presence at their schools; and withal so much importun'd me that—I protest to you as I am a gentleman—I was asham'd of their rude demeanor, out of all measure. Well, I told 'em that to come to a public school, they should pardon me; it was opposite in diameter to my humor; but if so they would give their attendance at my lodging, I protested to do them what right or favor I could, as I was a gentleman, and so forth.

EDWARD KNO'WELL. So, sir, then you tried their skill?

BOBADILL. Alas, soon tried! You shall hear, sir. Within two or three days after, they came; and by honesty, fair sir, believe me, I grac'd them exceedingly, show'd them some two or three tricks of prevention, have purchas'd 'em since a credit to admiration, they cannot deny this; and yet now they hate me, and why? Because I am excellent, and for no other vile reason on the earth.

EDWARD KNO'WELL. This is strange and barbarous as ever I heard!

BOBADILL. Nay, for a more instance of their preposterous natures but note, sir. They have assaulted me, some three, four, five, six of them together, as I have walk'd alone in divers skirts i'the town; as Turnbull, Whitechapel, Shoreditch, which were then my quarters, and since upon the Exchange, at my lodging, and at my ordinary; where I have driven them afore me the whole length of a street, in the open view of all our gallants, pitying to hurt them, believe me. Yet all this lenity will not o'ercome their spleen: they will be doing with the pismire, raising a hill a man may spurn abroad with his foot at pleasure. By myself, I could have slain them all, but I delight not in murder. I am loath to bear any other than this *bastinado* for 'em; yet I hold it good polity not to go disarm'd, for, though I be skilful, I may be oppress'd with multitudes.

EDWARD KNO'WELL. Ay, believe me, may you, sir; and, in my conceit, our whole nation should sustain the loss by it, if it were so.

BOBADILL. Alas, no: what's a peculiar man to a nation? Not seen.

EDWARD KNO'WELL. Oh, but your skill, sir.

BOBADILL. Indeed, that might be some loss; but who respects it? I will tell you, sir, by the way of private, and under seal: I am a gentleman, and live here obscure and to myself; but were I known to Her Majesty and the Lords, observe me, I would undertake, upon this poor head and life, for the public benefit of the state, not only to spare the entire lives of her subjects in general, but to save the one half, nay, three parts of her yearly charge in holding war, and against what enemy soever. And how would I do it, think you?

EDWARD KNO'WELL. Nay, I know not, nor can I conceive.

BOBADILL. Why, thus, sir. I would select nineteen more to myself, throughout the land; gentlemen they should be of good spirit, strong and able constitution; I would choose them by an instinct, a character that I have; and I would teach these nineteen the special rules, as your *punto,* your *reverso,* your *stoccata,* your *imbroccata,* your *passada,* your *montanto,* till they could all play very near or altogether as well as myself. This done, say the enemy were forty thousand strong, we twenty would come into the field the tenth of March, or thereabouts; and we would challenge twenty of the enemy; they could not, in their honor, refuse us. Well, we would kill them; challenge twenty more, kill them; twenty more, kill them; twenty more, kill them, too; and thus would we kill every man his twenty a day, that's twenty score; twenty score, that's two hundred; two hundred a day, five days, a thousand; forty thousand; forty times five, five times forty, two hundred days kills them all up, by computation. And this will I venture my poor gentlemanlike carcase to perform—provided there be no treason practic'd upon us—by fair and discreet manhood; that is, civilly, by the sword.

EDWARD KNO'WELL. Why, are you so sure of your hand, Captain, at all times?

BOBADILL. Tut, never miss thrust, upon my reputation with you.

EDWARD KNO'WELL. I would not stand in Downright's state, then, an' you meet him, for the wealth of any one street in London.

BOBADILL. Why, sir, you mistake me. If he were here now, by this welkin, I would not draw my weapon on him. Let this gentleman do his mind; but I will *bastinado* him, by the bright sun, wherever I meet him.

MATTHEW. Faith, and I'll have a fling at him, at my distance.

Downright *walks over the stage.*

EDWARD KNO'WELL. Godso, look where he is: yonder he goes.

DOWNRIGHT. What peevish luck have I, I cannot meet with these bragging rascals! [*Exit.*]

BOBADILL. It's not he, is it?

EDWARD KNO'WELL. Yes, faith, it is he.

MATTHEW. I'll be hanged, then, if that were he.

EDWARD KNO'WELL. Sir, keep your hanging good for some greater matter; for I assure you, that was he.

STEPHEN. Upon my reputation, it was he.

BOBADILL. Had I thought it had been he, he must not have gone so; but I can hardly be induc'd to believe it was he, yet.

[*Enter* Downright.]

EDWARD KNO'WELL. That I think, sir. But see, he is come again!

DOWNRIGHT. Oh, Pharaoh's foot, have I found you? Come, draw, to your tools; draw, gipsy, or I'll thresh you.

BOBADILL. Gentleman of valor, I do believe in thee; hear me—

DOWNRIGHT. Draw your weapon, then.

BOBADILL. Tall man, I never thought on it till now: body of me, I had a warrant of the peace served on me even now, as I

came along, by a water-bearer; this gentleman saw it, Master
Matthew.

DOWNRIGHT. 'Sdeath, you will not draw, then?

BOBADILL. Hold, hold; under thy favor, forbear.

> *He beats him and disarms him:* Matthew *runs away*.

DOWNRIGHT. Prate again as you like this, you whoreson foist,
you. You'll control the point, you? Your consort is gone? Had
he stay'd, he had shar'd with you, sir.   [*Exit*.]

BOBADILL. Well, gentlemen, bear witness, I was bound to the
peace, by this good day.

EDWARD KNO'WELL. No, faith, it's an ill day, Captain; never
reckon it other. But, say you were bound to the peace, the
law allows you to defend yourself: that'll prove but a poor
excuse.

BOBADILL. I cannot tell, sir. I desire good construction, in fair
sort. I never sustain'd the like disgrace, by heaven; sure, I was
struck with a planet thence, for I had no power to touch my
weapon.

EDWARD KNO'WELL. Ay, like enough; I have heard of many
that have been beaten under a planet; go, get you to a surgeon.
'Slid, an' these be your tricks, your *passadas* and your *montantos*,
I'll none of them.   [*Exit* Bobadill.]
Oh, manners! That this age should bring forth such creatures!
That nature should be at leisure to make 'em! Come, coz.

STEPHEN. Mass, I'll ha' this cloak.

EDWARD KNO'WELL. God's will, 'tis Downright's.

STEPHEN. Nay, it's mine now; another might have ta'en 't up
as well as I; I'll wear it, so I will.

EDWARD KNO'WELL. How an' he see it? He'll challenge it,
assure yourself.

STEPHEN. Ay, but he shall not ha' it; I'll say I bought it.

EDWARD KNO'WELL. Take heed you buy it not too dear,
coz.   [*Exeunt*.]

[IV.vi]

Enter Kitely, Wellbred, Dame Kitely, [*and*] Bridget.

KITELY. Now trust me, brother, you were much to blame
T'incense his anger and disturb the peace

Of my poor house, where there are sentinels
That every minute watch to give alarms
Of civil war, without adjection
Of your assistance or occasion.

WELLBRED. No harm done, brother, I warrant you; since there is no harm done, anger costs a man nothing; and a tall man is never his own man, till he be angry. To keep his valor in obscurity is to keep himself, as it were, in a cloak-bag. What's a musician, unless he play? What's a tall man, unless he fight? For indeed, all this my wise brother stands upon absolutely; and that made me fall in with him so resolutely.

DAME KITELY. Ay, but what harm might have come of it, brother!

WELLBRED. Might, sister? So might the good warm clothes your husband wears be poison'd, for anything he knows; or the wholesome wine he drunk even now at the table.

KITELY [aside]. Now, God forbid! Oh me! Now I remember,
My wife drunk to me last; and chang'd the cup;
And bade me wear this cursed suit today.
See, if heav'n suffer murder undiscover'd!—
I feel me ill; give me some mithridate,
Some mithridate and oil, good sister, fetch me.
Oh, I am sick at heart! I burn, I burn.
If you will save my life, go, fetch it me.

WELLBRED. Oh, strange humour! My very breath has poison'd him.

BRIDGET. Good brother, be content; what do you mean?
The strength of these extreme conceits will kill you.

DAME KITELY. Beshrew your heart-blood, brother Wellbred, now,
For putting such a toy into his head!

WELLBRED. Is a fit simile a toy? Will he be poison'd with a simile?
Brother Kitely, what a strange and idle imagination is this!
For shame, be wiser. O' my soul, there's no such matter.

KITELY. Am I not sick? How am I, then, not poison'd?
Am I not poison'd? How am I, then, so sick?

DAME KITELY. If you be sick, your own thoughts make you sick.

WELLBRED. His jealousy is the poison he has taken.

[*Enter* Brainworm.] *He comes disguised like Justice Clement's man.*

BRAINWORM. Master Kitely, my master, Justice Clement, salutes you, and desires to speak with you with all possible speed.

KITELY. No time but now? When, I think, I am sick? Very sick. Well, I will wait upon his worship. Thomas, Cob!   [*Aside.*] I must seek them out, and set 'em sentinels till I return.—Thomas! Cob! Thomas!   [*Exit.*]

WELLBRED [*aside to* Brainworm]. This is perfectly rare, Brainworm! But how got'st thou this apparel of the Justice's man?

BRAINWORM. Marry, sir, my proper fine penman would needs bestow the grist o' me at the Windmill, to hear some martial discourse; where so I marshal'd him that I made him drunk, with admiration. And because too much heat was the cause of his distemper, I stripp'd him stark naked as he lay along asleep, and borrowed his suit to deliver this counterfeit message in, leaving a rusty armor and an old brown bill to watch him till my return; which shall be when I ha' pawn'd his apparel and spent the better part o'the money, perhaps.

WELLBRED. Well, thou art a successful merry knave, Brainworm; his absence will be a good subject for more mirth. I pray thee, return to thy young master, and will him to meet me and my sister Bridget at the Tower instantly; for here, tell him, the house is so stor'd with jealousy there is no room for love to stand upright in. We must get our fortunes committed to some larger prison, say; and than the Tower, I know no better air; nor where the liberty of the house may do us more present service. Away.

[*Exit* Brainworm.]

[*Enter* Kitely *and* Cash.]

KITELY. Come hither, Thomas. Now my secret's ripe,
And thou shalt have it. Lay to both thine ears:
Hark what I say to thee: I must go forth, Thomas.
Be careful of thy promise, keep good watch;
Note every gallant and observe him well,
That enters in my absence to thy mistress;
If she would show him rooms, the jest is stale;
Follow 'em, Thomas, or else hang on him,
And let him not go after; mark their looks;
Note, if she offer but to see his band,

Or any other amorous toy about him;
But praise his leg; or foot; or if she say
"The day is hot," and bid him feel her hand,
How hot it is: oh, that's a monstrous thing!
Note me all this, good Thomas; mark their sighs,
And, if they do but whisper, break 'em off:
I'll bear thee out in it. Wilt thou do this?
Wilt thou be true, my Thomas?

    CASH.   As truth's self, sir.

    KITELY. Why, I believe thee. Where is Cob, now? Cob!
                                                [*Exit.*]

    DAME KITELY. He's ever calling for Cob. I wonder how he employs Cob so.

    WELLBRED. Indeed, sister, to ask how he employs Cob is a necessary question for you that are his wife, and a thing not very easy for you to be satisfied in; but this I'll assure you, Cob's wife is an excellent bawd, sister; and oftentimes your husband haunts her house; marry, to what end I cannot altogether accuse him; imagine you what you think convenient. But I have known fair hides have foul hearts ere now, sister.

    DAME KITELY. Never said you truer than that, brother; so much I can tell you for your learning, Thomas, fetch your cloak, and go with me. I'll after him presently. I would to fortune I could take him there, i'faith: I'd return him his own, I warrant him.

                        [*Exeunt* Dame Kitely *and* Cash.]

    WELLBRED. So, let 'em go; this may make sport anon. Now, my fair sister-in-law, that you knew but how happy a thing it were to be fair and beautiful!

    BRIDGET. That touches not me, brother.

    WELLBRED. That's true; that's even the fault of it: for indeed, beauty stands a woman in no stead, unless it procure her touching. But, sister, whether it touch you or no, it touches your beauties; and, I am sure, they will abide the touch; an' they do not, a plague of all ceruse, say I: and it touches me too in part, though not in the ———. Well, there's a dear and respected friend of mine, sister, stands very strongly and worthily affected toward you, and hath vow'd to inflame whole bonfires of zeal at his heart in honor of your perfections. I have already engag'd my promise to bring you where you shall hear him confirm much more. Ned Kno'well is the man, sister: there's no exception against the party. You are ripe for a husband, and a minute's loss to such an occasion is a great trespass in a wise beauty. What say you, sister? On my soul, he loves you. Will you give him the meeting?

BRIDGET. Faith, I had very little confidence in mine own constancy, brother, if I durst not meet a man; but this motion of yours savors of an old knight-adventurer's servant a little too much, methinks.

WELLBRED. What's that, sister?

BRIDGET. Marry, of the squire.

WELLBRED. No matter if it did, I would be such an one for my friend; but see, who is return'd to hinder us!

[*Enter* Kitely.]

KITELY. What villainy is this? Call'd out on a false message? This was some plot: I was not sent for. Bridget, Where's your sister?

BRIDGET.   I think she be gone forth, sir.

KITELY. How! Is my wife gone forth? Whither, for God's sake?

BRIDGET. She's gone abroad with Thomas.

KITELY. Abroad with Thomas? Oh, that villain dors me. He hath discover'd all unto my wife. Beast that I was to trust him! Whither, I pray you, went she?

BRIDGET.   I know not, sir.

WELLBRED. I'll tell you, brother, whither I suspect she's gone.

KITELY. Whither, good brother?

WELLBRED. To Cob's house, I believe; but keep my counsel.

KITELY. I will, I will. To Cob's house? Doth she haunt Cob's? She's gone a-purpose now to cuckold me With that lewd rascal, who, to win her favor, Hath told her all.   [*Exit.*]

WELLBRED.   Come, he's once more gone. Sister, let's lose no time; th'affair is worth it.

                                              [*Exeunt.*]

[*IV. vii*]

[*Enter*] Matthew [*and*] Bobadill.

MATTHEW. I wonder, Captain, what they will say of my going away, ha?

BOBADILL. Why, what should they say, but as of a discreet gentleman, quick, wary, respectful of nature's fair lineaments? And that's all.

MATTHEW. Why, so; but what can they say of your beating?

BOBADILL. A rude part, a touch with soft wood, a kind of gross battery us'd, laid on strongly, borne most patiently; and that's all.

MATTHEW. Ay, but would any man have offer'd it in Venice, as you say?

BOBADILL. Tut, I assure you, no: you shall have there your *Nobilis,* your *Gentilezza,* come in bravely upon your reverse, stand you close, stand you firm, stand you fair, save your *retricato* with his left leg, come to the *assalto* with the right, thrust with brave steel, defy your base wood! But wherefore do I awake this remembrance? I was fascinated, by Jupiter, fascinated; but I will be unwitch'd, and reveng'd by law.

MATTHEW. Do you hear? Is't not best to get a warrant, and have him arrested and brought before Justice Clement?

BOBADILL. It were not amiss; would we had it.

[*Enter* Brainworm *disguised as Formal.*]

MATTHEW. Why, here comes his man, let's speak to him.

BOBADILL. Agreed; do you speak.

MATTHEW [*to* Brainworm]. Save you, sir!

BRAINWORM. With all my heart, sir!

MATTHEW. Sir, there is one Downright, hath abus'd this gentleman and myself, and we determine to make our amends by law; now, if you would do us the favor to procure a warrant to bring him afore your master, you shall be well considered, I assure you, sir.

BRAINWORM. Sir, you know my service is my living; such favors as these gotten of my master is his only perferment; and therefore you must consider me as I may make benefit of my place.

MATTHEW. How is that, sir?

BRAINWORM. Faith, sir, the thing is extraordinary, and the gentleman may be of great account; yet, be what he will, if you will lay me down a brace of angels in my hand you shall have it; otherwise not.

MATTHEW [*to* Bobadill, *aside*]. How shall we do, Captain? He asks a brace of angels. You have no money?

BOBADILL. Not a cross, by fortune.

MATTHEW. Nor I, as I am a gentleman, but two pence, left of my two shillings in the morning for wine and radish: let's find him some pawn.

BOBADILL. Pawn? We have none to the value of his demand.

MATTHEW. Oh yes, I'll pawn this jewel in my ear, and you may pawn your silk stockings, and pull up your boots; they will ne'er be miss'd. It must be done now.

BOBADILL. Well, an' there be no remedy, I'll step aside and pull 'em off.

MATTHEW [*to* Brainworm]. Do you hear, sir? We have no store of money at this time, but you shall have good pawns: look you, sir, this jewel, and that gentleman's silk stockings, because we would have it dispatch'd ere we went to our chambers.

BRAINWORM. I am content, sir; I will get you the warrant presently. What's his name, say you? Downright?

MATTHEW. Ay, ay; George Downright.

BRAINWORM. What manner of man is he?

MATTHEW. A tall, big man, sir; he goes in a cloak most commonly, of silk russet, laid about with russet lace.

BRAINWORM. 'Tis very good, sir.

MATTHEW. Here, sir, here's my jewel.

BOBADILL. And here are stockings.

BRAINWORM. Well, gentlemen, I'll procure you this warrant presently; but who will you have to serve it?

MATTHEW. That's true, Captain: that must be consider'd.

BOBADILL. Body o' me, I know not: 'tis service of danger!

BRAINWORM. Why, you were best get one o'the varlets o'the city, a serjeant; I'll appoint you one, if you please.

MATTHEW. Will you, sir? Why, we can wish no better.

BOBADILL. We'll leave it to you, sir.

[*Exeunt* Bobadill *and* Matthew.]

BRAINWORM. This is rare! Now will I go pawn this cloak of the Justice's man's at the broker's for a varlet's suit, and be the varlet myself; and get either more pawns, or more money of Downright for the arrest.   [*Exit.*]

[*IV.viii*]

[*Enter*] Kno'well.

KNO'WELL. Oh, here it is; I am glad; I have found it now.
[*Knocks.*]   Ho! Who is within here?

[Tib *opens the door.*]

TIB. I am within, sir; what's your pleasure?
KNO'WELL. To know who is within besides yourself.
TIB. Why, sir, you are no constable, I hope?
KNO'WELL. Oh, fear you the constable? Then I doubt not
You have some guests within, deserve that fear.
I'll fetch him straight.
TIB.   O' God's name, sir!
KNO'WELL. Go to. Come, tell me, is not young Kno'well here?
TIB. Young Kno'well! I know none such, sir, o' mine honesty.
KNO'WELL. Your honesty! Dame, it flies too lightly from you.
There is no way, but fetch the constable.
TIB. The constable? The man is mad, I think.

[*Claps to the door.*]

[*Enter* Dame Kitely *and* Cash.]

CASH. Ho, who keeps house here?
KNO'WELL [*aside*]. Oh, this is the female copesmate of my son!
Now shall I meet him straight.
DAME KITELY.   Knock, Thomas, hard.
CASH [*knocking*]. Ho, good wife!
TIB [*within*].   Why, what's the matter with you?
DAME KITELY. Why, woman, grieves it you to ope your door?
Belike you get something to keep it shut.

[*Enter* Tib.]

TIB. What mean these questions, 'pray ye?
DAME KITELY. So strange you make it? Is not my husband
here?
KNO'WELL [*aside*]. Her husband!
DAME KITELY.   My tried husband, Master Kitely.
TIB. I hope he needs not to be tried here.

DAME KITELY. No, dame: he does it not for need, but pleasure.

TIB. Neither for need nor pleasure is he here.

KNO'WELL [*aside*]. This is but a device to balk me withal.
Soft, who is this? 'Tis not my son, disguis'd?

[*Enter* Kitely *in his cloak.*]
She spies her husband come, and runs to him.

DAME KITELY. Oh, sir, have I forestall'd your honest market?
Found your close walks? You stand amaz'd now, do you?
I'faith, I am glad I have smok'd you yet at last!
What is your jewel, trow? In: come, let's see her;
Fetch forth your huswife, dame; if she be fairer,
In any honest judgment, than myself,
I'll be content with it. But she is change,
She feeds you fat, she soothes your appetite,
And you are well? Your wife, an honest woman,
Is meat twice sod to you, sir? Oh, you treacher!

KNO'WELL [*aside*]. She cannot counterfeit thus palpably.

KITELY. Out on thy more than strumpet's impudence!
Steal'st thou thus to thy haunts? And have I taken
Thy bawd, and thee, and thy companion,

                           Pointing to Old Kno'well.

This hoary-headed lecher, this old goat,
Close at your villainy, and wouldst thou 'scuse it
With this stale harlot's jest, accusing me?
(*To him.*)   Oh, old incontinent, dost not thou shame,
When all thy powers' inchastity is spent,
To have a mind so hot? And to entice
And feed th'enticements of a lustful woman?

DAME KITELY. Out, I defy thee, I, dissembling wretch!

KITELY. Defy me, strumpet?   (*By* Thomas.)   Ask thy pander
here,
Can he deny it? Or that wicked elder?

KNO'WELL. Why, hear you, sir.

KITELY.   Tut, tut, tut, never speak.
Thy guilty conscience will discover thee.

KNO'WELL. What lunacy is this that haunts this man?

KITELY. Well, good-wife Bad, Cob's wife, and you
That make your husband such a hoddy-doddy;
And you, young apple-squire; and old cuckold-maker;

I'll ha' you every one before a justice:
Nay, you shall answer it; I charge you, go.

KNO'WELL. Marry, with all my heart, sir; I go willingly;
Though I do taste this as a trick put on me
To punish my impertinent search, and justly;
And half forgive my son for the device.

KITELY. Come, will you go?

DAME KITELY.   Go? To thy shame, believe it.

[Enter Cob.]

COB. Why, what's the matter here? What's here to do?

KITELY. Oh, Cob, art thou come? I have been abus'd,
And i'thy house. Never was man so wrong'd!

COB. 'Slid, in my house? My master Kitely, who wrongs you
in my house?

KITELY. Marry, young lust in old, and old in young, here:
Thy wife's their bawd, here have I taken 'em.

COB. How, bawd? Is my house come to that? Am I preferr'd
thither?

He falls upon his wife and beats her.

Did I charge you to keep your doors shut, Is'bel? And do you
let 'em lie open for all comers?

KNO'WELL. Friend, know some cause before thou beat'st thy
wife;
This's madness in thee.

COB.   Why, is there no cause?

KITELY. Yes; I'll show cause before the Justice, Cob.
Come, let her go with me.

COB.   Nay, she shall go.

TIB. Nay, I will go. I'll see an' you may be allow'd to make a
bundle o' hemp o' your right and lawful wife thus, at every
cuckoldly knave's pleasure. Why do you not go?

KITELY. A bitter quean. Come, we'll ha' you tam'd.

[Exeunt.]

[*IV.ix*]

[*Enter*] Brainworm [*disguised as a city serjeant*].

BRAINWORM. Well, of all my disguises yet, now am I most like myself, being in this serjeant's gown. A man of my present profession never counterfeits, till he lays hold upon a debtor and says he rests him, for then he brings him to all manner of unrest. A kind of little kings we are, bearing the diminutive of a mace, made like a young artichoke, that always carries pepper and salt in itself. Well, I know not what danger I undergo by this exploit; pray heaven I come well off.

[*Enter* Bobadill *and* Matthew.]

MATTHEW. See, I think yonder is the varlet, by his gown.
BOBADILL. Let's go in quest of him.
MATTHEW [*to* Brainworm]. 'Save you, friend, are not you here by appointment of Justice Clement's man?
BRAINWORM. Yes, an't please you, sir: he told me two gentlemen had will'd him to procure a warrant from his master, which I have about me, to be serv'd on one Downright.
MATTHEW. It is honestly done of you both; and see where the party comes you must arrest: serve it upon him quickly, afore he be aware—
BOBADILL. Bear back, Master Matthew!

[*Enter* Stephen *in Downright's cloak*.]

BRAINWORM. Master Downright, I arrest you i'the Queen's name, and must carry you afore a Justice by virtue of this warrant.
STEPHEN. Me, friend? I am no Downright, I. I am Master Stephen, you do not well to arrest me, I tell you truly. I am in nobody's bonds nor books, I, would you should know it. A plague on you heartily, for making me thus afraid afore my time.
BRAINWORM. Why, how are you deceived, gentlemen?
BOBADILL. He wears such a cloak, and that deceived us. But see, here 'a comes indeed! This is he, officer.

[*Enter* Downright.]

DOWNRIGHT. Why, how now, Signior Gull! Are you turn'd filcher of late? Come, deliver my cloak.

STEPHEN. Your cloak, sir? I bought it even now, in open market.

BRAINWORM. Master Downright, I have a warrant I must serve upon you, procur'd by these two gentlemen.

DOWNRIGHT. These gentlemen? These rascals!

BRAINWORM. Keep the peace, I charge you, in Her Majesty's name.

DOWNRIGHT. I obey thee. What must I do, officer?

BRAINWORM. Go before Master Justice Clement, to answer what they can object against you, sir. I will use you kindly, sir.

MATTHEW. Come, let's before, and make the Justice, Captain—

BOBADILL. The varlet's a tall man, afore heaven!

[*Exeunt* Bobadill *and* Matthew.]

DOWNRIGHT. Gull, you'll gi' me my cloak?

STEPHEN. Sir, I bought it, and I'll keep it.

DOWNRIGHT. You will?

STEPHEN. Ay, that I will.

DOWNRIGHT. Officer, there's thy fee; arrest him.

BRAINWORM. Master Stephen, I must arrest you.

STEPHEN. Arrest me? I scorn it. There, take your cloak, I'll none on't.

DOWNRIGHT. Nay, that shall not serve your turn now, sir. Officer, I'll go with thee to the Justice's; bring him along.

STEPHEN. Why, is not here your cloak? What would you have?

DOWNRIGHT. I'll ha' you answer it, sir.

BRAINWORM. Sir, I'll take your word; and this gentleman's, too, for his appearance.

DOWNRIGHT. I'll ha' no words taken. Bring him along.

BRAINWORM. Sir, I may choose to do that: I may take bail.

DOWNRIGHT. 'Tis true, you may take bail and choose, at another time; but you shall not now, varlet. Bring him along, or I'll swinge you.

BRAINWORM. Sir, I pity the gentleman's case. Here's your money again.

DOWNRIGHT. 'Sdeynes, tell not me of my money; bring him away, I say.

BRAINWORM. I warrant you, he will go with you of himself, sir.

DOWNRIGHT. Yet more ado?

BRAINWORM [*aside*]. I have made a fair mash on't.

STEPHEN. Must I go?

BRAINWORM. I know no remedy, Master Stephen.

DOWNRIGHT. Come along, afore me here. I do not love your hanging look behind.

STEPHEN. Why, sir, I hope you cannot hang me for it.—Can he, fellow?

BRAINWORM. I think not, sir. It is but a whipping matter, sure.

STEPHEN. Why, then, let him do his worst; I am resolute.

[*Exeunt.*]

[*V. i*]

[*Enter* Justice] Clement, Kno'well, Kitely,
Dame Kitely, Tib, *Cash,* Cob, [*and*] *Servants.*

CLEMENT. Nay, but stay, stay, give me leave; my chair, sirrah. You, Master Kno'well, say you went thither to meet your son?

KNO'WELL. Ay, sir.

CLEMENT. But who directed you thither?

KNO'WELL. That did mine own man, sir.

CLEMENT. Where is he?

KNO'WELL. Nay, I know not now; I left him with your clerk, and appointed him to stay here for me.

CLEMENT. My clerk? About what time was this?

KNO'WELL. Marry, between one and two, as I take it.

CLEMENT. And what time came my man with the false message to you, Master Kitely?

KITELY. After two, sir.

CLEMENT. Very good; but, Mistress Kitely, how that you were at Cob's, ha?

DAME KITELY. An' please you, sir, I'll tell you: my brother Wellbred told me that Cob's house was a suspected place—

CLEMENT. So it appears, methinks; but on.

DAME KITELY. And that my husband us'd thither daily.

CLEMENT. No matter, so he us'd himself well, mistress.

DAME KITELY. True, sir, but you know what grows by such haunts, oftentimes.

CLEMENT. I see; rank fruits of a jealous brain, Mistress Kitely; but did you find your husband there in that case, as you suspected?

KITELY. I found her there, sir.

CLEMENT. Did you so? That alters the case. Who gave you knowledge of your wife's being there?

KITELY. Marry, that did my brother Wellbred.

CLEMENT. How, Wellbred first tell her? Then tell you after? Where is Wellbred?

KITELY. Gone with my sister, sir; I know not whither.

CLEMENT. Why, this is a mere trick, a device; you are gull'd in this most grossly, all.   [*To* Tib.]   Alas, poor wench, wert thou beaten for this?

TIB. Yes, most pitifully, an't please you.

COB. And worthily, I hope; if it shall prove so.

CLEMENT. Ay, that's like, and a piece of a sentence.

[*Enter a* Servant.]

How now, sir? What's the matter?

SERVANT. Sir, there's a gentleman i'the court without, desires to speak with your worship.

CLEMENT. A gentleman? What's he?

SERVANT. A soldier, sir, he says.

CLEMENT. A soldier? Take down my armor, my sword, quickly. A soldier speak with me! Why, when, knaves?   (*He arms himself.*) Come on, come on, hold my cap there, so; give me my gorget, my sword; stand by, I will end your matters anon.—Let the soldier enter.   [*Exit* Servant.]

[*Enter*] Bobadill [*and*] Matthew.

Now, sir, what ha' you to say to me?

BOBADILL. By your worship's favor—

CLEMENT. Nay, keep out, sir; I know not your pretense; you send me word, sir, you are a soldier: why, sir, you shall be answer'd here; here be them have been amongst soldiers. Sir, your pleasure?

BOBADILL. Faith, sir, so it is: this gentleman and myself have been most uncivilly wrong'd, and beaten, by one Downright, a coarse fellow, about the town here; and for mine own part I protest, being a man in no sort given to this filthy humour of quarreling, he hath assaulted me in the way of my peace; dispoil'd me of mine honor; disarm'd me of my weapons; and rudely laid

me along in the open streets; when I not so much as once offer'd
to resist him.

CLEMENT. Oh, God's precious! Is this the soldier? Here, take
my armor off quickly, 'twill make him swoon, I fear; he is not
fit to look on't, that will put up a blow.

MATTHEW. An' please your worship, he was bound to the
peace.

CLEMENT. Why, an' he were, sir, his hands were not bound,
were they?

[*Enter* Servant.]

SERVANT. There's one of the varlets of the city, sir, has brought
two gentlemen here, one upon your worship's warrant.

CLEMENT. My warrant?

SERVANT. Yes, sir. The officer says, procur'd by these two.

CLEMENT. Bid him come in.   [*Exit* Servant.]
Set by this picture.

[*Enter*] Downright, Stephen, [*and*]
Brainworm [*disguised as a city serjeant.*]

What, Master Downright! Are you brought at Master Fresh-
water's suit here?

DOWNRIGHT. I'faith, sir. And here's another brought at my
suit.

CLEMENT [*to* Stephen]. What are you, sir?

STEPHEN. A gentleman, sir.   [*Seeing* Kno'well.]   Oh, uncle!

CLEMENT. Uncle? Who? Master Kno'well?

KNO'WELL. Ay, sir. This is a wise kinsman of mine.

STEPHEN. God's my witness, uncle, I am wrong'd here
monstrously; he charges me with stealing of his cloak, and would
I might never stir, if I did not find it in the street by chance.

DOWNRIGHT. Oh, did you find it, now? You said you bought
it erewhile.

STEPHEN. And you said I stole it; nay, now my uncle is here,
I'll do well enough with you.

CLEMENT. Well, let this breathe a while. You that have cause
to complain there, stand forth: had you my warrant for this
gentleman's apprehension?

BOBADILL. Ay, an't please your worship.

CLEMENT. Nay, do not speak in passion so: where had you it?

BOBADILL. Of your clerk, sir.

CLEMENT. That's well, an' my clerk can make warrants, and my hand not at 'em! Where is the warrant? Officer, have you it?

BRAINWORM. No, sir; your worship's man, Master Formal, bid me do it for these gentlemen, and he would be my discharge.

CLEMENT. Why, Master Downright, are you such a novice, to be serv'd, and never see the warrant?

DOWNRIGHT. Sir, he did not serve it on me.

CLEMENT. No? How then?

DOWNRIGHT. Marry, sir, he came to me and said he must serve it, and he would use me kindly, and so—

CLEMENT. Oh, God's pity, was it so, sir? He must serve it? Give me my long-sword there, and help me off; so. Come on, sir varlet.

He flourishes over him with his long-sword.

I must cut off your legs, sirrah: nay, stand up, I'll use you kindly; I must cut off your legs, I say.

BRAINWORM. Oh, good sir, I beseech you; nay, good Master Justice.

CLEMENT. I must do it; there is no remedy. I must cut off your legs, sirrah; I must cut off your ears, you rascal; I must do it; I must cut off your nose; I must cut off your head.

BRAINWORM. Oh, good your worship!

CLEMENT. Well, rise; how dost thou do now? Dost thou feel thyself well? Hast thou no harm?

BRAINWORM. No, I thank your good worship, sir.

CLEMENT. Why, so! I said, I must cut off thy legs, and I must cut off thy arms, and I must cut off thy head; but I did not do it: so, you said you must serve this gentleman with my warrant; but you did not serve him. You knave, you slave, you rogue, do you say you must? Sirrah [*to a servant*], away with him to the jail; I'll teach you a trick for your "must," sir.

BRAINWORM. Good sir, I beseech you, be good to me.

CLEMENT. Tell him he shall to the jail; away with him, I say!

BRAINWORM. Nay, sir, if you will commit me, it shall be for committing more than this. I will not lose, by my travail, any grain of my fame, certain.

[*He throws off his disguise.*]

CLEMENT. How is this?

KNO'WELL. My man Brainworm!

STEPHEN. Oh yes, uncle: Brainworm has been with my cousin Edward and I all this day.

CLEMENT. I told you all there was some device.

BRAINWORM. Nay, excellent Justice, since I have laid myself thus open to you, now stand strong for me; both with your sword and your balance.

CLEMENT. Body o' me, a merry knave! Give me a bowl of sack. If he belong to you, Master Kno'well, I bespeak your patience.

BRAINWORM. That is it I have most need of.   [*To* Kno'well.] Sir, if you'll pardon me only, I'll glory in all the rest of my exploits.

KNO'WELL. Sir, you know I love not to have my favors come hard from me. You have your pardon; though I suspect you shrewdly for being of counsel with my son against me.

BRAINWORM. Yes, faith, I have, sir; though you retain'd me doubly this morning for yourself: first, as Brainworm, after, as Fitzsword. I was your reform'd soldier, sir. 'Twas I sent you to Cob's upon the errand without end.

KNO'WELL. Is it possible! Or that thou shouldst disguise thy language so, as I should not know thee?

BRAINWORM. Oh sir, this has been the day of my metamorphosis! It is not that shape alone that I have run through today. I brought this gentleman, Master Kitely, a message, too, in the form of Master Justice's man here, to draw him out o'the way, as well as your worship, while Master Wellbred might make a conveyance of Mistress Bridget to my young master.

KITELY. How! My sister stol'n away?

KNO'WELL. My son is not married, I hope!

BRAINWORM. Faith, sir, they are both as sure as love, a priest, and three thousand pound, which is her portion, can make 'em; and by this time are ready to bespeak their wedding supper at the Windmill, except some friend here prevent 'em, and invite 'em home.

CLEMENT. Marry, that will I; I thank thee for putting me in mind on't.
Sirrah, go you and fetch 'em hither, upon my warrant.

[*Exit* Servant.]

Neither's friends have cause to be sorry, if I know the young couple aright. Here, I drink to thee for thy good news. But I pray thee, what hast thou done with my man Formal?

BRAINWORM. Faith, sir, after some ceremony past, as making him drunk, first with story, and then with wine, but all in kindness, and stripping him to his shirt, I left him in that cool vein, departed, sold your worship's warrant to these two, pawn'd his livery for that varlet's gown to serve it in; and thus have brought myself, by my activity, to your worship's consideration.

CLEMENT. And I will consider thee, in another cup of sack. Here's to thee.—Which having drunk off, this is my sentence.—Pledge me.—Thou hast done or assisted to nothing, in my judgment, but deserves to be pardon'd for the wit o'the offense. If thy master, or any man here, be angry with thee, I shall suspect his ingine while I know him for't. How now! What noise is that?

[*Enter* Servant, *then* Formal *in armor.*]

SERVANT. Sir, it is Roger is come home.
CLEMENT. Bring him in, bring him in.

[Formal *comes forward.*]

What, drunk in arms, against me? Your reason, your reason for this?

FORMAL. I beseech your worship to pardon me: I happen'd into ill company by chance, that cast me into a sleep, and stripp'd me of all my clothes—

CLEMENT [*to* Servant]. Well, tell him I am Justice Clement, and do pardon him. But what is this to your armor! What may that signify?

FORMAL. An't please you, sir, it hung up i'the room where I was stripp'd; and I borrow'd it of one o'the drawers to come home in, because I was loath to do penance through the street i' my shirt.

CLEMENT. Well, stand by a while.

[*Enter*] Edward Kno'well, Wellbred, [*and*] *Bridget.*

Who be these? Oh, the young company; welcome, welcome. Gi' you joy. Nay, Mistress Bridget, blush not; you are not so fresh a bride but the news of it is come hither afore you. Master Bridegroom, I ha' made your peace, give me your hand. So will I for all the rest, ere you forsake my roof.

EDWARD KNO'WELL. We are the more bound to your humanity, sir.

CLEMENT. Only these two have so little of man in 'em, they are no part of my care.

WELLBRED. Yes, sir, let me pray you for this gentleman; he belongs to my sister, the bride.

CLEMENT. In what place, sir?

WELLBRED. Of her delight, sir; below the stairs and in public: her poet, sir.

CLEMENT. A poet? I will challenge him myself presently, at *extempore.*

> Mount up thy Phlegon muse, and testify
>   How Saturn, sitting in an ebon cloud,
> Disrob'd his podex white as ivory,
>   And through the welkin thunder'd all aloud.

WELLBRED. He is not for *extempore,* sir. He is all for the pocket muse; please you, command a sight of it.

CLEMENT. Yes, yes; search him for a taste of his vein.

WELLBRED. You must not deny the Queen's Justice, sir, under a writ o' rebellion.

[*They search Matthew's pocket.*]

CLEMENT. What, all this verse? Body o' me, he carries a whole realm, a commonwealth of paper, in's hose! Let's see some of his subjects.   [*Reads.*]

> Unto the boundless ocean of thy face
> Runs this poor river, charg'd with streams of eyes.

How! This is stol'n.

EDWARD KNO'WELL. A parody! A parody! With a kind of miraculous gift to make it absurder than it was.

CLEMENT. Is all the rest of this batch? Bring me a torch; lay it together, and give fire. Cleanse the air. Here was enough to have infected the whole city, if it had not been taken in time!   [*The papers are burnt.*]   See, see, how our poet's glory shines! Brighter and brighter! Still it increases! Oh, now it's at the highest; and now it declines as fast. You may see: *Sic transit gloria mundi.*

KNO'WELL. There's an emblem for you, son, and your studies!

CLEMENT. Nay, no speech or act of mine be drawn against such as profess it worthily. They are not born every year, as an alderman. There goes more to the making of a good poet than a sheriff, Master Kitely. You look upon me! Though I live i'the city here amongst you, I will do more reverence to him, when I meet him, than I will to the Mayor, out of his year. But these paper-peddlers, these ink-dabblers! They cannot expect reprehension or reproach. They have it with the fact.

EDWARD KNO'WELL. Sir, you have sav'd me the labor of a defense.

CLEMENT. It shall be discourse for supper between your father and me, if he dare undertake me. But to dispatch away these. You, sign o'the soldier, and picture o'the poet—but both so false, I will not ha' you hang'd out at my door till midnight—while we are at supper you two shall penitently fast it out in my court without; and if you will, you may pray there that we may be so merry within as to forgive or forget you when we come out. Here's a third, because we tender your safety, shall watch you; he is provided for the purpose. Look to your charge, sir.

STEPHEN. And what shall I do?

CLEMENT. Oh, I had lost a sheep, an' he had not bleated! Why, sir, you shall give Master Downright his cloak; and I will entreat him to take it. A trencher and a napkin you shall have i'the buttery, and keep Cob and his wife company here; whom I will entreat first to be reconcil'd, and you to endeavor with your wit to keep 'em so.

STEPHEN. I'll do my best.

COB. Why, now I see thou art honest, Tib, I receive thee as my dear and mortal wife again.

TIB. And I you, as my loving and obedient husband.

CLEMENT. Good complement! It will be their bridal night, too. They are married anew. Come, I conjure the rest to put off all discontent. You, Master Downright, your anger; you, Master Kno'well, your cares; Master Kitely and his wife, their jealousy. For, I must tell you both, while that is fed,
Horns i'the mind are worse than o'the head.

KITELY. Sir, thus they go from me: kiss me, sweetheart.—
See, what a drove of horns fly in the air,
Wing'd with my cleansed and my credulous breath!
Watch 'em, suspicious eyes, watch where they fall:
See, see, on heads that think th' have none at all!

Oh, what a plenteous world of this will come;
When air rains horns, all may be sure of some.—
I ha' learn'd so much verse out of a jealous man's part in a play.

CLEMENT. 'Tis well, 'tis well! This night we'll dedicate to friendship, love, and laughter. Master Bridegroom, take your bride and lead: every one, a fellow. Here is my mistress— Brainworm! To whom all my addresses of courtship shall have their reference. Whose adventures this day, when our grandchildren shall hear to be made a fable, I doubt not but it shall find both spectators and applause.   [*Exeunt.*]

THE END

This Comedy was first
acted in the year
1598.
By the then Lord Chamberlain
his Servants.

The principal Comedians were

Will. Shakespeare.	Ric. Burbadge.
Aug. Philips.	Joh. Hemings.
Hen. Condel.	Tho. Pope.
Will. Slye.	Chr. Beeston.
Will. Kempe.	Joh. Duke.

With the allowance of the Master of Revels.

FICTION

FLATLAND: A ROMANCE OF MANY DIMENSIONS, Edwin A. Abbott. (0-486-27263-X)

PRIDE AND PREJUDICE, Jane Austen. (0-486-28473-5)

CIVIL WAR SHORT STORIES AND POEMS, Edited by Bob Blaisdell. (0-486-48226-X)

THE DECAMERON: Selected Tales, Giovanni Boccaccio. Edited by Bob Blaisdell. (0-486-41113-3)

JANE EYRE, Charlotte Brontë. (0-486-42449-9)

WUTHERING HEIGHTS, Emily Brontë. (0-486-29256-8)

THE THIRTY-NINE STEPS, John Buchan. (0-486-28201-5)

ALICE'S ADVENTURES IN WONDERLAND, Lewis Carroll. (0-486-27543-4)

MY ÁNTONIA, Willa Cather. (0-486-28240-6)

THE AWAKENING, Kate Chopin. (0-486-27786-0)

HEART OF DARKNESS, Joseph Conrad. (0-486-26464-5)

LORD JIM, Joseph Conrad. (0-486-40650-4)

THE RED BADGE OF COURAGE, Stephen Crane. (0-486-26465-3)

THE WORLD'S GREATEST SHORT STORIES, Edited by James Daley. (0-486-44716-2)

A CHRISTMAS CAROL, Charles Dickens. (0-486-26865-9)

GREAT EXPECTATIONS, Charles Dickens. (0-486-41586-4)

A TALE OF TWO CITIES, Charles Dickens. (0-486-40651-2)

CRIME AND PUNISHMENT, Fyodor Dostoyevsky. Translated by Constance Garnett. (0-486-41587-2)

THE ADVENTURES OF SHERLOCK HOLMES, Sir Arthur Conan Doyle. (0-486-47491-7)

THE HOUND OF THE BASKERVILLES, Sir Arthur Conan Doyle. (0-486-28214-7)

BLAKE: PROPHET AGAINST EMPIRE, David V. Erdman. (0-486-26719-9)

WHERE ANGELS FEAR TO TREAD, E. M. Forster. (0-486-27791-7)

BEOWULF, Translated by R. K. Gordon. (0-486-27264-8)

THE RETURN OF THE NATIVE, Thomas Hardy. (0-486-43165-7)

THE SCARLET LETTER, Nathaniel Hawthorne. (0-486-28048-9)

SIDDHARTHA, Hermann Hesse. (0-486-40653-9)

THE ODYSSEY, Homer. (0-486-40654-7)

THE TURN OF THE SCREW, Henry James. (0-486-26684-2)

DUBLINERS, James Joyce. (0-486-26870-5)

DOVER THRIFT EDITIONS

FICTION

THE METAMORPHOSIS AND OTHER STORIES, Franz Kafka. (0-486-29030-1)

SONS AND LOVERS, D. H. Lawrence. (0-486-42121-X)

THE CALL OF THE WILD, Jack London. (0-486-26472-6)

GREAT AMERICAN SHORT STORIES, Edited by Paul Negri. (0-486-42119-8)

THE GOLD-BUG AND OTHER TALES, Edgar Allan Poe. (0-486-26875-6)

ANTHEM, Ayn Rand. (0-486-49277-X)

FRANKENSTEIN, Mary Shelley. (0-486-28211-2)

THE JUNGLE, Upton Sinclair. (0-486-41923-1)

THREE LIVES, Gertrude Stein. (0-486-28059-4)

THE STRANGE CASE OF DR. JEKYLL AND MR. HYDE, Robert Louis Stevenson. (0-486-26688-5)

DRACULA, Bram Stoker. (0-486-41109-5)

UNCLE TOM'S CABIN, Harriet Beecher Stowe. (0-486-44028-1)

ADVENTURES OF HUCKLEBERRY FINN, Mark Twain. (0-486-28061-6)

THE ADVENTURES OF TOM SAWYER, Mark Twain. (0-486-40077-8)

CANDIDE, Voltaire. Edited by Francois-Marie Arouet. (0-486-26689-3)

THE COUNTRY OF THE BLIND: and Other Science-Fiction Stories, H. G. Wells. Edited by Martin Gardner. (0-486-48289-8)

THE WAR OF THE WORLDS, H. G. Wells. (0-486-29506-0)

ETHAN FROME, Edith Wharton. (0-486-26690-7)

THE PICTURE OF DORIAN GRAY, Oscar Wilde. (0-486-27807-7)

MONDAY OR TUESDAY: Eight Stories, Virginia Woolf. (0-486-29453-6)

NONFICTION

POETICS, Aristotle. (0-486-29577-X)

MEDITATIONS, Marcus Aurelius. (0-486-29823-X)

THE WAY OF PERFECTION, St. Teresa of Avila. Edited and Translated by E. Allison Peers. (0-486-48451-3)

THE DEVIL'S DICTIONARY, Ambrose Bierce. (0-486-27542-6)

GREAT SPEECHES OF THE 20TH CENTURY, Edited by Bob Blaisdell. (0-486-47467-4)

THE COMMUNIST MANIFESTO AND OTHER REVOLUTIONARY WRITINGS: Marx, Marat, Paine, Mao Tse-Tung, Gandhi and Others, Edited by Bob Blaisdell. (0-486-42465-0)

INFAMOUS SPEECHES: From Robespierre to Osama bin Laden, Edited by Bob Blaisdell. (0-486-47849-1)

GREAT ENGLISH ESSAYS: From Bacon to Chesterton, Edited by Bob Blaisdell. (0-486-44082-6)

GREEK AND ROMAN ORATORY, Edited by Bob Blaisdell. (0-486-49622-8)

THE UNITED STATES CONSTITUTION: The Full Text with Supplementary Materials, Edited and with supplementary materials by Bob Blaisdell. (0-486-47166-7)

GREAT SPEECHES BY NATIVE AMERICANS, Edited by Bob Blaisdell. (0-486-41122-2)

GREAT SPEECHES BY AFRICAN AMERICANS: Frederick Douglass, Sojourner Truth, Dr. Martin Luther King, Jr., Barack Obama, and Others, Edited by James Daley. (0-486-44761-8)

GREAT SPEECHES BY AMERICAN WOMEN, Edited by James Daley. (0-486-46141-6)

HISTORY'S GREATEST SPEECHES, Edited by James Daley. (0-486-49739-9)

GREAT INAUGURAL ADDRESSES, Edited by James Daley. (0-486-44577-1)

GREAT SPEECHES ON GAY RIGHTS, Edited by James Daley. (0-486-47512-3)

ON THE ORIGIN OF SPECIES: By Means of Natural Selection, Charles Darwin. (0-486-45006-6)

NARRATIVE OF THE LIFE OF FREDERICK DOUGLASS, Frederick Douglass. (0-486-28499-9)

THE SOULS OF BLACK FOLK, W. E. B. Du Bois. (0-486-28041-1)

NATURE AND OTHER ESSAYS, Ralph Waldo Emerson. (0-486-46947-6)

SELF-RELIANCE AND OTHER ESSAYS, Ralph Waldo Emerson. (0-486-27790-9)

THE LIFE OF OLAUDAH EQUIANO, Olaudah Equiano. (0-486-40661-X)

WIT AND WISDOM FROM POOR RICHARD'S ALMANACK, Benjamin Franklin. (0-486-40891-4)

THE AUTOBIOGRAPHY OF BENJAMIN FRANKLIN, Benjamin Franklin. (0-486-29073-5)

NONFICTION

THE DECLARATION OF INDEPENDENCE AND OTHER GREAT DOCUMENTS OF AMERICAN HISTORY: 1775-1865, Edited by John Grafton. (0-486-41124-9)

INCIDENTS IN THE LIFE OF A SLAVE GIRL, Harriet Jacobs. (0-486-41931-2)

GREAT SPEECHES, Abraham Lincoln. (0-486-26872-1)

THE WIT AND WISDOM OF ABRAHAM LINCOLN: A Book of Quotations, Abraham Lincoln. Edited by Bob Blaisdell. (0-486-44097-4)

THE SECOND TREATISE OF GOVERNMENT AND A LETTER CONCERNING TOLERATION, John Locke. (0-486-42464-2)

THE PRINCE, Niccolò Machiavelli. (0-486-27274-5)

MICHEL DE MONTAIGNE: Selected Essays, Michel de Montaigne. Translated by Charles Cotton. Edited by William Carew Hazlitt. (0-486-48603-6)

UTOPIA, Sir Thomas More. (0-486-29583-4)

BEYOND GOOD AND EVIL: Prelude to a Philosophy of the Future, Friedrich Nietzsche. (0-486-29868-X)

TWELVE YEARS A SLAVE, Solomon Northup. (0-486-78962-4)

COMMON SENSE, Thomas Paine. (0-486-29602-4)

BOOK OF AFRICAN-AMERICAN QUOTATIONS, Edited by Joslyn Pine. (0-486-47589-1)

THE TRIAL AND DEATH OF SOCRATES: Four Dialogues, Plato. (0-486-27066-1)

THE REPUBLIC, Plato. (0-486-41121-4)

SIX GREAT DIALOGUES: Apology, Crito, Phaedo, Phaedrus, Symposium, The Republic, Plato. Translated by Benjamin Jowett. (0-486-45465-7)

WOMEN'S WIT AND WISDOM: A Book of Quotations, Edited by Susan L. Rattiner. (0-486-41123-0)

GREAT SPEECHES, Franklin Delano Roosevelt. (0-486-40894-9)

THE CONFESSIONS OF ST. AUGUSTINE, St. Augustine. (0-486-42466-9)

A MODEST PROPOSAL AND OTHER SATIRICAL WORKS, Jonathan Swift. (0-486-28759-9)

THE IMITATION OF CHRIST, Thomas à Kempis. Translated by Aloysius Croft and Harold Bolton. (0-486-43185-1)

CIVIL DISOBEDIENCE AND OTHER ESSAYS, Henry David Thoreau. (0-486-27563-9)

WALDEN; OR, LIFE IN THE WOODS, Henry David Thoreau. (0-486-28495-6)

NARRATIVE OF SOJOURNER TRUTH, Sojourner Truth. (0-486-29899-X)

THE WIT AND WISDOM OF MARK TWAIN: A Book of Quotations, Mark Twain. (0-486-40664-4)

UP FROM SLAVERY, Booker T. Washington. (0-486-28738-6)

A VINDICATION OF THE RIGHTS OF WOMAN, Mary Wollstonecraft. (0-486-29036-0)

PLAYS

THE ORESTEIA TRILOGY: Agamemnon, the Libation-Bearers and the Furies, Aeschylus. (0-486-29242-8)

EVERYMAN, Anonymous. (0-486-28726-2)

THE BIRDS, Aristophanes. (0-486-40886-8)

LYSISTRATA, Aristophanes. (0-486-28225-2)

THE CHERRY ORCHARD, Anton Chekhov. (0-486-26682-6)

THE SEA GULL, Anton Chekhov. (0-486-40656-3)

MEDEA, Euripides. (0-486-27548-5)

FAUST, PART ONE, Johann Wolfgang von Goethe. (0-486-28046-2)

THE INSPECTOR GENERAL, Nikolai Gogol. (0-486-28500-6)

SHE STOOPS TO CONQUER, Oliver Goldsmith. (0-486-26867-5)

GHOSTS, Henrik Ibsen. (0-486-29852-3)

A DOLL'S HOUSE, Henrik Ibsen. (0-486-27062-9)

HEDDA GABLER, Henrik Ibsen. (0-486-26469-6)

DR. FAUSTUS, Christopher Marlowe. (0-486-28208-2)

TARTUFFE, Molière. (0-486-41117-6)

BEYOND THE HORIZON, Eugene O'Neill. (0-486-29085-9)

THE EMPEROR JONES, Eugene O'Neill. (0-486-29268-1)

CYRANO DE BERGERAC, Edmond Rostand. (0-486-41119-2)

MEASURE FOR MEASURE: Unabridged, William Shakespeare. (0-486-40889-2)

FOUR GREAT TRAGEDIES: Hamlet, Macbeth, Othello, and Romeo and Juliet, William Shakespeare. (0-486-44083-4)

THE COMEDY OF ERRORS, William Shakespeare. (0-486-42461-8)

HENRY V, William Shakespeare. (0-486-42887-7)

MUCH ADO ABOUT NOTHING, William Shakespeare. (0-486-28272-4)

FIVE GREAT COMEDIES: Much Ado About Nothing, Twelfth Night, A Midsummer Night's Dream, As You Like It and The Merry Wives of Windsor, William Shakespeare. (0-486-44086-9)

OTHELLO, William Shakespeare. (0-486-29097-2)

AS YOU LIKE IT, William Shakespeare. (0-486-40432-3)

ROMEO AND JULIET, William Shakespeare. (0-486-27557-4)

A MIDSUMMER NIGHT'S DREAM, William Shakespeare. (0-486-27067-X)

THE MERCHANT OF VENICE, William Shakespeare. (0-486-28492-1)

HAMLET, William Shakespeare. (0-486-27278-8)

RICHARD III, William Shakespeare. (0-486-28747-5)

PLAYS

THE TAMING OF THE SHREW, William Shakespeare. (0-486-29765-9)

MACBETH, William Shakespeare. (0-486-27802-6)

KING LEAR, William Shakespeare. (0-486-28058-6)

FOUR GREAT HISTORIES: Henry IV Part I, Henry IV Part II, Henry V, and Richard III, William Shakespeare. (0-486-44629-8)

THE TEMPEST, William Shakespeare. (0-486-40658-X)

JULIUS CAESAR, William Shakespeare. (0-486-26876-4)

TWELFTH NIGHT; OR, WHAT YOU WILL, William Shakespeare. (0-486-29290-8)

HEARTBREAK HOUSE, George Bernard Shaw. (0-486-29291-6)

PYGMALION, George Bernard Shaw. (0-486-28222-8)

ARMS AND THE MAN, George Bernard Shaw. (0-486-26476-9)

OEDIPUS REX, Sophocles. (0-486-26877-2)

ANTIGONE, Sophocles. (0-486-27804-2)

FIVE GREAT GREEK TRAGEDIES, Sophocles, Euripides and Aeschylus. (0-486-43620-9)

THE FATHER, August Strindberg. (0-486-43217-3)

THE PLAYBOY OF THE WESTERN WORLD AND RIDERS TO THE SEA, J. M. Synge. (0-486-27562-0)

TWELVE CLASSIC ONE-ACT PLAYS, Edited by Mary Carolyn Waldrep. (0-486-47490-9)

LADY WINDERMERE'S FAN, Oscar Wilde. (0-486-40078-6)

AN IDEAL HUSBAND, Oscar Wilde. (0-486-41423-X)

THE IMPORTANCE OF BEING EARNEST, Oscar Wilde. (0-486-26478-5)